MAP SCRIPTING 101

MAP SCRIPTING 101

An Example-Driven Guide to Building Interactive Maps with Bing, Yahoo!, and Google Maps

by Adam DuVander

no starch
press

San Francisco

MAP SCRIPTING 101. Copyright © 2010 by Adam DuVander.

14 13 12 11 10   1 2 3 4 5 6 7 8 9

ISBN-10: 1-59327-271-5
ISBN-13: 978-1-59327-271-5

Publisher: William Pollock
Production Editor: Ansel Staton
Cover and Interior Design: Octopod Studios
Developmental Editor: Tyler Ortman
Technical Reviewer: Derek Fowler
Copyeditor: LeeAnn Pickrell
Compositors: Serena Yang and Riley Hoffman
Proofreader: Linda Seifert
Indexer: Nancy Guenther

For information on book distributors or translations, please contact No Starch Press, Inc. directly:

No Starch Press, Inc.
38 Ringold Street, San Francisco, CA 94103
phone: 415.863.9900; fax: 415.863.9950; info@nostarch.com; www.nostarch.com

Library of Congress Cataloging-in-Publication Data:

DuVander, Adam.
 Map scripting 101: an example-driven guide to building interactive maps with Bing, Yahoo!, and Google Maps
/ by Adam DuVander.
      p. cm.
 Map scripting one hundred one
 Includes index.
 ISBN-13: 978-1-59327-271-5
 ISBN-10: 1-59327-271-5
 1. Cartography. I. Title. II. Title: Map scripting one hundred one.
 GA105.3.D88 2010
 526--dc22
                                            2010024113

Printed in Canada.

For my mother, who would have read this book from cover to cover,
even if she didn't understand it.

BRIEF CONTENTS

CONTENTS IN DETAIL

3
GEOCODING   43

4
LAYER IT ON   61

8
DATA FORMATS
173

9
GO SERVER-SIDE
205

A
JAVASCRIPT QUICK START

B
MAPSTRACTION REFERENCE

INDEX

ACKNOWLEDGMENTS

For a number of years I've kept a personal blog called *Simplicity Rules* where I've covered ways to raise productivity and decrease stress at the same time. From that frame of reference, I am now able to report that there is no simple way to write a book. However, the following people and organizations made it a whole lot easier for me than it might have been.

My wife, Jenny. You supported me in many ways, including one that I didn't expect: You were always there to encourage me to write the "bockety first draft" of a chapter. Somehow, you knew I'd be able to eventually turn it into something worth reading.

The entire staff of No Starch Press. If there's anybody that makes creating books look easy, it's you guys. Bill Pollock, thanks for getting this thing started; Tyler Ortman, your guidance is immeasurable; Ansel Staton, you made this book look sharp.

LeeAnn Pickerell's copy editing went well beyond finding typos and sentence fragments. Among her many talents, she destroys clichés like they're going out of style. (You can leave this one, LeeAnn.)

Derek Fowler, a major contributor to Mapstraction and the dedicated technical reviewer of this book. Thanks for making me smarter.

Mike Calore, my longtime editor at Wired and Webmonkey. I'm certain that whatever "instincts" I have about my audience are merely lessons you've taught me (perhaps more than once).

Bert Sperling. You got me excited about location in the first place.

The always positive Portland tech community, who never stopped asking about my book, even when I had been writing it for an awkwardly long time. In particular, I'm grateful to my teahouse buddy, Andy Baio. You offered just the balance of encouragement and kick-in-the-pants I needed.

La Bonita, a Mexican restaurant (with delicious cod tacos) where I wrote the bulk of this book. Thanks for making me feel like Coppola.

INTRODUCTION

The Web has changed our lives in many ways. The first online, on-demand driving directions from MapQuest very nearly rendered traditional road atlases obsolete. Today, many websites that provide driving directions also make their maps available to developers. Using these mapping APIs, you can plot your own points or make a mashup with geo-data from other websites.

This book shows you how to take advantage of these services and include their maps on your site. Instead of limiting you to one provider, I'll show you how to use all of them via an open source library called *Mapstraction*. Write your code once and watch it work in Google Maps, Bing, MapQuest, Yahoo!, OpenStreetMap, and more.

In addition to teaching you how to work with maps from these providers, I'll show you many other common geographic projects. You'll learn how to calculate the distance between locations and embed driving directions on your own site. You'll also learn how to customize the way your map looks by adding your own icons, adding large graphic overlays, or even completely changing the underlying map imagery.

Bringing location to the Web by embedding maps is an important part of most sites now, but there's also an increasing need to bring the Web "on location" to smartphones running mobile browsers. You can add maps to mobile versions of your site using the techniques shown in this book. And I'll show you how to use a convenient geolocation standard to find your user's location, whether he's using a phone, a tablet, or even a regular computer.

You are just pages away from adding some *where* to your website. This book is designed to help you quickly get to work on an application you already have in mind or inspire your next map. To that end, I've organized the book into projects. And once you become a map scripting wizard, I hope this book will be useful enough as a reference to earn a spot on your bookshelf.

About This Book

The book's project-based approach starts off with basic examples then picks up speed quickly. If you're one to jump ahead, I'd recommend you at least read "Create a Mapstraction Map" on page 10 first. Almost every example in the book builds upon the map you will create in that section.

In Chapter 1 you'll learn the basics of constructing online maps. I'll introduce Mapstraction and show how to add controls, such as a zoom interface, to your maps.

In Chapter 2 you'll start adding your own points to the map. You'll create custom icons and add message boxes to describe locations.

In Chapter 3 you'll learn many ways to convert addresses and city names to coordinates that mapping providers can understand. This process, called *geocoding*, is a big part of making mapping human-friendly.

In Chapter 4 you'll add more complex layers to your map. You'll learn how to draw lines to describe routes and shapes to outline borders. You'll even see how to take large graphics, geo-reference them, and then add them as a map overlay.

In Chapter 5 you'll make your maps respond to events, such as drags, clicks, and zooms. These hooks allow you to create an even more interactive experience for your users.

In Chapter 6 we'll explore proximity. You'll learn how to create driving directions or search around a point. You'll also dive into some more advanced topics, such as determining whether a location is within a shape (known as a *hit test*).

In Chapter 7 you'll learn several simple ways to access your user's location with various degrees of accuracy. I'll cover using the geolocation standard, falling back on IP address data, and integrating with location sharing services.

In Chapter 8 you'll focus on common location data formats used on the Web. You'll learn to parse GeoRSS, Google Earth's KML, and XML output from most GPS devices.

In Chapter 9 it's time to go server side. You'll get a crash course in PHP and MySQL, two technologies provided by many web hosts. We'll then use these languages for common location tasks, such as finding the closest points from your own database.

In Chapter 10 you'll put it all together with five fun mashups. You'll create a Twitter tweet finder, an interactive weather map, and a way to find a coffee shop between two locations (so you can meet a friend in the middle). There's also a local concert finder and a way to visualize earthquakes around the world.

How to Use This Book

This book introduces cartography to web developers, and shows cartographers and other geo-folks how to move their maps online. It is written for beginning and advanced programmers alike—your skill level and knowledge of mapping will impact how you use the book. Chapter 1 is a good place for everyone to start, because most of the later examples build upon the basic maps presented there.

If you haven't used JavaScript before, or if you need a refresher, be sure to read Appendix A. This will give you a primer on the concepts used throughout the book and provide a quick introduction to the JavaScript framework jQuery.

Each chapter builds upon earlier chapters, so you can read from beginning to end as you expand your mapping knowledge. This book also works well as a reference—you can skip around to find the concepts you want to learn, or find the chapter or project you need for your current application.

Another part of the book that you'll find useful is Appendix B, a reference that details the classes and functions within Mapstraction. This reference serves as a quick way to check syntax and gives examples of how to use each function.

About the Website

I encourage you to take advantage of this book's companion website at *http://mapscripting101.com/* (Figure 1). Among other things, you'll find live examples of every project in the book—so you can save yourself some typing by downloading or copying the code.

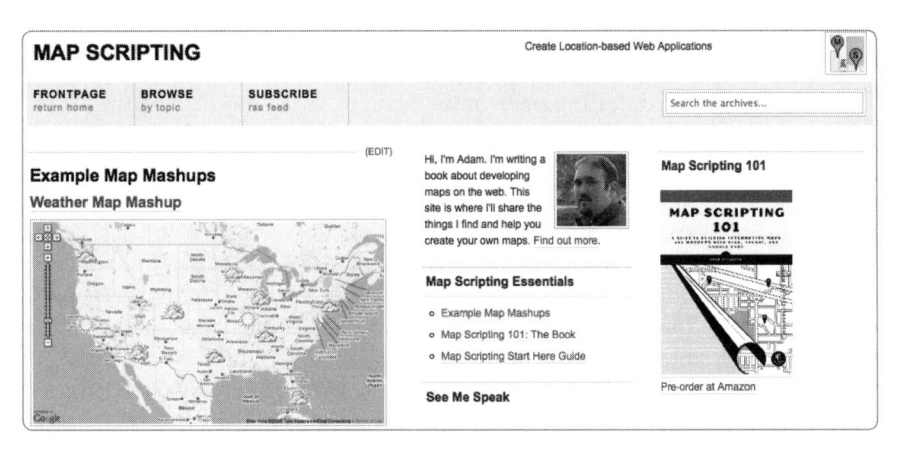

Figure 1: The companion website

Also, since map scripting technology and the Web are both changing so quickly, you'll want to check the website to see what's new so you can keep your chops fresh. I'll be posting updates and tutorials to help you take your knowledge beyond the pages of this book.

1

MAPPING BASICS

X marks the spot, right? That's the old pirate saying. Have you ever wondered who made maps for the pirates? The pirates had to do it themselves. No wonder they were so cranky! If they'd only had today's technology, the pirates could have used someone else's map and only had to mark the *X* themselves, leaving the intricate coastline detail to the cartographer.

Luckily, you live in the present day and have all sorts of mapping options. You can use Google Maps, Yahoo! Maps, and many others. And these maps make mapping easy; all you need are just a few lines of code to include a map on your web page. Figure 1-1 shows a page from Yelp, a restaurant review site and one of thousands of sites that use maps to mark locations.

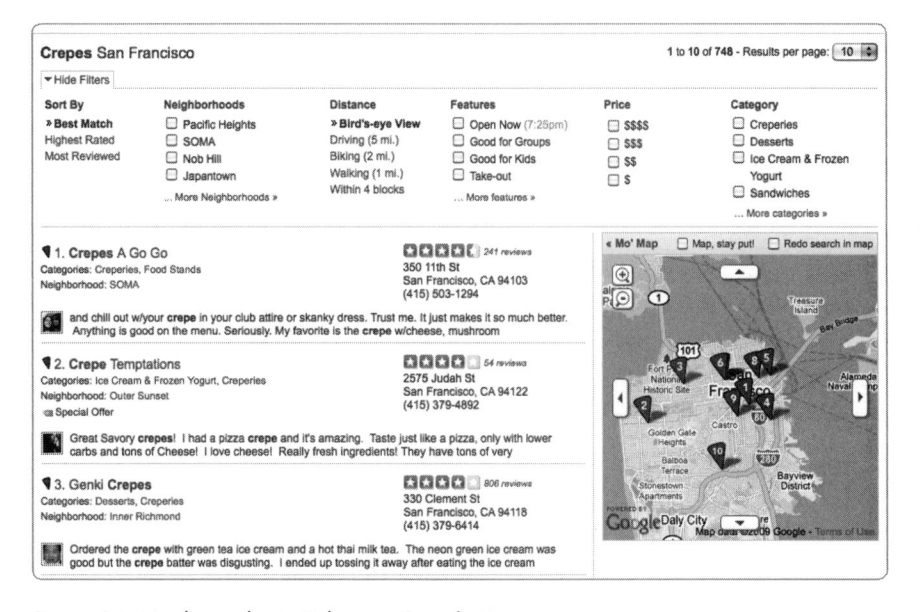

Figure 1-1: Local search site Yelp uses Google Maps.

To embed a map, you need to use an API. An AP . . . what? API stands for *Application Programming Interface*, and it consists of a collection of functions that make creating maps easier. You'll still have to do some programming, but writing your code will be trivial compared to what you'd have to do if you had to do everything yourself. Sound familiar, matey?

The Mapping APIs: Google, Yahoo!, and Mapstraction

As I mentioned, you can choose from a number of mapping API providers. The features and the style of the maps vary, though the APIs share a number of elements. This book will cover mapping tools from Google and Yahoo!, but most of the code examples will use a JavaScript library called Mapstraction, which is also an API, but different from the others. Mapstraction is not a mapping service itself; instead, it is a wrapper for other APIs. You write the code once, and it will work on Google Maps, Yahoo! Maps, and ten other providers.[1]

Mapstraction doesn't always support every provider's features, but it covers those features the services share and more. For the majority of mapping projects, using Mapstraction makes sense. Every now and then, you'll come across an example that only works with one provider. In those cases, I will clearly indicate where the Mapstraction code ends and the proprietary code begins.

Using Mapstraction is about foresight. How much code will you need to rewrite if, for example, Google shuts down its Maps API? If that sounds

---

1. CloudMade, FreeEarth, Map24, MapQuest, Microsoft, MultiMap, OpenLayers, OpenSpace, OpenStreetMap, and ViaMichelin

far-fetched, then consider instead what might happen if your mapping provider starts showing annoying ads or another comes along that has maps with colors more suitable to your design. Mapstraction allows you to switch seamlessly between providers. So you write the code once, and it works everywhere.

Before you can begin plotting locations on a map, however, you need to understand mapping basics. One of the most important concepts is the coordinate system used to describe a point on the earth. Let's look at how that is done.

Describe a Point on the Earth

Geographers have a difficult job, taking a round earth and giving it meaning on a flat map. For those with the skills, the job is an exercise in accepting imprecision. Because, despite what Columbus said, the earth is not round; it's not even a sphere. The earth is an ellipsoid, slightly wider than it is tall. We owe the astronomers and mathematicians who have worked hard over the past few hundred years to help us pinpoint a location as accurately as we can a great many "thank yous."

The most common way to describe a point on the earth is to use latitude and longitude coordinates. This system is used by GPS devices, every web mapping API provider, and this book. With it, we can convert a complicated ellipsoid into a standard coordinate frame like we used in algebra class to create graphs. A world map is shown in Figure 1-2 with the axes overlaid.

The points we plot indicate locations on earth, with an error of only two centimeters (0.8 of an inch). Rather than calling the axes x and y, as we did in school, we call them latitude and longitude. We can express coordinate pairs in several ways:

45° 33′ 25″ N, 122° 31′ 55″ W

45° 33.4′, –122° 31.9′ or 45d33.4m, –122d31.9m

45.55713, –122.53194

As you might have guessed, these coordinate pairs are all roughly equal ways of expressing the same point. The units are degrees (°), minutes (′), and seconds (″). Each degree is split into 60 minutes, and each minute is then further diced into 60 seconds. The decimal representation, in the third example, is used by mapping providers and is the style you will see most in this book.

Like the coordinate frame we're all familiar with, each axis has a zero point, with values increasing in one direction and decreasing in the other direction. Therefore, latitudes and longitudes can have both positive and negative numbers.

Latitude measures the vertical axis, which describes how far north or south a location is. The zero point for latitude is the equator. To the north, the values increase until reaching 90 degrees at the pole. South of the equator, latitude decreases, with –90 degrees being the other pole.

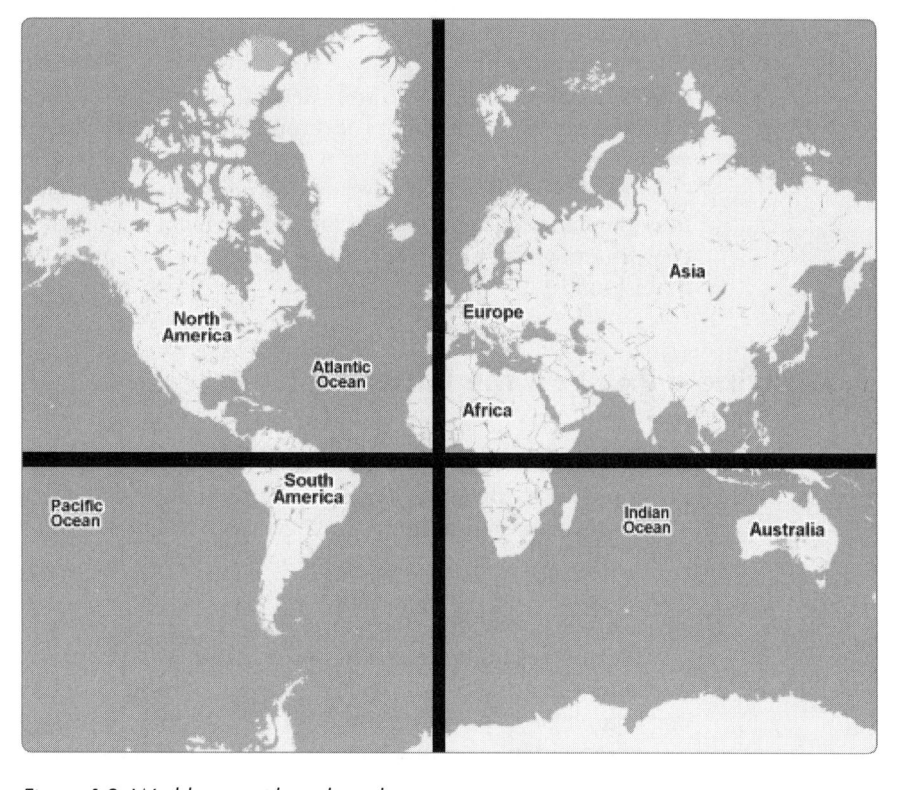

Figure 1-2: World map with grid overlay

The horizontal axis measurement is called *longitude*. Longitude describes how far west or east a location is. The earth does not have a natural vertical equator, so scientists and politicians had to decide on a zero point. They chose the location of astronomer George Biddell Airy's telescope in Greenwich, London (the Royal Observatory), to be the *Prime Meridian*. To the east of this spot, longitudes increase to 180 degrees on the other side of the earth. Similarly, longitude decreases to –180 degrees to the west, meeting positive longitudes opposite the Prime Meridian (called the *antipodal* meridian).

Why does latitude stop at 90 degrees and longitude continue to 180 degrees? The horizontal axis does not have any poles, so picking a place to stop would be as arbitrary as the meridians. Also, latitude degrees are parallel to one another, whereas longitudinal lines become closer to each other at the poles. Points along a specific latitude are symmetrical. If you traced the hypothetical 100 degrees latitude halfway around the earth, you would arrive at 80 degrees latitude, so you might as well just call it that.

Now that you have a feel for how coordinates are used, let's look at the different ways they are expressed and how you can switch between them.

Convert Between Decimal and Degree Formats

When I first introduced latitude and longitude points, I showed several examples. If you work with enough geographic data, you'll likely end up seeing each of those ways of expressing the same point. In this section, I'll show you how to convert between the two most common formats.

Mapping APIs accept latitude and longitude values as a pair of decimal numbers. For example, the No Starch Press office in San Francisco is situated at 37.7740486, −122.4101883. What does that mean? First, finding the major degrees is easy—these are the numbers before the decimal, so 37 and −122 in this case.

The remaining decimals describe how close this value is to the next degree. A latitude of 37.7740486 is more than halfway between the 37th and 38th degree. A portion of a degree is expressed as minutes and seconds.

Multiply the decimal portion of the coordinates by 60 to get the number of minutes:

0.7740486 × 60 = 46.442916 minutes

0.4101883 × 60 = 24.611298 minutes

Now we're getting somewhere. The latitude is 37 degrees, 46 minutes. The longitude is −122 degrees, 24 minutes. However, the answer has a decimal portion. We need to repeat the previous step, multiplying these new decimals by 60 to determine the number of seconds:

0.442916 × 60 = 26.57496 seconds

0.611298 × 60 = 36.67788 seconds

Again, we're left with a decimal portion. Unless we want to be extremely precise, we can just take the whole number at this point. The difference between 26.57496 seconds and 26 seconds is one hundredth of a mile. Some people choose to leave a single digit after the decimal point. Then our measurement is precise within about five feet, which is almost certainly less than a pixel on a web map.

The final answer after converting from point 37.7740486, −122.4101883 to degree, minute, second format is 37° 46′ 26″ N, 122° 24′ 36″ W.

Note the directions, which show this location is in the northern and western hemispheres. Also, the longitude is no longer expressed as a negative because the location is west of the Prime Meridian.

Converting from degree, minute, second to decimal format is even easier. As before, converting the degree is easy, as it becomes the whole number portion to the left of the decimal. Now we just have to remember to use a negative number to indicate the southern and western hemispheres.

Next, we convert the minutes portion into seconds (multiply by 60) and add that result to the existing seconds:

46 × 60 + 26 = 2,786 seconds latitude

24 × 60 + 36 = 1,476 seconds longitude

Finally, divide each of those results by the number of seconds in one degree, which is 3,600 (60 × 60):

2,786 / 3600 = 0.77389
1,476 / 3600 = 0.41000

The answer after converting point 37° 46′ 26″ N, 122° 24′ 36″ W to decimal format is 37.77389, –122.41000. The answer is roughly the same as the decimal version the section started with. The difference is the rounding error, which isn't very significant for this purpose. You will discover more about precision in the next project.

Determine Precision of Decimal Coordinates

The latitude and longitude format most commonly used expresses degrees as decimals. Mapping providers, and also most services, convert from degrees to decimals to provide location data.

You might remember a tricky little thing about decimals from learning real numbers in math class: they can go on forever. You have to decide how many digits to use, much like calculators only have room for a certain amount of numbers. At some point, decimals need to be chopped off.

The number of decimals in latitude and longitude points varies by service. However, most services provide at least five digits after the decimal. As you can see in Table 1-1, five digits is enough to get within four feet of the location. In other words, for plotting points on a web map, five digits is plenty.

Table 1-1: Latitude Precision by Number of Decimals

Digits after decimal	Possible error
1	7 miles (11 km)
2	¾ mile (1 km)
3	370 feet (110 meters)
4	37 feet (11 meters)
5	4 feet (1 meter)

City-level coordinates often have as few as one digit after the decimal. Only using one digit gives a possible error of 7 miles, but the coordinates will still be within the bounds of most cities. For example, Yahoo!'s weather API (used in "#69: Create a Weather Map" on page 237) gives city coordinates to only two digits of precision, which reduces the error to less than one mile.

Longitude precision is not as easy to calculate as latitude, because degrees of longitude are not parallel. At the equator, the latitude and longitude charts would be the same. As longitude lines near the poles, however, they come closer together. The good news is that the latitude error is the maximum that can exist for longitude, so, in most cases, the error is smaller for longitudes.

NOTE *The latitude error also varies by about 1 km between the equator and the poles, but this error is a much smaller variation than with longitude.*

You'll learn more about the strange quirks of longitude in "#36: Calculate Distance Between Two Points" on page 117, where I'll show how to adjust for the different distances between degrees based on latitude.

Create Your First Map

You are about to embark upon an education in neocartography, taking yourself from plain ol' web developer to a Geolocative Web Developer. We'll create a basic map in this section, and it will serve as a building block for future projects.

First, we'll use the Google Maps API to create a map centered on the No Starch Press offices in San Francisco. Then, I'll show you the changes necessary to create the same map using Yahoo!'s service. Finally, I'll show how nearly identical Mapstraction code can create both of those maps.

Create a Google Map

Google is the 500 pound gorilla in many areas of the Web, and mapping is no exception. Most map developers choose the Google Maps API, if only because of its ubiquity. In addition to being everywhere, Google Maps is fast and stable.

Google Maps has been around since 2005. That's not to say the Maps team isn't innovating. On the contrary, Google Maps is often the first to add new features to its API, such as driving directions and a 360-degree view of any address in many cities in the United States and select places across the globe.

Let's create a basic map using Google. Open a new HTML file and type the following:

```
<!DOCTYPE html PUBLIC "-//W3C//DTD XHTML 1.0 Strict//EN"
"http://www.w3.org/TR/xhtml1/DTD/xhtml1-strict.dtd">
<html xmlns="http://www.w3.org/1999/xhtml">
  <head>
    <title>Basic Google Map</title>
    <script
        src="http://maps.google.com/maps/api/js?sensor=false"
        type="text/javascript"></script>
    <style type="text/css">
    div#mymap {
        width: 400px;
        height: 350px;
    }
```

```
        </style>
        <script type="text/javascript">
        function create_map() {
❶          var opt = {center: new google.maps.LatLng(37.7740486,-122.4101883),
                      zoom: 15, mapTypeId: google.maps.MapTypeId.ROADMAP};
❷          var map = new google.maps.Map(document.getElementById("mapdiv"), opt);
        }
        </script>
    </head>
    <body onload="create_map()">
❸     <div id="mymap"></div>
    </body>
</html>
```

Save your file and load it in a browser. The result should look something like Figure 1-3, with your Google Map centered on No Starch Press's neighborhood in San Francisco.

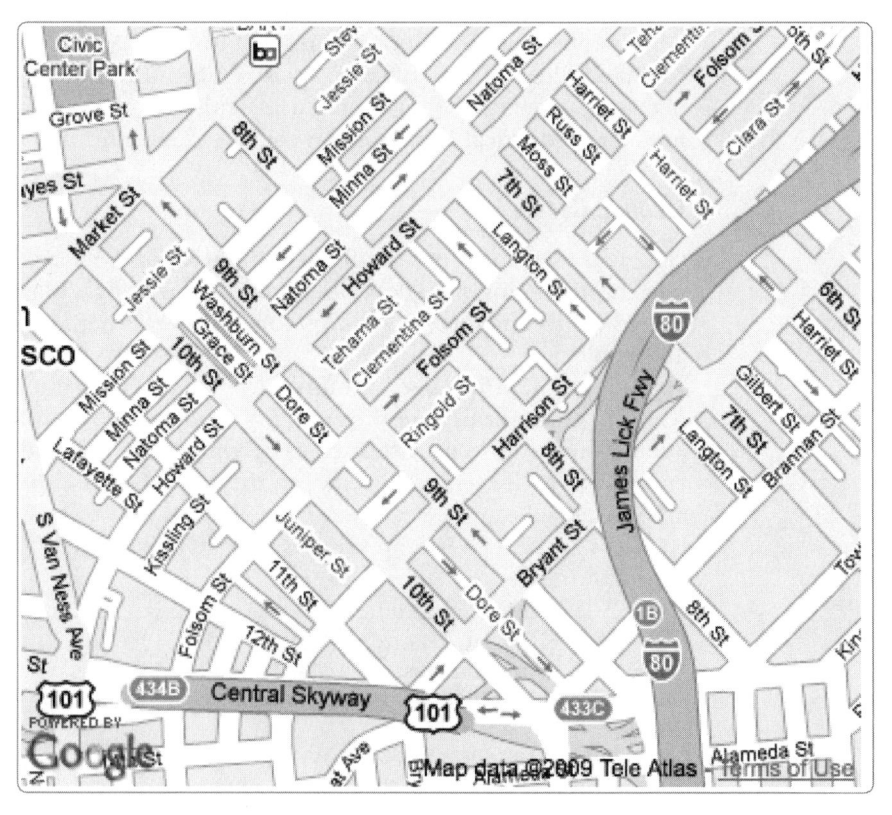

Figure 1-3: A basic Google Map

As you can see, the HTML hooks are minimal. An empty div tag ❸ with an id attribute is all that's required. The JavaScript function create_map() takes over and makes calls to the API. This function can have any name you want. In many examples in this book, I'll use this same name.

Before creating the map, we'll need to set some options ❶. The minimum amount of information needed is a center (using a latitude/longitude pair), a zoom level and a map type. Then, we pass those options and reference the div tag's id to create a map ❷.

And just like that you've created your first Google Map. Read on to see how this map is different from Yahoo! and how you can use Mapstraction to write code once that will work with any mapping provider.

Create a Yahoo! Map

Yahoo! released its mapping API around the same time as Google. Unfortunately, the first version was Flash-based and difficult to use. Google grabbed an early lead and Yahoo! has been playing catch-up ever since. Now Yahoo! has a JavaScript API with features similar to Google's.

You'll need an API key from Yahoo! and a Yahoo! account to use its maps. To register an application, which gives you a key, visit this web page: *https://developer.yahoo.com/wsregapp/*.

Select the option with no authentication because you will not be accessing Yahoo! user data. Fill out the rest of the form with information about your application, click the button, and you're set.

Once you get your API key, you're ready to create a Yahoo! Map. To do that, start with the Google example in the previous section. Replace the call to Google's JavaScript to instead include Yahoo!'s code (be sure to use your API key):

```
<script type="text/javascript"
  src="http://api.maps.yahoo.com/ajaxymap?v=3.8&appid=yourkeyhere"></script>
```

Next, alter the contents of the create_map function like so:

```
    function create_map() {
❶     var map = new Ymap(document.getElementById('mymap'));
❷     map.drawZoomAndCenter(new YGeoPoint(37.7740486,-122.4101883), 3);
    }
```

Save your file and load it in a browser. The result should look something like Figure 1-4, with your Yahoo! Map centered on No Starch Press's neighborhood in San Francisco.

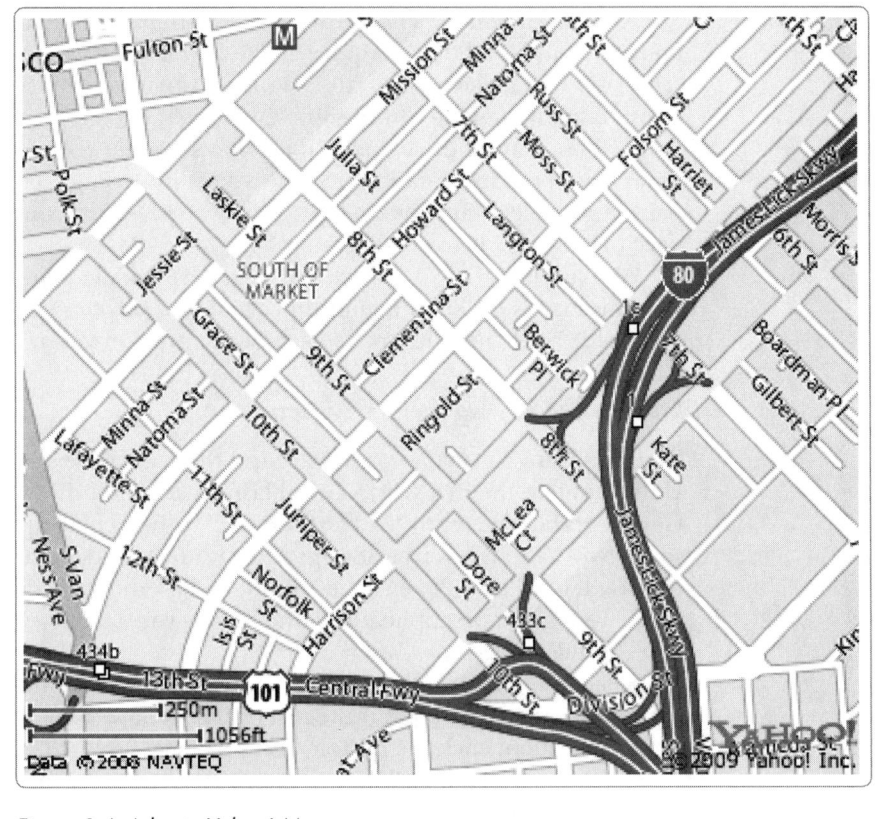

Figure 1-4: A basic Yahoo! Map

The code is not that different from Google Maps. You create a new map by referencing the div tag's id ❶. And you give the map a center by using a latitude/longitude pair ❷. The biggest differences are in terms of syntax and order. With Yahoo, you create a map, then add options, such as the zoom level and center.

The concept behind the two maps is very similar. But these minor differences compound to become a big pain, however, if you need to switch from one to the other. That's why Mapstraction is so powerful, as you will see in the next section.

Create a Mapstraction Map

Mapstraction is a little different from Google Maps and Yahoo! Maps. Mapstraction is an open source JavaScript library that ties into other mapping APIs. If you use Mapstraction, you can switch from one type of map to another with very little work, as opposed to rewriting your code completely.

Using Mapstraction limits your risk to changes being made to an API. For example, if your site's traffic takes you beyond the limit for your chosen provider, or the provider begins placing ads on the map, Mapstraction lets you switch providers quickly and inexpensively.

To use Mapstraction, you must first choose a provider. In this example, I'm using Mapstraction to create a Google Map.

Open a new HTML file and type the following:

```
<html>
  <head>
    <title>Basic Mapstraction Map</title>
    <script
❶  src="http://maps.google.com/maps/api/js?sensor=false"
      type="text/javascript"></script>
 <script type="text/javascript" src="mxn.js?(❷googlev3)"></script>
    <style type="text/css">
      div#mymap {
        width: 400px;
        height: 350px;
      }
    </style>
    <script type="text/javascript">
      function create_map() {
        var mapstraction = new mxn.Mapstraction('mymap', '❸googlev3');
        mapstraction.setCenterAndZoom(
          new mxn.LatLonPoint(37.7740486,-122.4101883), 15);
      }
    </script>
  </head>
  <body onload="create_map()">
    <div id="mymap"></div>
  </body>
</html>
```

Just like you would for a normal Google Map, we include Google's JavaScript ❶. For this code to work, you also need to download the Mapstraction files. Go to *http://mapstraction.com/*, and follow the instructions to save the files in the same directory as your HTML file. Best practices would dictate that you keep JavaScript files in their own directory, separate from your HTML, but I'm simplifying things for this example.

The Mapstraction files you should have, at minimum, are *mxn.js*, *mxn.core.js* and *googlev3.core.js*. You may also have files for other providers, such as *yahoo.core.js*. The only one we need to reference in our HTML code is *mxn.js*, which loads the other files that it needs, including those that we pass it in the filename ❷. Then, in the create_map function, we let it know which type of map ❸ we are creating.

Once you have your Mapstraction map, save your HTML file and load it in a browser. The result should look exactly like the Google Map in Figure 1-4. This Google Map, created via Mapstraction, should be centered on No Starch Press's neighborhood in San Francisco.

Use Yahoo! Maps with Mapstraction

To get an idea of how powerful the Mapstraction library is, let's try using Yahoo! Maps instead of Google Maps. You only have to change a few bits in the code. And the best part is even if you have a lot of Mapstraction code, you will still only need to change this one line.

As when switching from a standard Google Map to a Yahoo! Map, you need to include Yahoo!'s JavaScript. Before moving on, ensure the following lines are in your file:

```
<script
    src="http://api.maps.yahoo.com/ajaxymap?v=3.8&appid=yourkeyhere"
    type="text/javascript"></script>
<script type="text/javascript" src="mxn.js?(❶yahoo)"></script>
```

Note that rather than loading the Mapstraction JavaScript with Google support, we specified the Yahoo! version of Mapstraction ❶. Although the core of Mapstraction is provider agnostic, you need to tell it which of the providers you want to use. You also need to make sure you have *yahoo.core.js* in the same directory as *mxn.js*.

Now let's look at the Mapstraction code itself inside the create_map function:

```
function create_map() {
    var mapstraction = new mxn.Mapstraction('mymap', ❷'yahoo');
    mapstraction.setCenterAndZoom(
        new mxn.LatLonPoint(37.7740486,-122.4101883), 15);
}
```

Here, the only difference between the Mapstraction map made with Google and this map is we've noted we're making a Yahoo! map ❷. That's it. No need to change the setCenterAndZoom or LatLonPoint functions. The syntax is the same because Mapstraction is wrapped around the providers.

Save and reload your file and what was once a Google Map should be replaced with a Yahoo! Map instead, exactly like Figure 1-5. It is the same Yahoo! Map, only this one was created through Mapstraction.

Mapstraction is like magic, only better. In fact, you don't even have to choose Google *or* Yahoo!. You could have both within the same map or one of each on a page.

Find the Underlying Map Tiles

A web map's draggability might be its best attribute. I often find myself dragging a map just because I can. The feature also turns out to be a really good illusion.

What looks like one seamless map is actually many small tiles, placed next to each other. You might have noticed this in a moment of network lag, when a section of your map failed to load. Network lag is most likely to happen after you've changed the zoom level or if you quickly drag the map far from its original location.

Providers often attempt to avoid disrupting the illusion of seamlessness by preloading all the tiles that touch the tiles in your current area.

Each tile has a standard size of 256 pixels square. In the basic map example, six tiles are at least partially visible. If Google is the provider, it also loads additional surrounding tiles. Figure 1-5 shows how the visible portion of the map corresponds to its tiles. In the original view, we only see slivers of the top two tiles.

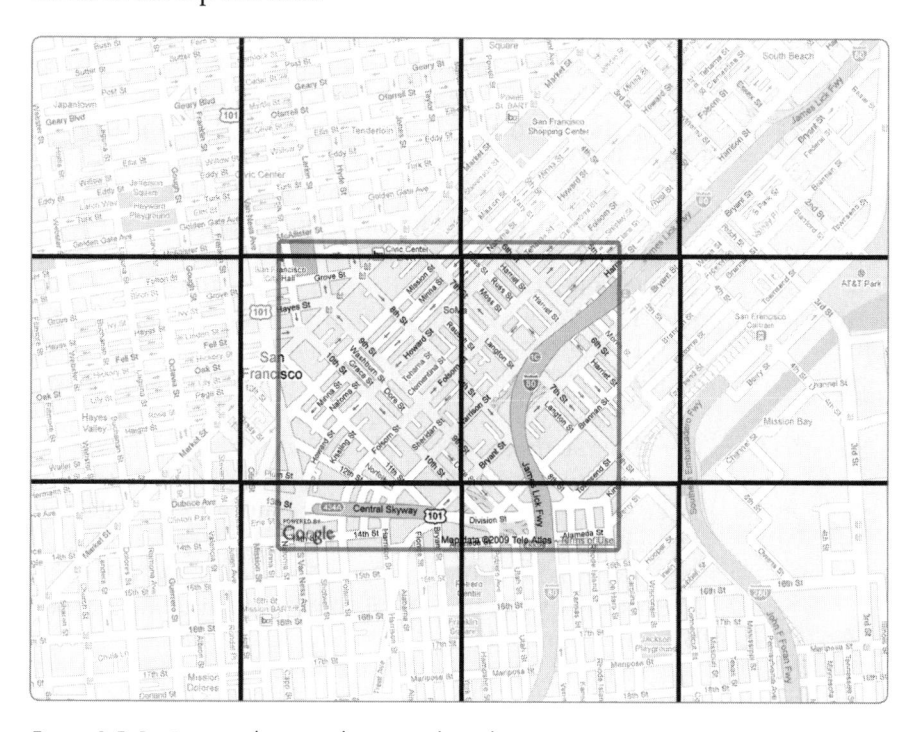

Figure 1-5: Basic map shown with surrounding tiles

What happens when we change zoom levels? We need to download a completely new set of tiles. The details shown are different for each zoom level, and each tile now represents a different amount of the earth.

Due to copyright concerns, providers tend to make it difficult to access their tiles directly. You can, however, look at the tiles that are downloaded to your browser when you access a provider's maps. Doing this will give you a better idea of how the tile system works.

Though you can get at the files in a number of ways, I'll show you a very easy method using the Firefox browser and the Firebug developer add-on. You can find them at *http://www.getfirefox.com/* and *http://www.getfirebug .com/*, respectively.

In Firefox, load an embedded map, such as the one in the basic map example. Click the Firebug icon in the lower-right corner, or choose **Firebug ▸ Open Firebug** from the Tools menu. In the Firebug panel, click the **Inspect** button, which allows you to see highlighted page elements. Hover your mouse over the center of the map, and a blue border should appear around a portion of the map. You have found a tile!

With a tile highlighted, click the mouse, and you will be taken to HTML code with an image tag, as shown in Figure 1-6. At first, this tag may seem confusing because you didn't add this image to your code. Unlike simply viewing source code in a browser, Firebug shows the page with the elements added by JavaScript. To create a map, your provider had to inject images as child elements of the map div tag.

In the src attribute of the image, you'll see the URL to the single tile that you highlighted with Firebug. You can copy that URL into a new window or tab to see only that tile, without including the context of its surrounding brethren. Also, you can doctor the parameters in the URL to view other tiles.

The earth is made up of thousands or millions of tiles, depending on the zoom level. Mapping providers refer to tiles based on a simple grid system. You can think of this as similar to a paper map, which helps you identify areas by referencing them based on a letter-number combination. For example, you might look in (K, 18) to find Maple Street.

Tiles are called by their grid reference, too; only these are usually numbered in the thousands. For example, my San Francisco example might contain a tile that is at (5241, 3718). The grid is different for each zoom level, so that reference is an important third piece of information needed to call a particular tile. To call the tile to the right of the example tile, I would look for (5242, 3718) at the same zoom level. Only the first number changes because it represents the horizontal portion of the grid. Vertically, both tiles are in row 3718.

To recap, you'll usually find three numbers in the tile URLs: the horizontal grid reference (often called X), the vertical grid reference (Y), and the zoom level.

Mapstraction provides a way to use whatever tiles you would like, regardless of the provider. Again, most providers don't support direct access to the tiles. Many times you might find they use methods to prevent you from calling them. You could always create your own tiles. I show you how to do that and how to connect them to Mapstraction in "#26: Use Custom Tiles" on page 90.

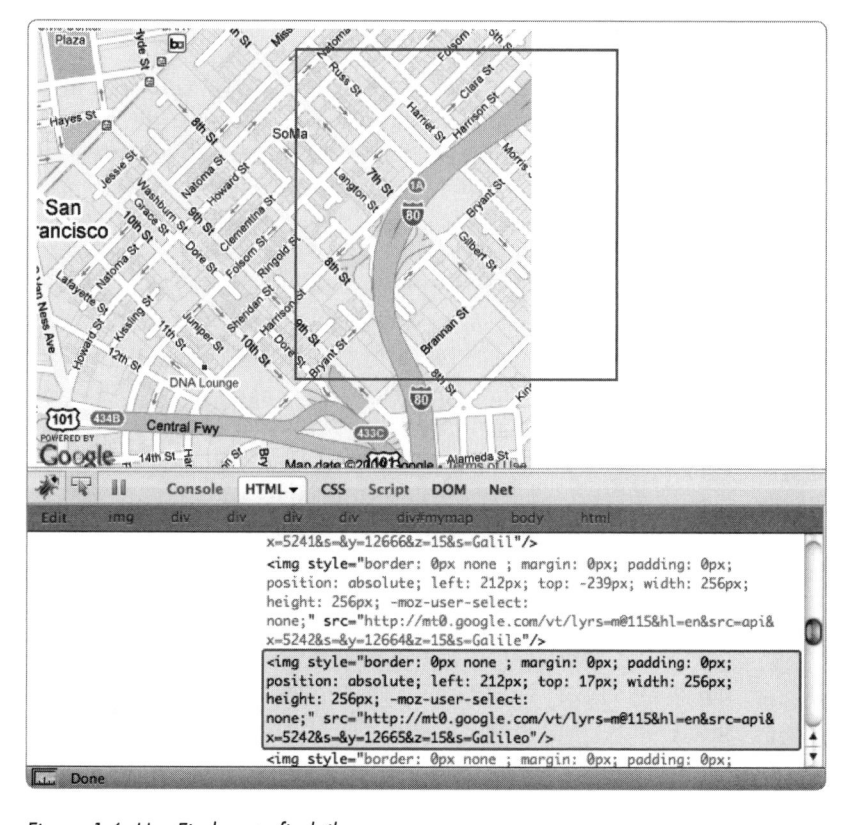

Figure 1-6: Use Firebug to find tiles.

Change the Map Size

The initial map size is determined by CSS styles for the div tag. You can change the size of the map programmatically with Mapstraction, however.

Add the following line to the create_map function, or include it as a click event in a link (see Appendix A):

```
mapstraction.resizeTo(200, 300);
```

When the resizeTo function is called, you pass a width and height. Mapstraction then immediately sets the size of the map to the desired pixels. Note the center of the map is not reset. If you shrink the map, you may need to recenter the map to keep your same center-point in view.

Also, a word of caution about shrinking your map: Depending on the provider you use, interface elements may begin to collide. Be sure to test to see how small a map you can get away with.

Add Zoom and Other Controls

One of the best things about using maps on your website is that users can explore with them. They want to see what's nearby, look more closely at a particular location, or figure out where a spot is in relation to the city or country. The basic maps I've shown so far do not give users very much control.

Let's give the users an interface to click, so they can zoom and pan around the map. Mapstraction offers several ways to do this.

Small Controls

Small controls are useful when your map isn't very big, such as when you stick it in a sidebar. Also, if you don't expect users to perform many zooms, you might prefer to keep the interface clean.

To add small controls to your map, add this line in your create_map function after you have set the mapstraction variable:

```
mapstraction.addSmallControls();
```

Save and reload your file, and you should see a small set of buttons in the upper-left corner of your map. Exactly how the controls look will depend on which mapping provider you instruct Mapstraction to use. The map will likely contain plus and minus buttons for zooming and a collection of arrow buttons for panning.

Large Controls

If your map is the focal point of your website or page, you probably want large controls. While small controls only let users zoom in or out one level at a time, with large controls you can skip to any zoom level.

Add this line to your create_map function:

```
mapstraction.addLargeControls();
```

Save and reload your file. When using Google Maps, Mapstraction adds several other controls in addition to the larger zoom/pan tools. To see how small and large zoom/pan tools look, see Figure 1-7.

To only add the large versions of zoom/pan, try this function:

```
mapstraction.addControls({zoom:'large'});
```

Here, you pass an object (declared with curly braces) with a single option for large zoom controls.

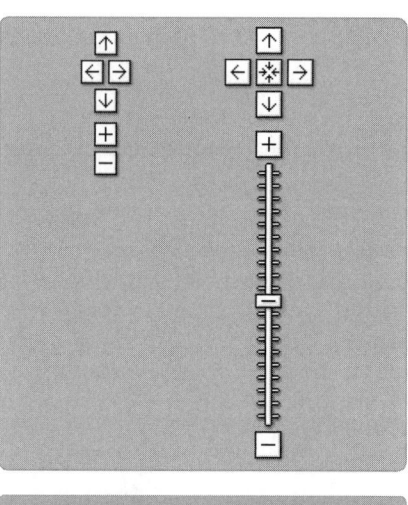

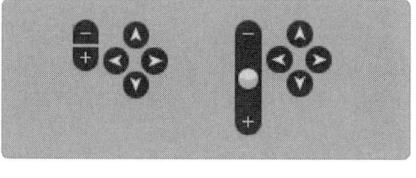

Figure 1-7: Small and large zoom controls in
Google Maps (top) and Yahoo! Maps (bottom)

Map-Type Controls

Mapping providers often let users choose which type of map to view. In
addition to a normal map, a satellite view and a hybrid of normal and satellite view are common. Not every map provider has all of these views. For
example, some use aerial photography instead of satellite or don't have
photographic imagery at all.

Use this command to add a map-type control to your map, like the one
in Figure 1-8, so users can choose how they want to see your map:

```
mapstraction.addMapTypeControls();
```

Save and reload your file to see the buttons in the upper-right corner of
your map (with most providers).

Figure 1-8: Map type controls in Google Maps

Set Zoom Level

Now you've added some controls to your map, and users can change the zoom level. In most projects, you'll want to give users this power. Regardless, you need to set an initial zoom level, so the mapping provider knows what to show.

Zoom levels determine how much detail is shown. A map of the entire world cannot contain streets or parks. Showing country borders is about as complex as that map can get—even most cities are smaller than a pixel. When zoomed in to a city-level map, you'll see major streets, but perhaps not neighborhood features.

In the basic map, you set the center and the zoom at the same time. Mapstraction also has a function that only sets the zoom level, while keeping the center the same:

```
mapstraction.setZoom(10);
```

As with the setCenterAndZoom function, the zoom level is communicated as an integer. In this example, I set a zoom level of 10, whereas I used 15 in the basic map. What do these numbers mean? Which one is zoomed in closer?

Mapstraction uses zoom levels 0–16, with the larger numbers corresponding to being more zoomed in—a greater level of detail. With satellite view, you may be able to zoom in even further. Table 1-2 shows an approximate correspondence between zoom levels and the area usually shown. Naturally, the exact level is determined by the size of a country, state, or city.

Table 1-2: Mapstraction Zoom Levels

Geography description	Zoom level
World	0
Country	4
State	7
City	13
Street	16

Another reason to appreciate Mapstraction is it accommodates the different ways mapping providers handle zoom levels. Yahoo!, for example, uses a reverse numbering system, where larger numbers mean the map is more zoomed out. MapQuest, on the other hand, counts the same as Mapstraction, but has fewer levels with minimal detail. Through its single interface, Mapstraction takes care of these discrepancies.

Just as you can set the zoom level, Mapstraction has a very similar command to retrieve the current zoom level:

```
var currentzoom = mapstraction.getZoom();
```

The integer returned is within the 0–16 Mapstraction range, converting from the provider's zoom system, if necessary. You can use a combination of setZoom and getZoom to create your own controls, rather than sticking with the mapping provider's defaults. "#23: Create Your Own Zoom Interface" on page 79 shows how to do this with step-by-step instructions.

Set Map Type

Most mapping providers offer three options for determining the look of maps. You can choose a simple map, which is the default, a satellite view, or a combination of the two. As I showed previously, you can let the user decide which map type to view by adding a control, usually to the upper-right corner of the map. The map type can also be set programmatically, which is what we'll do in this section.

You can set the map type at any time, though the most common situation is declaring something other than the default type when the map is loaded. For example, add this line to the create_map function of your basic map to show the satellite view layered with street information:

```
mapstraction.setMapType(Mapstraction.HYBRID);
```

The argument that the setMapType function accepts is just a simple integer, but as you can see, we passed it some other type of variable. Mapstraction has *constants*—special variables that are created to give more meaning than simple numbers—that make choosing a map type easy. Setting the map type to HYBRID makes more sense than remembering that you need to pass along the number 3 when you want both street and satellite views. Table 1-3 shows all the map-type options and their corresponding numeric values.

Table 1-3: Mapstraction Map Types

Name	Value
Mapstraction.ROAD	1
Mapstraction.SATELLITE	2
Mapstraction.HYBRID	3

Map-type constants are also useful when retrieving the current map type from Mapstraction. Just as you can both *set* and *get* the zoom level, you can access the map type. Add this line sometime after you've created your map:

```
var maptype = mapstraction.getMapType();
```

Remember, the setMapType function accepts an integer value as an argument. The value returned from getMapType is 1, 2, or 3. Again, referring to map types by the Mapstraction constants is much easier. For example, you can use a switch... case statement to perform different actions based on the map type:

```
switch (maptype) {
  case Mapstraction.ROAD:
    // Run this code only when it is a road map type
  break;
  case Mapstraction.SATELLITE:
    // Run this code only when it is a satellite map type
  break;
  case Mapstraction.HYBRID:
    // Run this code only when it is a hybrid map type
  break;
}
```

Replace the comments (the lines that start with two slashes) with the code you would want to use in the circumstances described. For example, you might want to remove driving directions from a map if only the satellite map is showing, because showing driving directions when no streets are visible makes less sense.

Recenter the Map

If you're already displaying a map, then you gave it a center with the setCenterAndZoom function. You never know when users will drag the map away from your center. Knowing how to reset the center—and just the center—can be useful.

Add the following line to the create_map function, or include it as a click event in a link:

```
mapstraction.setCenter(new mxn.LatLonPoint(37.7740486,-122.4101883));
```

Of course, snapping a map directly to a point can be jarring. Luckily, the user can pan to the new center point, as if he or she dragged the map there:

```
mapstraction.setCenter(new mxn.LatLonPoint(37.7740486,-122.4101883), {pan:true});
```

Here we're passing an options object to the setCenter function. The curly braces declare an object in JavaScript with values set by key:value pairs. Mapstraction will look for whether pan exists. If pan is set to true, then the map will pan smoothly to the new point.

Retrieve the Center of the Map

When you load a new map, you need to give it a center. Then you give up control, as your users drag and pan that map to their heart's content. That's good, because maps are interactive. On the other hand, you may want to know the map's current center.

Mapstraction has a simple command to retrieve the map's center:

```
var centerpoint = mapstraction.getCenter();
```

The variable created, centerpoint, holds the result from the call to getCenter() as a LatLonPoint, which is the way Mapstraction stores coordinates. Keeping coordinates in a variable is handy because you can turn around and pass that to other functions. Or you can access the latitude and longitude directly:

```
centerpoint.lat
centerpoint.lon
```

Now, you can use those values to add a marker to your map, plot local results on a map, or for some other purpose.

Find Point Where User Clicked

Out-of-the-box interactivity makes mapping APIs pretty special. Using built-in controls, users can drag and pan the map, zoom in, and change map types. Users can also click, but nothing will happen unless you help them out.

To find the point where a user clicks, you need to "listen" for the click event:

```
mapstraction.addEventListener('click', function(clickpoint) {
    alert('latitude: ' + clickpoint.lat + '\nlongitude: ' + clickpoint.lon);
});
```

When the user clicks anywhere within the map, an anonymous function is called with clickpoint as an argument. Similar to when you retrieve the center of a map, the variable is a LatLonPoint. This example uses a JavaScript alert to display the latitude and longitude of the point where the user clicked, as shown in Figure 1-9.

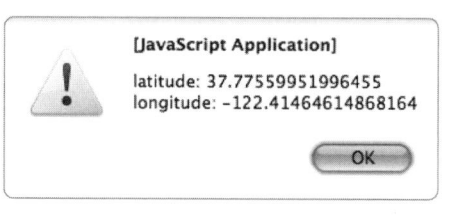

Figure 1-9: JavaScript alert showing latitude and longitude of click point

Of course, you'll want to do something more useful than a JavaScript alert. For example, you could add a marker to your map at that point. As it happens, the next chapter shows you how to do that and more.

2

PLOTTING MARKERS AND MESSAGE BOXES

Creating simple maps is a cool and useful way to see the area around a location, but you'll find creating maps even more fun and useful when you plot your own points on a map. Using mapping APIs you can overlay small graphics to call attention to locations (determined by latitude and longitude coordinates). Optionally, you can create messages that describe a location when the marker is clicked.

You've seen these principles in action on just about any chain store's website, among many others. If you're looking to shop in person, you've probably used the Find a Store link. From there, you enter your city, ZIP Code, address, or some other determination of your location. Then a map appears showing the closest stores, with each store's location marked, often with a number that matches a results list. If the number is clickable, you will likely find that store's address, telephone number, or other information.

This chapter will get you started creating tools like store locators. You will learn to add markers, create custom icons, show messages in hovering boxes, and more. Mapping providers implement similar, but slightly different ways, of plotting markers on your map. Mapstraction wrangles these differences into a single set of functions that can add markers and message boxes no matter the underlying map type.

#1: Add a Marker to Your Map

The basic marker is a staple of web maps. Markers bring the user's attention to one or more points on the map. For many projects, you won't need to get any more complicated than a map and a handful of basic markers.

Although we'll be using Mapstraction to produce our markered maps, the underlying work is being done by whichever mapping service we're using. Just like the look of the map is determined by the provider, so will the default style of the basic marker. Figure 2-1 shows the differences among the markers from major map services.

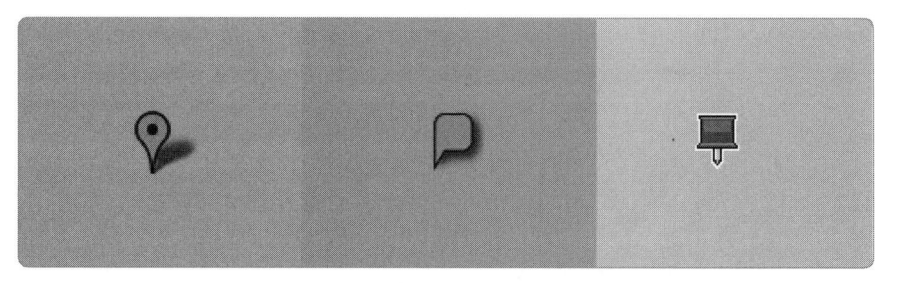

Figure 2-1: Default markers from different providers: Google, Yahoo!, and Microsoft

To add a simple marker to your map, you just need to use two Mapstraction functions. First, create the marker. Next, add it to the map. The reason for these two distinct steps will become clear in further projects when we start to use advanced options, such as custom marker icons.

Let's see what creating the marker looks like in code. Start with the basic Mapstraction map you created in "Create a Mapstraction Map" on page 10, and add these lines to the create_map() function:

```
marker = new mxn.Marker(new mxn.LatLonPoint(37.7740486,-122.4101883));
// marker options will go here
mapstraction.addMarker(marker);
```

The first line creates a marker object, passing latitude/longitude coordinates for the No Starch Press offices in San Francisco. Remember this is the same point we used as the center of our map in Chapter 1. By drawing attention to the graphical marker, we are essentially marking that spot as important.

The second line is a placeholder for any marker options we want to add later. (Any JavaScript line that begins with two slashes is a comment, and the browser ignores them.) The marker options are where we tell Mapstraction which icon to use or add a message to be displayed when the marker is clicked.

Finally, the third line adds the marker to the map. Once this happens, no additional options can be added. The reason is that the marker object is used only by Mapstraction. Once the marker is added to the map, however, Mapstraction makes the appropriate calls to the mapping provider. Mapstraction plots the marker based on all options set beforehand. In this case, we don't have options to add, but we'll add to this map in future projects.

If you're using Google as your mapping provider, your new map will look like Figure 2-2. The default Google icon sits in the center of the map. Although the marker is clickable, this marker is very simple and nothing actually happens if you click it. Read on to learn other cool things you can do with markers.

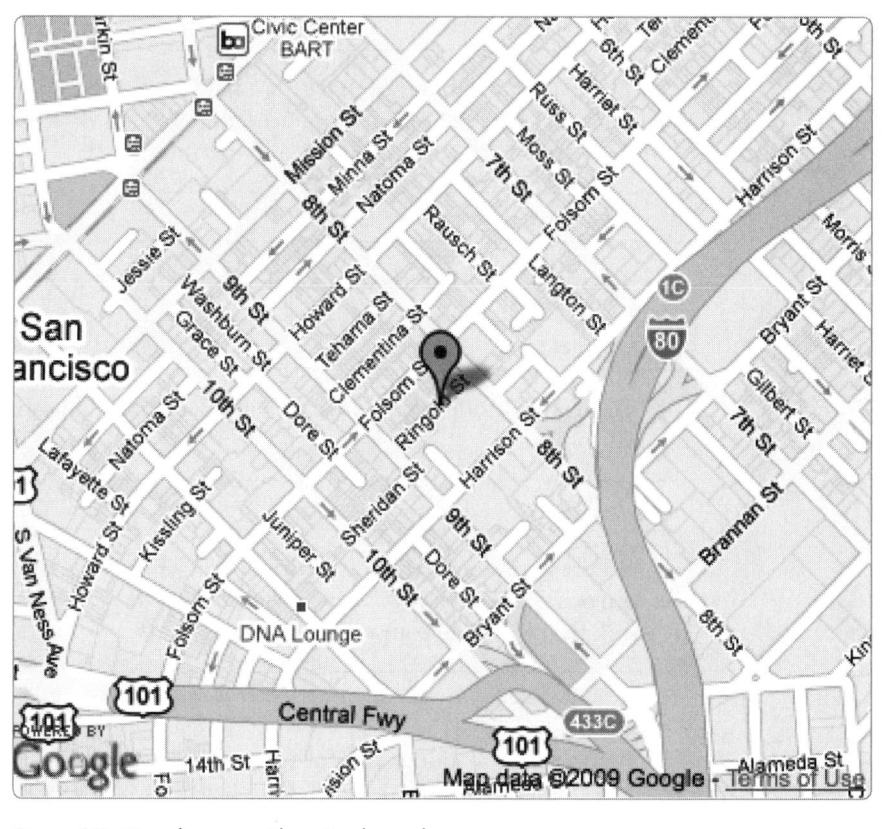

Figure 2-2: Google map with a simple marker

#2: Remove or Hide a Marker

Once your map has markers, you may wish to remove them from the map selectively. You might replace the current markers with new results. Or maybe the user added a filter that does not include the current marker. Mapstraction provides three functions to make markers disappear and reappear. Though *removing* and *hiding* may sound like similar terms, understanding the differences between them is important. Removing a marker from a map means the marker is gone for good. Simply hiding the marker allows you to make it visible again.

To use the functions to remove, hide, and show markers, you need access to Mapstraction and marker objects. These objects are generated when you create your new map and whenever you create a new marker. Whether they become available to the rest of your script, however, depends on the variable's scope.

Scope refers to the parts of code where a variable can be accessed. Any variable created inside the create_map function can only be used inside that function. To remove or hide markers, we need to make our Mapstraction and marker objects global. To do this, add this declaration right above the create_map function:

```
var mapstraction, marker;
```

These two variables now have a global scope, meaning we can use the variables outside of the create_map function. To remove a marker, you call the removeMarker function on the Mapstraction object:

```
mapstraction.removeMarker(marker);
```

To simply hide a marker, you call the hide function on the marker object:

```
marker.hide();
```

To make a hidden marker reappear, you call the show function on the marker object:

```
marker.show();
```

Where do you call these functions? Anywhere they're needed. For testing purposes, create a link anywhere after the <body> tag. For example, here is a link that will hide your marker:

```
<a href="javascript:marker.hide();">hide marker</a>
```

Again, this location is just for testing. You want unobtrusive JavaScript that isn't called from a link's href. One barrier to using all three of these functions is having access to the marker object.

This single marker example only requires the variable be within a global scope. As you've seen, that's easy enough. When you start using many markers, you'll need a way to organize them beyond declaring dozens of variables.

Mapstraction's built-in ability to filter out certain markers (see "#9: Filter Out Certain Markers" on page 36) may be the easiest solution. If it does not provide all the features you need, you can always access all the markers that Mapstraction has added:

```
var allmarkers = mapstraction.markers;
```

Mapstraction's markers object gives you an array of markers. From here, you can remove, hide, or show them as you wish.

#3: Show a Message Box When Your Marker Is Clicked

Markers alone are useful because they identify spots on the map. Once your map has more than one, viewers will start wondering what each marker means. Sure, you could use custom icons to differentiate markers and we'll see how to do that shortly. But you can provide more information by showing descriptive text when the user clicks a marker.

Each mapping provider has a way to show a message box. Like markers themselves, the box looks different depending on the provider. Figure 2-3 shows the differences among the message boxes from the major map services.

Figure 2-3: Message boxes from different providers

Mapstraction provides an interface, called an *InfoBubble*, that works with all providers. To create an InfoBubble for a marker, you add a marker option like so:

```
marker.setInfoBubble("Look ma, No Starch!");
```

The setInfoBubble function takes a string of text (HTML works, too) and saves it in connection with the marker. The line must be inserted after the marker object is created but before the marker is added to the map. If you have the code from creating a basic marker ("#1: Add a Marker to Your Map" on page 24), you can just add the setInfoBubble line in place of the comment about marker options.

For clarification, here are the commands necessary to create a brand new marker, include an InfoBubble, and place the marker on the map:

```
marker = new mxn.Marker(new mxn.LatLonPoint(37.7740486,-122.4101883));
marker.setInfoBubble("Look ma, No Starch!");
mapstraction.addMarker(marker);
```

Great! Now if you load this file, you see a basic marker in the No Starch Press neighborhood. Where is the InfoBubble? Click the marker, and you see something similar to Figure 2-4. Mapstraction and the mapping provider do all the work of capturing the click event and displaying the InfoBubble. All you need to do is provide the content. If you're hoping to open the InfoBubble automatically or from code, read on; I'll show you how to display a message box without making the user click in the next project.

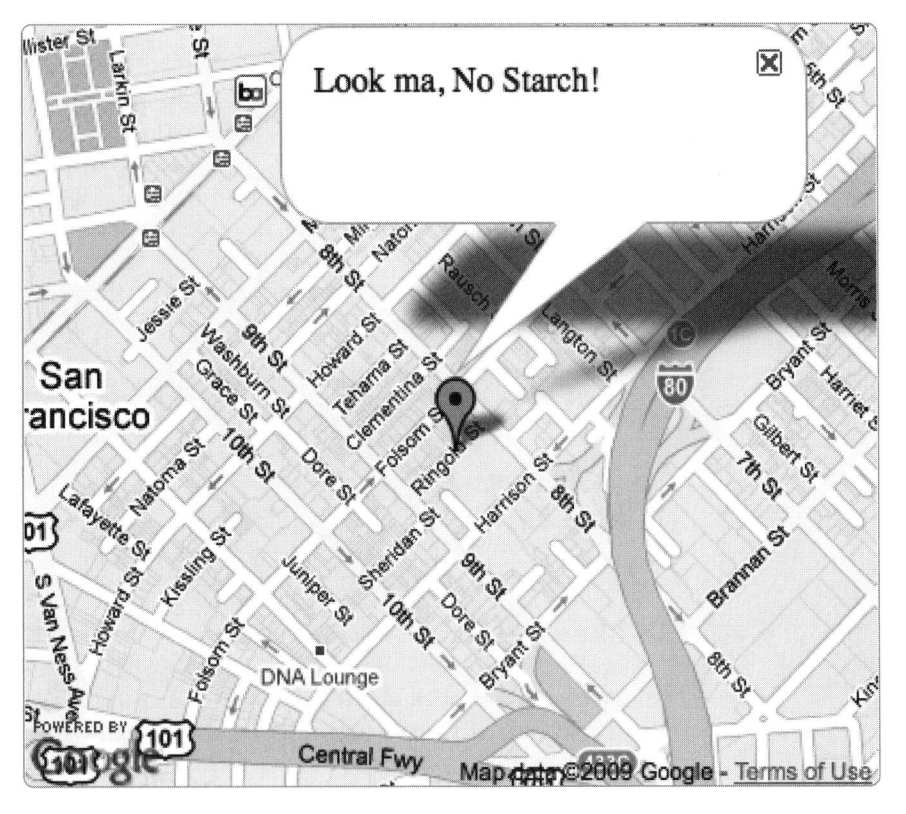

Figure 2-4: Message box with message displayed

#4: Show and Hide Message Boxes Without Clicking the Marker

Maps let users click around and interact with a location. You've seen how you can add clickable markers that provide more information about the spots you've plotted. But sometimes you want a little bit more control. Sometimes you want to open up that InfoBubble *without* the user's permission.

For example, if your map shows search results, you might duplicate the locations in a list format beside the map. Then users can choose a location from the list and its corresponding marker opens a message box on the map.

The basic setup for displaying a message box from code is the same as a standard clickable marker. You can just set some text as a marker option:

```
marker.setInfoBubble("Look ma, No Starch!");
```

This ensures that a clicked marker will still show your message. Then, from elsewhere in your code (such as when the user clicks one of the search results), you can tell the marker to open the InfoBubble:

```
marker.openBubble();
```

You can close the InfoBubble with a similar command:

```
marker.closeBubble();
```

The `openBubble` and `closeBubble` functions require the marker variable to be accessible globally. That is, the marker object needs to be declared at the top of your code, or you need to find another way to access it. In "Functions" on page 297, I describe variable scope and how to declare variables so they can be accessed anywhere in your code.

#5: Create a Custom Icon Marker

The quickest way to make a map feel like your own is to change the default icon used for markers. Mapstraction has simple marker options that make the technical process of using custom icons a cinch. The more laborious part may be creating the icon file itself. To avoid this, you can find icons others have made online for free. I list several resources at *http://mapscripting.com/download-custom-markers/*.

Still want to create your own? Read on.

Get Out the Image Editor

To create your own marker icon, you just need to have a graphics program that can save a transparent *.png* file. The icon can be whatever size you want, but keeping each dimension between 20 and 50 pixels is probably best. If the icon is too small, clicking it becomes difficult; too big, and the icon obscures the location you're attempting to call out.

If you're using Google as your mapping provider, you also want to create an image to use as your marker's shadow. This step isn't necessary if your marker is a similar shape to the Google default or if you're using another provider.

NOTE　*Not much of an image magician? You can find an online service to create a shadow at* http://www.cycloloco.com/shadowmaker/.

Add Your Icon to the Map

Now that you have an icon, the easy part is adding it to the marker options. All it takes is setting a few values to tell Mapstraction where the icon image files resides. Your best bet is to keep custom marker icons in a special directory on your server. If you're testing locally, you can use local copies, accessed by their location relative to the page containing the map. For simplicity, I have the HTML file and the icon files in the same directory in this example. In reality, you might prefer to be more organized.

I decided to use a teensy No Starch Press logo for my custom icon. It's 27 pixels wide by 31 pixels high. Like I said, the icon is teensy. Then, I used a shadow-maker service to create a file that is 43×31 including the marker's shadow.

Finally, it's time to code. Add these lines as marker options. These lines are inserted after a marker has been created but before the marker has been added to the map:

```
marker.setIcon(❶'nostarch-logo.png', ❷[27,31]);
marker.setShadowIcon('nostarch-shadow.png', [43,31]);
```

The only parameter that you need to include is the path to the image ❶ for both the icon and the shadow. Notice that the dimensions of each graphic get passed as an inline array ❷. This parameter is optional but recommended. If you leave it out, some providers will assume the dimensions of the default marker, which could mean a poorly scaled graphic.

The results of the custom marker code are shown in Figure 2-5. The No Starch Press office is marked by the company's logo, a little iron icon. Notice the shadow, as well, which makes the graphic pop out from the map.

Omit the shadow icon at your own risk. Some mapping providers will assume the default shadow, which might look silly with your icon. Not every mapping provider uses shadows, but planning for one is good. If you really don't want a shadow, consider using a completely transparent graphic. I show an example of shadowless icons in "#69: Create a Weather Map" on page 237.

Figure 2-5: Custom marker shows the No Starch Press logo

#6: Create Numbered Markers

When you have a list of locations on your web page that you also want to plot on a map, provide users with numbered markers. For example, when displaying search results, you want a matching label both on and off the map so users can easily identify what's what.

Numbered markers are not any different from any other custom marker. You'll need to create a graphic icon for each number you want. Numerous icon sets are available online that you can use, or you can create them dynamically with the Google Charts API.

Generate the Numbered Icon

The Google Charts API generates reverse teardrop–style pins that look like the default Google marker. Using these Google-generated icons does not mean you have to use Google Maps. Mapstraction will add the icon for any provider to your map.

You control the marker's background and border color, as well as what the label reads. The criteria you require are sent in the URL of the icon itself. For example, here is the URL for a red marker labeled with a number one:

```
http://chart.apis.google.com/chart?chst=d_map_pin_letter&chld=❶1|❷FF3333|❸000000
```

The final argument of the URL contains all the important information for the marker: the label text ❶ (in this case, the number one), the background color, ❷ and the border ❸ color. The colors are represented as hex values, similar to how colors are declared in CSS.

The individual pieces of the chld argument are separated by the pipe character, |. In a way, the final argument is really three arguments with its own way of segmenting the values.

Custom markers added to a map when using Google as a mapping provider also require a shadow. Because the shapes of these dynamic markers are all the same, the shadow can be static. The Google Charts API provides this URL:

```
http://chart.apis.google.com/chart?chst=d_map_pin_shadow
```

Now that you can generate the icons, you need to place them on the map. To do this, we'll call these Google Charts URLs on the fly.

Add the Icon to the Map

Armed with dynamically generated marker URLs from Google Charts, the process of adding these numbered markers to a map is much like adding any custom icon. Here is the code listing that creates five random points within San Francisco. Each marker is given an icon with a label numbered one through five based on the order that it is created:

```
mapstraction = new mxn.Mapstraction('mymap', 'googlev3');
mapstraction.setCenterAndZoom(new mxn.LatLonPoint(37.7740486,-122.4101883), 11);
mapstraction.addLargeControls();
for (i=1; i<=5; i++) {
    var rndlatlon = get_random_by_bounds(mapstraction.getBounds());
    marker = new mxn.Marker(rndlatlon);
    marker.setIcon(
      'http://chart.apis.google.com/chart?chst=d_map_pin_letter&chld=' + i +
      '|FF3333|000000', [21,32]);
    marker.setShadowIcon(
      'http://chart.apis.google.com/chart?chst=d_map_pin_shadow');
    mapstraction.addMarker(marker);
}
mapstraction.autoCenterAndZoom();
```

The lines in bold set the generated icon and its shadow. The rest either sets up the map or creates the random points. For the code to work, you need a JavaScript function, get_random_by_bounds, which is discussed in Chapter 6 but which I have reprinted next. Put the previous code inside the create_map function used in all examples so far, and then make sure the following function is included somewhere in the JavaScript (but outside of other functions):

```
function get_random_by_bounds(bounds) {
  var lat = bounds.sw.lat + (Math.random() * (bounds.ne.lat - bounds.sw.lat));
  var lon = bounds.sw.lon + (Math.random() * (bounds.ne.lon - bounds.sw.lon));
  return new mxn.LatLonPoint(lat, lon);
}
```

Save your file. You'll see a map like the one shown in Figure 2-6 (marker locations vary—remember, they're random).

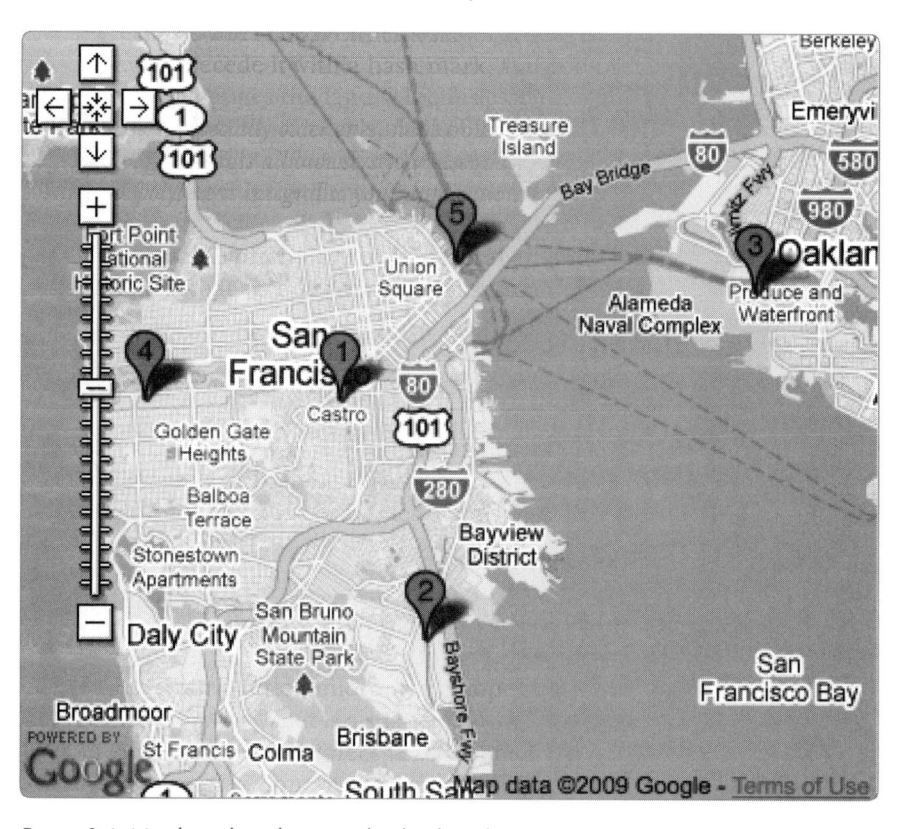

Figure 2-6: Numbered markers, randomly plotted

Use numbered markers when the order matters, such as when displaying nearby locations. Numbering is also helpful when users will match search results or another list from outside the map to the individual markers.

#7: Loop Through All Markers

When you've added a bunch of markers to the map, you may want a way to access them all. For example, you might be looking for outliers or determining which marker is the farthest north.

Mapstraction provides a property that holds an array of every marker plotted on the map. You can then reference an individual marker from within that array using standard JavaScript code to pull out a value at a specific index. Doing this for each marker on the map lets you loop through and perform an action on all the markers.

Add these lines to your code wherever you need to do something to each marker:

```
❶ var allm = mapstraction.markers;
❷ for (var i=0; i<allm.length; i++) {
❸   var thism = allm[i];
    // Any code for thism variable goes here
  }
```

The first thing we do is reference the array of all markers from Mapstraction ❶ with a new variable name, allm. The saves us some typing, as we'll need to use the marker variable several times. Next, we use JavaScript's for statement ❷ to loop through the array. A temporary variable, i, keeps track of the index, as we count from zero (the first element in an array is at zero) up to the total number of markers.

As each marker becomes available, we place a reference to it inside the temporary thism variable ❸, a name I chose because it describes "this marker," as in the marker we are currently utilizing. Anything within the braces, { and }, of the for loop now has access to this new variable.

We can look up marker options or call functions on the marker (such as showBubble or hide, for example). In most cases, we cannot *add* options because options need to be added before the marker is added to the map. For example, we cannot change the marker's icon without removing and re-adding the marker.

Despite these few limitations, looping through the markers is a useful trick to add to your mapping tool bag. Many of Mapstraction's functions, such as filtering or autocentering, use a loop internally.

#8: Determine the Correct Zoom Level to Use Based on Markers

Once your map has several markers, ensuring that all of them can be viewed becomes a chore. This is especially true when your locations are being served up by a database ("#66: Plot Locations from a Database" on page 226). Markers start to fall outside of your manually set center and zoom levels.

You may have tried to fix this on your own by changing the zoom level. If you zoom out, your markers can end up scrunched together, with lots of room to zoom in. The only way to achieve a good zoom level for any marker is to determine it programmatically after all the markers are added to the map.

Mapstraction makes setting the zoom level as easy as one function call. Add the following line to the create_map function from the basic map after you have added some markers:

```
mapstraction.autoCenterAndZoom();
```

You can also use a similar function that only works on displayed markers. That is, if you've hidden or filtered out some markers, you will probably want to zoom in to the ones that are still on the map. Instead of the previous function, use this:

```
mapstraction.visibleCenterAndZoom();
```

If these functions feel like magic, that's okay. Mapstraction makes it easy, but a lot is going on behind the curtain. Here's the run-down of how Mapstraction makes auto-zooming happen:

1. Loops through all the markers (or just the visible ones), and determines the maximum and minimum latitude and longitude of the markers. This measurement is called the *bounding box* and consists of four numbers that describe each edge of the box.
2. Finds the center of the bounding box by averaging the two latitudes and the two longitudes.
3. Checks zoom levels until it finds one that displays the entire bounding box.

Actually, Mapstraction does not need to perform the last two steps for very many mapping providers. Most already have something that does the auto-zooming work within their own library. That wasn't always the case, however, and it points to the power of Mapstraction. Mapstraction is able to add these indispensable functions before they're available in all map APIs.

To get a feel for how auto-zooming works, insert this code in the basic map's create_map function to add random markers:

```
❶ var num_markers = 5;
❷ var bigbounds = new mxn.BoundingBox(37.766, -122.400, 37.784, -122.418);
  for (i=1; i<=num_markers; i++) {
      var rndlatlon = ❸get_random_by_bounds(bigbounds);
      marker = new mxn.Marker(rndlatlon);
      mapstraction.addMarker(marker);
  }
❹ mapstraction.autoCenterAndZoom();
```

This code chooses five random markers, but you can change the first variable ❶ to any number you want. I've also created a bounding box ❷ that is larger than the basic map's visible area (you can learn more about bounds in Chapter 6). These bounds are used to produce a new random point for each of my markers. You actually need to include a special function ❸ to create the point. We'll get to that in a moment.

First, note the last line ❹, the one that auto-zooms. Try commenting it out by placing a // at the front of the line to see how the markers look without auto-zooming. Reload the map a few times with and without the comment slashes. Figure 2-7 shows an example comparison of the maps in each of these situations.

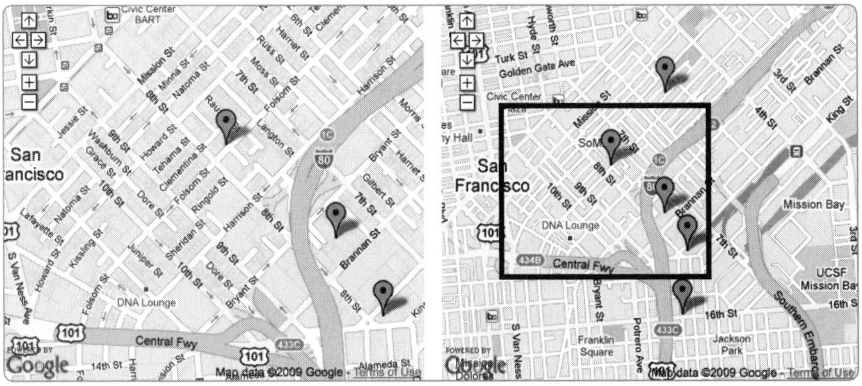

Figure 2-7: Difference between markers without and with automatic centering and zooming

Of course, you need that special function, get_random_by_bounds. Unlike in the previous code, add this outside of the create_map function but within the JavaScript section:

```
function get_random_by_bounds(bounds) {
  var lat = bounds.sw.lat + (Math.random() * (bounds.ne.lat - bounds.sw.lat));
  var lon = bounds.sw.lon + (Math.random() * (bounds.ne.lon - bounds.sw.lon));
  return new mxn.LatLonPoint(lat, lon);
}
```

This function is described in detail in "#44: Get a Random Point in a Bounding Box" on page 140.

As for the automatic centering and zooming, now that you can do it in a single function call, you'll likely include it for all but the simplest maps—it's really that useful.

#9: Filter Out Certain Markers

You must have a map with a whole bunch of markers by now, right? That means you're getting the hang of this mapping stuff. With a full screen of markers, users will likely want to way to see only what they care about. That's where you'll find Mapstraction's filtering options handy.

Keeping track of many markers without the filtering options is a pain. You need to maintain global arrays or make use of the `mapstraction.markers` object. In either case, you need a way to distinguish the type of marker or some data associated with it.

The first step in filtering is to create a new attribute and add it to your new marker. You do this by adding some marker options, which has to happen after a marker is created but before you add it to the map. Here, I'll set the price to be 1000—maybe the marker represents an apartment and this attribute is its rent:

```
marker.setAttribute('price', '1000');
```

If you'd like to add more attributes, such as number of bedrooms, you can do that with additional `setAttribute` lines. Once you've added the data for several markers, you can move on to filtering.

Filters are applied after the markers have been added to the map. In fact, filtering usually happens in response to user behavior, such as when a user clicks a filter button or enters search terms.

To show only markers with a price attribute greater than or equal to 1000, use this code:

```
mapstraction.removeAllFilters();
mapstraction.addFilter(❶'price', ❷'ge', ❸1000);
❹ mapstraction.doFilter();
```

First, use `removeAllFilters` unless you know no filters are applied. The reason is that filters are additive, meaning a second filter does not remove the first. You could end up with fewer results than you expect because of a previously applied filter.

Once filters are removed, you can continue. To add the filter requires three parameters: the attribute name ❶, the operator (in this case **greater than or equal to**) ❷, and the number ❸ to use as a comparison. Finally, the map will not change at all unless you apply the filter ❹.

Table 2-1: Filtering Operators

Operator	Description
ge	Greater than or equal to—use on numbers.
le	Less than or equal to—use on numbers.
eq	Equal to—use on numbers or with words (such as tags or types).

Once a filter is applied, the markers that *don't* match the filter will disappear. In our example, anything with a price attribute less than 1000 (or without a price attribute) will be removed. Thus, filtering can be thought of as filtering *in* rather than *out*.

Mapstraction provides three operators to use to filter markers, as seen in Table 2-1. You can combine filters to achieve more granular results.

Sticking with the apartment search theme, you might add a neighborhood attribute, so users can view apartments in a certain neighborhood that are below a certain price, for example.

Mapstraction filters are a speedy way to show only a subset of markers based on simple criteria. They do not require any additional communication with the server because Mapstraction stores information about every marker in memory. For an example of filtering used in a real project, see "#71: Search Music Events by Location" on page 260.

#10: Remove or Hide All Markers

Need to start fresh, or want to show a clear map in some situations? We all can use a little spring cleaning from time to time. I've already shown how to remove or hide a single marker in this chapter. Now we'll get rid of them all.

Again, make sure you understand that when you remove a marker it is gone forever. Removing a marker is sometimes desired, such as when the user activates a new search. Mapstraction has a function to achieve a clean slate. A hidden marker, on the other hand, can always be shown again. We'll have to write our own function to hide all markers and make the slate *appear* clean.

First, let's be destructive and remove all the markers from our map. Add this line wherever you want to axe all the markers:

```
mapstraction.removeAllMarkers();
```

That's it—they're gone. "#71: Search Music Events by Location" on page 260 shows an example of this function in use every time a user starts a search. By removing the markers, we ensure the previous search results don't get mixed up with the new ones.

If we only want to hide all markers, we need to write our own function. To do this, we need to loop through all markers (described in detail in "#7: Loop Through All Markers" on page 34) and hide each one.

```
function hideAllMarkers() {
❶    var allm = mapstraction.markers;
     for (var i=0; i<allm.length; i++) {
❷      var thism = allm[i];
❸      thism.hide();
     }
}
```

So far, much of our code has been used inside the create_map function. Because hideAllMarkers is a new function, we need to add it in its own place outside of other functions but still in the JavaScript section of the page.

The function itself is straightforward. It first grabs a reference to the marker object ❶ from Mapstraction, which holds an array of every marker added to the map. Then, using that array of markers, the function goes through them one by one. Each time through the loop, the function takes another marker and puts it in a temporary variable named thism ❷ (for "this marker"). Finally, it calls the hide function ❸ on this marker.

By the end of the function, no markers will be displayed on the map. We've looped through every marker and hidden them one at a time.

To write the function is not enough. We need to call the function from somewhere else in our code:

```
hideAllMarkers();
```

Notice that this call looks very similar to the call for removing all the markers. One major difference is that removeAllMarkers was called on the Mapstraction object. This new function is merely called on its own. The difference is that we wrote hideAllMarkers in our own code, whereas Mapstraction's functions are part if its package.

Writing utility functions, as we did here to hide every marker, is an important part of programming. Now that we've written the function once, we can call it any time we need it.

#11: Handle Clusters of Markers

This chapter has already covered several ways to make sense of a map with many markers plotted. You can number them and filter them. You can automatically zoom to show all the markers within the visible portion of the map. These tools are all good to have, but you'll find that sometimes your markers are still scrunched together and overlapping. You can't avoid it, but you can make it less of a problem.

Instead of showing every single marker, you can use a special icon to represent a cluster of markers. Then, when users zoom in, the cluster will disappear and be replaced by the actual markers. You can see an example of many markers, with and without clustering, in Figure 2-8.

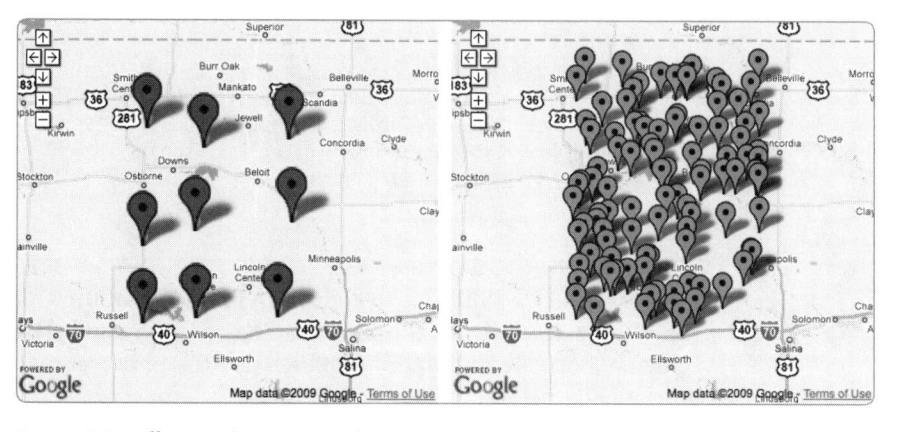

Figure 2-8: Difference between markers with and without clustering

The code behind marker clustering is surprisingly complicated, but the concept is simple. Although many approaches exist, commonly the map is divided into a grid. If one *cell* of the map contains more than one marker (or more than a certain number—you may prefer a cutoff of five markers per cell), they're replaced by a cluster.

Rather than write this algorithm ourselves, we'll use a utility that is already written to work directly with Google Maps, called *ClusterMarker*. You can download the code from *http://www.acme.com/javascript/* and save it in a file named *clusterer2.js*.

Unlike most examples in this book, you'll work with Google Maps directly, as you did in "Create a Google Map" on page 7. In addition to including the Google Maps API JavaScript in the header, you also need to reference the new cluster file. Add this to the header section of your HTML:

```
<script type="text/javascript" src="clusterer2.js"></script>
```

The cluster code is similar to Mapstraction in that it wraps itself around Google Maps. The code to add markers will go through the cluster functions and then be routed to Google Maps. Replace your create_map function with this one, which will place 100 random markers on the map and cluster where necessary:

```
function create_map() {
  if (GBrowserIsCompatible()) {
    // Basic Google Map
    var map = new Gmap2(document.getElementById("mymap"));
    var center_point = new GLatLng(39.34, -98.26);
    map.setCenter(center_point, 8);
    map.addControl(new GsmallMapControl());
    // Cluster settings
❶    var clustobj = new Clusterer(map);
❷      clustobj.SetMaxVisibleMarkers(50);
❸      clustobj.SetMinMarkersPerCluster(2);
    // Add Markers
    for (var i=1; i<=100; i++) {
      var lat = center_point.lat() + Math.random() - 0.5;
      var lon = center_point.lng() + Math.random() - 0.5;
      var gmk = new GMarker(new GLatLng(lat, lon));
❹      clustobj.AddMarker(gmk, 'Marker #' + i);
    }
  }
}
```

I've centered this map roughly in the middle of the United States (hello, Kansas!). Once the basic map has been created, we need to tell the cluster code where to find it ❶, which creates an object that is put into a variable named clustobj.

Before we add any markers, we want to reset some properties of the clusterer. The first ❷ sets the number of markers when the cluster code will begin clustering. The default is 150, which means every single one of our 100 markers will be shown without clustering if we don't change this setting. The next setting ❸ declares how many markers need to occupy a grid cell before clustering takes over. The default is 5 and, for our example, seems a little too crowded. Experiment with what works best for your map.

Now we're ready to add markers to the map. I wrote a for loop that creates 100 markers at random points near the center of our map. Then, instead of adding them directly to the map, we add them to the clusterer ❹.

Save your file, and load it in a browser to see the large clustered markers. You may also see a few stray normal markers—these markers didn't need to be clustered because other markers weren't nearby. The map looks a whole lot cleaner, doesn't it? Zoom in and some of the clusters will disappear, as the map is able to display the actual markers without crowding them.

Change the Cluster Icon

Out of the box, your cluster code uses a large, blue icon for cluster markers. If you have another graphic you would rather use, you can include it instead.

Add the following code after your other cluster settings but before you start adding markers:

```
var cicon = new GIcon();
cicon.image = 'icon.png';
cicon.iconSize = new GSize(27,31);
cicon.shadow = 'shadow.png';
cicon.shadowSize = new Gsize(43,31);
clusterer.SetIcon(cicon);
```

Clustering icons solves the marker overload problem, in which the markers are so numerous they become meaningless. Clustering is also a quick way to still show everything without overwhelming your users.

3

GEOCODING

I've demonstrated some fun map examples in the first two chapters of this book, but there's been an elephant in the room. Those latitude and longitude points I explained in "Describe a Point on the Earth" on page 3 are obviously useful to a computer, but not to humans. How often have you been invited to a party at a location designated by only geographic coordinates?

In this chapter, I'll show how you can take something that makes sense to you—addresses, city names, and even postal codes—and turn them into the latitude and longitude points that Mapstraction needs. The conversion is called *geocoding*, and we'll look at several methods you can put to use in your own mapping projects.

How Do Geocoders Work?

At first glance, a geocoder looks like an oracle. You pass it an address, it looks into its crystal ball, and then it replies with a pair of numbers. Like magic, the coordinates, when plotted on a map, are exactly where the address is located. Let's take a look behind the curtain and see how a geocoder works.

As with most magic, you may be disappointed to find out that most geocoding is really just estimation. Geocoding isn't elegant—it's sort of brute force.

First, the geocoder breaks the address into pieces. For example, consider Graceland's address:

> 3734 Elvis Presley Blvd, Memphis, TN
> Street number, Street name, Suffix, City, State

The city is important because, believe it or not, other cities have an Elvis Presley Blvd. When you think of even more common names (say, Main Street), you can see how this step becomes important. In fact, within cities a road's suffix can be an issue, with a single street name being an Avenue, Street, Circle, and more. If you think those variations are confusing while navigating, think about how they confuse a geocoder.

A street name match might be the toughest part of fixing a location. Dealing with misspellings and other ways of formatting a name can be difficult. Like many other major cities, my hometown of Portland, Oregon, has a street named after Martin Luther King, Jr. The street, both in Portland and in other cities, is commonly referred to as *MLK*. Whether a geocoder should recognize this abbreviation is debatable, but that gives you an idea of the sort of things you have to consider.

Now that you've zeroed in on the correct street and know its city, you need to find the actual address on the street. Storing every last address in the world isn't necessary and would be difficult since new ones are created all the time. Instead, most geocoders use street segments, as shown in Figure 3-1.

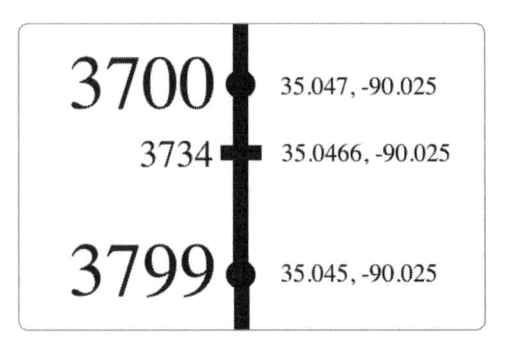

Figure 3-1: Geocoders use street segments to estimate location.

Using our Graceland example, we might know that a segment of Elvis Presley Blvd begins at 3700 and ends at 3799. We also know the latitude and longitude points at each end of the segment. Using those pieces of information, we can estimate that Graceland, at 3734, is about a third of the way between 3700 and 3799. Using the two points, the geocoder can then calculate an approximate location.

JavaScript vs. HTTP Geocoding

In this chapter, I will cover two major methods of retrieving latitude and longitude results from an address: via a JavaScript geocoding API or via a geocoding web service over HTTP. On the surface, these methods are very similar because the data that comes back is the same. The difference is in what you can do with the results.

JavaScript geocoders call an external server with client-side code, meaning the code runs in the browser. This method is the same one used by Mapstraction and every mapping API. In this sense, JavaScript geocoders are extremely convenient for the web-mapping developer.

HTTP geocoders also call an external server, but do so from your server, so the code runs outside the browser. This method is similar to the one used by PHP, the web programming language I've employed to show examples in Chapter 9. In fact, you might use PHP to interpret the results from an HTTP geocoder.

Why would you use one type of geocoder over another? The quality of the data is similar, assuming the geocoders come from the same provider (i.e., Google). A JavaScript geocoder is usually just a wrapper for a server-side geocoder. In other words, both types end up calling upon the same dataset.

The decision about which geocoder to use comes down to how much freedom you want with input and output. You can use a JavaScript geocoder in only a narrow band of ways. The input likely comes from the user via a form. The output almost certainly goes to a web page or to a map on the web page.

Most of your location data will end up on a map, of course. You may want to do many things before that happens, however. Gaining control of the output is the biggest reason why you would use an HTTP geocoder. When the result is retrieved server-side, you have the option to store it to a database, cache the data, share the data over SMS or email, or send it off to a third-party service. Some of these options may be possible with a JavaScript geocoder, but they aren't easy to implement because they are outside the JavaScript geocoder's normal use—inside the browser.

By using an HTTP geocoder, you control where you get your input. For example, you might retrieve it from a database, a third-party service, or a list of addresses. With a JavaScript geocoder, the input likely comes directly from data the user enters in an input box on a website. For many uses, that's all you'll need, but other times you'll want more freedom.

If you spend enough time producing web maps, you'll probably combine JavaScript and HTTP geocoding. The rest of this chapter will focus on the different services you can use as you convert human-readable addresses to geographic coordinates (and vice versa).

#12: Geocode with JavaScript

When you want geocoding that stays within the web browser, you use JavaScript, the same programming language used by Mapstraction and every mapping provider it supports. You can retrieve a city name or address from a user and send it off to be geocoded. The response goes to a JavaScript callback function that you declare.

As with mapping APIs, you can choose your own JavaScript geocoder. Predictably, I'll show Mapstraction's geocoder, which will use whichever provider you specify and give you the same flexibility that you get from using Mapstraction for creating maps: Write the code once and easily switch between providers.

Because not every map requires geocoding, the geocoder is kept separate from the main Mapstraction code. Also, not every provider has a geocoder, so each is stored individually. In this example, we'll be using Google. You can download mxn.google.geocoder.js from *http://mapstraction.com/*.

You include the Mapstraction geocoder in your code much like you include your mapping provider and Mapstraction proper. Add this line (assuming the file is in the current directory) within the <head> section of your basic map:

```
<script src="mxn.google.geocoder.js"></script>
```

With the script included, use this code to initialize the map, geocode an address, and mark the result on the map:

```
var mapstraction, geocoder;
function create_map() {
  mapstraction = new mxn.Mapstraction('mymap', 'googlev3');
  geocoder = new MapstractionGeocoder(❶add_point, ❷'googlev3');
  // Create address object
❸ var address = {
    street : "38 Ringold Street",
    locality : "San Francisco",
    region : "CA",
    country : "US"
  };
❹ geocoder.geocode(address);
}
function add_point(loc) {
  var mk = new mxn.Marker(❺loc.point);
  mk.setInfoBubble(❻loc.address);
  mapstraction.addMarker(mk);
```

```
  mk.openBubble();
  mapstraction.autoCenterAndZoom();
}
```

As with most map examples in this book, I use the `create_map` function to initialize the map. You can name this function whatever you want, as long as the function is called when the page loads.

To create the Mapstraction geocoder object, we need to provide a callback function ❶ and tell Mapstraction which provider ❷ we want to use (the provider's JavaScript still needs to be included). The callback function receives the geocoded results. First, we need to give an address or city name to the geocoder.

We create a generic JavaScript object ❸ to hold the textual location information. Then, we add attributes for the parts of the address. The names may be slightly odd because Mapstraction is attempting to work not just in your country but around the world.

Once the address's parts are filled in, you can send it to the geocoder ❹. Then, your callback function will be passed the results as a location object, which itself has some attributes of interest. Most important is the `LatLonPoint` of the address ❺. In this example, I've used the point to create a new marker.

The marker needs a description, which I'll put inside a message box. I'm using the full address ❻, which the geocoder has cleaned up. As you can see in Figure 3-2, the geocoder has added the ZIP Code, converted "Street" to "St" and refers to the country as "USA" instead of "US."

Figure 3-2: Geocoded results of No Starch Press offices

Of course, this example is only so useful. The address is hard-coded. You will likely be taking input from a user.

Geocode User Input

JavaScript geocoders most commonly require user input to be helpful. Let's tweak the code from the previous section to take a textual location from an input box and geocode it.

To start, you'll need a place for the user to enter data. Let's add a form to our HTML, either above or below the map div:

```
<form id="addrform">
  <input type="text" id="newpt" />
  <input type="submit" id="butnew" value="Geocode" />
</form>
```

Now we need to do something when the user types in an address or city name. Here's a new version of the create_map function with a few changes:

```
function create_map() {
    mapstraction = new mxn.Mapstraction('mymap', 'googlev3');
    mapstraction.setCenterAndZoom(new mxn.LatLonPoint(0, 0), 1);
    mapstraction.addSmallControls();
    geocoder = new MapstractionGeocoder(add_point,'google');
❶  document.getElementById('addrform').onsubmit = function() {
    var address = {
❷  document.getElementById('newpt').value
    }
    geocoder.geocode(address);
    return false; // avoids posting form to the server
    };
}
```

We can't geocode until we get input, which won't happen until the user submits the form. So we wait for submission ❶ and then jump into action with an anonymous function. We could have used a named function, but with only a few lines writing the code inline is easiest.

In the previous section, I separated each piece of the address. In the case of input from a user, that is not always possible. Instead, I've provided the entire value of the input box to the geocoder ❷.

The callback function, add_point, can remain the same. Enter an address and it adds a marker to the geocoded point. Do it again and now you have two markers. This geocoding could get addicting.

#13: Geocode with an HTTP Web Service

JavaScript is convenient when you want to geocode in the browser. You gain more control of your geocoding by using a web service, however. The addresses can come from anywhere, including a list of places. The results can be stored anywhere, including a database, so you can access them anytime and plot them on a map.

Several geocoders are available to choose from, including one each from Google and Yahoo!. The input for each is slightly different, as are the results. In the next sections, I outline how to use these two geocoders and point you to a few others.

Use Google's Geocoding Web Service

Google is the king of the web-mapping world, so of course, Google has a geocoding web service. You can use it to convert an address or city into latitude and longitude points and grab the result in one of several data formats. As an added benefit, Google pretties up the address for you and provides multiple options when the query is ambiguous.

One of the additional freedoms of using a web service to geocode is that you can look at results in a web browser, without writing any actual code. Check out the following URL in your browser:

```
http://maps.google.com/maps/geo?q=38+Ringold+Street+San+Francisco+CA&output=xml&sensor=false
```

The parameters you can send to Google are shown in bold, along with all possible parameters that are shown in Table 3-1. The entire address is passed as the q query argument. You could also simply include a city name or postal code here.

Table 3-1: Google Geocoder Parameters

Parameter	Description
q	*Required.* Query to search, such as address or city name
sensor	*Required.* Whether from a mobile device: true or false
output	Format of results: json (default), xml, kml, or csv
gl	Country code as a top-level domain. E.g., us, ca, uk

The output we want is XML, which can be read by most any programming language. And unless you are using this geocoder from a mobile device, set sensor to false.

Now let's look at the XML results from the above call to Google's HTTP geocoder:

```
<?xml version="1.0" encoding="UTF-8" ?>
<kml xmlns="http://earth.google.com/kml/2.0">
  <Response>
    <name>37.7740486,-122.4101883</name>
    <Status>
      <code>200</code>
      <request>geocode</request>
    </Status>
❶  <Placemark id="p1">
❷    <address>38 Ringold St, San Francisco, CA 94103, USA</address>
      <AddressDetails Accuracy="8"
                      xmlns="urn:oasis:names:tc:ciq:xsdschema:xAL:2.0">
        <Country>
          <CountryNameCode>US</CountryNameCode>
          <CountryName>USA</CountryName>
          <AdministrativeArea>
❸          <AdministrativeAreaName>CA</AdministrativeAreaName>
            <Locality>
❹            <LocalityName>San Francisco</LocalityName>
              <Thoroughfare>
❺              <ThoroughfareName>38 Ringold St</ThoroughfareName>
              </Thoroughfare>
              <PostalCode>
❻              <PostalCodeNumber>94103</PostalCodeNumber>
              </PostalCode>
            </Locality>
          </AdministrativeArea>
        </Country>
      </AddressDetails>
      <ExtendedData>
        <LatLonBox north="37.7773156" south="37.7710204"
                   east="-122.4071324" west="-122.4134276" />
      </ExtendedData>
      <Point>
❼        <coordinates>-122.4102800,37.7741680,0</coordinates>
      </Point>
    </Placemark>
  </Response>
</kml>
```

The results are actually in *Keyhole Markup Language* (KML), a flavor of XML (see "#55: Use KML" on page 188). The coordinates and other information about the geocoded place are stored as Placemarks. In our example, we only have one Placemark ❶, because only one result is possible for a complete address. In ambiguous cases (say we searched for simply "Springfield"—many places have that name), the best result will be listed as the first Placemark, with others receiving incremented ids (i.e., p2, p3, etc.).

In fact, if you want your application to show possible results, as *http://maps.google.com/* does, use the full formatted address ❷ of each Placemark. You can see here that Google cleaned up even my specific address, converting the "Street" to "St" and adding the postal code.

The pieces of the address can also be accessed individually, yet the tag names might seem strange to you. That's because Google has made them generic, so the tags aren't confusing to people not in the United States. The state abbreviation ❸ is called an *Administrative Area Name*, for example.

Accessing the values individually makes showing just the city ❹ or only the address ❺ easier. Also, accessing them individually is a quick way to determine a place's postal code ❻ (called a ZIP Code in the US).

Finally, the most important part of geocoding is the latitude and longitude points. These points are stored together within a single tag ❼. You can use a split function (one using PHP is shown in the next section) to retrieve the coordinates' individual pieces.

Did you notice that Google provides three numbers instead of just two? The third represents altitude and is a property of the KML format. The geocoder does not send this value, so it will always be zero.

If you need help bringing these geocoder results into your applications, Chapter 9 can show you how to do so in PHP. Or, if you only need the coordinates, read on to see Google's approach to really simple geocoding.

Alternate Data Formats

I love XML, but it's not always the preferred data format. Google's web service geocoder gives you a choice of several formats, including JavaScript Object Notation (JSON) and comma-separated values (CSV). The latter is great when you want "just the facts."

Plop an `output` argument in the URL and set its value to be the desired format, for example:

```
http://maps.google.com/maps/geo?q=38+Ringold+St+San+Francisco+CA&output=csv&sensor=false
```

Here, we ask for CSV. Unlike other result formats, we don't get a rewritten address, a postal code, or any other niceties. We do, however, get the four most important values separated by commas:

```
200,8,37.7741680,-122.4102800
```

The first part is the code from the server. A `200` means we have a good result. Anything else, and we likely have an error.

The second part is a number that represents the granularity of our result. Is it street-level (an address), postal-level, or city-level? The possible results are roughly equivalent to zoom levels, as shown in Table 3-2.

Table 3-2: Levels Codes for Geocoding Accuracy

Code	Description
0	Unknown
1	Country
2	State (or similar region)
3	County (or other subregion)
4	City
5	Postal code
6	Street
7	Intersection
8	Address
9	Building (such as landmarks)

The last two numbers of the CSV results might look familiar. They are the latitude and longitude points (in that order). These results are probably the most important because geocoding is all about turning a city name or address into plotable coordinates.

Here's some simple PHP code that calls out to the Google geocoder web service, parses the CSV results, and saves the coordinates to variables:

```php
<?
$url = "http://maps.google.com/maps/geo?q=38+Ringold+St+San+Francisco+CA";
❶ $url += "&output=csv&sensor=false";
$csvtxt = ❷get_url($url);
$llarray = ❸explode(",", $csvtxt);
if (❹count($llarray) == 4 && ❺$llarray[0] == "200") {
  $lat = $llarray[2];
  $lon = $llarray[3];
  // Now do something here with the $lat and $lon variables
}
// Additional PHP code/functions could go here
?>
```

This code is just a snippet to give you an idea of how to separate simple CSV results like those in this example. If you run this code, nothing will happen because all I have shown here is storing the results in variables.

To begin, we create a variable to hold the URL we'll use to call Google. Because the variable is long and this book's pages are only so wide, I split it into two lines ❶, but to PHP, the variable is all one text string.

The URL is then passed to the get_url function ❷, one I will show you how to write in "#61: Retrieve a Web Page" on page 215. You'll need to include a file with that code or paste a copy of the function near the bottom of your PHP file.

Once we have a result from Google, we explode the text ❸ into several pieces, all stored in a single array variable. Because a comma is used to separate the data, that's the delimiter we'll use to split the text.

With the pieces stored as elements of an array, we're almost ready to get our latitude and longitude. We need to make sure the array variable has four results ❹, as expected. Also, the first number in the results needs to be 200 ❺, the code for a good result.

Because arrays in PHP start counting at the zeroth spot, our latitude and longitude are stored as the second and third indexes of the explode result variable. With very little PHP code and even less text, you've now successfully turned an address into geographic coordinates.

Use Yahoo!'s Geocoding Web Service

Though Google may get the lion's share of the press, Yahoo's geo-developer tools are exceptional. Such is the case with its easy-to-use, full-featured geocoding web service. You pass a city name or full address and Yahoo! spits out simple XML with coordinates and other geographic data.

Because the result is just plain XML, you can check it out in your web browser to get a feel for how the service works. Visit this URL:

```
http://local.yahooapis.com/MapsService/V1/geocode?appid=YOURKEY&street=38+Ringold+St
&city=San+Francisco&state=CA
```

The arguments are shown in bold. You'll need your API key as the appid. This ID is the same as for the Yahoo! Maps API. I showed you how to sign up for an ID in "Create a Yahoo! Map" on page 9.

In this example, the pieces of the address are segmented into street, city, and state. You can also use a single argument for an address, similar to Google's geocoder:

```
http://local.yahooapis.com/MapsService/V1/geocode?appid=YOURKEY&location=38+Ringold+St+San+
Francisco+CA
```

The location argument contains all the pieces in the previous example but puts them in one place. If you are receiving an address as input from a user, you will prefer this option unless you have a way to separate the address into pieces (such as multiple form fields).

No matter which way you call the API, the results will be formatted the same way:

```
<?xml version="1.0"?>
<ResultSet ...>
  <Result precision="address">
    <Latitude>37.774155</Latitude>
    <Longitude>-122.410230</Longitude>
```

```
      <Address>38 Ringold St</Address>
      <City>San Francisco</City>
      <State>CA</State>
      <Zip>94103-4403</Zip>
      <Country>US</Country>
   </Result>
</ResultSet>
```

Compared to Google's XML results, these results are very simple. The latitude and longitude are shown separately, as are the pieces of the address (even if you send the location as one string of text, Yahoo! separates things out for you). Each field makes sense as long as you are geocoding addresses or cities in the United States. In Canada, for example, you have to know that provinces are stored in the <state> tag.

If your search has ambiguous results, such as a non-unique city name, Yahoo! will put the best result first. Other results will follow inside their own <Result> tag.

Because you're working with simple XML here, you can parse them as you would any other XML. "#52: Use XML" on page 174 shows this process in PHP and JavaScript. If you want other formats, Yahoo! does provide results as JSON or Serialized PHP. The first is covered in "#53: Use JSON" on page 180, whereas the second is explained at *http://developer.yahoo.com/common/phpserial.html/*.

Other Geocoding Web Services

The previous examples show the two most likely choices for geocoders, but you have other options, especially if you are willing to pay for the service. Why shell out dough when Google and Yahoo! give away geocoding? Your choice really comes down to the terms of service and rate limits, which can restrict your use of a geocoder for high traffic, commercial purposes.

You won't necessarily need to crush that piggy bank to use a for-pay geocoder. For example, *geocoder.us* only charges a quarter of a US cent to geocode an address. For an up-to-date list of geocoder services, see *http://mapscripting.com/geocoders/*.

#14: Reverse Geocoding: Get an Address from a Point

So far we have used human-readable information—a city name or address—to retrieve latitude and longitude points, which are easier for a computer to understand. From time to time, you may want to go the other way. If all you have is a set of coordinates, you can use them to reverse geocode to get the address and other geographic information that will make sense to a human.

Regular geocoding is complicated and imprecise, but reverse geocoding is more so. First, the geocoder finds the street that is closest to the coordinates; then, it determines which address belongs to that point. Truthfully, the result is more often a range of addresses.

Reverse geocoding may seem a little silly given that it is imperfect. But as location becomes more prevalent on the Web, reverse geocoding will become more common. For example, consider "#48: Get Location Using JavaScript" on page 157. In many cases, the GPS or other device reporting someone's whereabouts will only provide the latitude and longitude points. That information is enough to plot it on a map, but not enough to make much sense to humans viewing the information.

In the following sections, I'll show two services, both from Google, that will provide reverse geocoding, helping you create geographic information from computer-readable data.

Reverse Geocode with JavaScript

If you use Google as your mapping provider, reverse geocoding can happen within your JavaScript code without even loading Mapstraction's geocoder (which only supports *forward* geocoding). In this example, we'll still use Mapstraction because the reverse geocoding is only a small part of a map's code.

Let's create a basic Mapstraction map, with Google as the provider. We'll convert the center of the map to a Google point and send it off to be reverse geocoded.

Assuming you have your HTML set up as in "Create a Mapstraction Map" on page 10, here is the JavaScript to create the map and call the Google geocoder:

```
var mapstraction;
function create_map() {
  mapstraction = new mxn.Mapstraction('mymap', 'googlev3');
  mapstraction.setCenterAndZoom(
    new mxn.LatLonPoint(37.7740486,-122.4101883), 15);
  // Google-specific calls
❶ var geocoder = new GclientGeocoder();
  geocoder.getLocations(❷mapstraction.getCenter().toProprietary(mapstraction.api),
    ❸found_address);
}
function found_address(response) {
  if (response && ❹response.Status.code == 200) {
❺   var pt = response.Placemark[0].Point;
    var marker = new mxn.Marker(new mxn.LatLonPoint(pt.coordinates[1], pt.coordinates[0]));
    marker.setInfoBubble(❻response.Placemark[0].address);
    mapstraction.addMarker(marker);
    marker.openBubble();
  }
}
```

As promised, much of this code is comprised of Mapstraction functions. The Google-specific calls are separated out. For example, we create a geocoder object ❶ and then make the call to get the location. Even this contains some Mapstraction, as we use it to get the center of the map ❷ and convert that point to one Google understands.

With the call to the geocoder, we need to provide a callback function ❸. This function is used when the result comes back from Google. Because we created a named function, we also need to create the function with that name.

The found_address function takes one argument, which is the results object that Google's geocoder sends to us. Once we've determined we have a good response ❹ (a status code of 200), we can grab the point ❺, which contains our coordinates.

You might wonder why the point is even necessary, seeing as this is the piece of data that you started with. In many cases, Google isn't able to find an address at your *exact* point (imagine the center of a large park, for example), so it chooses one nearby. In that case, you'll want to know the point it used, so you can plot accordingly.

Google might actually send multiple results, which would be stored in the response.Placemark array. The first is its best guess and probably the one to use, though in some situations you could allow the user to select the most accurate result.

Most of the remaining code in found_address will look familiar, as it's standard Mapstraction functions from Chapter 2. We put a marker at the location Google returned. Then, we use the most important piece of information, the address ❻, as the message inside the marker's box.

To get a good feel for reverse geocoding, try changing the coordinates you pass to Google by altering the center of the map. Or, read on to make a map that reverse geocodes wherever you click.

Reverse Geocode in a Click

Want to play around with reverse geocoding? Attempting to click exactly on your own address to see how close you can come to your exact location can be fun. Also, giving yourself quick access to reverse geocoding can be a good developer tool to get a better idea of how the process works.

You can use most of the previous example. In fact, found_address can stay exactly the same. Replace the create_map function with this slightly altered version:

```
function create_map() {
  mapstraction = new mxn.Mapstraction('mymap', 'googlev3');
❶ mapstraction.addSmallControls();
  mapstraction.setCenterAndZoom(
    new mxn.LatLonPoint(37.7740486,-122.4101883), 15);
❷ mapstraction.addEventListener('click', function(clickpoint) {
    // Google-specific calls
    var geocoder = new GclientGeocoder();
    geocoder.getLocations(❸clickpoint.toProprietary(mapstraction.api), found_address);
  });
}
```

I added some zoom controls ❶ to the map, so you can find specific places to click (in San Francisco, unless you change the map's center or scroll the map to another location). Then I wrote some code that waits for a click event ❷ on the map. When the click occurs, it calls an anonymous, inline function. This function could be named, but with only a few simple lines, writing it inline is easier.

Within the anonymous function, we make a call to the Google geocoder very similar to the one we used before. In this instance, we pass the point where the user clicked ❸ instead of the center of the map. Note that we need to convert the point to the proprietary Google coordinate type because Mapstraction captures the clickpoint but then needs to pass it off to a Google geocoder. Mapstraction speaks Google, but Google does not speak Mapstraction.

Because the other code is the same, clicking the map adds a marker with the address in an opened message box. Click a few more times and additional markers will appear on the map, containing the geographic information provided by the reverse geocoder.

Are you beginning to see the usefulness of a reverse geocoder? In the next section, you'll be able to access that data outside of JavaScript, with Google's HTTP geocoder.

Reverse Geocode with Google's Web Service

As I've mentioned elsewhere in this chapter, power and flexibility come from being able to control the input and output of a geocoder. You can have the same freedom using the reverse geocoding provided by Google's web service.

With a tiny tweak to the URL, Google's geocoder becomes a reverse geocoder:

```
http://maps.google.com/maps/geo?q=37.7740486,-122.4101883&output=xml&sensor=false
```

We're still using the q query argument, as we did in the Google portion of "#13: Geocode with an HTTP Web Service" on page 49. Instead of passing an address, we send the latitude and longitude, in that order and separated by a comma (bolded in the above URL).

The results are virtually the same as with the forward geocoder:

```
<?xml version="1.0" encoding="UTF-8" ?>
<kml xmlns="http://earth.google.com/kml/2.0">
  <Response>
    <name>37.7740486,-122.4101883</name>
    <Status>
      <code>200</code>
      <request>geocode</request>
    </Status>
```

```
      <tPlacemark id="p1">
        <address>38 Ringold St, San Francisco, CA 94103, USA</address>
        <AddressDetails Accuracy="8"
                        xmlns="urn:oasis:names:tc:ciq:xsdschema:xAL:2.0">
          ...
        </AddressDetails>
        <Point>
          <coordinates>-122.4102800,37.7741680,0</coordinates>
        </Point>
      </Placemark>
      <Placemark id="p2">
        ...
      </Placemark>
      ...
    </Response>
</kml>
```

The biggest difference is that you are bound to have multiple Placemarks, because reverse geocoding is much less precise than standard geocoding. Otherwise, the content you receive within each Placemark is the same, right down to the postal code—as, of course, is the address (or range), which is the entire point of the process in the first place.

No longer will you have to leave users attempting to decipher strange numbers that are made for a computer to understand. Whether you choose JavaScript or a server-side web service, you can go from coordinates to text with a quick call to a reverse geocoder.

#15: Get Postal Code Coordinates

Have you ever been to a website that asked you to enter your ZIP Code to find a store's nearest location? Probably yes, I'd guess. This section will help you take the first step toward creating something like that yourself. You need a way to turn a postal code into geographic coordinates.

You may be thinking that a large area cannot be turned into a single geographic point. You're right, though the same could be said about any address where the geocode result tends to be a point near the street. What about your backyard?

Remember, geocoding is not a precise science. For an address, a point is chosen that makes sense. For a postal code, the most logical point is somewhere near the center. Even the center is difficult to determine for the amorphous boundaries of some places, however. Hence, the latitude and longitude represent a spot *near* the center.

The easiest method for getting coordinates of a postal code is to search using a geocoding service. For example, if you wanted to look up the most famous ZIP Code in Beverly Hills using a Yahoo! geocoder, you'd use this URL:

```
http://local.yahooapis.com/MapsService/V1/geocode?appid=YOURKEY&location=90210
```

And your results would look something like this:

```xml
<?xml version="1.0"?>
<ResultSet ...>
  <Result precision="zip">
    <Latitude>34.092807</Latitude>
    <Longitude>-118.411115</Longitude>
    <Address />
    <City>Beverly Hills</City>
    <State>CA</State>
    <Zip>90210</Zip>
    <Country>US</Country>
  </Result>
</ResultSet>
```

Note that the precision is ZIP-level and the address tag is empty. Otherwise, the results are similar to what gets returned when you search for a complete address.

Install a Postal Code Database

If you need to perform a lot of lookups, or want faster access to the results, having a database table to geocode postal codes without the use of another service makes sense. The United States has fewer than 50,000 ZIP Codes, a reasonably small number of records to store and access. Other countries have more unique postal codes (Canada, for example, has nearly a million, which is still small enough to be worth it).

You will need a database to keep your postal codes and their corresponding coordinates. In Chapter 9, I describe how to install MySQL and import data from a CSV file. The book's website contains links where you can download postal code databases for free. See *http://mapscripting.com/postal-code-database*.

The fields contained in the databases will vary, but here's an example structure of a US ZIP Code database:

ZIP Code The postal code

name A textual description of this ZIP Code, such as neighborhood or city name

latitude The north/south portion of the coordinates

longitude The east/west portion of the coordinates

A very basic database may not even contain a name field, as the most important part of a postal code database is converting from the code to a point.

NOTE *You'll want to pay attention to whether the ZIP Code field is stored as text or a number. Some prefer text because text can better represent ZIP Codes that begin with a zero. Databases are able to search for numbers more efficiently, however, so you'll need to make sure to strip off any zeros at the beginning of user input.*

With a full database of postal codes loaded into the zipcoord table (a name I made up), the SQL to find the coordinates for Beverly Hills, 90210, would look something like this:

```
select latitude, longitude from zipcoord where zipcode='90210';
```

You should only get one set of coordinates from that database call because only one 90210 postal code exists. To learn more about accessing the SQL results with PHP, see "#65: Use MySQL from PHP" on page 225.

Now that you can get postal code coordinates, you're ready to do something with them. At the beginning of this project, I mentioned websites that have a search box to find locations near your ZIP Code. Combine your postal code result with "#46: Get Nearest Locations from Your Own Database" on page 150, and you'll have built a store locator, just like you've seen on those sites.

4

LAYER IT ON

Mapping is like painting on a geo-referenced canvas. The most common brushes are markers and message boxes, which is the bulk of what we've used so far. To achieve a different texture, you'll need to switch it up. In this chapter, we'll branch out with some specialized layers that will improve the look of your maps.

To start, we'll simply draw lines. A lot can be represented simply by connecting geographic coordinates together: routes, political boundaries, and even individual buildings. This chapter even has a project to color states or countries on a map, which could be used to make an election map like the ones that have become popular in recent US presidential races.

We'll also add images to the map. Didn't we do that with custom markers? Yes, but the images we'll be adding will be larger and act like your own map's imagery. In fact, we'll also create custom tiles, still utilizing a mapping API but bypassing (or augmenting) its own maps.

Creating layers on your map is a huge step toward making your maps stand out as a masterpiece. Get out those new brushes and let's start mapping.

#16: Draw Lines on a Map

What's the shortest distance from point A to point B? Here's a hint: After reading this section, you'll be able to represent it on a map.

Drawing lines, which Mapstraction calls *polylines*, is very useful. With them, you can outline a route, such as driving directions or a hiking trail. Like a marker, a line uses latitude and longitude points. Of course, you can't have a line with a single point, so you'll need at least two pairs of coordinates to draw a line.

Mapstraction lets you have an unlimited number of points, but let's start simply. This example will draw a line between the capitals of Georgia (the US state) and Georgia (the country). Add the following code to your create_map function after your map has been initialized:

```
var georgias = ❶[new LatLonPoint(33.754487, -84.389663),
                new LatLonPoint(41.709981, 44.792998)];
var poly = ❷new Polyline(georgias);
❸ mapstraction.addPolyline(poly);
mapstraction.autoCenterAndZoom();
```

The first thing I've done is declare the two points ❶, storing them in an array variable. Note the square brackets—[and]—that create the array and that the two LatLonPoints inside the array are separated by a comma. Mapstraction requires an array with at least two LatLonPoints to create a polyline.

Next, I actually create the Polyline object ❷ using the array. Like a marker object, this object is Mapstraction's way of representing the data so it can be reproduced with multiple mapping providers, if necessary. Creating a polyline is not enough to draw the line, however. I also need to add it to the map ❸.

Finally, I automatically center the map using the same function described in "#8: Determine the Correct Zoom Level to Use Based on Markers" on page 34. In this case, Mapstraction uses polylines instead of markers to determine the zoom level.

The resulting map is shown in Figure 4-1 with a line drawn across the Atlantic Ocean, connecting the two Georgias. Let's see if we can make something a little more useful by adding more points to our line.

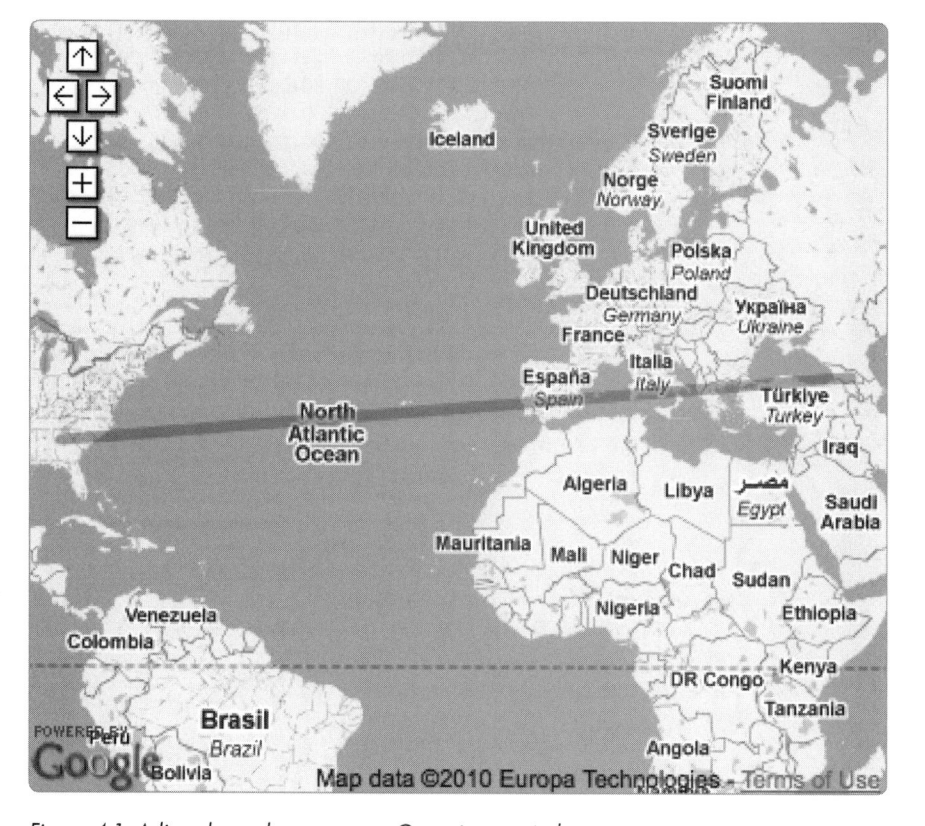

Figure 4-1: A line drawn between two Georgian capitals

Draw Multiple Line Segments

When you think of a line, you probably picture something like what we created in the previous section: the connection between two points. Polylines, however, can have unlimited segments, which means you can use them to create paths and routes.

In fact, Google uses a polyline to display its driving directions. Using polylines makes sense because very few streets are perfectly straight. Most have at least slight meanderings from side to side. In San Francisco, a couple of streets are even known for their crookedness, most notably a short section of Lombard.

Here's some code to create a polyline that very roughly follows the curves of Lombard Street, from the top to the bottom:

```
var lombard = [new LatLonPoint(37.802010, -122.419635),
            new LatLonPoint(37.802036, -122.419463),
            new LatLonPoint(37.802120, -122.419356),
```

```
            new LatLonPoint(37.802010, -122.419184),
            new LatLonPoint(37.802137, -122.419034),
            new LatLonPoint(37.802053, -122.418841),
            new LatLonPoint(37.802197, -122.418701),
            new LatLonPoint(37.802087, -122.418519),
            new LatLonPoint(37.802231, -122.418401),
            new LatLonPoint(37.802120, -122.418186),
            new LatLonPoint(37.802214, -122.417993)];
var poly = new Polyline(lombard);
mapstraction.addPolyline(poly);
mapstraction.autoCenterAndZoom();
```

As you can see from Figure 4-2, those 11 latitude and longitude points create a polyline that traces along Lombard's eight turns. As with the Georgia example, the points are stored within brackets to create the JavaScript array that Mapstraction needs to make a polyline.

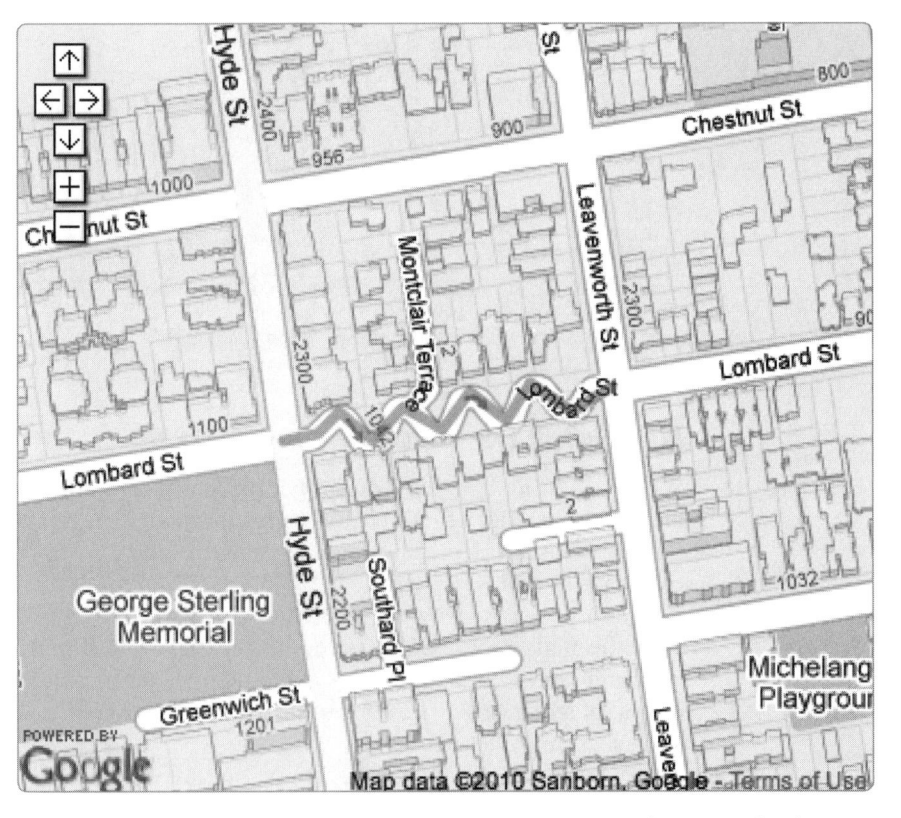

Figure 4-2: A polyline with several points to trace San Francisco's famous Lombard Street

Lombard Street is still a fairly simple example. We've covered less than a quarter mile—and that includes the twists and turns. You could use polylines to trace entire highways, rivers that flow for hundreds of miles, or even the Great Wall of China.

Set the Color and Thickness

Like markers and other aspects of a map, polylines come with a standard look you may want to change. For example, you can alter the color and thickness of the lines you draw.

Mapstraction has individual functions to set the criteria you want. Each can be applied after you have created a polyline, but before you have added it to the map. This process is similar to the order in which Marker options have to be added.

Here is an example that makes a purple polyline that is five pixels thick (it assumes your polyline is stored in the poly variable):

```
poly.setColor(❶'#FF00FF');
poly.setWidth(5);
```

Note that the color is set as a hexadecimal value ❶, similar to how colors are declared in HTML. Either a six- or three-character value works, and you can even precede it with a hash mark, #, if you prefer.

NOTE   *Some browsers, especially older ones, have trouble with colored polylines. Be sure to check thoroughly across all browsers your user base commonly employs, especially if the color of the polyline is integral to your application.*

Because you'll often want to set several attributes at once, Mapstraction has a function that accepts many options, storing their values in a JavaScript object:

```
poly.addData({color: '#FF00FF', width: 5});
```

The curly brackets { and } are important, as they declare the JavaScript object. Then an attribute is set with the name of the option, a colon, and the value. You'll see more examples of adding styling options to polylines in the next project.

#17: Draw Shapes on a Map

Are you ready for a little philosophy? I hope so, because I have a philosophical question for you: What is a shape?

Before you answer that, let's list some names of shapes. Shapes include circles and triangles. Squares are popular, as are their relative the rectangles. If we continue to increase the number of sides, the names may sound familiar—pentagon, hexagon, heptagon, octagon—and then the names get a little strange.

Your philosophical answer may be different, but for our purposes, we'll create a shape with some number of sides. This shape is called a *polygon*. A polygon is made up of line segments that start and end at the same point. If you have mastered the previous project, you probably have a pretty good idea of how you could create a polygon using Mapstraction.

Surprisingly, creating shapes on a map is essentially the same process as drawing polylines. Take a look at this code, which draws an outline around the US Department of Defense headquarters ("The Pentagon"—get it?):

```
var pentagon = [new LatLonPoint(38.870253, -77.058491),
                new LatLonPoint(38.872725, -77.057955),
                new LatLonPoint(38.873059, -77.054715),
                new LatLonPoint(38.870804, -77.053320),
                new LatLonPoint(38.869000, -77.055616),
                new LatLonPoint(38.870253, -77.058491)];
var poly = new Polyline(pentagon);
mapstraction.addPolyline(poly);
mapstraction.autoCenterAndZoom();
```

As with standard polylines, we need to declare an array of LatLonPoints using square brackets [and] to show a JavaScript array. The big difference is that the first and last points (both shown in bold) are identical, signaling to Mapstraction that you are creating a polygon.

The outcome, as shown in Figure 4-3, is that the polyline is filled in to show that it's more than just a line—it's a shape. Shapes bring up a few more styling issues than normal lines, so Mapstraction provides some additional options.

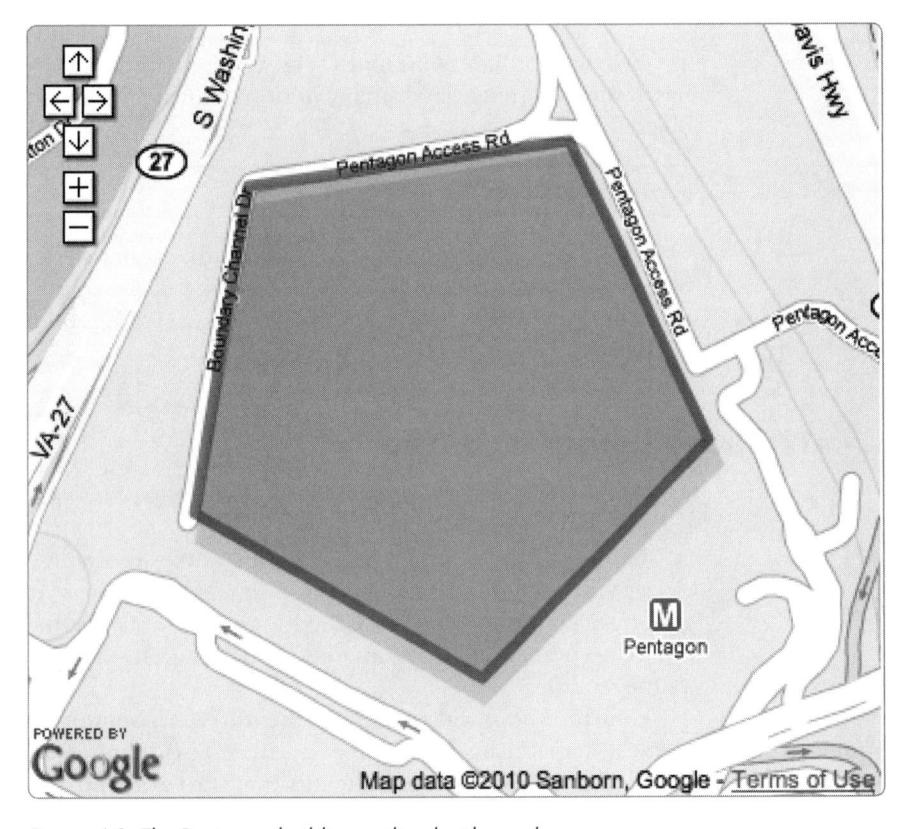

Figure 4-3: The Pentagon building outlined with a polygon

Set the Fill Color and Opacity

Now that your polyline has turned into a polygon, let's declare the color that fills its center. Also, with the fill covering such a large area, you may want to leave bits of the map under the polygon visible. That's where opacity comes in—it determines the opaqueness of the fill color.

If you are familiar with graphics programs, you'll likely be comfortable with opacity. You declare it with a percentage from 0 to 100, where 0 is invisible and 100 is not transparent at all.

Let's use a single function in Mapstraction to set all the options for the pentagon we made earlier:

```
poly.addData({❶opacity: 0.9, ❷fillColor: '#00FF00', color: '#009900', width: 5});
```

Here, we have declared an opacity of 90 percent ❶, so we can barely see through it. Notice that we use a decimal between 0 and 1 to show the percentage. Though mathematically correct, you may find this a little confusing.

The fill color is declared with a CSS-like hexadecimal value ❷. This value is separate from the color of the polyline, which can be the same or different. In this example, the fill color is a bright green, whereas the border is a slightly darker green.

#18: Add Circles to Show Search Radius

Drawing lines and polygons is fairly easy. They are made up of a series of connected points. A circle is a little more difficult to express. A circle has no points that make up its border. Instead, it's declared by a center point and a radius.

Circles are useful in mapping, because you can use them to show an area you are searching. For example, if you are looking for places within five miles of a point, your circle would be ten miles wide (and tall—a circle is perfectly round), with the search point right at the center.

Mapstraction offers two ways to create a circle. First, we can approximate with a many-sided polygon. Second, we could use a graphic and layer it on top of the map. In this section, I'll show you how to do both.

Approximate with a Polygon

Creating a fake circle by connecting points along the circle looks better than you might imagine it would. Of course, the more points you use, the better the circle looks. Mapstraction has a built-in function to perform the computations, and you can set the quality.

Remember, a circle requires two pieces of information: a center and a radius. In this example, we'll show just how big the state of Texas is by drawing a circle 500 miles in diameter starting from its capital near the center of the state.

Add these lines to your map initialization function, which I've called create_map throughout this book:

```
var radius_object = ❶new Radius(new LatLonPoint(30.268259, -97.744674), ❷10);
var poly = radius_object.getPolyline(❸mxn.fn.milesToKM(250), ❹'#990066');
mapstraction.addPolyline(poly);
mapstraction.setCenterAndZoom(center, 5);
```

This code is all that's necessary to add a circle-ish polygon to your map. First, you need to create a Radius object ❶, which is part of the Mapstraction library. This object does some important calculations to determine the circle's edges. Then you pass the object two values: the center point (downtown Austin, Texas) and a quality number ❷.

The lower the quality number, the more your polygon will look like a circle. The number represents the degrees between each point in the polygon. You can use this to determine the number of sides your "circle" will have. A circle is 360 degrees total, so if you divide by 10, that's 36 points, which means you're creating a 36-sided polygon in this instance. Using this method, you've done a pretty good job of approximating a circle, as you can see in Figure 4-4. The more sides you have, the longer it takes to create the circle, so you have to make a trade-off.

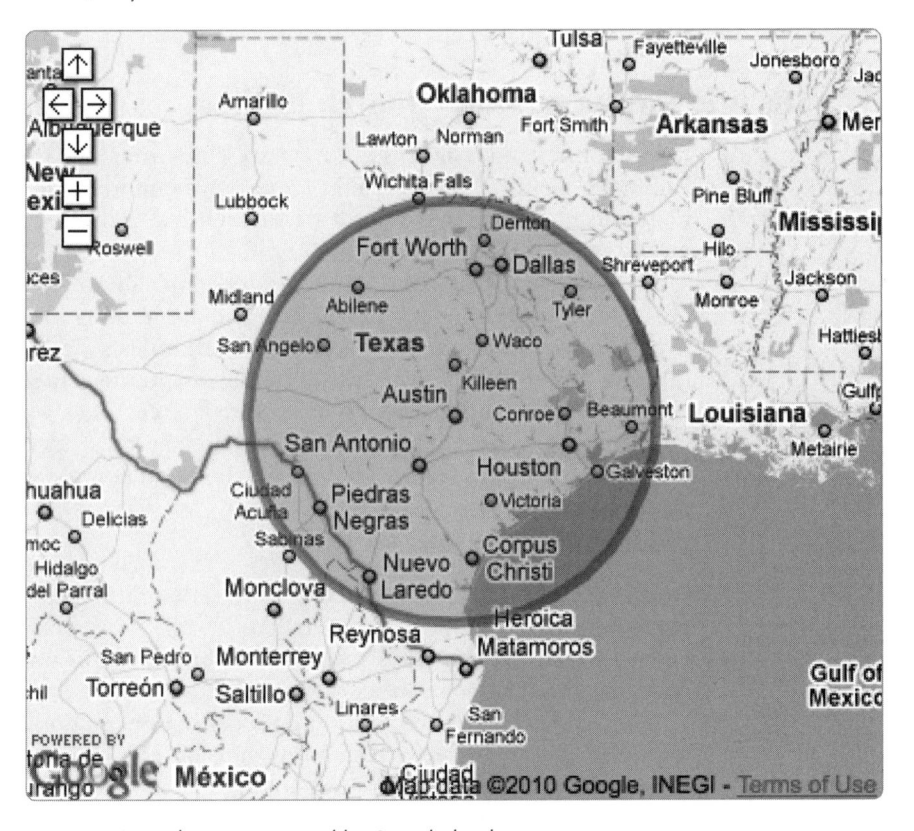

Figure 4-4: Circle approximated by 36-sided polygon

Now that you have a Radius object, you can create the polygon, which is a Polyline object. You use a Mapstraction function to convert miles to kilometers ❸. Here, I've passed it the number of miles of the radius, which is half of the diameter of the eventual circle. Also, I've passed a hexadecimal value for the color ❹ of the circle, in this case, a shade of purple.

You can create as many circles as you want from the radius object, so you could show several levels of distance from Austin. If you want to move the center (or change the quality of the circle), however, you'll need to re-create the radius object.

Overlay a Circle Image

The polygonized circle may still be too jagged for you, or perhaps you want more control over how the circle looks. In that case, overlaying an image on your map is your best choice.

First, you'll need a circle image, likely saved as a transparent PNG file. Transparency is important because graphics are stored as rectangles, so you definitely don't want the area outside of the circle to be visible. Also, since you'll be referencing this on the map as a rectangle, your circle should be up against the four edges of the graphic. I've included several sample circle graphics for download on the book's website at *http://mapscripting.com/circle-overlays.*

Once you have your circle graphic, you can figure out where to place it on the map. A graphic is referenced by the four sides of its rectangle, so you need to determine the north, south, east, and west points. Usually, a circle is determined by its center and radius. You can calculate the side values by measuring in four directions from the center.

Add these lines to your map code:

```
    var center = new LatLonPoint(30.268259, -97.744674);
❶  var dist_lat = 250 / 69.2;
    var dist_lon = ❷mxn.fn.metresToLon(❸mxn.fn.milesToKM(250)*1000, center.lat);
❹  var n = center.lat + dist_lat;
    var s = center.lat - dist_lat;
    var e = center.lon + dist_lon;
    var w = center.lon - dist_lon;
    mapstraction.addImageOverlay(❺'searchradius', 'circle.png', ❻75, w, s, e, n);
    mapstraction.setCenterAndZoom(center, 5);
```

To be able to determine the geographic borders of your circle image, you need to calculate how many degrees of latitude and longitude make up the radius, which is 250 miles. The latitude distance ❶ is easier, because latitude is nearly constant throughout the world at 69.2 miles per degree.

Longitude depends on where you are on earth because the degrees are closer to each other as you near a pole. Mapstraction has a handy function ❷ for converting meters to longitude based on a latitude. In order to pass the function 250 miles in meters, you must first convert to kilometers ❸ and then multiply by 1000.

At this point, you have your distances, so now you just need to calculate the four sides. For example, the northern border ❹ of the graphic will be at the center point latitude plus the number of degrees latitude we determined are in 250 miles. South will also use that latitude distance (only this distance is subtracted from the center's latitude. East and west borders will use the longitude distance.

Armed with your four geographic borders, you can apply your image overlay. Mapstraction needs a lot of information, including an identifier for the image ❺ and an opacity level ❻ (for this example, I've chosen 75 percent). The results are shown in Figure 4-5, where you can see a perfect circle atop Texas. The area it covers, you'll notice, is identical to the area covered by the polygon circle in Figure 4-4.

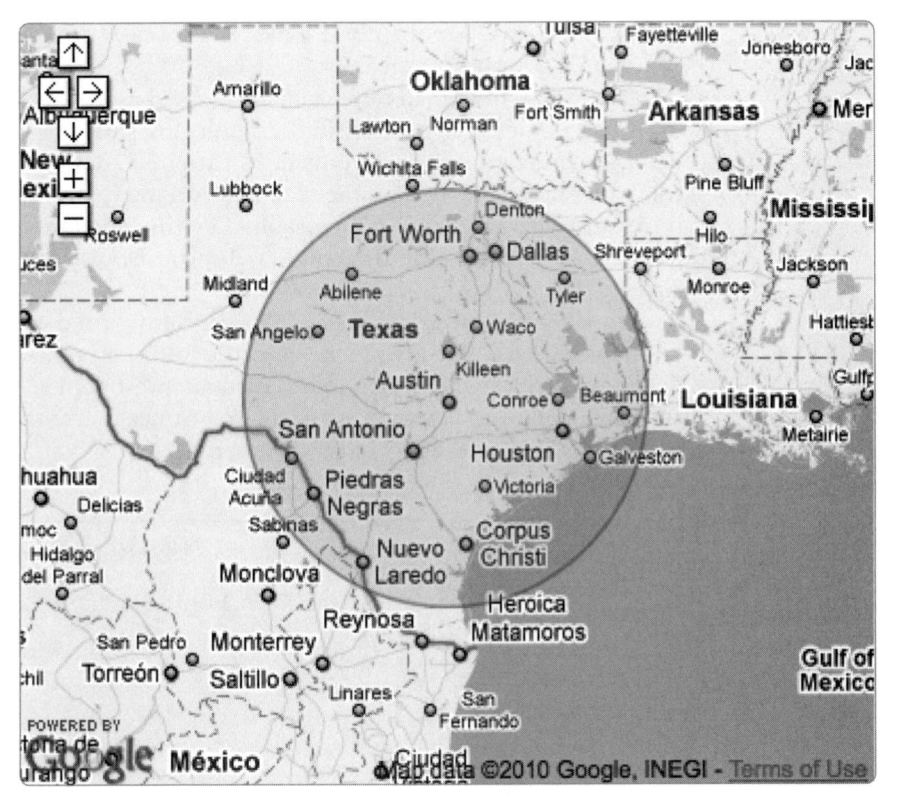

Figure 4-5: Transparent circle image overlay

No matter which type of circle you choose to use, Texas is a big state.

#19: Draw a Rectangle to Declare an Area

In Chapter 2, I discussed the bounding box, a set of coordinates that roughly describes a geographic area. I write *roughly* because bounds are visually rectangular, so they can only be used to declare the simplest of areas. Of course, with every map we have been indirectly creating bounds. The visible portion of the map is a rectangular portion of the greater map.

Mapstraction uses the BoundingBox class to describe an area. As a data structure, this class is made up of two LatLonPoints. One declares the southwest corner (the lower left) and the other the northeast corner (the upper left). From those two values, we can figure out the remaining two corners. And we'll do just that in this project.

You may find yourself wanting to declare an area of the map visually. Because a BoundingBox is simply a data representation of an area, we need to convert to a Polyline. Add this function to your JavaScript (outside the create_map function) to perform the conversion:

```
function BoundingBox_to_Polyline(box) {
  var points = [❶box.sw, ❷new mxn.LatLonPoint(box.ne.lat, box.sw.lon), box.ne,
            new mxn.LatLonPoint(box.sw.lat, box.ne.lon),
            new mxn.LatLonPoint(box.sw.lat, ❸box.sw.lon-.0001)];
  var poly = new mxn.Polyline(points);
  return poly;
}
```

Drawing a rectangle on a map requires five points. At first, this requirement may seem a bit strange—doesn't a rectangle have four corners? Of course. We aren't violating basic rules of geometry. We need to declare the start and the finish points separately, however. And because these are the same point (or, as you'll see, nearly the same), we include it twice.

The array of points begins, simply enough, with the southwest point ❶. Then we want to draw a line directly north, which means we need to keep the same longitude while increasing the latitude. We only have two points to work with, so we create a new point ❷ using the southwest's longitude and the northeast's latitude.

The third point is the northeast point itself. Then we can use a similar process to determine the fourth point. Finally, we need to draw the final side of the rectangle back to the southwest point. But this is where things get strange. If we use exactly the southwest point, Mapstraction will fill in the area. To get an unfilled box, we create a final point with a longitude almost imperceptibly off ❸ from the starting point.

Now that we've written our new function, we need to call it. From within your create_map function, add the following lines:

```
❹ var bounds = mapstraction.getBounds();
❺ var poly = BoundingBox_to_Polyline(bounds);
  mapstraction.addPolyline(poly);
  mapstraction.setZoom(mapstraction.getZoom()-1);
```

We could create new bounds if we wanted, but instead we are taking them from the map itself ❹. Then we use those bounds to call our function to convert to a `Polyline` ❺. As you saw earlier, creating the object is just the first step. We also need to add it to the map. The final line zooms out so we can see the rectangle, as shown in Figure 4-6. Without zooming, the rectangle would be right at the edges of our map.

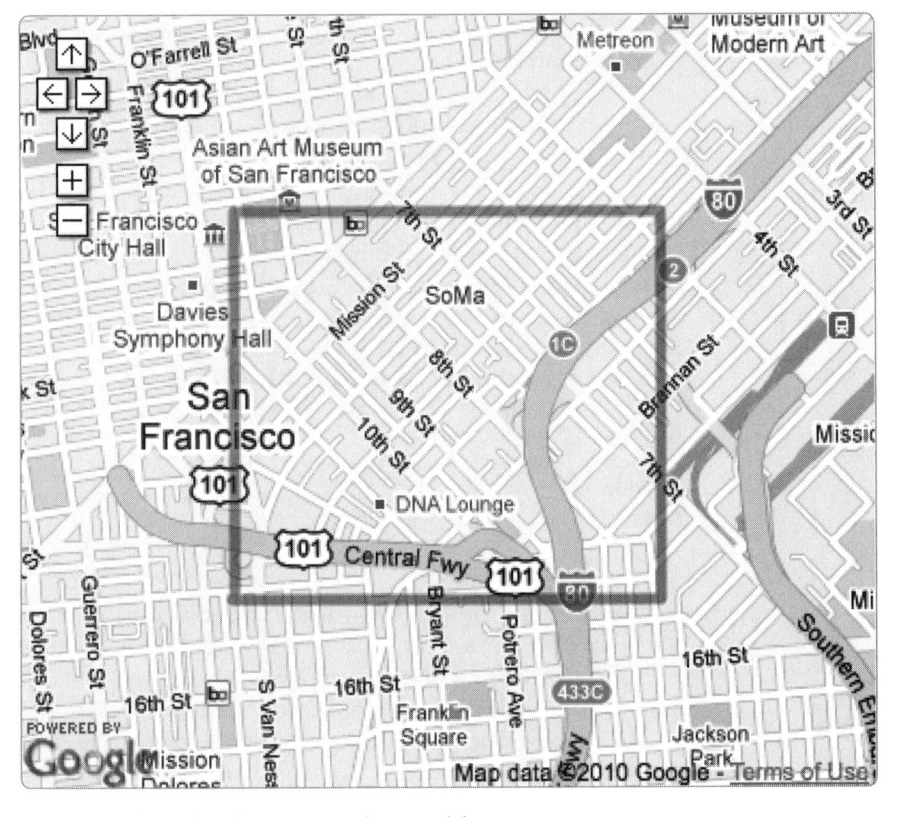

Figure 4-6: Bounding box converted to a polyline

Use this snippet of code to clearly show bounds. For an example of this project in action, see "#43: Check Whether a Point Is Within a Bounding Box" on page 137.

#20: Draw Lines Along Clicks

The biggest stumbling block to creating your own lines on a map is finding the latitude and longitude points. With this project, you (or your users) will be able to draw lines simply by clicking the map. Gmap Pedometer (*http://gmap-pedometer.com/*) popularized this technique in the earliest days of mapping APIs, and now you can use it, too.

Reacting to a click event is at the center of this method. You will find events covered in detail in Chapter 5. We want to store all the click points in an array. Because we'll be accessing this from an event, the variable we create needs to be public, meaning it is declared outside of any function. Include this line at the beginning of your JavaScript:

```
var cpts = [];
```

This variable will hold every point that is clicked. Right now it is an empty array (there's nothing between those square brackets). With every click, however, we'll add a new LatLonPoint to the array.

From within your map initialization code, add these lines to react to clicks:

```
mapstraction.click.addHandler(function(event_name, event_source, event_args) {
    var clickpoint = event_args.location;
❶  cpts.push(clickpoint);
    if (cpts.length == 1) {
❷  var mk = new Marker(clickpoint);
      mapstraction.addMarker(mk);
    }
    else {
      ❸var poly = new Polyline(❹cpts.slice(cpts.length-2));
      mapstraction.addPolyline(poly);
    }
});
```

Here, I have included the code that runs when the user clicks the map in an anonymous, inline function. This is about as long as I would make a function without explicitly naming it.

The very first thing that happens is we "push" the new point into the array ❶. The push function is built into JavaScript for every array variable and always adds it on to the end of the array.

The minimum number of points before we can draw a line is two. This requirement causes a bit of an issue because we need the user to know we have recorded the first click. To deal with this, we added a marker ❷ to the map only if the length of the array is one. In other words, a marker is added only on the first click.

On subsequent clicks, we create a new polyline ❸ with the two most recent points. To do this, we connect the last point in the array ❹ to the next-to-last point in the array (because arrays in JavaScript begin counting at zero, the last element is always one less than the length). Also, remember that a polyline is created with an array itself, so we need to surround those two numbers with brackets. The code starts to look a little messy.

After several clicks, the map will look something like Figure 4-7. Internally, we'll have all the points stored in our array. Mapstraction, however, is treating each line segment as its own polyline. From a visual perspective, it still looks like one big line.

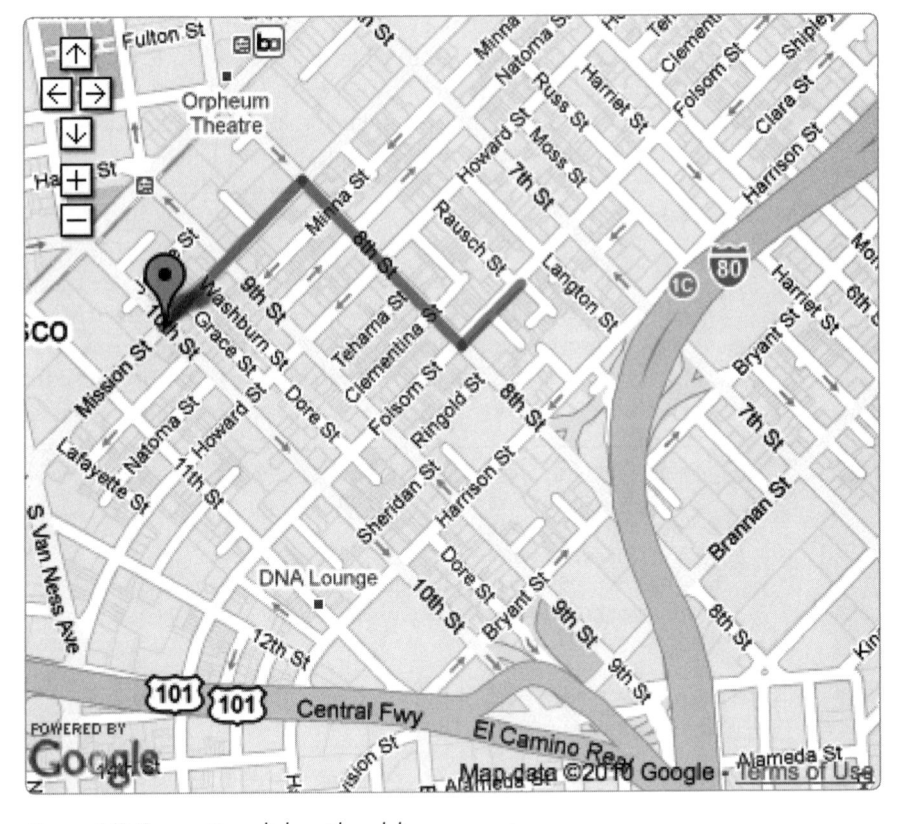

Figure 4-7: Connecting clicks with polyline segments

#21: Color States/Countries on a Map

If you've paid attention to recent US politics, you've likely seen red and
blue state maps. During the 2004 and 2008 presidential campaigns, these
became common across the Web. And believe it or not, if you've read
this far in the chapter, you already know how to make a colored map of
your own.

All you need are the points that make up the outline of each state.
Then, you create a polygon for each state, giving it the proper fill color.
Before you can start coloring states, you'll need the points that make up
the outline of each state. You can get this data in a number of ways. For
example, you could create it on your own using code similar to that in the
previous project.

You could also take it directly from the government, but you'd likely
need to convert it to a format that's easy for Mapstraction to use. I have
data sources available at the book's website at *http://mapscripting.com/
state-boundaries*.

If you want to try it out, start with just a few states. In this example, I'll
use the four-corner states of Utah, Colorado, Arizona, and New Mexico.

They have relatively few points, and they all come together neatly. The first step is declaring the points that make up each state boundary as a JavaScript array:

```
var utah = [new LatLonPoint(36.99, -114.05), new LatLonPoint(36.99, -109.04),
            new LatLonPoint(40.99, -109.05), new LatLonPoint(40.99, -111.05),
            new LatLonPoint(41.99, -111.05), new LatLonPoint(41.99, -114.04),
            new LatLonPoint(36.99, -114.05)];
var colorado = [new LatLonPoint(41.00, -102.05), new LatLonPoint(40.99, -109.04),
                new LatLonPoint(37.00, -109.04), new LatLonPoint(36.99, -102.04),
                new LatLonPoint(41.00, -102.05)];
var arizona = [new LatLonPoint(33.95, -114.52), new LatLonPoint(34.00, -114.47),
               new LatLonPoint(34.02, -114.43), new LatLonPoint(34.08, -114.43),
               ...
               new LatLonPoint(33.92, -114.53), new LatLonPoint(33.95, -114.52)];
var newmexico = [new LatLonPoint(32.00, -106.62), new LatLonPoint(31.99, -103.06),
                 new LatLonPoint(36.99, -103.00), new LatLonPoint(36.99, -109.04),
                 new LatLonPoint(36.99, -109.04), new LatLonPoint(31.33, -109.04),
                 new LatLonPoint(31.33, -108.21), new LatLonPoint(31.77, -108.20),
                 new LatLonPoint(31.78, -106.53), new LatLonPoint(32.00, -106.62)];
```

Arizona is just a little too complex to show all of its points in the book, but the others are complete. Like declaring other shapes using points, we include a list of LatLonPoints within square brackets to designate an array. To create a complete shape (and, therefore, include a fill color), the first and last points in the array must be identical. The identical points tell Mapstraction that the polyline begins and ends at the same place.

Because we are going to be performing the same actions multiple times, this is an appropriate occasion to create our own function. Here is the code to color in a state:

```
function color_state(❶pts, ❷color) {
  var poly = new Polyline(pts);
  poly.addData({❸opacity: 0.9, ❹fillColor: color, ❺width: 0});
  mapstraction.addPolyline(poly);
}
```

We'll call this function four times—once for each state. Or, if you're doing the whole United States, you'd call the function fifty times. This function's three lines mean our code will only take up one-third of the space. If you're going to run the same code many times, you'll want to avoid duplication and create your own function.

We'll need to pass the function two arguments. First, we pass it a list of points ❶—a state boundary array. Then, because we're filling in the map with different colored states, we'll need to let the function know what color ❷ to make the current state.

The function then goes to work creating a Polyline and adding data to it. We've set the opacity to 90 percent ❸, which means the filled state shape will be slightly transparent, just enough to see the state name underneath. The color is set ❹ to the argument that we received. We made the width zero ❺, meaning the state will not have a border. You may prefer to have a border, so try out a few different values. This argument takes integers, which refer to thickness in number of pixels.

Nothing we've done so far will actually do anything yet. For that, we need to call this function, passing a state boundary array and color. Add this code to your map initialization section:

```
color_state(utah, '#00ff00');
color_state(colorado, '#006600');
color_state(arizona, '#009900');
color_state(newmexico, '#00cc00');
mapstraction.autoCenterAndZoom();
```

As you see, this calls the color_state function four times, using a different point array variable and color each time. To keep this example apolitical, I've used shades of green. Feel free to insert your own red ('ff0000') or blue ('0000ff') values.

To be sure every state is within view, I autocentered the map after adding the four states. As you can see from Figure 4-8, our map looks pretty snazzy. But if you zoom in, the borders of each state might not completely touch. That's a precision issue, which you may not care about. Its importance depends on how closely you expect users to view your borders. For the case of a colored election map, which is viewed at country-level, we don't need perfection.

Another issue you may notice with creating a state map is that not all states are one perfect shape. Hawaii is a series of islands, and Michigan's two pieces are separated by a Great Lake. Again, how you handle this depends on how big of a deal it is to you. You may be fine connecting the portions so they can be one state. Or, you may use multiple polygons to represent these complex states.

#22: Add Custom Controls

Everything we have layered on the map so far has been geo-referenced. In other words, when the user drags the map to the side, the thing we've layered also moves. In this section, we'll create some interface elements that don't move, but instead are anchored to a specific spot in the map window.

The controls we'll be creating are similar to map type controls, which are in the upper-right corner of the map. In "Add Zoom and Other Controls" on page 16, I showed how to include these (and other) controls. Now, we'll be making our own buttons that live in the same spot.

For this example, we'll make a button that gives users the option to center the map automatically so all the markers and lines are visible. Better yet, we'll write the code so you can create any number of these custom controls with a simple function call.

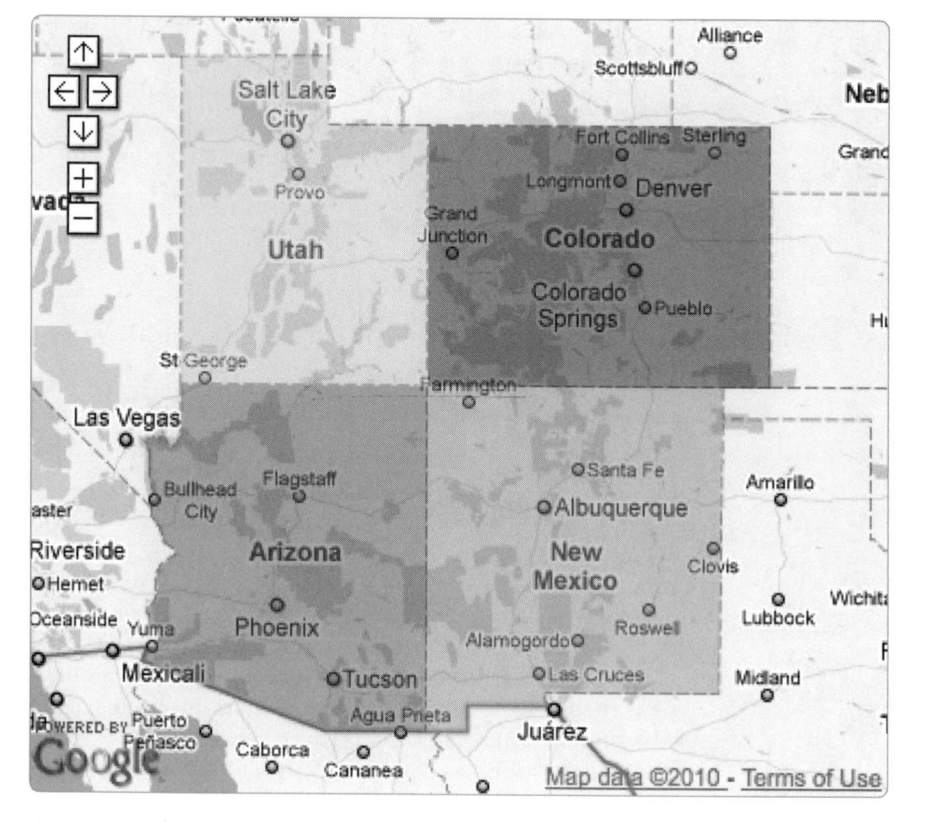

Figure 4-8: Polygons of four US states

Here's the code for creating a control:

```
function create_control(❶txt, ❷func) {
❸ var newcontrol = document.createElement("a");
❹ newcontrol.className = 'googlecontrol';
❺ newcontrol.appendChild(document.createTextNode(txt));
❻ newcontrol.onclick = func;
❼ mapstraction.currentElement.appendChild(newcontrol);
}
```

This function needs two pieces of data in order to create the control and add it to the map: It needs the text ❶ that will be written inside the button, and it needs the function ❷ that it will call when the button is clicked.

With those pieces of information, we can go about creating this control. In terms of how the browser interprets it, we are creating a simple <a> tag programmatically ❸. We give it a class name ❹ so we can style it with CSS. Then we add the label to it ❺.

At this point, the control has been created, but it isn't on the map, nor does it do anything. To fix these two issues, we set the function ❻ that will be called when the user clicks and then append the object as a child of the map object ❼.

Now we can style the control. Add these CSS lines to your style sheet:

```
a.googlecontrol {
  position: relative;
  float: right;
  width: 63px;
  height: 15px;
  margin: 5px 3px 0 0;
  border: 1px solid #b0b0b0;
  background-color: white;
  color: black;
  font-size: 12px;
  text-align: center;
}
a.googlecontrol:hover {
  cursor: pointer;
}
```

This CSS is designed to make our controls look similar to Google's map type controls. Only the first two lines (in bold) are necessary to position it in the upper-right corner. Everything else is styling.

All of the hard work is now done, and we're ready to use our custom control. From within the initialization code for our map, add these lines to create an autocentering control:

```
create_control("auto-center", function() {
  mapstraction.autoCenterAndZoom();
});
```

This code passes the label for our new control (autocenter) and an anonymous, inline function reference, which decides what to do when the user clicks the new control button. In this case, it fires off the Mapstraction code to show all the markers and lines on the map automatically. See Figure 4-9 for a before and after example of clicking the button.

You could do anything you want when the user clicks your custom control button. One common choice might be showing only markers of a particular type. I demonstrate how to do this in "#9: Filter Out Certain Markers" on page 36. With a marker-filled map, you might also create specific areas to zoom into, as I do in "#70: Display Recent Earthquakes Worldwide" on page 247.

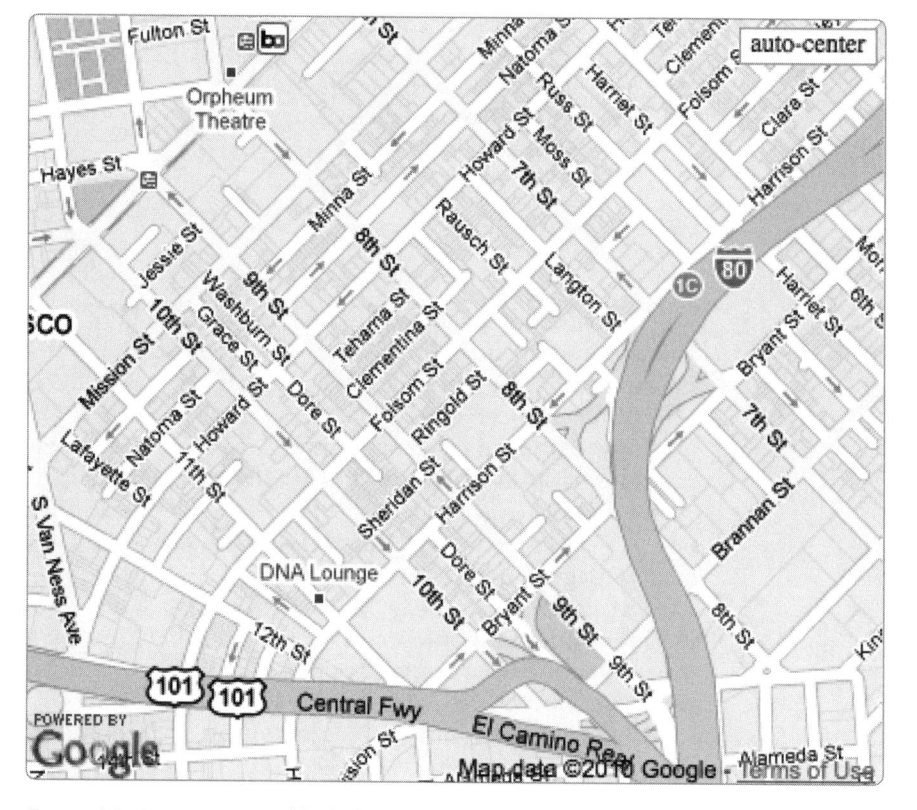

Figure 4-9: A custom control looks like a Google control

#23: Create Your Own Zoom Interface

When you choose a mapping provider, certain elements of how the map looks cannot be easily changed. The zoom interface may be one of these things you've accepted as being unchangeable. In this project, I'll show how you can include your own zoom in/out buttons to give you even more control over the look of your map.

The approach is similar to the previous project. We'll make a function that adds a new object to the page, and we'll position and style it using CSS. Instead of a text button, we'll make an image button. And, as before, each new object will react to a click.

First, you need two images: one will be your zooming-in button and the other the zooming-out button. You can see the two unassuming graphics I chose in Figure 4-10.

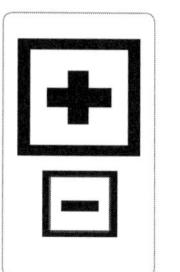

Figure 4-10: Two zoom graphics to be used as custom controls

Here is the generic code for creating an image control:

```
function create_image_control(❶src, ❷func) {
❸ var newcontrol = document.createElement("img");
❹ newcontrol.className = 'imgcontrol';
❺ newcontrol.src = src;
❻ newcontrol.onclick = func;
❼ mapstraction.currentElement.appendChild(newcontrol);
}
```

This function needs two pieces of data in order to create the control and add it to the map. It needs the image source ❶, which is a path to the image file we'll be using for this control. It also needs the function ❷ that it will call when the image is clicked.

Now we're ready to create this control. We create an image element programmatically ❸, just as we did with the <a> tag when making a custom control. Then we give the image a class name ❹ so we can style it with CSS. Finally we add the image URL ❺. This URL can be full or relative to the current page.

At this point, the image is created, but it's neither on the map, nor does it do anything. To fix those two issues, we set the function ❻ to be called when the user clicks and then append the image object as a child of the map object ❼.

Let's make sure our new image controls are positioned correctly. Add these CSS lines to your style sheet:

```
img.imgcontrol {
  position: relative;
  float: right;
  margin: 2px;
}
```

Now we can add our custom zoom controls to the map. From within the initialization code for your map, add these lines:

```
create_image_control(❶"zoom-plus.png", function() {
❷ mapstraction.setZoom(mapstraction.getZoom()+1);
});
create_image_control("zoom-minus.png", function() {
  mapstraction.setZoom(mapstraction.getZoom()-1);
});
```

Here, I've created two image controls, as shown in Figure 4-11. The first is for zooming in. The CSS will place the control furthest to the right. I send it the name of my image ❶, which assumes it is stored in the same directory as the HTML page. Then I pass it an anonymous, inline function. Here, I set the zoom level ❷ using Mapstraction, passing a number one greater than the current zoom level.

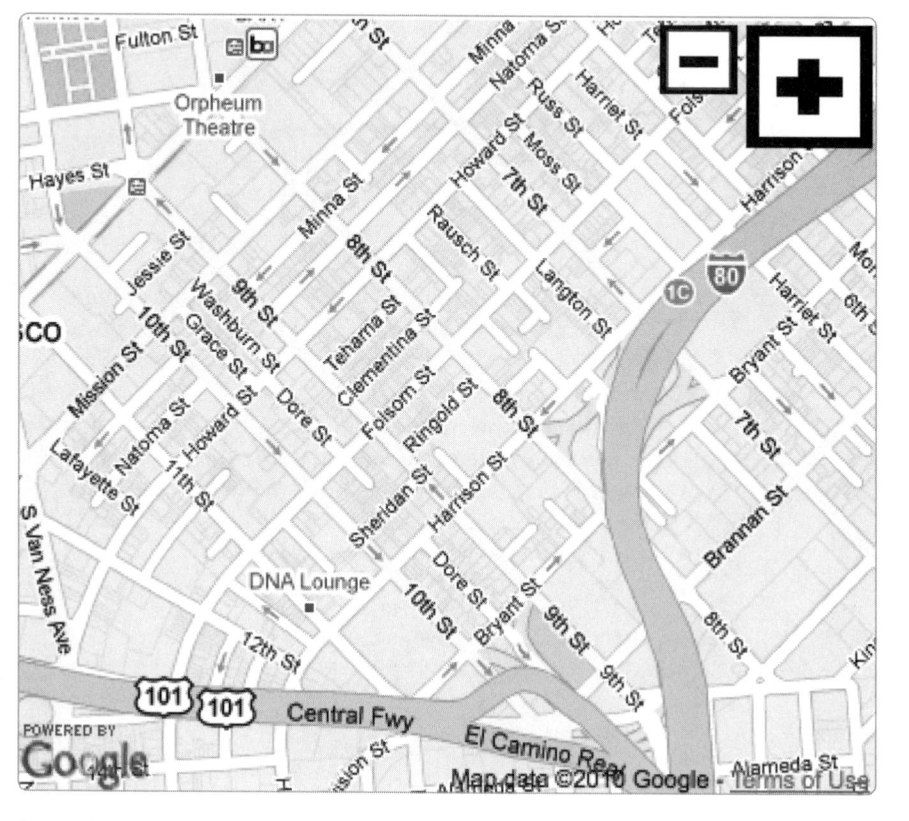

Figure 4-11: Custom zoom images on a map

The second image control is similar. It is given a different image, and when clicked, it sets the zoom to one *less* than the current zoom level.

#24: Plot Image Thumbnails on a Map

A picture may not be quite worth a thousand geographic points, but it's close. A map is a great way to show photos that have been *geo-tagged*. Geo-tagging is associating latitude and longitude coordinates with images. Full-size photos may not be ideal, however, as they would take up too much space. Instead, a popular method is to display much smaller versions—thumbnails—that the viewer can expand.

Of course, you'll need photos. You can use some that you have as a test or search the photo sharing site Flickr. I was able to find some good shots, already geo-tagged, by searching for Orlando, Florida. I looked specifically for photos that are licensed as Creative Commons, meaning they have less rigid copyright restrictions.

Though we will link to larger versions of each picture, we'll need separate files to store the smaller versions. Another plus to using Flickr is that it creates these thumbnails and a midsize image, too, automatically.

For each Orlando photo we plot, we're going to need the following:

- Photo thumbnail
- Latitude and longitude
- Medium-sized photo
- Dimensions of medium photo
- Link to full photo

At the very least you need the first two items, though you'll create a better user experience the more items from this list you can include. If, like me, you're using Flickr, then you'll need that link to avoid violating Creative Commons.

My three plotted thumbnails are shown on a map in Figure 4-12. As in other situations where we may be doing one action many times, creating a function is best. Add this to your JavaScript code:

```
function plot_thumbnail(pt, thumbimg, medimg, medw, medh, link) {
    var mk = new Marker(pt);
❶  mk.setIcon(thumbimg, [50, 50]);
❷  mk.setShadowIcon('outline.png', [52, 52]);
    mk.setInfoBubble('<a href=\"' + ❸link + '\">' +
                     '<img src=\"' + ❹medimg + '\" width=\"' + ❺medw + '\"' +
                     ' height=\"' + ❻medh + '\" /></a>');
    mapstraction.addMarker(mk);
}
```

As arguments to the function, we need to pass all the items I mentioned in the list. Then we create a custom marker using the thumbnail image ❶. Notice that I set the dimensions of the marker to be 50×50. You can use whatever size you want, but make sure the image itself is close to that size. Flickr's are 75 pixels square, so a little downsizing is okay.

Next, we want to set a shadow ❷ or else the default will be used (in Google Maps the default is a reverse teardrop, which would look funny underneath a square photo). I've created an outline graphic that gives a slight border to the image. I set the size to be slightly bigger than the thumbnail itself.

Finally, we add a message box. Remember, you can include any HTML inside, so we'll link to the full image ❸, as well as display the medium image ❹. To help the mapping provider determine how big to make the message box, we include the width ❺ and height ❻ of the midsized image.

Now we're ready to call the function:

```
plot_thumbnail(new LatLonPoint(28.4736, -81.4651),
             'http://farm3.static.flickr.com/2578/3769139951_954a782886_s.jpg',
             'http://farm3.static.flickr.com/2578/3769139951_954a782886_m.jpg',
             240, 180,
             'http://www.flickr.com/photos/lancerrevolution/3769139951/');
```

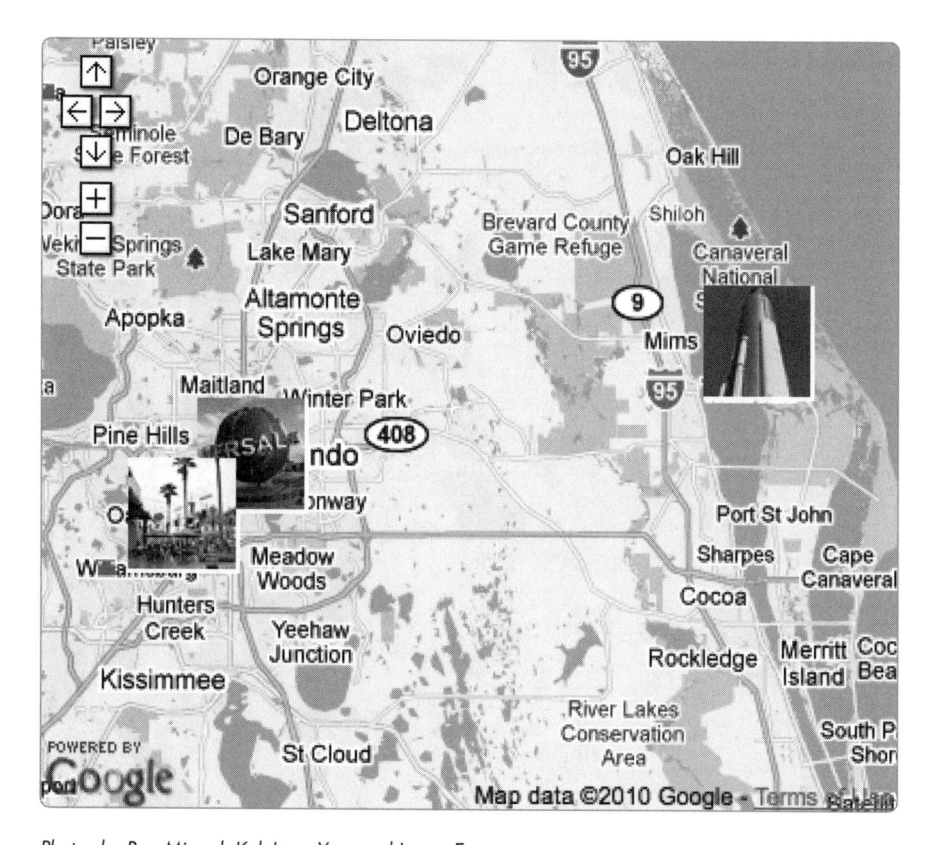

Photos by Ron Miguel, Kok Leng Yeo, and LancerE

Figure 4-12: Thumbnails overlaid as custom markers

This function plots a single photo thumbnail on the map. Click the tiny version and it opens a message box showing the midsized version. Then, when you click the image, the Flickr link opens.

Now simply call that function two more times—or twenty. You can use the Flickr shots from my map as examples:

- *http://www.flickr.com/photos/kamoteus/2421383748/*
- *http://www.flickr.com/photos/yeowatzup/461692550/*

For a more advanced project, you could automate the process of finding images by tapping into the Flickr API to search near a geographic point. The API then responds back with XML or JSON, both of which you can parse using the techniques shown in Chapter 8.

#25: Overlay an Image on a Map

You can add an image to a map in a number of ways. In "#5: Create a Custom Icon Marker" on page 29, you used an image as the icon for a

Placemark. In this section, we'll do something a bit different—overlaying an image over a larger area of the map, where it will replace or augment the existing map.

You're actually familiar with this process, as we used it earlier in this chapter, in "#18: Add Circles to Show Search Radius" on page 67. There, we used a circle image and geo-referenced it so the image was centered on a point and covered a specific area. That example was easier than what we want to do now because a circle is the same distance in every direction and it doesn't matter where it's pointing.

Consider, for example, the map of New York's Central Park in Figure 4-13. It contains some buildings and landmarks that may not be on your standard web map. This map has the park perfectly oriented to be running north and south. In reality, the streets that border the long side of the park are slightly east of north (and west of south).

Mapstraction is only able to overlay a graphic if the top of its rectangle is at north exactly. To get the Central Park map to match the rest of New York, we need to geo-reference it.

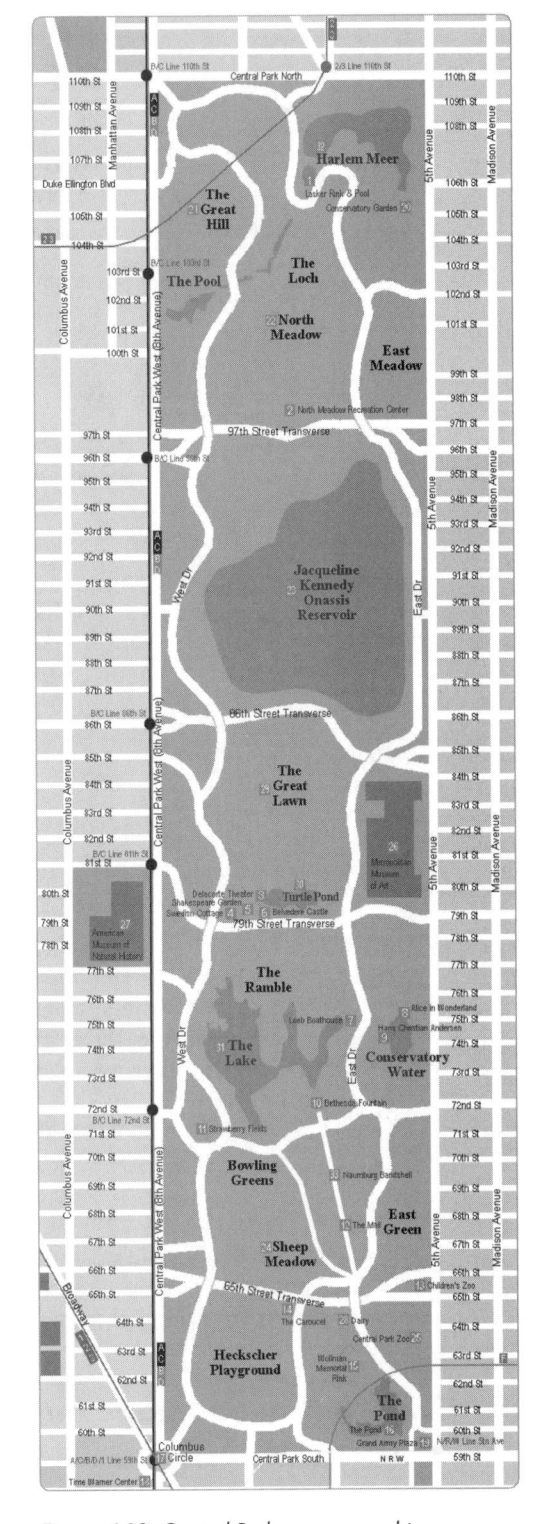

Figure 4-13: Central Park source graphic

Geo-Reference Your Map

At the heart of the geo-referencing technique is the ability to determine the latitude and longitude of points on the graphic. Then, using those points, you can bend and warp the map so the top and bottom borders of the graphic are static latitudes (and the other two static longitudes).

This process is often called *rubbersheeting*, because you are taking a two-dimensional reference, stretching it across a spherical earth, and then unfolding it so it's flat again. The result is a warped image, as if it were made of rubber.

You can geo-reference a graphic to a map in a number of ways. Microsoft has a program called MapCruncher that works well. In this case, you'll need a Windows machine and the resulting graphic can only be used for noncommercial purposes. MetaCarta also has a web tool called Map Rectifier.

For this project, I'll be using a web application called Map Warper, which can be found at *http://warper.geothings.net/*. Map Warper was built by Tim Waters and is open source and meant to free you from worries over how you can use the end result. You will need to create a free account to store your map images. Once you do, click the **Add Map** link to start a new map.

After you provide the name and other metadata to the map, you include a graphic. Browse your hard drive for the image you want to use. You can find the Central Park graphic that I'm using in this example at *http://mapscripting.com/image-overlay/*.

Click the **Rectify** tab and you'll see your image on the left and a map on the right (see Figure 4-14). Move and zoom the map provided until you can see Central Park or the area you are geo-referencing. Now you want to add *control points* wherever you can identify a spot in the left graphic whose coordinates you can determine in the map on the right.

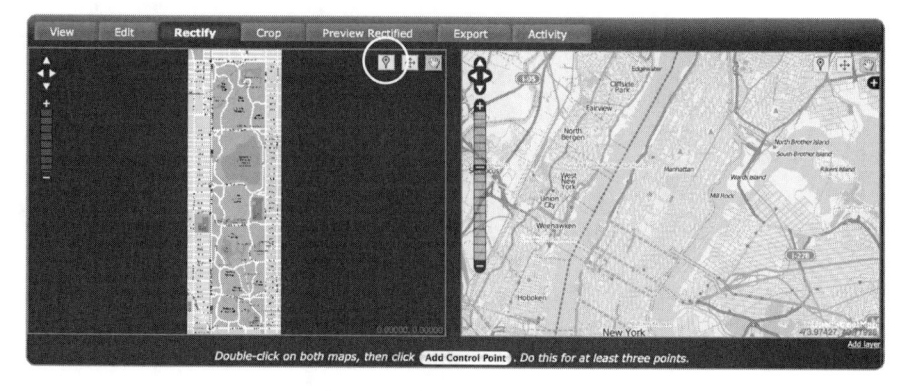

Figure 4-14: Map Warper interface

For example, I chose my first point at Columbus Circle in the lower left of the Central Park graphic. Once I can see Columbus Circle on both screens, I click the marker button (see the circle in Figure 4-14) and the spot on the left. Then I click the same spot on the right side. Finally, I click the **Add Control Point** button and the marker changes so the number 1 appears inside it, as shown in Figure 4-15.

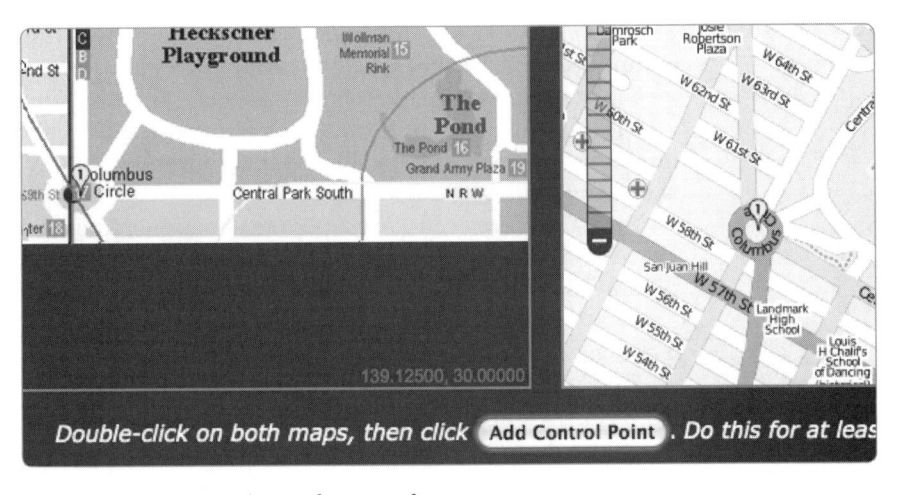

Figure 4-15: First control point for geo-referencing

To find additional points that are off the screen, remember to switch from the marker to the hand, which will allow you to move the image again. You'll need to do the same thing with the map on the right. Continue this process until you have a handful of points. Map Warper suggests at least three points, but I've found it often takes more.

The Central Park example is easier than some, as New York City has a nice set of grid streets to use as references. Figure 4-16 shows the seven points I chose for this example. When you are finished adding control points, scroll to the bottom and click **Warp Image**.

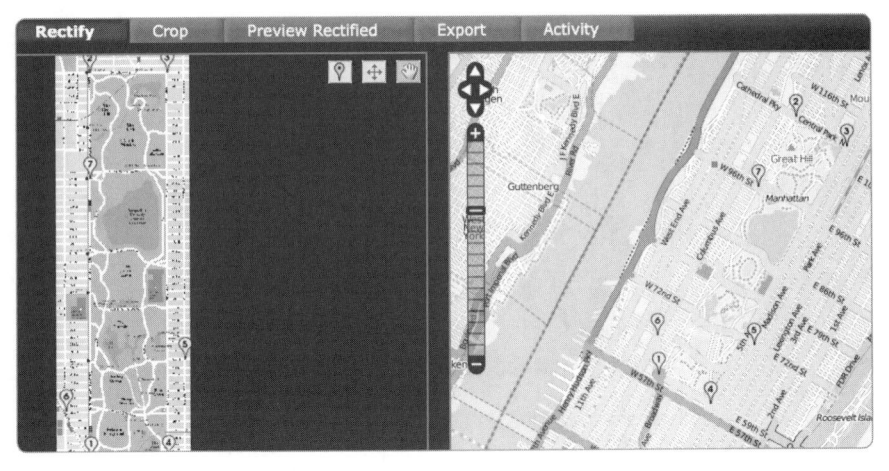

Figure 4-16: More control points produces a better rectified map

The system will whirl and whiz for a bit. When it responds that the map has been rectified, you can scroll back to the top and click the **Preview Rectified** tab. A map with your image warped and overlaid on top will appear, as shown in Figure 4-17. You can move the slider at the bottom to change your image's opacity. Moving the marker all the way to the right makes the image completely opaque, meaning it completely covers the original map.

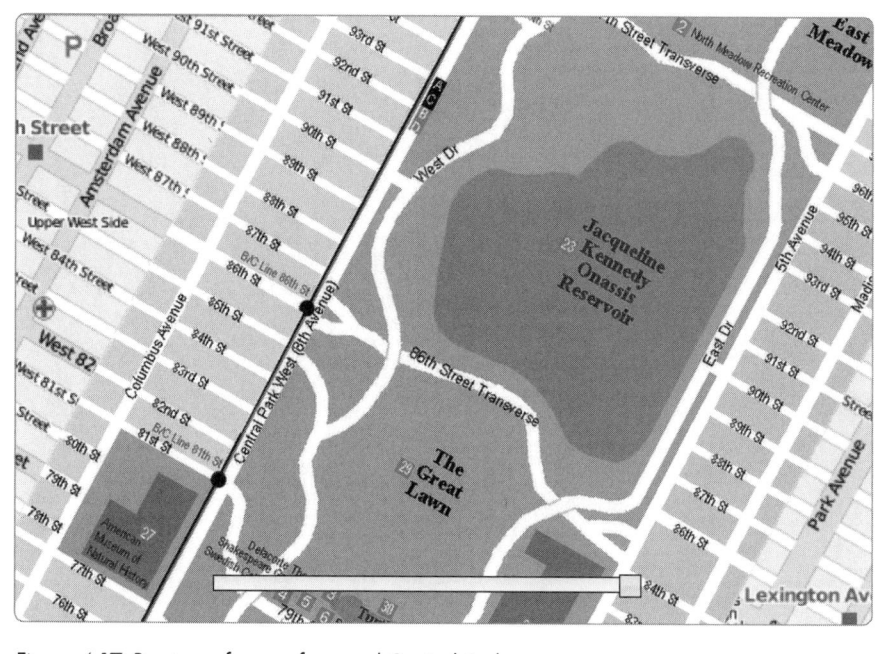

Figure 4-17: Preview of geo-referenced Central Park map

Move the slider back and forth to determine how well your image matches the source map. If you aren't satisfied with the results, click the **Rectify** tab and add a few more points.

Apply Warped Map

When you're happy with the result of your warped image, click the **Export** link to download the image to use it in your own project. You'll want to get the PNG-formatted version. Figure 4-18 shows how different my Central Park graphic is now that it has been geo-referenced.

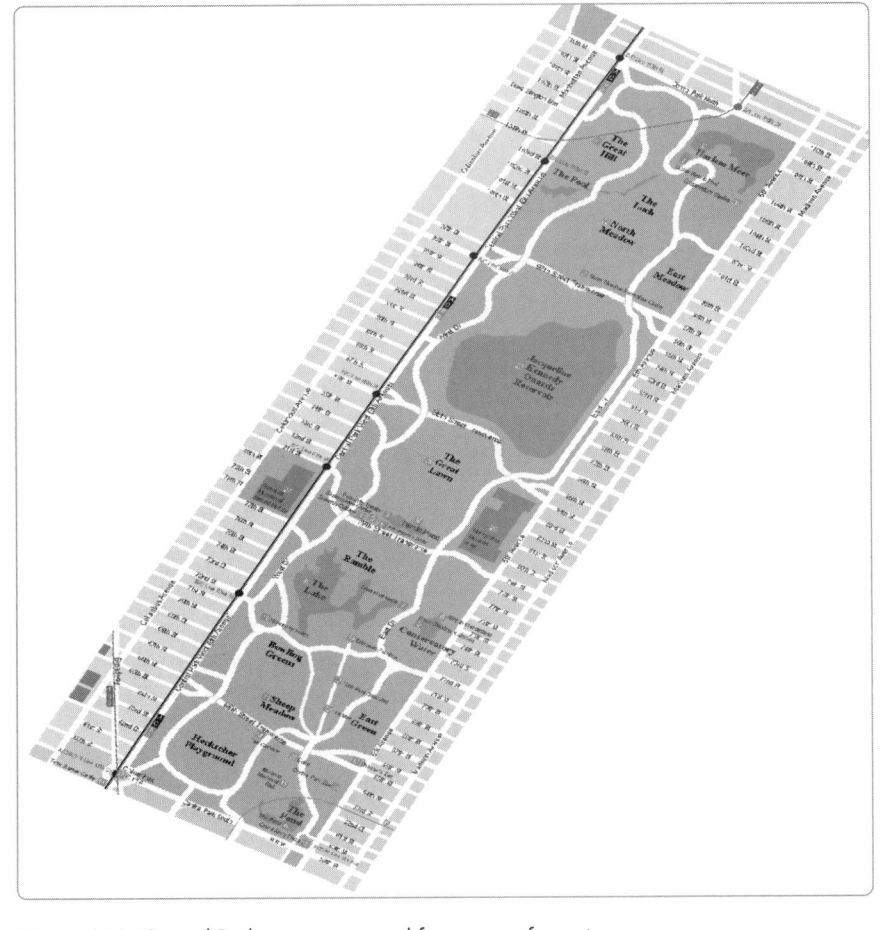

Figure 4-18: Central Park image, warped from geo-referencing

In order to overlay the warped image on your map using Mapstraction, you need to know the boundaries of the image rectangle. To find this information within Map Warper, click the **Activity** tab, where you'll see a table showing the timeline of your geo-referencing session. The topmost item is likely Map Successfully Rectified. Click the **Further Details** link for that row and you'll see more details, including a box with a list of four decimal numbers. Highlight and copy these, which should already be in order: west, north, east, and south.

Now you can add the overlay code to your Mapstraction map:

```
mapstraction.addImageOverlay(❶'centralpark', ❷'centralpark-warped.png', ❸100,
                ❹-73.9867415, 40.7622753, -73.9460798, 40.8032834);
```

In order to add our warped image to the map, we need to give it an identifier ❶. We let Mapstraction know the path to the warped image ❷ (here, I've assumed the image is in the same directory as the HTML file). Then, we give an opacity percentage ❸ between 0 (invisible) and 100 (hidden—no map can be seen under the image). Finally, we add the four numbers from Map Warper ❹ that describe the geographic box where the image will reside.

Figure 4-19 shows the finished map, with the Central Park graphic completely obscuring the Google Map under it.

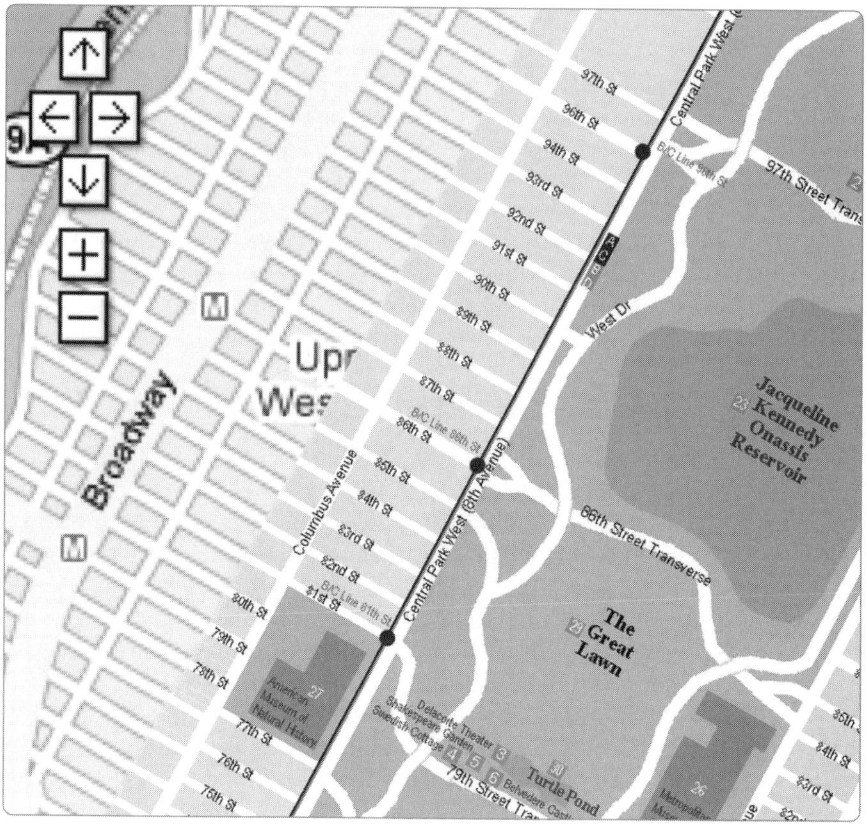

Figure 4-19: Central Park geo-referenced image overlay on a Google Map

You can use your own map imagery over larger areas as well. Storing an entire city or more of data in a single image won't work very well, however. Instead, see the next project, which shows how to create your own imagery to display a little bit at a time.

#26: Use Custom Tiles

Most providers allow you to choose from a handful of imagery types for your maps. You can show satellite view, road maps, or a hybrid version. You're not the cookie-cutter type though, are you? You like the glitz and glamour of choosing your own shade of green for parks or your own thickness for roads. To do this, you'll need custom tiles. And what better place for your glitz and glamour than the Las Vegas strip?

To create Vegas tiles, we'll need the data about streets and other features. Although mapping providers are liberal in what they allow you to do with their APIs, most hold the underlying data like a poker player does his or her cards. One that makes its data widely available is OpenStreetMap, the free editable map of the world. Of course, distributing the details of every street on earth means the file is pretty big, so region-specific downloads are also available. In this project, for example, we'll just use the data for Nevada, the state where Las Vegas is located.

To create the tiles, we'll plug the data into an open source program called Mapnik. Because Mapnik can be a bit complicated to install and configure, we'll take advantage of another project called Tile Drawer, which provides an Amazon EC2 machine image to do much of the technical work. First, let's get a feel for how tiles are used by mapping providers.

How Many Pixels Wide Is the Earth?

As described in Chapter 1, a map is made up of tiles arranged to appear as one large image. Each tile is 256 pixels square and organized as a grid. Most providers reference the grid left to right and north to south, beginning in the Arctic Ocean above Alaska. Tiles are referenced by their number in the grid, such as (14, 34).

The number of tiles required to display the entire earth depends on the zoom level. For example, at its most zoomed out, which is zoom level 0 in Mapstraction, the earth can be shown on a single tile. Each time you zoom in, it takes four tiles to show the detail that was previously displayed on one tile. You can find the number of tiles used in each direction by determining 2 to the *zoom level* power ($2zoom\ level$). Table 4-1 shows tile and pixel information at each zoom level.

When a mapping provider loads map tiles, it uses three numbers: the zoom level, the number of tiles from the left, and the number of tiles from the top. All of these numbers begin at zero, so the upper left of the map at every zoom level is (0, 0). The upper right at level 6, for example, is (16383, 0).

Table 4-1: Tiles and Pixels at Each Zoom Level

Zoom level	Tiles wide/tall	Pixels wide/tall
0	1	256
1	2	512
2	4	1,024
3	8	2,048
4	16	4,096
5	32	8,192
6	64	16,384
7	128	32,768
8	256	65,536
9	512	131,072
10	1,024	262,144
11	2,048	524,288
12	4,096	1,048,576
13	8,192	2,097,152
14	16,384	4,194,304
15	32,768	8,388,608
16	65,536	16,777,216
17	131,072	33,554,432
18	262,144	67,108,864

Thankfully, you don't need to reference the tiles by their grid location. The mapping provider does all this for you. Understanding how it works is important because you'll need to use this knowledge to create custom tile URLs later in this project.

As for the question at the top of this section—how many pixels wide is the earth? It depends on the zoom level, but for most providers, the earth is between 256 and 67,108,864 pixels wide.

Start a Tile Drawer EC2 Instance

Tile Drawer helps you create your own custom map tiles and runs a tile server in the cloud. It runs on top of Amazon EC2, which is an *elastic compute cloud*, that is, an expandable web server. Another feature of EC2 is the ability to save preconfigured servers, Amazon Machine Images (AMIs), and make them available to others. That's what the creators of Tile Drawer have done. Handy!

You will need an Amazon account (be prepared to provide your email address and a few other bits of information) and then sign up for EC2. Amazon charges for this service, but does so for cents per hour, so you'll be able to try this project for less than a dollar. This page will walk you through the signup process: *http://aws.amazon.com/ec2/*.

Log in to the AWS Management Console from this page. Click the **Launch Instance** button. Then search the Community AMIs for the Tile Drawer machine image. Look for *tiledrawer*, or find the ID, such as `ami-e1ea0a88`, listed on *http://tiledrawer.com/*. When you find the Tile Drawer AMI, click the **Select** button.

On the Instance Details screen, only create one instance, as shown in Figure 4-20. Because you'll be using a very small area to start, you can get away with a small instance type. Click the **Continue** button, and then on the next screen, you mostly leave the default settings in place. You'll need to add some user data, however.

Figure 4-20: Create a single Amazon EC2 Tile Drawer instance

Declare User Data for Your Instance

The Tile Drawer server is fairly plug and play. Just a few settings are necessary to make it run. As you'll see later, these settings also allow you to fully customize your map tiles.

You can use the wizard on *http://tiledrawer.com/* to help you create the user data automatically. Or to continue following along with this example, paste the following data in the User Data box on the EC2 setup page (see Figure 4-21):

```
{
  "style": "http://tiledrawer.com/mapscratch.mml",
  "bbox": [-115.2, 36.10, -115.1, 36.15],
  "source": "http://downloads.cloudmade.com/north_america/united_states/nevada/nevada.osm.bz2",
  "coast": "http://hypercube.telascience.org/~kleptog/processed_p.zip"
}
```

This data has four preferences. First, the style of the map, which uses a CSS-like style sheet. We'll stick with the basic look from Tile Drawer for this first example and make changes later. Next, we declare a BoundingBox, similar to those we've used with Mapstraction. The difference here is that longitudes are listed before latitudes. The two points we use are still southwest followed by northeast.

The last two items are URLs to files that Tile Drawer will download and use. The first is the data itself. We're using the data for Nevada, which is hosted by CloudMade. You can find the data you need at *http://downloads .cloudmade.com/*. Look for files of type *.osm.bz2*. The final URL is the coastline data, which is hosted separately.

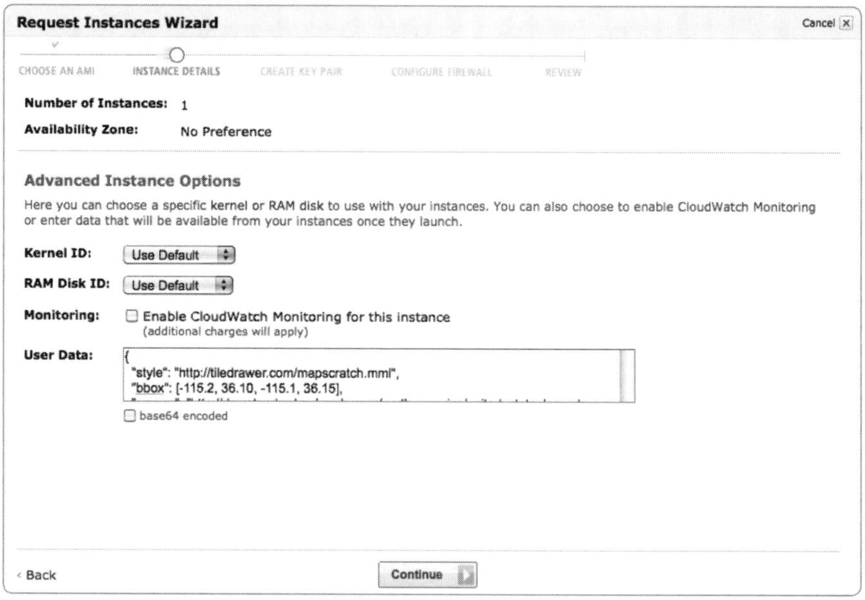

Figure 4-21: Adding user data to the EC2 instance

With the user data set, click **Continue** again. The next screen will prompt you to create a key pair. The key pair enables you to connect to the server's backend. This advanced feature may be useful at some point in the future. For now, select **Proceed without a Key Pair**, and click **Continue**.

On the firewall screen, make sure you select the webserver security group. This group opens up the appropriate ports for running a web server, which is necessary for accessing your tiles from any computer, including your own. Click **Continue** and you'll be on the final screen. Take a deep breath and then click **Launch**.

Tile Drawer Does Its Job

Your EC2 instance will not instantly start up. Although it's a virtual computer, it still takes a few minutes to boot. Once it is available, creating all the tiles will take some additional time. This is a great time for a break!

But you shouldn't need *too* long of a break. With only one state of data to download and a small area to prepare, Tile Drawer should be ready in less than 15 minutes. From your EC2 dashboard, you should be able to click the **Running Instances** link under My Resources. From there, you can see the status of your new instance. When the server has booted up, it should switch from yellow and pending to green and running.

When the server is running, click your instance and a description will appear in the pane below. Scroll down and locate the Public DNS address, as shown in Figure 4-22. This address is the equivalent of a domain name for your new virtual server. Enter that address in your web browser and you should see a page that says, "It works!"

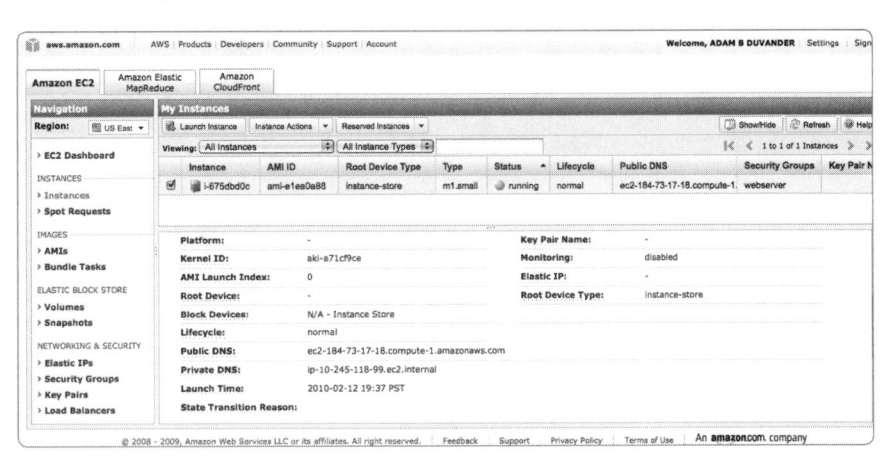

Figure 4-22: Instance details shows your Public DNS address.

Next, add */status.php* to the end of your address to get Tile Drawer's status. Tile Drawer goes through to create tiles: Getting Started, Downloading Source, Extracting Data, Creating Tables, Importing Coastline, Downloading Stylesheet, and Creating TileCache. As it completes each step, it will become grayed out, as shown in Figure 4-23. When Tile Dawer is done, you can click the link or go to your address followed by */preview.php*.

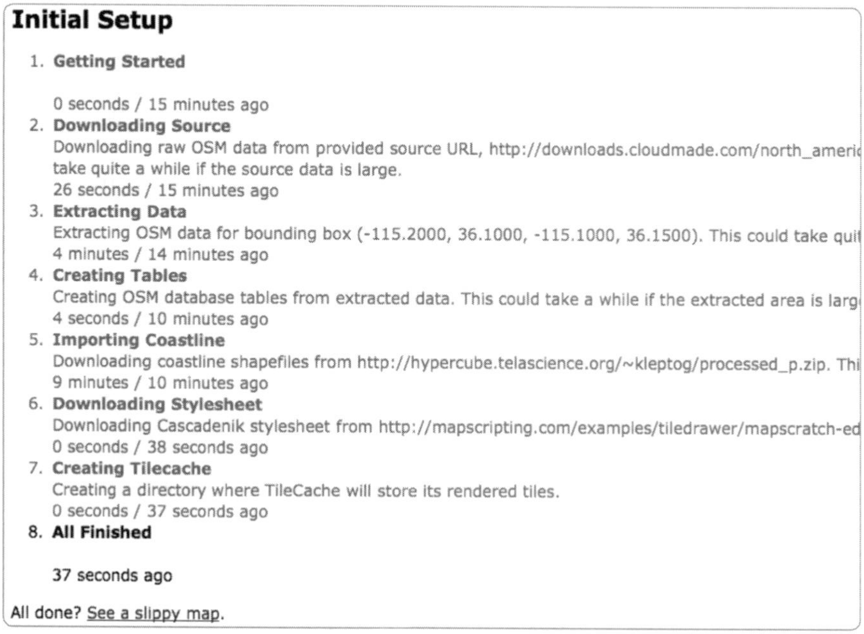

Initial Setup

1. **Getting Started**

   0 seconds / 15 minutes ago
2. **Downloading Source**
   Downloading raw OSM data from provided source URL, http://downloads.cloudmade.com/north_america take quite a while if the source data is large.
   26 seconds / 15 minutes ago
3. **Extracting Data**
   Extracting OSM data for bounding box (-115.2000, 36.1000, -115.1000, 36.1500). This could take quite
   4 minutes / 14 minutes ago
4. **Creating Tables**
   Creating OSM database tables from extracted data. This could take a while if the extracted area is large
   4 seconds / 10 minutes ago
5. **Importing Coastline**
   Downloading coastline shapefiles from http://hypercube.telascience.org/~kleptog/processed_p.zip. This
   9 minutes / 10 minutes ago
6. **Downloading Stylesheet**
   Downloading Cascadenik stylesheet from http://mapscripting.com/examples/tiledrawer/mapscratch-ed
   0 seconds / 38 seconds ago
7. **Creating Tilecache**
   Creating a directory where TileCache will store its rendered tiles.
   0 seconds / 37 seconds ago
8. **All Finished**

   37 seconds ago

All done? See a slippy map.

Figure 4-23: Tile Drawer's status updates as each section finishes.

You'll see a quick preview of your new tiles on the Tile Drawer server. You can double-click to zoom in. If everything looks good, the time has come to put those tiles on a Mapstraction map.

Add Tile Overlays to Your Map

The process of including your tiles in Mapstraction is as easy as a single line of code. The hard work is behind you with setting up the tile server—and also ahead of you in creating the styles, which can be a tedious.

Create a new basic map using the following code:

```
function create_map() {
  mapstraction = new mxn.Mapstraction('mymap', 'googlev3');
  mapstraction.setCenterAndZoom(
    new mxn.LatLonPoint(36.123, -115.167), 13);
  mapstraction.addSmallControls();
  mapstraction.addTileLayer(
    "http://yourserver.amazonaws.com/tilecache/1.0.0/osm/❶{Z}/{X}/{Y}.png", ❷1.0);
}
```

Here we have created a map centered on the Las Vegas strip. Then, in the line in bold, we tell Mapstraction where to find our tiles. Our URL contains placeholders for zoom level ❶ and the tile grid coordinates.

These values, {z}, {x}, and {y}, are filled in with actual numbers. You can see an example tile by going to *yourserver.amazonaws.com/tilecache/1.0.0/ osm/13/1475/3213.png*. Be sure to replace *yourserver* with the Public DNS address of your EC2 instance.

The second argument that we pass to Mapstraction's tile layer function is an opacity. Like in "#25: Overlay an Image on a Map" on page 83, we can make our tiles semitransparent so we can still see some of the provider imagery underneath. Here I made our tiles completely opaque ❷ by choosing a value of one. A number between zero and one sets the percentage. For example, 0.6 would be 60 percent opaque.

Save your map and load it in a browser. You should now see your custom Las Vegas tiles instead of the Google imagery, like in Figure 4-24. You may catch a glimpse of the default look before your tiles load. That's because the custom tiles are being placed on top of Google, so both sets still need to load.

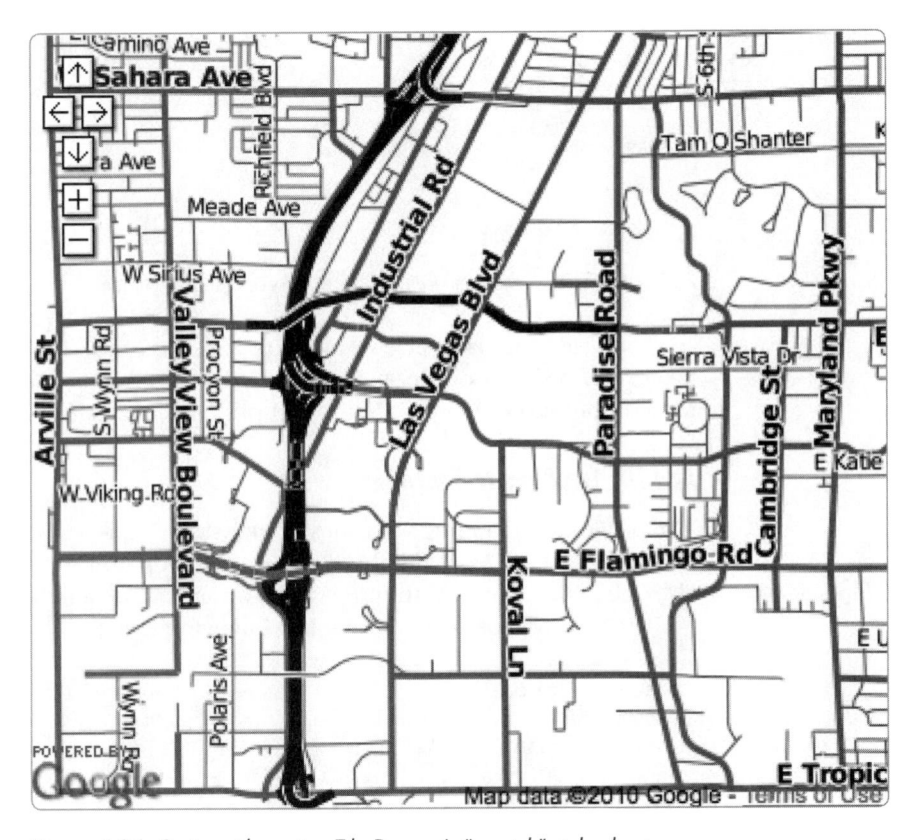

Figure 4-24: Custom tiles using Tile Drawer's "scratch" style sheet

Create Your Own Tile Styles

If you are familiar with CSS for styling web pages, you will likely feel comfortable with the way Tile Drawer applies colors and other styles to maps. It uses Cascadenik to convert into the file format necessary to work with the Mapnik tile generator. Earlier in this project, we used a basic example provided by Tile Drawer. Now we'll try changing a few of the colors and road widths.

The first thing you'll need is to copy *http://tiledrawer.com/mapscratch.mml* to your own server. Or you can use the version I have edited for this section at *http://mapscripting.com/examples/tiledrawer/mapscratch-edits.mml*.

Because Vegas is famous for its neon lights, let's aim to make the roads pop out from the map. To do this, we'll use bright colors and a dark background. Find the line that begins with #land and change it, using this styling data:

```
#land { polygon-fill: #333; }
```

This data changes the land, which is essentially the background color, from a very light color to nearly black. Black is very Vegas, especially when we include the bright colors. For these next changes, you'll need to use the styles that begin with the #lines. Be sure your code matches these settings:

```
#lines[❶highway=motorway],
#lines[highway=motorway_link]
{
❷  line-width: 6;
❸  line-color: #f00;
   }
#lines[highway=primary],
#lines[highway=secondary],
#lines[highway=tertiary]
{
   line-width: 4;
   line-color: ❹#ff0;
   }
#lines[highway=residential],
#lines[highway=unclassified],
#lines[highway=service]
{
   line-width: 2;
   line-color: ❺#00f;
   }
```

Cascadenik style sheets use OpenStreetMap tags inside the square brackets to determine which elements you want to style. In all these examples, we're styling highways, a generic term for any road. In the first set, we apply the styles only to motorways ❶ and motorway "links" (such as off-ramps). Since everything is bigger and brighter in Vegas, we make the motorways wider ❷ and then color them a bright red ❸.

In the next two sections, we set the larger streets to be yellow ❹. Residential and other small streets are set to blue ❺. As the streets get smaller, so do their widths on the map. Seeing as we're doing this Vegas-style, however, they're still larger than the styles we're editing.

You can do some powerful things with these styles to make your maps look unlike any imagery available. As one example of how specific you can get with styles, try adding these lines to your style sheet:

```
#lines[zoom=13][highway=motorway]
{
  line-color: #ff8000;
}
```

At first glance, this code is similar to some we've already done. Pay attention to the bolded section; it tells the tile server to only apply this style when the zoom level is 13. At all other zoom levels, our other styles will take precedence. But when our map is at level 13, the motorways will be orange instead of red.

I didn't reset the line width, as I did in other sections, which means the line width already set for motorways will remain the same for zoom level 13. Only the color will change. In addition to =, you can use >, >=, <, and <= to style at certain zoom levels.

With a few styles changed, let's see Tile Drawer in action. Create a new EC2 instance (remember to terminate those not in use to avoid the hourly charges) with the following data:

```
{
  "style": "http://mapscripting.com/examples/tiledrawer/mapscratch-edits.mml",
  "bbox": [-115.2, 36.10, -115.1, 36.15],
  "source": "http://downloads.cloudmade.com/north_america/united_states/nevada/nevada.osm.bz2",
  "coast": "http://hypercube.telascience.org/~kleptog/processed_p.zip"
}
```

If you've made changes that I didn't include here, good for you! In that case, replace the URL in bold with the address of the map style sheet on your own server. To get a feel for how these few changes alters the look of our tiles, see Figure 4-25.

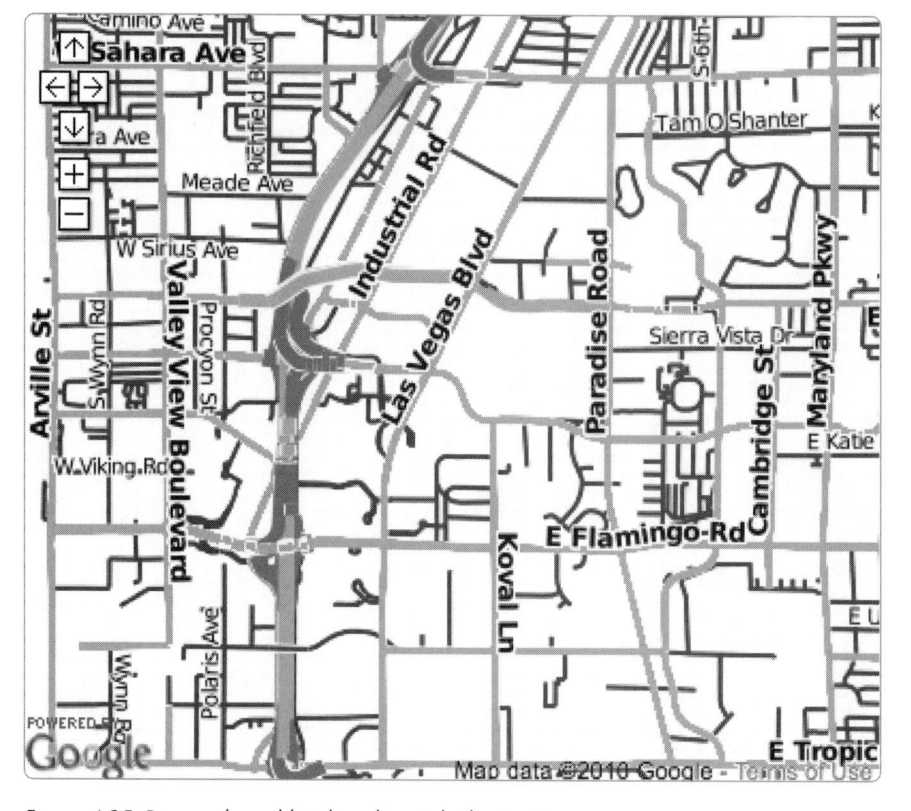

Figure 4-25: Big roads and bright colors style the Las Vegas map

After a short wait as your virtual server boots and Tile Drawer does its work, your newly styled Las Vegas tiles should be ready. Update the address of your server in the Mapstraction file you used to create a tile layer. Load it up and you should see the bright roads of Vegas popping out from your new map.

5

HANDLE MAP EVENTS

Web-based maps are highly interactive. They make users want to drag them, click them, and zoom them. That's all part of the fun, but this interactivity also makes them more useful. By tapping into this interactivity, you can design those little user movements to provide an even better interface; for instance, changing the visible markers when users drag the map or changing the search radius along with the zoom level.

Events control all the potential ways a user can interact with your map. You can run special code any time a user drags the map, zooms in, or clicks. Events are also specific to markers, message boxes, and polylines. Read on for a quick introduction to the way Mapstraction organizes events and for examples of each.

Mapstraction's Event Model

Events happen, regardless of whether we're paying attention. To be able to react to an event, we need to tell Mapstraction that we care about that particular event. We do this by setting a function for Mapstraction to call when an event happens. This function is called a *handler*.

To create an event handler, we need to know the event type we're looking for and the object from which the event will be originating. We register our interest in the event using the following form:

```
object.event.addHandler(function (event_name, event_source, event_args) {
  // Code to perform after the event
});
```

The potential events that can occur for each object are shown in Table 5-1. The addHandler function accepts one argument—a reference to a function that will handle the event. In the case of the previous example, and most examples in this chapter, I'm using an anonymous, inline function. You can also use named functions, as I do in most examples that involve markers. If you are going to call the same function on many objects, you'll find it more memory efficient to use a named function.

Whether you use an anonymous or named function to handle events, however, the function accepts three arguments: an event name, an event source, and additional event arguments. Those values are passed automatically by Mapstraction. The name will always be the same as *event*, whereas the source will always be the *object*. Additional data, if it exists, is included in the arguments object.

Table 5-1: Objects and Their Events

Object	Event
Mapstraction	click
Mapstraction	endPan
Mapstraction	changeZoom
Mapstraction	markerAdded
Mapstraction	markerRemoved
Mapstraction	polylineAdded
Mapstraction	polylineRemoved
Marker	click
Marker	openInfoBubble

Each event is covered in depth in the sections of this chapter.

#27: The User Clicks the Map

Out-of-the-box interactivity makes mapping APIs pretty special. Using built-in controls, users can drag and pan a map, zoom in, and change map types. Users can also click, but nothing will happen unless you help them out.

Mapstraction's click event is what reacts to a user's click. Unlike some other events shown in this chapter, knowing that your users clicked is not enough. You need to know *where* they clicked.

To find out when and where a user clicks, add the following code to your create_map function:

```
mapstraction.click.addHandler(function(event_name, event_source, event_args) {
    var clickpoint = event_args.location;
    var mk = new mxn.Marker(clickpoint);
    mapstraction.addMarker(mk);
});
```

Here, we add a handler for Mapstraction's click event. To react to this event, I've used an anonymous inline function. If you have more than a couple lines of code to run, you'll want to use a standard named function, because long anonymous functions are hard to read. I'm pushing the limits here.

When the user clicks anywhere within the map, Mapstraction calls our function with three pieces of data, the last of which contains the event arguments. The key piece of information we want is inside those arguments: the click location, which is stored as a LatLonPoint. The previous example uses that point to create a new marker.

Each click adds another marker to the map. Do this a few times and your map will look something like Figure 5-1.

#28: The User Drags the Map

If you're a developer who likes to be in control, you may not immediately appreciate the interactivity of maps. Users can move the viewable portion of a map to wherever they want, forgoing your perfectly designed experience. What a drag! In fact, literally a drag, as the user drags the map this way and that. You can use an event, however, to help you gain back a little of that control.

You can write code to react to a even the smallest movement of the map. You can use this to force the map back to where you put it, if that's what you prefer. A more friendly reaction is to find a way to recognize the area of the map where the user moved. For example, if you are showing search results, try reloading them with the new center.

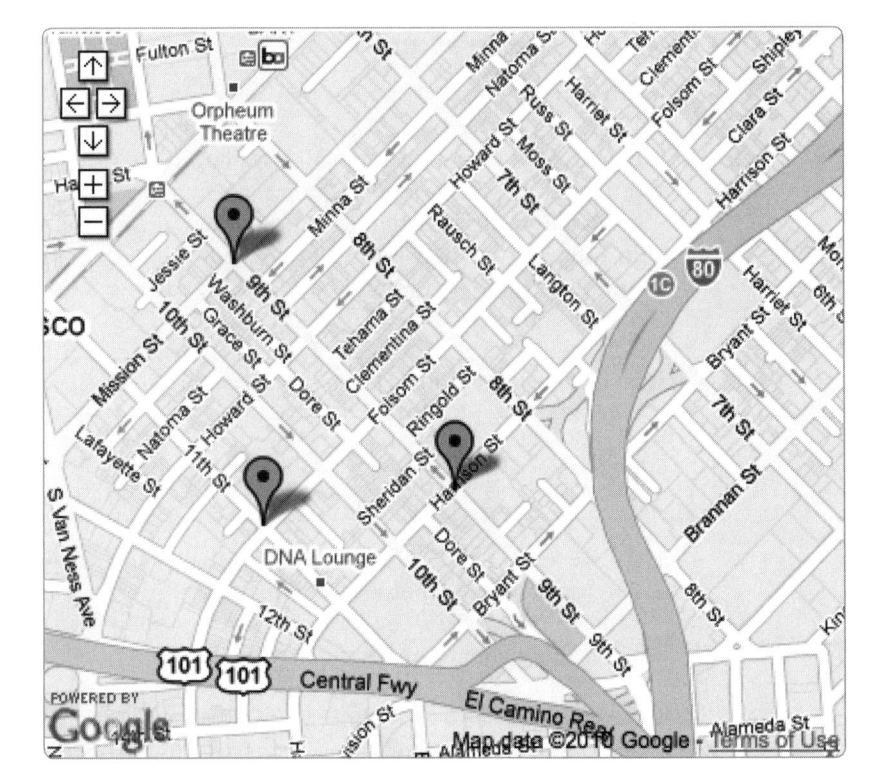

Figure 5-1: Each click adds a new marker.

For this example, we'll merely create a JavaScript alert whenever we notice the map has moved. And how do we know when a map has moved? Add these lines to your basic map:

```
mapstraction.endPan.addHandler(function(event_name, event_source, event_args)
{
  alert('The map just moved!');
});
```

Here, we add a handler for Mapstraction's endPan event. To react to this event, I've used an anonymous inline function. If you have more than a couple lines of code to run, you'll want to use a standard named function.

With this code implemented, any time the user moves the map, this event will fire, and the alert box will pop up. Programmatically setting the center will also trigger the event because the map has been panned (just not directly by the user). The event does not fire when you initially set the center of the map, however, only because that code comes before Mapstraction knows to look out for map movement.

NOTE   *With some providers, such as Google, the endPan event will also be triggered when the zoom level changes.*

As soon as the endPan event fires, you'll have access to the current map data, such as the center, via the Mapstraction object. Here's an example that creates a new marker at the new center whenever the user drags the map:

```
mapstraction.endPan.addHandler(function(event_name, event_source, event_args)
{
  var mk = new mxn.Marker(mapstraction.getCenter());
  mapstraction.addMarker(mk);
});
```

Enter this into your basic map's create_map function, and load it into a browser. Try moving the map and each time you'll find a brand new marker at its center.

#29: The Zoom Level Changes

"Let's take a closer look," she thinks, clicking the plus-sign button to zoom closer into the map. Assuming you provide the interface to do so, your users will be doing a lot of zooming in and zooming out. In some maps, reacting to those sometimes drastic changes in the map's bounds is important, which is where Mapstraction's zoom event can be your best friend.

You can make your map handle the zoom event and do something useful, such as reset your search radius. Or, as shown later in this chapter, determine whether the user moves the map outside preset bounds.

For this example, we'll create a JavaScript alert whenever the map is zoomed, so you can get a feeling for when this event is triggered. Add the following code to your basic map's create_map function:

```
mapstraction.changeZoom.addHandler(function(event_name, event_source, event_args) {
  alert('Zoom level changed!');
});
```

Here, we add a handler for Mapstraction's changeZoom event. To react to this event, I've used an anonymous inline function. If you have more than a couple lines of code to run, you'll want to use a standard named function.

Try loading your map with this code included. Change the zoom on your map a few times, and watch it respond. If your provider interprets a double-click as a zoom in (and most do), try that, too. Your users won't be able to zoom in or out without you knowing about it!

Do you want to respond with something a little more useful? How about an alert displaying the new zoom level? Try the following code:

```
mapstraction.changeZoom.addHandler(function(event_name, event_source, event_args) {
  alert('Changed zoom to level ' + mapstraction.getZoom());
});
```

Now, each time your users zoom in or out, a message doesn't just say that the zoom level changed; it also shows the new zoom level. If your map has large zoom controls, try zooming in quickly from your current level to one very close in or try zooming extremely far out. An alert will pop up with the new zoom level number. If you'd like to make more sense of zoom levels, see "Set Zoom Level" on page 18.

#30: A Marker Is Added to or Removed from the Map

Markers, markers everywhere. Once your mapping application becomes large, you might be adding markers from many different areas of your code. The same could be true of removing markers. You can take advantage of two events that will call a function you specify when a marker is added or removed.

Add the following code to your basic map's create_map function:

```
mapstraction.markerAdded.addHandler(function(event_name, event_source, event_args) {
  alert('Added marker at ' + event_args.marker.location);
});
mapstraction.markerRemoved.addHandler(function(event_name, event_source, event_args) {
  alert('Removed marker at ' + event_args.marker.location);
});
```

Of course, using a JavaScript alert to let the user know a marker has been added or removed is probably not that helpful. Instead, you might update your own metadata on markers or autocenter the map based on the new or remaining markers.

You can access the affected marker via the event_args object, which contains one property called marker. You may find it more intuitive to access the marker from the event_source object. Though these events are related to markers, they are initiated by the Mapstraction object, which is passed as the source.

Because the only way to add or remove markers is through your code, plenty of other non-event-based ways available to perform an action when a marker is added or removed. As mentioned, you might only find this useful if you have a large application.

#31: A Polyline Is Added to or Removed from the Map

Do you use lots of polylines on your maps? You can use an event to run a special function every time you add or remove a polyline. This feature is especially useful for large mapping applications, where many different places create new lines or when you need to nix unnecessary ones.

To create functions for the two Polyline events, add the following code to your `create_map` function:

```
mapstraction.polylineAdded.addHandler(function(event_name, event_source, event_args) {
  alert('Added polyline starting at ' + event_args.polyline.points[0]);
});
mapstraction.polylineRemoved.addHandler(function(event_name, event_source, event_args) {
  alert('Removed polyline starting at ' + event_args.polyline.points[0]);
});
```

I have created a JavaScript alert to show the first point of the polyline that has been added or removed. You'll want to include something more useful than JavaScript alerts, which users would see as overkill in most situations. You might choose to autocenter the map based on the new or removed polyline, for example.

You can access the affected polyline via the event_args object, which contains one property called polyline. You may find it more intuitive to access the polyline from the event_source object. Though these events are related to polylines, they are initiated by the Mapstraction object, which is passed as the source.

Like adding and removing markers, your code is the only way to add new polylines to (or remove unwanted ones from) the map. Due to this fact, other methods are available for running code in these events. For large applications, however, you may prefer this event-based approach.

#32: The User Opens or Closes a Message Box

Your map's markers can only do so much to communicate a location's meaning. The rest happens in a message box, which users can open by clicking a marker. If you want to react when a message box is opened or closed, you'll need to write event handlers for each marker.

A common use case is to update a section of the website outside the map when a message box is opened. For example, perhaps you want to highlight the result related to that marker in search results. Or you may want to hide each marker once its message box has been viewed. Here, we'll stick with our method of showing a JavaScript alert.

Add the following code to your basic map's `create_map` function:

```
var mk = new mxn.Marker(mapstraction.getCenter());
mk.setInfoBubble('Look ma, No Starch!');
mk.openInfoBubble.addHandler(myboxopened);
mk.closeInfoBubble.addHandler(myboxclosed);
mapstraction.addMarker(mk);
```

And include this function within the JavaScript section, but outside of other functions:

```
function myboxopened(event_name, ❶event_source, event_args) {
  alert('Opened bubble attached to marker at ' + ❷event_source.location);
}
function myboxclosed(event_name, event_source, event_args) {
  alert('Closed bubble attached to marker at ' + event_source.location);
}
```

Here, I've created a simple marker in the center of the map with a message box, similar to what we created in "#3: Show a Message Box When Your Marker Is Clicked" on page 27. The events for opening and closing message boxes are shown in bold. For this particular marker, we're waiting to react to either of these events.

When the event fires, we call the named functions, either myboxopened or myboxclosed. You can name these functions anything you want. When the appropriate function is called, the marker is passed to the event_source variable ❶. At this point, we have access to any of this marker's attributes, including the location ❷. We can do anything with this marker that we can do with any other marker, including hide it, removing it, or setting new attributes (perhaps tracking which message boxes have been opened?).

NOTE   *Unlike some of the previous examples, we add handlers for these events to the marker object, not the Mapstraction object. If you want to run similar code for every marker, you need to add an event to each marker.*

As you can see from comparing the code for the two events, reacting to a closed message box uses almost identical code. You can see a more advanced example of the closeInfoBubble event later in this chapter.

#33: The User Clicks a Marker

Your users see all those markers on the map and many will want to click them to learn more about a particular location. That's what the message box is for, right? Well, you may want to do a little more. In those cases, you'll need a way to tell when a marker has been clicked. As you might have guessed, Mapstraction has an event for just this occasion.

The marker click event, like the other marker events, is attached to the marker itself. So, if you want to perform the same action for every marker, you'll need to add a handler individually.

For this example, we'll simply use a single marker and create a JavaScript alert to share its location. Add the following code to the create_map function of your basic map:

```
var mk = new mxn.Marker(mapstraction.getCenter());
mk.click.addHandler(mymarkerclicked);
```

And include this function within the JavaScript section but outside of other functions:

```
function mymarkerclicked(event_name, ❶event_source, event_args) {
  alert('Clicked the marker at ' + ❷event_source.location);
}
```

When the event fires, the `mymarkerclicked` function is called with three arguments. The marker is then passed to the event_source variable ❶. At this point, we have access to any of this marker's attributes, including the location ❷. We can do anything with this marker that we can do with any other marker, but here we've just created a JavaScript alert.

NOTE   *This event is different than Mapstraction's main click event, which fires whenever the map is clicked. In this case, the event is attached to a particular marker, and your code only runs when that marker is clicked.*

Here's the truth: You won't use this event very often because a message box is the best way to show information about a marker. The marker click event is a useful tool, however, for the times when you want to do something a bit different.

#34: Return to the Center When the Message Box Is Closed

Have I sung the praises of message boxes enough yet? They help explain what your markers represent. They provide additional information about a location yet only at the moment the user wants it. They make your maps more informative and more interactive. But they can also get in the way, as shown in Figure 5-2.

Depending on your provider, opening a message box can cause your map to pan ungracefully, leaving a messy map when the user has closed the message box. A little code and the help of an event already covered in this chapter can improve the user's experience. Re-enter the `closeInfoBubble` event.

Let's say you've laid out your markers so they fit perfectly within the map, as shown in "#8: Determine the Correct Zoom Level to Use Based on Markers" on page 34. If you make that code run again whenever the user closes a message box and after each new marker is added, your map will always look organized.

Add this code after creating a marker:

```
mk.closeInfoBubble.addHandler(myboxclosed);
```

And add the function to handle the event:

```
function myboxclosed(event_name, event_source, event_args) {
  mapstraction.autoCenterAndZoom();
}
```

This code assumes a marker named mk, but you'll want to change that to match whatever variable name you choose for your marker. Also remember that the closeInfoBubble event is set for a single marker. In order for the event to fire for every marker, you need to set it for every marker.

Preserve the Previous Center

Re-autocentering code might be very useful for most situations because users can still see every marker. In some cases, however, you might want to give the user a little more control, while still maintaining the benefit of reorganizing your map when a message box is closed. Here, you want to remember where the map was before the user opened the message box.

To achieve this result, you'll need to use the two message box events in tandem. This method is a simple and effective way to preserve the map's center. Add the following code after creating each marker:

```
mk.openInfoBubble.addHandler(myboxopened);
mk.closeInfoBubble.addHandler(myboxclosed);
```

And then include these handler functions:

```
function myboxopened(event_name, event_source, event_args) {
❶   mapcenter = mapstraction.getCenter();
}
function myboxclosed(event_name, event_source, event_args) {
    mapstraction.setCenter(mapcenter, ❷{pan: true});
}
```

As with the previous example, I'm assuming a marker named mk. Additionally, I've added a global variable named mapcenter to hold the LatLonPoint of the map's center.

Whenever a message box is opened, the openInfoBubble event fires *before* the provider moves the map to make room for the message box. This is important: Now we have a chance to record the map's center ❶, which will allow us to reset it later.

When the message box is closed, the closeInfoBubble event fires. Instead of autocentering, we set the center to the one stored when the message box was opened, as shown in Figure 5-3. To be extra kind to the user's eyes, we pan the map ❷ instead of setting the center directly.

Now you've used events to subtly improve your users' interactions with your maps.

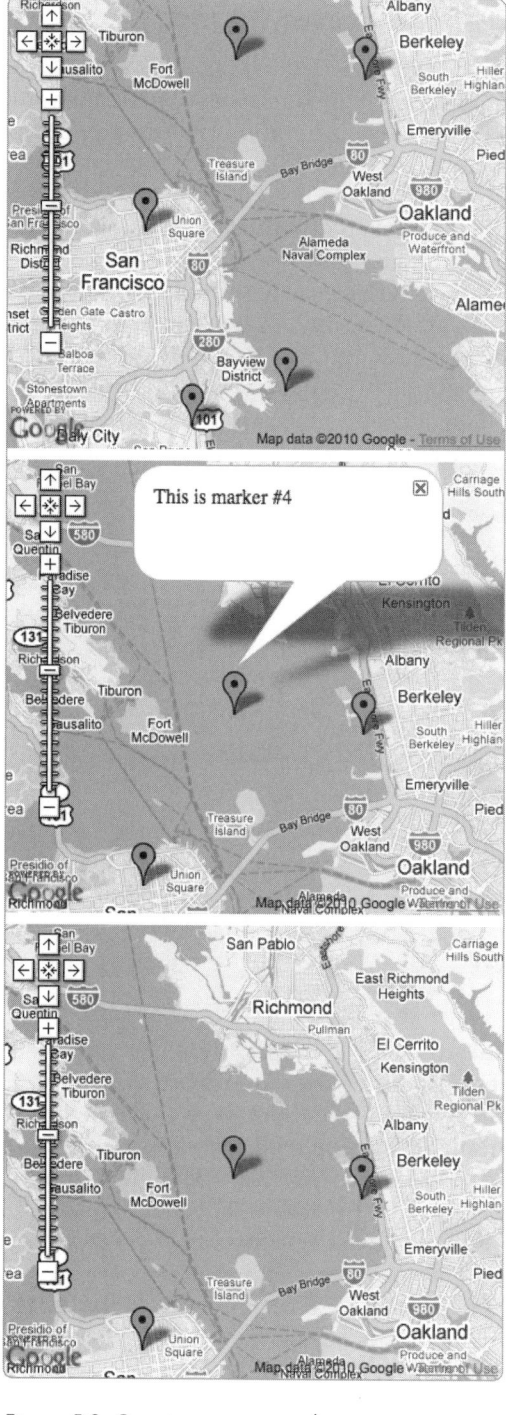

Figure 5-2: Opening a message box can move your map.

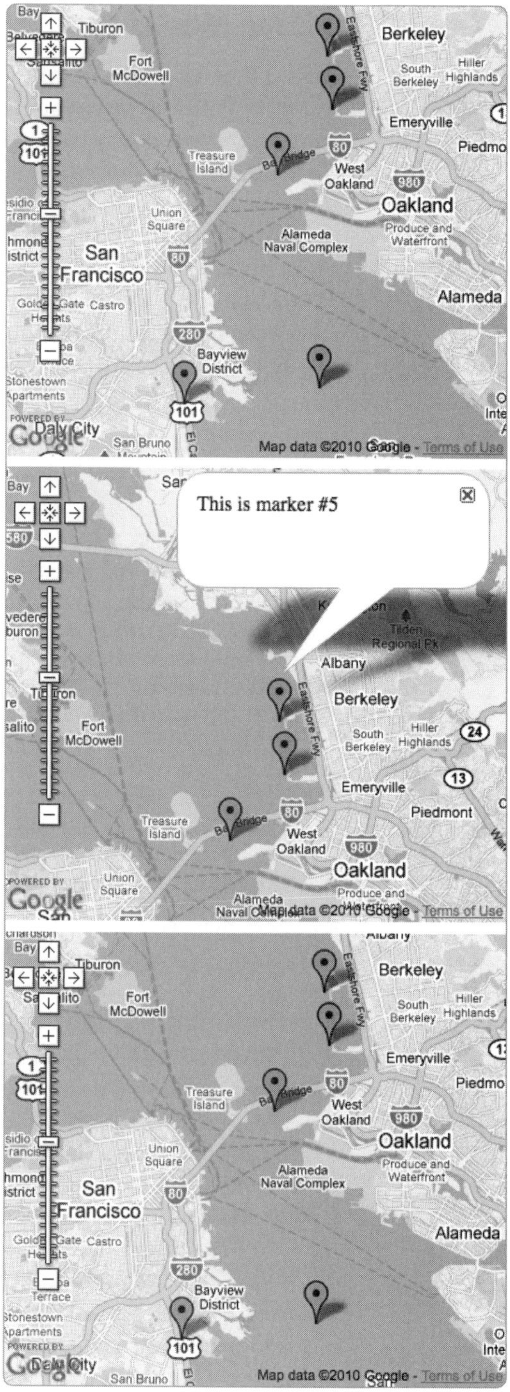

Figure 5-3: Return to the previous center when the message box is closed.

#35: The User Moves the Map Outside Preset Bounds

Drag that map all you want, users. But don't drag it too far or we won't have anything else to show you. Providers have mapped the whole earth, but your map may only contain data for a particular neighborhood or city. You can use events to let you know when the user has moved outside of a predetermined area.

Let's say you're creating a sightseeing map of Yellowstone National Park. You'd include Old Faithful geyser and Mammoth Hot Springs because they're both within Yellowstone. You wouldn't include the Statue of Liberty because that's thousands of miles away. We want to warn users that if they drag the map away from Yellowstone, they won't find anything there.

To start, let's get a basic map centered on Yellowstone. Add the following code to your JavaScript, replacing any other map code:

```
  var mapstraction;
❶ var yellowstone = new mxn.BoundingBox(43.7, -111.8, 45.5, -109.3);
  function create_map() {
    mapstraction = new mxn.Mapstraction('mymap', 'google');
    mapstraction.addLargeControls();
    // Add Old Faithful marker
    var ofmk = new mxn.Marker(new mxn.LatLonPoint(44.46270, -110.81153));
    ofmk.setInfoBubble('Old Faithful');
    mapstraction.addMarker(ofmk);
    // Add Mammoth Hot Springs marker
    var mammk = new mxn.Marker(new mxn.LatLonPoint(44.97682, -110.70425));
    mk.setInfoBubble('Mammoth Hot Springs');
    mapstraction.addMarker(mk);
    mapstraction.autoCenterAndZoom();
    // Event code below here
❷
  }
  // Additional functions below here
❸
```

First, we make a global variable to hold the BoundingBox to describe Yellowstone ❶. We'll use these bounds in the next step. Within the create_map function, you'll see a marker for each of the two sights I mentioned. After that, the map is automatically centered to show just those locations. I left two lines to indicate where we'll soon be adding additional code. One spot ❷ is for event code, and the other ❸ is for functions we'll use to determine whether the map is outside of Yellowstone.

Save the code and load it into a browser. Your map should look something like Figure 5-4. Try dragging the map to show more area to the north. Drag far enough and the map will be in Canada, far away from Yellowstone. Let's see what we can do to provide users with a warning.

The act of dragging the map is what moves users far from Yellowstone, so we need to handle the endPan event, as described earlier in this chapter. Add the following within the create_map function in the section we set aside for event code:

```
mapstraction.endPan.addHandler(function(event_name, event_source, event_args)
{
  if (❹!boundsInBounds(mapstraction.getBounds(), yellowstone)) {
    alert('Watch out! You might be leaving Yellowstone...');
  }
});
```

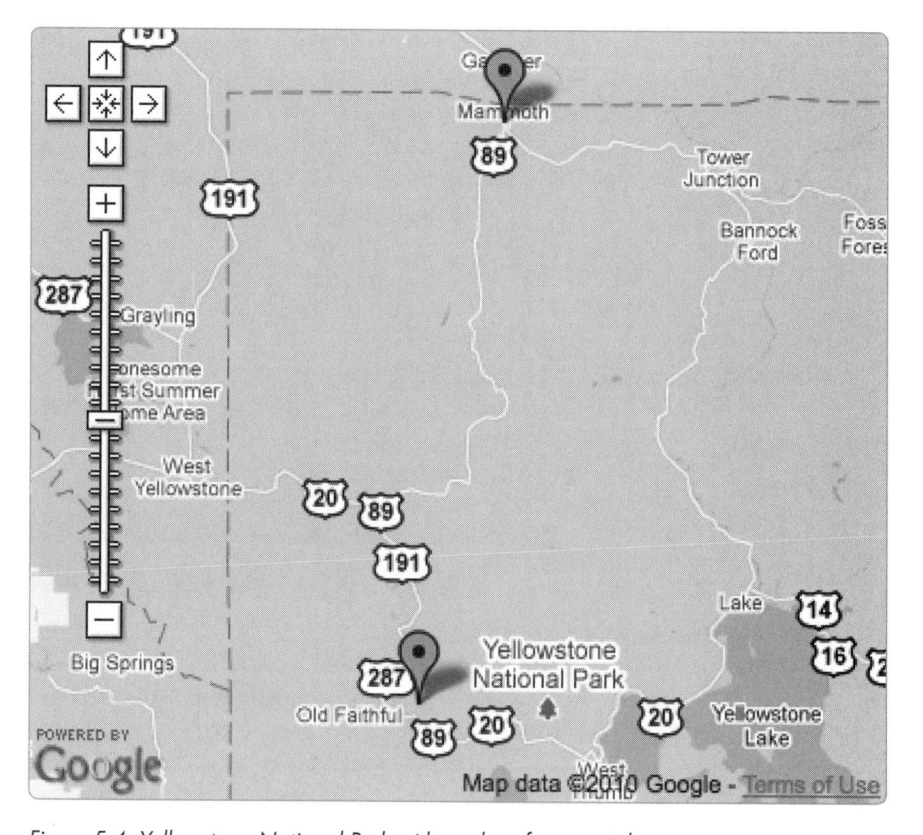

Figure 5-4: Yellowstone National Park with markers for two sights

Here we've created code that runs each time the user finishes dragging the map. It uses the global yellowstone variable, which is the BoundingBox that describes Yellowstone. The bounds is only data and not visible on the map. Figure 5-5 shows the area our bounds cover, however. You can see I've made the bounds big enough to include a reasonable buffer around Yellowstone. We want users to be able to see what's nearby. We only want to warn them when they're obviously off course.

To check if our map is still within our Yellowstone bounds, we need to compare the new variable to the map's bounds. To do so, we pass each of these to a function called boundsInBounds, which we still need to write. If that function returns false ❹ (the exclamation point in the code is read as "not"), then we create a JavaScript alert to warn the user.

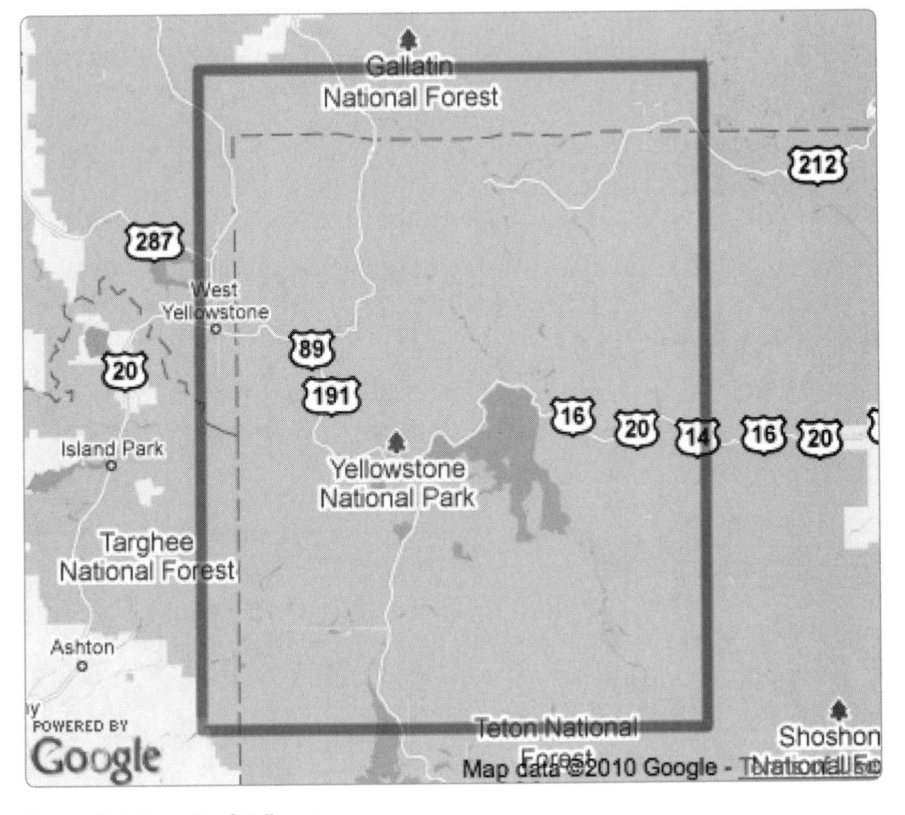

Figure 5-5: Bounds of Yellowstone

Let's include the new function outside of create_map, in the section we set aside for function code:

```
function boundsInBounds(smaller, larger) {
  if (larger.contains(smaller.sw) && larger.contains(smaller.ne)) {
    return true;
  }
  return false;
}
```

The function accepts two `BoundingBox` variables as arguments. The first is the one we *expect* to be smaller, in this case the map's bounds. The second is the bounds we're checking, in this case Yellowstone. Because a `BoundingBox` is made up of two points (its southwest and northeast corners), we know that one `BoundingBox` is inside another only if the larger bounds contains both points.

The event code that we wrote previously will only create an alert if this function returns false, meaning the user has dragged the map outside of Yellowstone. Try it yourself. Drag the map north. Once you leave Yellowstone, you'll receive a warning after each drag of the map, as shown in Figure 5-6.

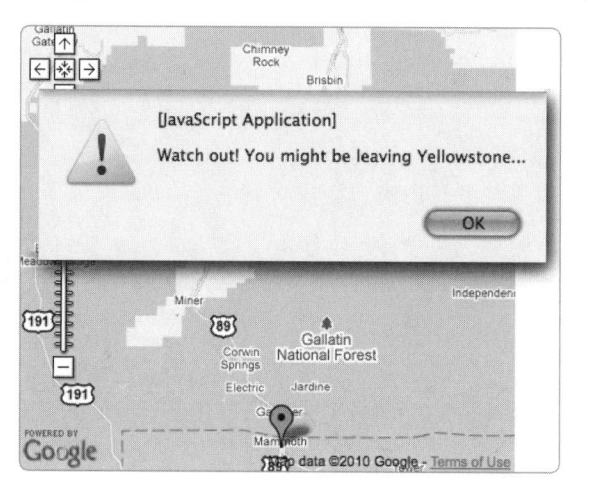

Figure 5-6: JavaScript alert triggered when the user moves outside of Yellowstone bounds

6

EXPLORE PROXIMITY

Maps are all about proximity. What's nearby? How far is it from one location to another? This chapter will help you answer those questions with your own maps.

In some cases, you'll be using another service, such as Yahoo!'s Local Search API. In others, Mapstraction comes through with some handy functions. We'll also rely on some mathematicians far smarter than I am to help us make sense of a two-dimensional coordinate system applied to earth's three-dimensional sphere.

#36: Calculate Distance Between Two Points

In the ancient times of paper maps, determining the distance between two places on a map required using the map's scale and some measuring device. I would often use a scrap of paper or my finger to duplicate the length for the number of times necessary to calculate the distance. Without a ruler, calculating the distance was not an exact science. Some providers still show scales, but Mapstraction makes performing the calculation yourself unnecessary.

Let's say you have a map with two markers: `marker1` and `marker2`. You can determine the latitude and longitude points of these markers and, from there, derive the distance. Or, you can let Mapstraction do it for you:

```
var dist_km = marker1.location.distance(marker2.location);
```

The result is the number of kilometers from `marker1`'s location to `marker2`'s location. The `distance` function can be called on any `LatLonPoint`, with a second `LatLonPoint` passed as an argument. A marker's `LatLonPoint` is stored in the `location` property.

What's really happening with this calculation? Isn't it the simple Pythagorean Theorem that we all learned in grade school—$a^2 + b^2 = c^2$? Unfortunately, not quite. Pythagoras was working in two dimensions and the earth is a three-dimensional ellipsoid—that is, a slightly warped sphere.

In Chapter 1, I described the latitude and longitude system, where the distance between degrees of longitude gets smaller the farther a point is from the equator. In other words, Pythagoras will get you *close enough* if you're in Ecuador, but your calculation would be way off in Sweden.

You need another strangely named formula—the *Haversine*. This function uses the radius of the earth and some fancy spherical trigonometry. Here is a slightly altered version of Mapstraction's distance function:

```
function LatLonPoint_distance(pt1, pt2) {
❶   var rads = Math.PI / 180;
    var diffLat = (pt1.lat-pt2.lat) * rads;
    var diffLon = (pt1.lon-pt2.lon) * rads;
    var a = Math.sin(diffLat / 2) * Math.sin(diffLat / 2) +
            Math.cos(pt1.lat * rads) * Math.cos(pt2.lat * rads) *
            Math.sin(diffLon/2) * Math.sin(diffLon/2);
    return 2 * Math.atan2(Math.sqrt(a), Math.sqrt(1-a)) * ❷6371;
}
```

The very first thing this function does is calculate the multiplier ❶ needed to convert degrees into radians, which the trigonometry functions use to calculate the distance required. A radian is about 57 degrees (180 degrees divided by pi). To convert latitude and longitude decimal degrees to radians, we need to multiply by the number of radians in a degree, which is roughly 1/57 (pi divided by 180 degrees).

Then we get into the Haversine formula, which determines the shortest distance between two points on a sphere. To get a usable distance, we must know the radius of the sphere. In this case, we use the radius of the earth in kilometers ❷. To get miles, use a radius of 3958. Or multiply the kilometer result by 0.6213. Mapstraction also has two helper functions, `KMToMiles` and `milesToKM`, to perform these conversions.

Could You Throw an Object Across a River?

This math makes my head hurt, so let's look at a practical example. Well, throwing things may not be practical in your locale, but in Portland, the Willamette River runs through the middle of the city. Naturally, I often wonder whether something could be thrown across the river.

The farthest distance a human has thrown an object was when Erin Hemmings threw a disc 1333 feet, over a quarter mile (0.4 km). In this example, we'll see if the distance from Portland's downtown west bank to the east bank of the Willamette is less than Hemmings' toss.

Naturally, we want to visualize this on a map, so we add the following code to the JavaScript section of our basic map, replacing any JavaScript already there:

```
var mapstraction;
var dist;
var wportland, eportland;
function create_map() {
  mapstraction = new mxn.Mapstraction('mymap', 'google');
  mapstraction.addSmallControls();
  // Declare points for each side of the river
  wportland = new mxn.LatLonPoint(45.52822, -122.67195);
  eportland = new mxn.LatLonPoint(45.52933, -122.66957);

❶ dist = eportland.distance(wportland); // Calculate distance

  // Show points on the map
  mapstraction.addMarker(new mxn.Marker(wportland));
  mapstraction.addMarker(new mxn.Marker(eportland));
❷ mapstraction.addPolylineWithData(new mxn.Polyline([wportland, eportland]));
  mapstraction.autoCenterAndZoom();

  var disttext = document.createTextNode("Distance is " + dist + " km.");
❸ mapstraction.currentElement.parentNode.appendChild(disttext);
}
```

Be sure you call the `create_map` function when the page loads and that you have a `div` tag with its `id` set to `mymap`, just as you did with the basic map. Within the function, along with creating the Mapstraction map, this code creates two points, one for each side of the river. Then it calculates the distance between those two points ❶.

We could stop here, but let's add something visual to the map, so it makes more sense. Let's add a marker for each of the two points. Then, to make things really clear, let's draw a line between the points ❷. You can see how this map looks in Figure 6-1.

Below the map, we show the user the distance that we calculated. We do this by adding a new text node below the map div ❸. The text will show the distance, which is 0.22 km. Compare this to the record, and you can see that, if your name is Erin Hemmings, you can indeed throw an object across the Willamette River!

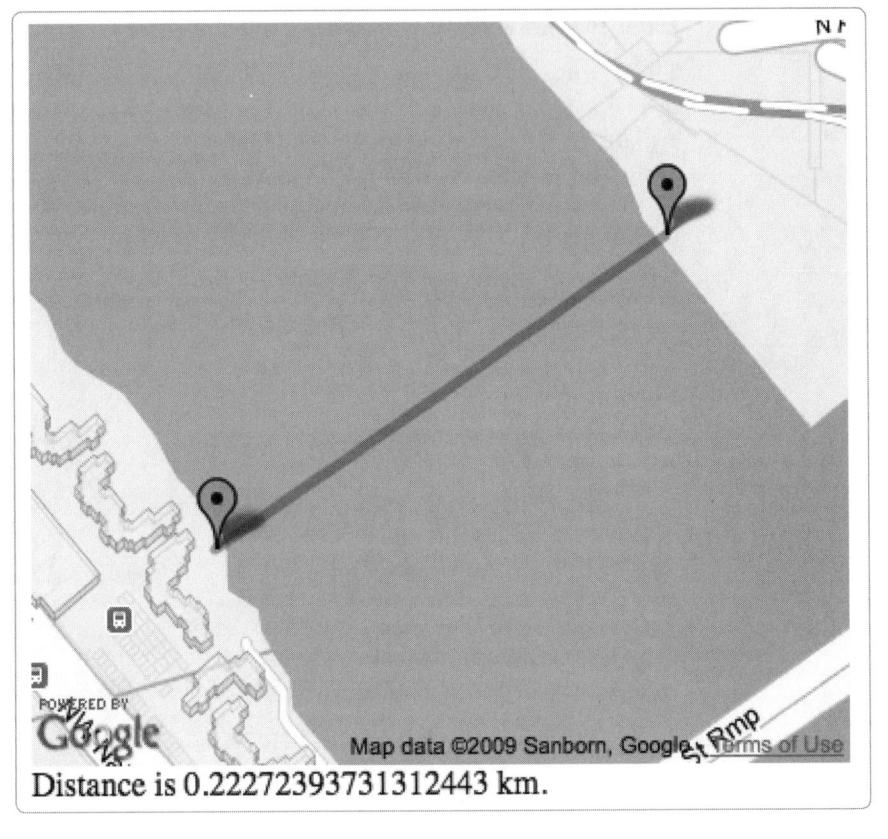

Figure 6-1: Two points and the distance between them

#37: Find True Distance with Routing

Determining the distance between two points is at the crux of searching. That's why Mapstraction gives you access to the distance function described in the previous project. However, this function only tells you the distance as the crow flies. I have yet to see any crows using maps.

To be able to determine the driving distance between two points, you need a lot of information. You need to have a map's underlying data that stores intersections and whether a street is one way or two way. Then you need an algorithm to determine optimal routes. Creating this on your own would be a chore, so in this example, you'll take advantage of the driving directions service from the Google Maps API.

For this example, you'll still be using Mapstraction, but you'll be counting on Google to calculate the distance. That means you'll need to load the Google API, so you'll likely use Google as your mapping provider. You could load a second provider and display the Google routing results on its map, however.

You need to understand what's going on here. Unlike calculating the simple distance between points, which relies on a formula, here you need to send the points to Google and wait for a reply. Due to the wait time for results, performing this over many points is not advisable.

Let's get to the routing code. For this example, I'll use the two points from the standard distance calculation and compare the results. Add this to the JavaScript section of your basic map, replacing any other code:

```
var mapstraction;
var gdir;
var dist, ddist;
var wportland, eportland;
function create_map() {
  mapstraction = new mxn.Mapstraction('mymap', 'google');
  mapstraction.addSmallControls();
  // Declare points for each side of the river
  wportland = new mxn.LatLonPoint(45.52822, -122.67195);
  eportland = new mxn.LatLonPoint(45.52933, -122.66957);
  dist = eportland.distance(wportland); // Calculate distance
  mapstraction.addPolylineWithData(new mxn.Polyline([wportland, eportland]));

  // Google-specific code for driving directions
❶  gdir = new google.maps.DirectionsService();
❷  var diropt = {
  origin: wportland.toProprietary(mapstraction.api),
  destination: eportland.toProprietary(mapstraction.api),
  travelMode: google.maps.DirectionsTravelMode.DRIVING
  };
  gdir.route(diropt, ❸setDDist);
}
function setDDist() {
  if (status == google.maps.DirectionsStatus.OK) {
    var directionsDisplay = new google.maps.DirectionsRenderer(
                          {map: mapstraction.getMap()});
❹    directionsDisplay.setDirections(response);
❺    ddist = response.routes[0].legs[0].distance.value / 1000;
    // driving distance in km
    var disttext = document.createTextNode("Normal distance is " + dist +
    " km, but driving distance is " + ddist + " km");
❻    mapstraction.currentElement.parentNode.appendChild(disttext);
  }
}
function handleErrors(){
  // Handle errors in this section
}
```

Because much of the setup is similar to the map in the previous distance project, let's start by discussing the Google-specific code. We can create a DirectionsService object ❶ because the Google API has been loaded. Even though we usually talk to Google through Mapstraction, here we're communicating with Google directly.

Once we've created the DirectionsService object, we can do something with it. The first thing we do is prepare options ❷, such as our starting and finishing points, for our directions search. Because our points were created for Mapstraction, we need to convert them to Google's proprietary format. Then we send those options to Google along with a callback function ❸ to receive the results.

When the directions have loaded, Google calls our setDDist function. We add the driving directions route to the map as a proprietary Google polyline ❹, which will help us visually compare the two distance methods. Then we can get the driving distance for these directions in meters ❺. To convert to kilometers, just divide by 1000.

Finally, we'll add a new text node below the map div ❻, which will communicate both distances to the user.

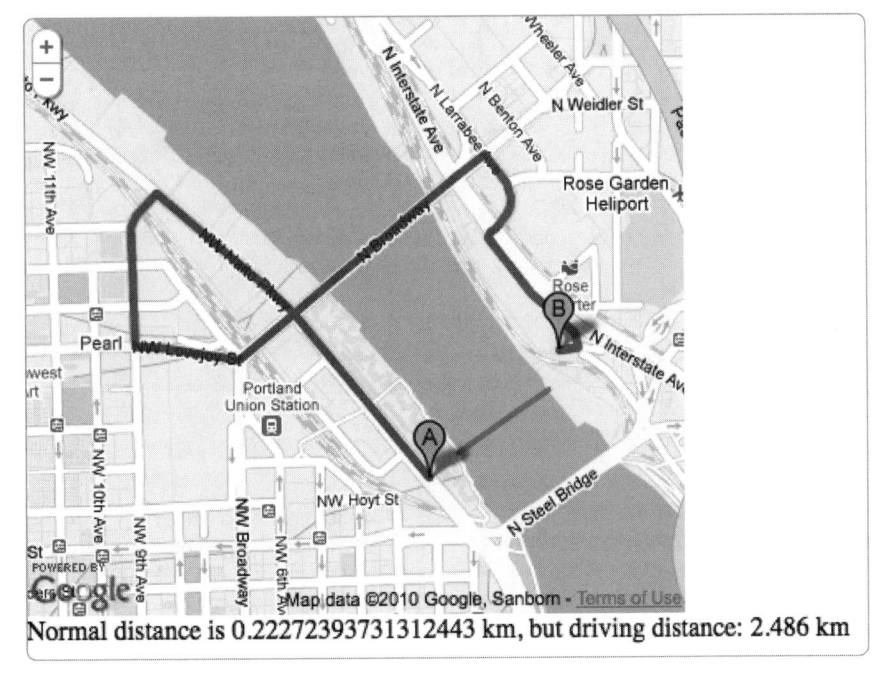

Normal distance is 0.22272393731312443 km, but driving distance: 2.486 km

Figure 6-2: Driving distance compared to Haversine distance

As you can see in Figure 6-2, the distance you have to drive is much farther than the lazy crow has to fly. Seeing as the shortest distance between two points is a straight line, the routing results will always be farther. In this case, because only so many bridges cross the Willamette River, the effect is magnified, at least until Google includes swimming directions in its API.

#38: Create Driving Directions

Perhaps the most useful feature of mapping websites has always been their driving directions. The routing technology behind driving direction is more advanced than most developers can take on, but Google provides access to driving directions via its API. In this section, I'll create a directions widget that could help any business show its customers the way to the store. In this case, I'll use La Bonita, a Mexican restaurant where I wrote much of this book.

This example depends heavily on the Google Maps API, so this project is one of the few where I won't use Mapstraction. To start, let's add some basic HTML to a new file:

```
<html xmlns="http://www.w3.org/1999/xhtml">
  <head>
    <title>Driving Directions with Google Maps</title>

    <script type="text/javascript" src="http://maps.google.com/maps/api/
js?sensor=false"></script>
    <style type="text/css">
    div#mymap {
      width: 400px;
      height: 350px;
    }
    div#mydir {
      width: 400px;
    }
    </style>
    <script type="text/javascript">
      ❶var myaddress = "2839 NE Alberta St, Portland, OR";
      // Google Maps Driving Directions Code Will Go Here
    </script>
  </head>
  <body ❷onload="create_map()" onunload="GUnload()">
    <h1>Venido a La Bonita</h1>

    <div id="mymap"></div>
    ❸<div id="mydir"></div>
  </body>
</html>
```

Most of this code is for a basic, pretty much empty HTML page. We'll fill it in with a form to accept user input and JavaScript to ask Google for driving directions. First, let's look at a few new elements, and I'll explain what they mean.

In the JavaScript section, I hard-coded La Bonita's address ❶. You can replace this with your business address or the location of a party. Then, customers or guests will later input their own address. Together, these two addresses will make up the start and end points for the driving directions.

When the page loads, we're calling the create_map function ❷, just as we've done in most Mapstraction examples. That's because I made this function up; I could have called anything, as it's not tied to Mapstraction.

Down in the HTML, I included a second div ❸. This tag will hold the driving direction text. This second div is after the map div, so the directions will be listed below the map. This part of the driving directions service is optional (in fact, I omitted it in "#37: Find True Distance with Routing" on page 120), but the text is important for this example.

Now that we've put the shell of an HTML page together, let's add the pieces that will make this map work. In the blank space above the map `div` (and just below the `<h1>` tag), include this form:

```
<form onSubmit="❹loadDir();return false;">
  Address: <input type="text" name="addr" />
  City: <input type="text" name="city" value="Portland" />
  ❺<select name="state">
    <option>OR</option>
    <option>WA</option>
  </select>
  <input type="submit" value="Go" />
</form>
```

Most forms send data to the server, but with this example, we want to use JavaScript. This means when the user submits the form, we need to call a JavaScript function ❹. Then we need to return false to keep the browser from sending the data to the server anyway.

This code asks for the user's location in three pieces: address, city, and state. You could use just one or two fields if you want, but separating them out into separate fields helps make your format expectations clear. On the other hand, prepping the call to the driving directions service will be more work.

The state is shown as a drop-down menu ❺. In the case of my example, I have only included Oregon and Washington. La Bonita's food is good, but nobody is going to travel very far to get it. You can include the states where your customers are most likely to live.

Now we'll hook everything together with JavaScript. At a minimum, we need to create the two functions we've already referenced in our HTML: create_map will get the Google Map ready, and loadDir will send the addresses to Google's driving directions service.

Add this to the JavaScript section, below La Bonita's address:

```
❶ var map, gdir;
  function create_map() {
    var opt = {center: new google.maps.LatLng(45.559192, -122.636049), zoom: 15,
               mapTypeId: google.maps.MapTypeId.ROADMAP};
    map = new google.maps.Map(document.getElementById("mymap"), opt);
❷  gdir = new google.maps.DirectionsService();
  }
  function loadDir() {
    var stateobj = document.getElementById('state');
❸  var fromaddress = document.getElementById('addr').value + " "
         + document.getElementById('city').value + ", "
         + stateobj.options[stateobj.selectedIndex].value;
❹  var diropt = {
       origin: fromaddress, destination: myaddress,
       travelMode: google.maps.DirectionsTravelMode.DRIVING
     }
     gdir.route(diropt, ❺setDir);
  }
```

```
function setDir(response, status) {
  if (status == google.maps.DirectionsStatus.OK) {
    var directionsDisplay = new google.maps.DirectionsRenderer(
        {map: map, panel: document.getElementById('mydir')});
    directionsDisplay.setDirections(response);
  }
}
```

First, we make the gdir variable global by declaring it outside of a function ❶. That way, the variable can be referenced from anywhere in the code. After creating the map, we also need to initialize the gdir variable ❷, so Google knows we're going to be asking for driving directions.

We are almost ready for a user to interact with our form. Let's look at the function, loadDir, that is called when the form is submitted. First, the function pieces together the address with the city/state ❸. You might prefer to check for empty or malformed content in these fields, but this simple example merely concatenates them together.

Next we set up the options ❹, including the two addresses, that tells Google what directions to find. Finally, the function sends the options to Google along with a callback function ❺. In the setDir function, which receives the driving directions, we simply tell Google to render the route on the map and the text below the map, as shown in Figure 6-3.

That's it. We've created driving directions to get anyone to La Bonita. To use it for your business, simply alter the myaddress variable and fill in the appropriate states. To see an example that digs a little deeper into driving directions, see "#73: Find a Coffee Shop to Meet in the Middle" on page 277.

Check out the full documentation for Google's driving directions: *http://code.google.com/apis/maps/documentation/javascript/reference.html #DirectionsService*

#39: Determine Closest Marker

Given a point and a whole bunch of markers, can you find the one closest to your point? In this project, we'll loop through every marker on the map and draw a line between wherever the user clicks and its closest marker, which we'll determine by calculating the distance between two points.

Before we can find the closest marker, however, we need a map with a handful of markers plotted. To do this, we'll get five random points, as shown earlier in the chapter. Here, I've reprinted the get_random_by_bounds function you'll need from that section. Add these lines to your JavaScript section at the top of your basic map, but make sure they are outside of the create_map function:

```
function get_random_by_bounds(bounds) {
  var lat = bounds.sw.lat + (Math.random() * (bounds.ne.lat - bounds.sw.lat));
          var lon = bounds.sw.lon + (Math.random() * (bounds.ne.lon - bounds.sw.lon));
  return new mxn.LatLonPoint(lat, lon);
}
```

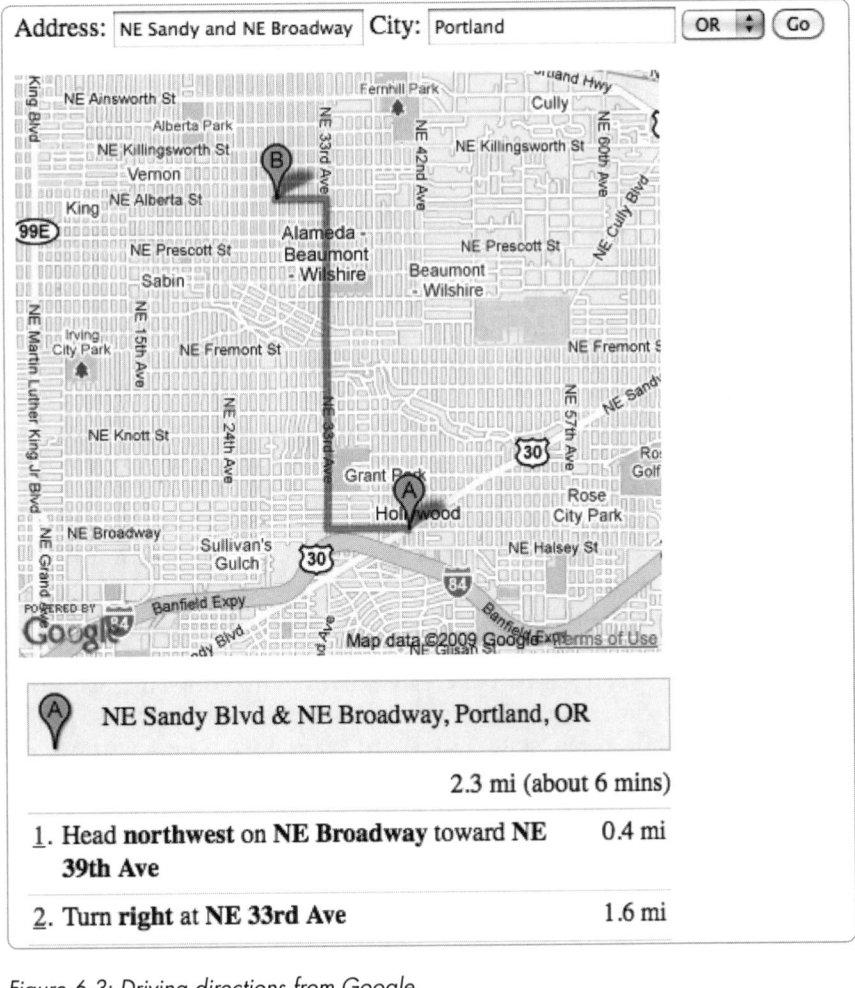

Figure 6-3: Driving directions from Google

With that helper function ready, add these lines to your basic map's create_map function:

```
❶ var bounds = new mxn.BoundingBox(32.4, -113.9, 40.9, -103.0);
❷ for (i=1; i<=5; i++) {
     var marker = new mxn.Marker(❸get_random_by_bounds(bounds));
     mapstraction.addMarker(marker);
   }
❹ mapstraction.setBounds(bounds);
   mapstraction.click.addHandler(❺find_closest_marker);
```

Assuming you've already initialized the map, you can almost dive into creating the markers. First, you need to create the bounds for the markers, which represents the area you'll use to create the random location. In this case, I used some points ❶ that roughly define the "four corners" states in the United States: Arizona, Utah, Colorado, and New Mexico.

Now we can create a loop ❷ to perform the same bit of code five times. Each time through the loop, we'll get a new random point ❸, so our markers could be anywhere within the bounds.

Normally, I'd ask Mapstraction to center and zoom automatically when using random markers. Here, however, I set the bounds to be the quartet of states ❹, the same area that could possibly hold a marker. This way, I know the markers will all be visible.

Lastly, we listen for the user to click the map. Upon a click, we tell Mapstraction to call a function to find the closest marker ❺. Now we need to write that function. Add these lines to your JavaScript, outside of the create_map function:

```
function find_closest_marker(event_type, event_source, event_args) {
  if (mapstraction.markers.length > 0) {
    var clickpoint = event_args.location;
    var closest_marker = mapstraction.markers[0];
    var closest_dist = clickpoint.distance(closest_marker.location);
    for (var i=1; i < mapstraction.markers.length; i++) {
      var thismarker = mapstraction.markers[i];
      var thisdist = clickpoint.distance(thismarker.location);
      if (thisdist < closest_dist) {
        closest_dist = thisdist;
        closest_marker = thismarker;
      }
    }
    if (closest_marker) {
      var poly = new mxn.Polyline([clickpoint, closest_marker.location]);
      mapstraction.addPolyline(poly);
    }
  }
}
```

In order to find the closest marker to the point the user clicked, we need to check the distance between each marker and the click point. We need to keep two pieces of data during our search: the current closest marker we have found and its distance to the point.

To begin, we create those two variables and assume the first marker (remember JavaScript array indexes start at zero) is currently closest ❻. So we know what distance to compare, we also calculate the first marker's distance to the point ❼. Now we're ready to loop through all the other markers ❽, starting with the second one.

Each time through the loop, we calculate the distance between the current marker and the click point. If the distance is farther than the closest distance we have found so far, we do nothing. If this current marker is now closer than the previous ❾ one, we replace our original two variables with new values.

After the loop, I created a new polyline between the point where the user clicked and the marker that we determined is closest ❿. Load this example into a web browser and click around a few times. You'll create several lines, connecting multiple markers if you move around enough (see Figure 6-4). Which marker is closest to Albuquerque? How about Denver?

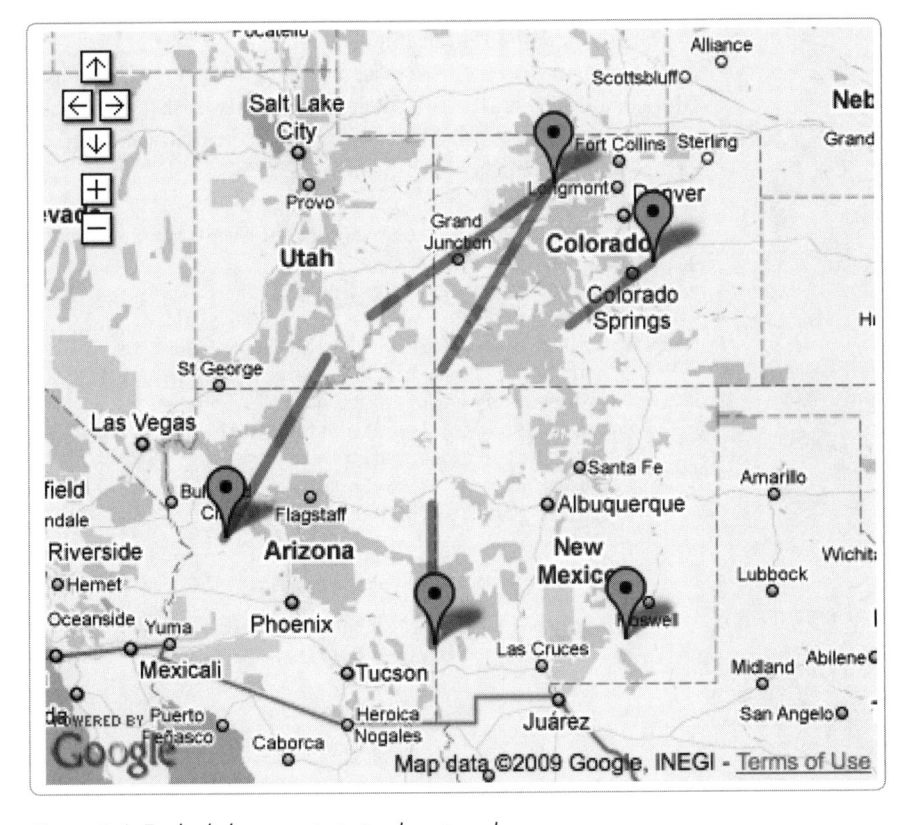

Figure 6-4: Each click connects to its closest marker.

#40: Find a Point Along a Line

Let's say you're taking a short flight with your forgetful pilot friend from Wichita, Kansas, to Tulsa, Oklahoma, about 140 miles. "Oops," he says nonchalantly after you're airborne, "I forgot to gas up." I know what you're thinking—turn around! But your friend assures you there is enough gas to go 80 miles, which should get you into Oklahoma where the gas is cheaper.

Knowing the distance between two points is useful, but sometimes you want to know the story between those points. For example, what's the midpoint between two cities? Or, given point A and point B, what are the coordinates of point C that is nine miles along that line? It's a math-heavy problem to solve, but doing so makes for some fun possibilities.

Fun might not be the right word if you were really flying on a near-empty tank from Wichita to Tulsa. But you would definitely want to know where along that route you will be after 80 miles when the engine starts to sputter. You would be smart to double-check: *will you get to Oklahoma, as your friend claims?* After all, this information is coming from the guy who forgot to put gas in his airplane.

To find out the answer to the question, we'll use a three step process:

1. Plot our starting and ending points on a map.
2. Calculate our bearing (direction) using the two points.
3. Use the bearing and starting point to find a new point 80 miles away.

Let's get started while there's still time to turn around.

Plot Your Route

Since planes fly in a straight line, we'll use a simple polyline, similar to the initial example in "#16: Draw Lines on a Map" on page 62. All we need are the starting and ending points for the two airports.

To draw a line between Wichita and Tulsa, add the following function to your basic map, replacing your current create_map function:

```
var mapstraction;
var wichita = new mxn.LatLonPoint(37.7454463, -97.4080747);
var tulsa = new mxn.LatLonPoint(36.0390101, -95.9936344);

function create_map() {
  mapstraction = new mxn.Mapstraction('mymap', 'google');
  mapstraction.setCenterAndZoom(wichita, 8);
  mapstraction.addPolyline(new mxn.Polyline([wichita, tulsa]));
  mapstraction.autoCenterAndZoom();
  // Find bearing

  // Find point X km along route

}
```

Save the file and load it up. Your map should look similar to Figure 6-5.

Do you think you can make it to Oklahoma? The 80 miles of fuel in the tank will take you almost 60 percent through your route. It's going to be close. Let's continue and find out.

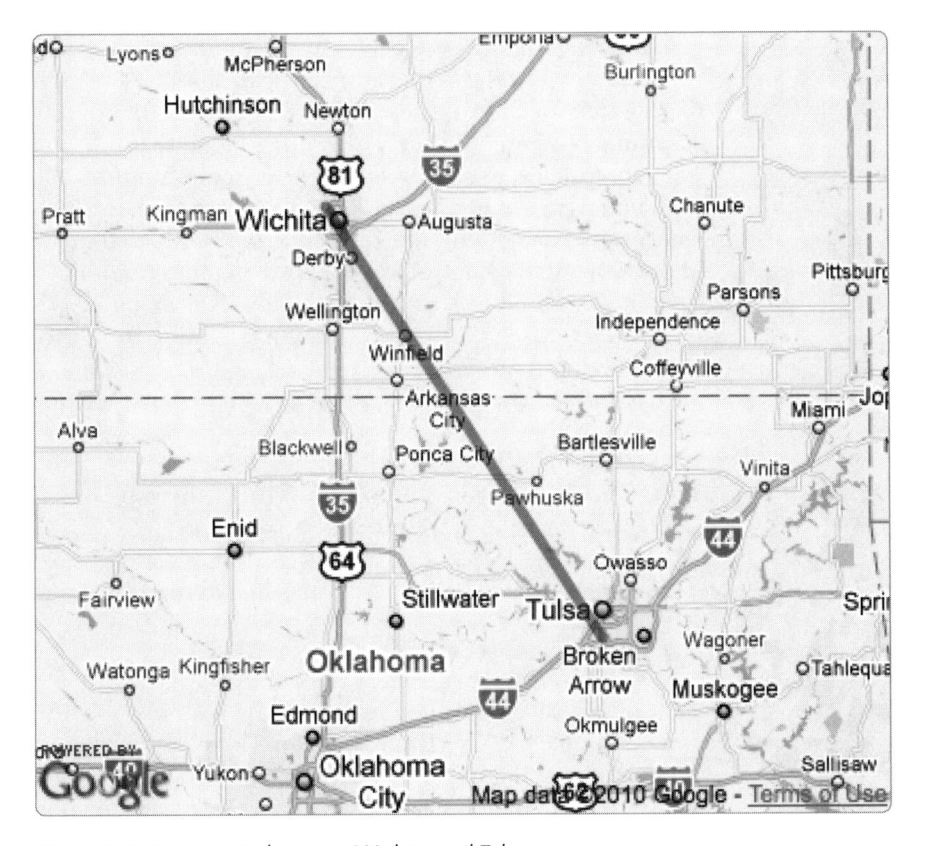

Figure 6-5: Direct route between Wichita and Tulsa

Find Your Bearing

In order to find a point along a line, you first need to know the direction that the line is pointed. The direction is called the bearing, and it is a number expressed in degrees, from 0 to 359. Most compasses mark these degrees around the outside, along with the four cardinal directions.

In this section, we'll write a function to calculate the bearing for us, based on the work of Chris Veness of Movable Type Ltd. (*http://movable-type .co.uk/*). Add the following code to the JavaScript section of your map file, but outside the create_map function:

```
function get_bearing(pt1, pt2) {
  var lat1 = degrees_to_radians(pt1.lat);
  var lat2 = degrees_to_radians(pt2.lat);
  var lon_diff = degrees_to_radians(pt2.lon - pt1.lon);
  var y = Math.sin(lon_diff) * Math.cos(lat2);
  var x = Math.cos(lat1) * Math.sin(lat2)
        - Math.sin(lat1) * Math.cos(lat2) * Math.cos(lon_diff);
  var bearing = Math.atan2(y, x);
  return (radians_to_degrees(bearing)+360) % 360;
}
```

```
function degrees_to_radians(deg) {
  return deg * Math.PI / 180;
}
function radians_to_degrees(rad) {
  return rad * 180 / Math.PI;
}
```

Along with the function to calculate the bearing, I've also included a couple helper functions to convert between degrees and radians. The trigonometry we use is less complicated when using radians (that's right—the math could be even more complicated). However, we also need to convert back since degrees are what Mapstraction expects.

Now, from within your create_map function, add this line:

```
var bearing = get_bearing(wichita, tulsa);
```

Here we call the get_bearing function, passing our two points. The result should be about 146 degrees. Notice that if you swap the order of the arguments to the function, the result will be different: about 326 degrees. That's because you travel a different direction to go from Tulsa to Wichita. Since it's the exact opposite direction, the two results are 180 degrees different.

We're going from Wichita to Tulsa, so we'll take that result and use it in the next section.

Determine New Point

Now we know the direction we're traveling. That's an important step toward finding the point that is 80 miles along our route. It's time to employ some more fancy math using the bearing and the coordinates of our starting point, Wichita.

In this section we'll write another function, again based on the work of Chris Veness. Add the following code to your JavaScript, taking care to not put it inside any other functions:

```
function get_destination(pt, dist, bearing) {
  var R = 6371; // radius of earth (km)
  var lat1 = degrees_to_radians(pt.lat);
  var lon1 = degrees_to_radians(pt.lon);
  bearing = degrees_to_radians(bearing);
  var cosLat1 = Math.cos(lat1);
  var sinLat1 = Math.sin(lat1);
  var distOverR = dist / R;
  var cosDistOverR = Math.cos(distOverR);
  var sinDistOverR = Math.sin(distOverR);

  var lat2 = Math.asin( sinLat1 * cosDistOverR

          + cosLat1 * sinDistOverR * Math.cos(bearing) );
  var lon2 = lon1 + Math.atan2( Math.sin(bearing) * sinDistOverR * cosLat1,
          cosDistOverR Ð sinLat1 * Math.sin(lat2) );
  lon2 = (lon2 + Math.PI) % (2 * Math.PI) Ð Math.PI;
```

```
lat2 = radians_to_degrees(lat2);
lon2 = radians_to_degrees(lon2);

return new mxn.LatLonPoint(lat2, lon2);
}
```

Now we need to call our newly created function. Add the following code inside the create_map function, just after the line that calculates the bearing:

```
var newpt = get_destination(wichita, 128, bearing);
var mk = new mxn.Marker(newpt);
mapstraction.addMarker(mk);
```

Notice that the distance we're passing to the new function is 128, not 80. That's because the function expects the distance in *kilometers*, not miles. This matches the way Mapstraction calculates distance. To convert miles to kilometers, multiply the miles by 1.6.

Take a deep breath before you load your changes. Along with determining the point 80 miles along the path, the code creates and adds a marker to the map, as shown in Figure 6-6.

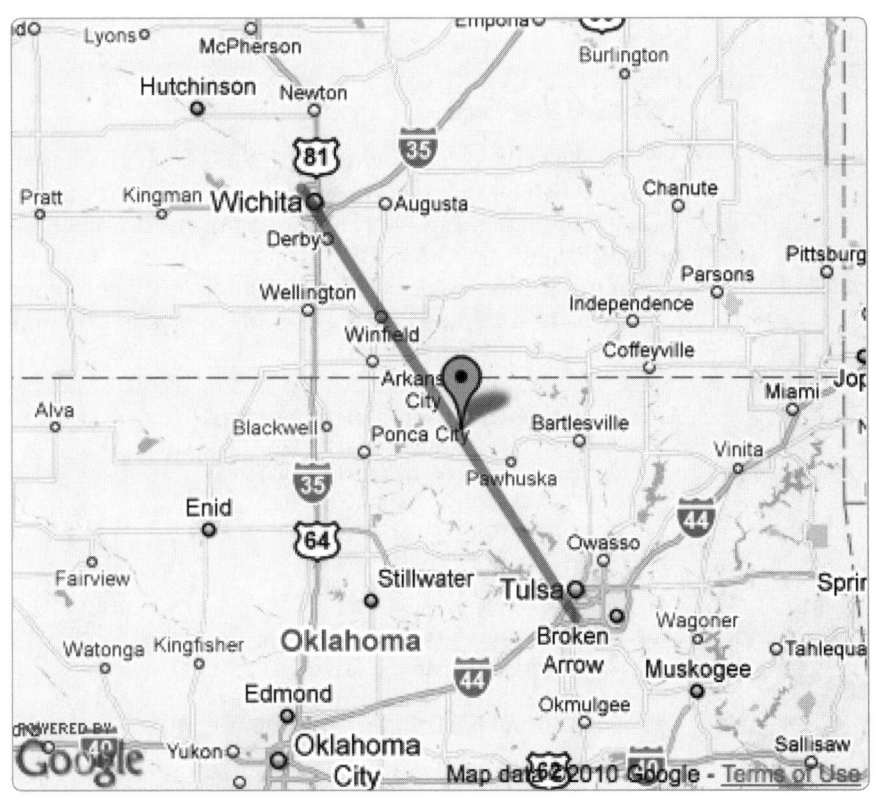

Figure 6-6: 80 Miles from Wichita gets you into Oklahoma!

And you can take another deep breath, because it looks like 80 miles of gas will get you from Wichita into Oklahoma where, according to your forgetful pilot friend, you can fill up for less. As for finding a landing strip, that's another issue.

Now that you know how to find a point along a line, try out a less hypothetical project. "#73: Find a Coffee Shop to Meet in the Middle" on page 277 combines the project you just finished with driving directions and local search results.

NOTE *The point you find will only appear directly on the line over short distances, like the 140-mile trip in this example. For larger distances, the point will be correct, but the line will be wrong. Standard polylines do not take the curvature of the earth into consideration. To get a line that follows the "great circle" shortest distance between two points, you'll need to use a geodesic polyline, which is supported by Google.*

#41: Plot Local Results on a Map

When you are searching nearby, sooner or later you want to find businesses that meet certain qualifications. For example, in Portland we're always looking for coffee. In San Francisco, where this example takes place, that means finding delicious, cheap burritos.

In this project we'll use JavaScript to perform a local search for the keyword *burritos*. Both Google and Yahoo! have APIs that allow for this type of search. In this example, we'll use Yahoo! because it is simple and to the point.

We're starting with a basic Mapstraction map, so we minimize the number of provider-specific calls. Because most of my examples have used Google as a provider, double-check that you're calling the Yahoo! Maps API:

```
<script type="text/javascript"
 src="http://api.maps.yahoo.com/ajaxymap?v=3.8&appid=yourkeyhere"></script>
```

With the external JavaScripts loaded, replace any existing inline JavaScript code with the following:

```
var mapstraction;
function create_map() {
  mapstraction = new mxn.Mapstraction('mymap', 'yahoo');
  mapstraction.setCenterAndZoom(new mxn.LatLonPoint(37.7740486,-122.4101883), 15);
  mapstraction.addLargeControls();
  // Yahoo-specific calls
❶ var ymap = mapstraction.getMap();
  YEvent.Capture(ymap, EventsList.onEndLocalSearch, ❷plotResults);
❸ ymap.searchLocal(ymap.getCenterLatLon(), 'burritos', ❹1, ❺5);
}
```

To be able to use Yahoo-specific calls, we need to grab the map object ❶. Then we need to let the map know that we're interested in an event, which will occur when our search is complete. We also reference a function where the results can be sent ❷. We'll create that function in a moment.

Now, we need to write the code that actually initiates a local search to Yahoo! ❸. The searchLocal function requires four values to be passed to it: We send the center of the map, the search query, the search radius (in miles) ❹, and the number of results ❺.

Then we write the plotResults function. Add the following lines below the create_map function:

```
   function plotResults(❶results) {
     if (results.Data) {
       var places = results.Data.ITEMS;
❷      for (i=0; i < places.length; i++) {
         var thisplace = places[i];
         var lat = ❸parseFloat(thisplace.LATITUDE);
         var lon = parseFloat(thisplace.LONGITUDE);
         var marker = new mxn.Marker(new mxn.LatLonPoint(lat, lon));
         marker.setInfoBubble(thisplace.TITLE + '<br />' + thisplace.ADDRESS);
         mapstraction.addMarker(marker);
       }
     }
❹    mapstraction.autoCenterAndZoom();
   }
```

The search results are passed from Yahoo! as a parameter ❶ to our function. The parameter is a special object that contains a number of pieces of information about each business we found. We want to extract the latitude, longitude, address, and business name from the object, which we do by looping ❷ through the results.

Each time through the loop, we access the four pieces of information we require for a business. To get usable latitude and longitude values, we need to use the JavaScript helper function parseFloat ❸. This function converts textual values into the floating point numbers required for coordinates.

The rest is probably old hat to you by now. We create a marker, put text in the message box (the name and address of the location), and when we've added all the markers, we make sure they can all be seen on the map ❹, as shown in Figure 6-7.

#42: Retrieve Local Results with HTTP

On many occasions you'll want to use something more powerful than Java-Script to perform a local search. For example, you may want to store the results in a database or output them into an RSS feed. In either case, the approach used in the previous project just won't do. Instead, we'll use Yahoo!'s Local Search API and access it with PHP, a popular server-side programming language available on many web hosts.

Figure 6-7: Local results plotted on a Yahoo! map

Before we bring the results into code, let's see what they look like. One of the great things about an API like the one we're using is that it outputs plain-text XML, which can be interpreted by a web browser and is human-readable.

NOTE   *Some of the concepts in this project may be considered advanced. They build upon those introduced in Chapters 8 and 9.*

Just like going to an ordinary web page, you can access the Local Search API by visiting a URL. Try typing this search for burritos in San Francisco into your location bar:

```
http://local.yahooapis.com/LocalSearchService/V3/localSearch?appid=yourkeyhere&query=burritos
&location=San+Francisco+CA
```

The request parameters are highlighted in bold. The first, your appid, is your Yahoo! API key. The query is what you're searching for and the location is where you're searching.

Once the results are loaded, you'll see something like this:

```
❶ <?xml version="1.0"?>
❷ <ResultSet ... totalResultsAvailable="553" totalResultsReturned="10">
❸   <Result id="21356805">
        <Title>El Farolito</Title>
        <Address>2777 Mission St</Address>
        <City>San Francisco</City>
        <State>CA</State>
        <Latitude>37.752713</Latitude>
        <Longitude>-122.41835</Longitude>
        ...
     </Result>
     <Result id="21342579">
        ...
     </Result>
     ...
  </ResultSet>
```

Like most XML documents, the results declare themselves to be XML ❶ on the first line. The second line is the root element ❷ of the document, meaning it contains all other tags below it. Every result is stored within a <Result> tag ❸, with data items stored within tags one level below.

For more on the terms used to describe XML, see "#52: Use XML" on page 174, which also contains a more in-depth description of parsing XML than I'll provide in the next section.

Parse Local Results with PHP

Viewing the XML that Yahoo! returns within a browser is one thing. Even more useful is to read it into PHP, which allows you to do even more. In this example, we'll get the same burrito results as in the previous section and print out the name of the first restaurant found.

Create a new PHP file and add the following lines:

```
<?
  $api_key = "yourkeyhere";
  $search_term = urlencode("burritos");
  $location = ❶"urlencode("San Francisco, CA");
  $url = "http://local.yahooapis.com/LocalSearchService/V3/localSearch";
❷ $url .= "?appid=$api_key&query=$search_term&location=$location";

❸ $xobj = get_xml($url);
  print $xobj->Result[0]->Title;
?>
```

I've stored the three parameters as PHP variables. This makes it easy for you to include your own API key and change the search terms. Go ahead and change what we're searching for, or include your own city. Notice that, even though we're hard-coding the search criteria, I've used the urlencode function to make sure the URL remains valid. For example, the encoding of the location ❶ will replace the spaces and comma with URL-friendly versions of those characters.

Next, I put the parameters together in URL form ❷, so we can retrieve the results. The actual call to download the web page happens in another function ❸, which you can find described in detail in "#61: Retrieve a Web Page" on page 215.

Finally, the PHP code prints out the name of the first result: El Farolito in the example results. You are more likely to want to do something more interesting with the results than print out the first name, but this gives you an idea of how to access the items.

Other Useful Parameters

In the previous example, I showed just three parameters that you can use to search with Yahoo!'s Local Search API: appid (required), query (required for most searches), and location.

Many more options are available, the most interesting of which I've included in Table 6-1.

Table 6-1: Additional Parameters Accepted by Yahoo! Local Search

Parameter name	Description
city, state, and zip	Any of these three can be used, alone or in combination, to replace the free-form location parameter used in the example.
latitude and longitude	If both of these are used, they take the place of any other location data and set the search center at the point created by the coordinates.
radius	Sets the maximum distance (in miles) from the search location.
results	Declares the number of results, from 1 to 20. The default value is 10.
sort	Indicates how the results will be sorted, using one of four options: distance, rating, relevance, or title. The default value is relevance.

More parameters are listed in Yahoo!'s documentation,[1] but with the examples here you should be able to get some interesting results. Where's your nearest taxidermist?

#43: Check Whether a Point Is Within a Bounding Box

Among the most important shapes in mapping is the rectangle. After centuries, we still view maps in a rectangular shape, even with today's fancy

---

1. *http://developer.yahoo.com/search/local/V3/localSearch.html*

JavaScript. A rectangle can also be easily described (you only need two points), and determining if a point is within a specific rectangle requires no fancy math.

As you'll see in later in this project, checking for a point within a BoundingBox is the first step. You might also use this to determine, for example, whether all the markers are on the screen.

Because finding if a point is within a rectangle is such a useful feature, Mapstraction has baked it in as a function. Given any BoundingBox object, you can pass a LatLonPoint and receive back either true (within the box) or false.

Here's code to determine whether a point is within the map view:

```
var box = mapstraction.getBounds();
var inview = box.contains(new mxn.LatLonPoint(37.7740486, -122.4101883));
```

What's happening? It's not that complicated. A BoundingBox is determined by its southwest and northeast points (see Figure 6-8). So to be within a box, your latitude must be between the latitude of those two points. Longitude is the same.

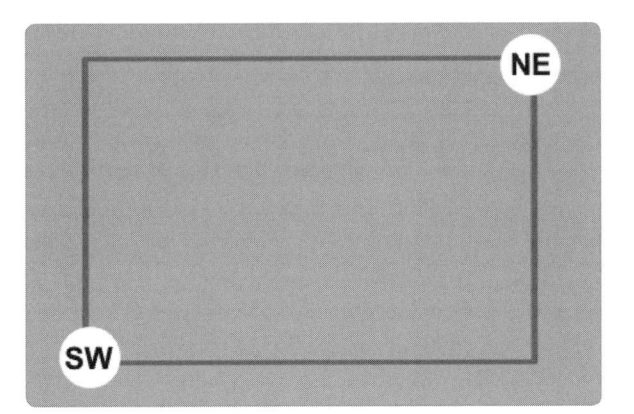

Figure 6-8: A BoundingBox is declared by its southwest and northeast points.

Here is a slightly altered version of Mapstraction's BoundingBox contains function:

```
function check_bounds(pt, box) {
  return (pt.lat >= box.sw.lat && pt.lat <= box.ne.lat
      && pt.lon >= box.sw.lon && pt.lon <= box.ne.lon);
```

Yes, the math is fairly straightforward, but that would be a lot of code to write out each time. I'm sure glad Mapstraction does it for us.

Can You Click Inside the Box?

Now that we know how to check for points inside a box, let's try it. This example will create a bounding box smaller than the viewable map. When the user clicks, we check whether the point where he or she clicked is inside our box.

To make things clear, we'll draw a polyline around the bounding box, making it easy to tell whether Mapstraction returns the correct results. Do you think you can click inside the box?

Add the following code into the JavaScript section of a basic map, replacing any existing code:

```
var mapstraction;
var box;
function create_map() {
  mapstraction = new mxn.Mapstraction('mymap', 'google');
  mapstraction.setCenterAndZoom(new mxn.LatLonPoint(37.7740486,-122.4101883), 9);
  mapstraction.addSmallControls();
❶ box = new mxn.BoundingBox(37.5, -122.8, 37.9, -122.2);
❷ var poly = BoundingBox_to_Polyline(box);
  mapstraction.addPolyline(poly);
❸ mapstraction.click.addHandler(function(event_type, event_source, event_args) {
    var reply = "";
    var clickpoint = event_args.location;
❹   if (box.contains(clickpoint)) {
      reply = "You clicked inside the box! ";
    }
    else {
      reply = "Sorry--You missed the box. ";
    }
    // Create marker at click
    var mk = new mxn.Marker(clickpoint);
    mk.setInfoBubble(reply);
    mapstraction.addMarker(mk);
❺   mk.openBubble();
  });
}
function BoundingBox_to_Polyline(box) {
  var points = [box.sw, new mxn.LatLonPoint(box.ne.lat, box.sw.lon), box.ne,
             new mxn.LatLonPoint(box.sw.lat, box.ne.lon),
             new mxn.LatLonPoint(box.sw.lat, box.sw.lon-.0001)];
  var poly = new mxn.Polyline(points);
  return poly;
}
```

After creating the map, we make a somewhat arbitrary bounding box ❶ around San Francisco. Then we take that same box and make it visible on the map by tracing its edges ❷. We use the BoundingBox_to_Polyline function, which I explain in detail in "#19: Draw a Rectangle to Declare an Area" on page 71. For convenience, I have reprinted it here.

Next we need to listen for clicks on the map ❸. When the user clicks, we need to see if the clicked point is within the box. To do this, we call the `contains` function on the `BoundingBox` object we created ❹. The outcome (true or false) will determine what message we display to the user.

To communicate the outcome to the user, we add a new marker where the user clicked and open up its message box ❺ to display whether the click was inside the bounds. Try it a few times. Click inside, click outside—it gets it right every time! An example result is shown in Figure 6-9.

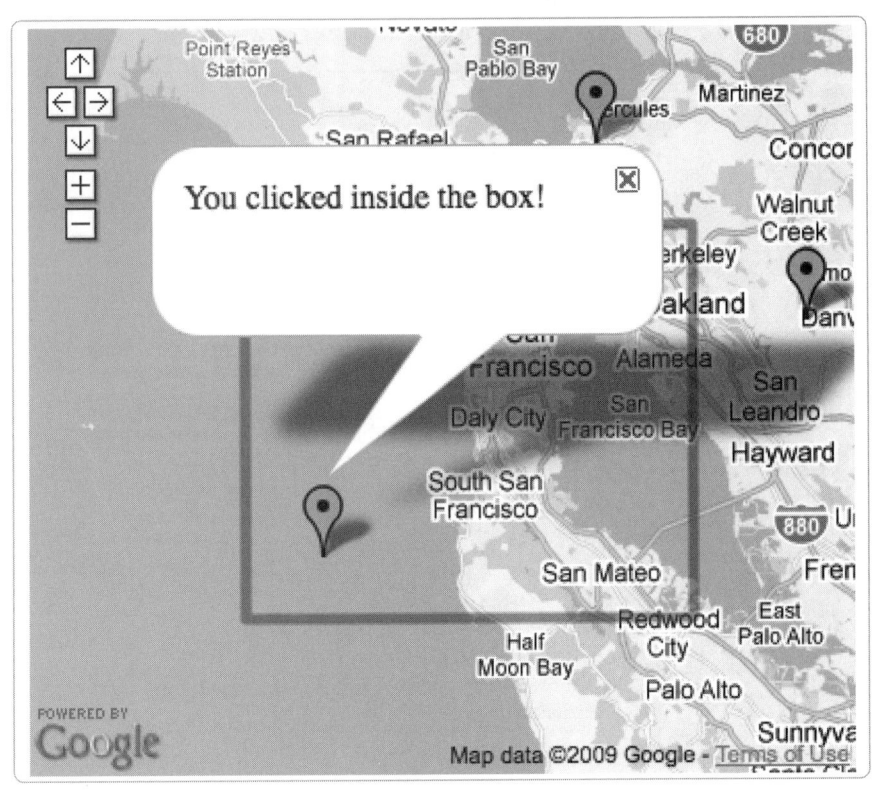

Figure 6-9: Clicking a point within the bounding box

#44: Get a Random Point in a Bounding Box

Quick! Think of a number between −122.9 and −122.8! Though not an ordinary question, you may find yourself asking it while creating maps. Especially for testing, you'll want to be able to generate random geographic points, often within a specific area. In a way, finding a random point within a box is the opposite of the previous project.

I've created a special function just for creating random points. You may have even seen it in other parts of this book. In this section, I'll describe it briefly, and then use it in an example.

Here is the code to get a random point:

```
function get_random_by_bounds(❶bounds) {
  var lat = bounds.sw.lat + (❷Math.random() * ❸(bounds.ne.lat - bounds.sw.lat));
  var lon = bounds.sw.lon + (Math.random() * (bounds.ne.lon - bounds.sw.lon));
❹ return new mxn.LatLonPoint(lat, lon);
}
```

The most important piece of information that this function needs is to know the general area, or the *bounds*, where you want the random point. This information is passed as the single parameter ❶ of this function, a Mapstraction BoundingBox object. The BoundingBox object is made up of the southwest (SW) and northeast (NE) corners of a rectangular area. Between those two points, you can determine the maximum and minimum values of the edges.

Now, we know where the point will be, but we still need to make the point random using a built-in JavaScript function ❷. The number returned by Math.random is a decimal between 0 and 1, which is not likely to be what you want. We can, however, use that number, multiplied by our range ❸, to determine the random coordinate.

For example, to get the random latitude, we take the NE latitude minus the SW latitude and multiply that answer (the distance in degrees between the two latitudes) by the random number. Then, we add the SW latitude (the smallest of the two) to the outcome. As a result, our smallest latitude (when the random number is zero) will be the same as the SW latitude; the largest latitude (when the random number is one) will be the same as the NE latitude.

The same process is then applied to the longitude but with a new random number. Now that we have a latitude and a longitude, we can return the two numbers as a new LatLonPoint ❹.

Here's an example using a random point. Be sure you have the get_random_by_bounds function in your JavaScript code and then add the following lines to the create_map function of a basic map:

```
   var b = new mxn.BoundingBox(❶45.5, -122.9, 45.6, -122.8);
❷ var pt = get_random_by_bounds(b);
   var mk = new mxn.Marker(pt);
   mapstraction.addMarker(mk);
```

We need some bounds to be able to pass to the random point function. In this case, I made up some points ❶, roughly located around my hometown of Portland, Oregon. When creating a new BoundingBox, we must pass four numbers in this order: SW latitude, SW longitude, NE latitude, and NE longitude.

Next we get the random point ❷ by passing the bounds we just created. Remember the function we created used a return to share the new random point. When we call the function, we can declare a variable (which I called pt) to store that returned value.

To show the random point, I used it to create a new marker and then placed the marker on the map. If you want to visually check that the point is really within your bounds, try incorporating "#19: Draw a Rectangle to Declare an Area" on page 71 with this one.

#45: Check Whether a Point Is Within a Shape

Did the user just click on Kansas? Is this address within the city limits? These questions are common ones you'll want to answer with a *hit test*, the process used to determine whether a point is inside a shape. To do so requires some data (the outline of the shape) and a little math. In this section, I'll show how you can crunch the coordinates and find the answers to these and other questions.

First, the data. A shape can be described as a series of latitude and longitude points, where the start and end are the same point, enclosing a polygon. You may be able to create the shape you want by tracing the border. You can likely find someone sharing their shape online. For example, polygons for all 50 US states can be found at *http://mapscripting.com/ state-boundaries*.

We'll perform a hit test to see if the point where a user clicks is inside a state. Seeing as Kansas is somewhat rectangular, let's choose a state that has a slightly more complex shape, such as Utah (see Figure 6-10). The edges of Utah are made up of six points, which means describing Utah as a line requires seven points (because the final point needs to reconnect with the first point).

Here is some Mapstraction code to describe the outline of Utah as a series of coordinates:

```
utah = [new mxn.LatLonPoint(36.99, -114.05), new mxn.LatLonPoint(36.99, -109.04),
        new mxn.LatLonPoint(40.99, -109.05), new mxn.LatLonPoint(40.99, -111.05),
        new mxn.LatLonPoint(41.99, -111.05), new mxn.LatLonPoint(41.99, -114.04),
        new mxn.LatLonPoint(36.99, -114.05)];
```

Now we want to write a function that determines whether a particular point is within the polygon that could be created with these points. Our point could be anywhere on the earth. Seeing as Utah is a relatively small area, our point is quite likely not in the state. Let's rule that out quickly— before getting to the advanced math.

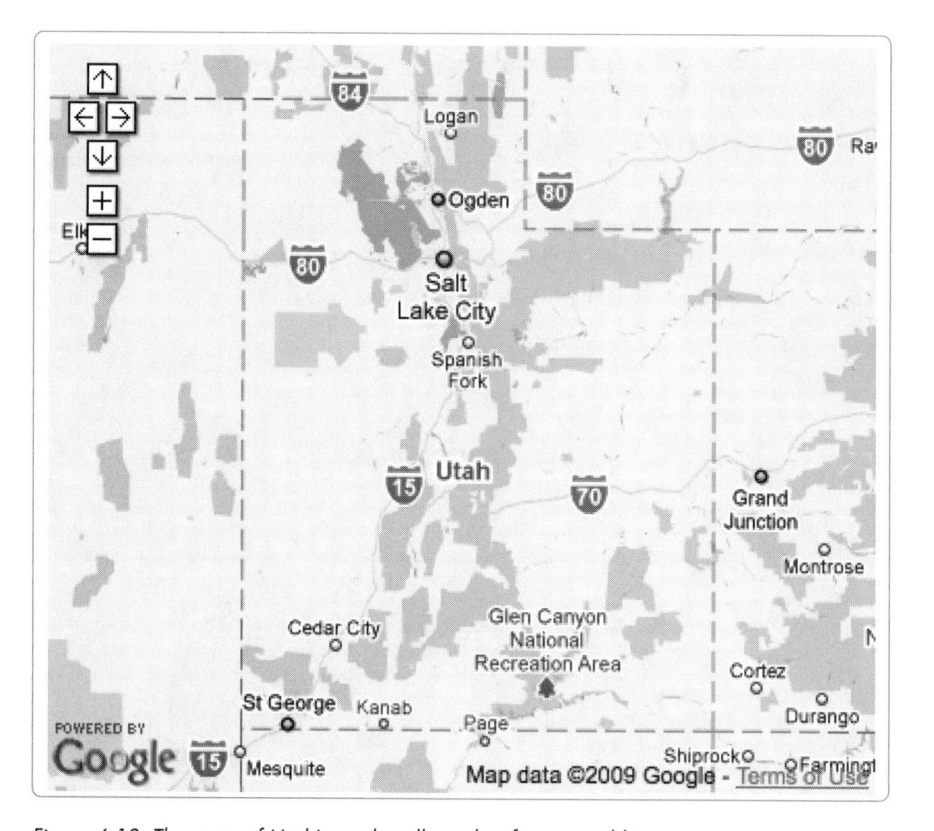

Figure 6-10: The state of Utah's panhandle makes for a good hit test.

Find the Polygon's Bounding Box

The easiest way to determine that a point is *not* within a polygon is to show the point lies outside the polygon's bounding box. To determine the rectangular bounds of a polygon, we must look through each point, so we can find the minimum and maximum values for both latitude and longitude.

Once we have those values, we'll know what to use to create the bounding box. An example of one is shown in Figure 6-11.

Let's write a function to create a new Mapstraction BoundingBox from a series of LatLonPoints. Here is the code for the entire function:

```
function points_to_bounds(pts) {
  if (pts.length > 0) {    var minlat = pts[0].lat
    var maxlat = minlat;
    var minlon = pts[0].lon
    var maxlon = minlon;
```

```
❶     for (var i = 1; i < pts.length; i++) {
         var pt = pts[i];
❷        if (pt.lat > maxlat) {
❸          maxlat = pt.lat;
          }
         if (pt.lon > maxlon) {
           maxlon = pt.lon;
          }
   if (pt.lat < minlat) {
         minlat = pt.lat;
          }
         if (pt.lon < minlon) {
           minlon = pt.lon;
          }
       }
❹     return new mxn.BoundingBox(minlat, minlon, maxlat, maxlon);
     }
    return null;
  }
```

Figure 6-11: A polygon's rectangular bounds

We want to determine four values: the smallest latitude, the largest latitude, the smallest longitude, and the largest longitude. Because we have to start somewhere, we begin with the assumption that the first point is both minimum and maximum. That's simply so we have something to compare.

Then, beginning with the second point (which has an index of one because JavaScript array indexes start at zero), we loop through all the other points ❶. Each time through the loop, we check whether we have found new minimum or maximum values. For example, if the current point has a latitude greater than what we currently think is the maximum ❷, then we need to set the maximum to be this value ❸.

Once we have completed the loop, the four values will be correct. Those values represent the corners of a BoundingBox. The SW corner is made up of the minimum values, the NE corner of the maximum. We can create the BoundingBox and return it for use elsewhere ❹.

Now that we have the bounds, we can check whether a point is within the polygon with the simple rectangle that surrounds our polygon. I covered this in detail earlier, and I'll demonstrate it again in a few sections when we perform the complete hit test.

Connect Our Point to an Outside Point

Okay, if we've gotten this far, we've determined that our point is inside the polygon's bounding box. This doesn't mean the point is within the polygon itself, but it's at least nearby. In our Utah example, our point is in the very northeast corner of the bounding box, but not inside the Utah polygon.

Now the tricky stuff begins, but within this trickery, you'll find simplicity. We need to make a temporary line for testing. This line connects our point (the one that may be inside the polygon) to a point that we can guarantee is outside the polygon.

When we draw the temporary line, it may intersect the line segments that make up our polygon. If the lines crosses the polygon an odd number of times, our point is inside. If it crosses the polygon an even number of times, or not at all, our point is outside. Figure 6-12 provides a visual of the Utah example.

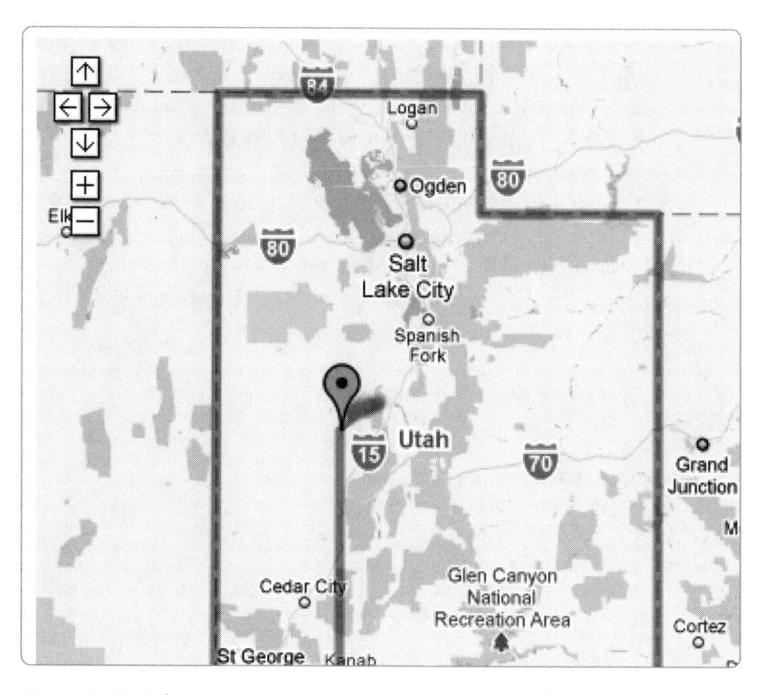

Figure 6-12: Polygon representing Utah only intersected once—the point is inside the shape.

The hit test is only conclusive if we can guarantee the new point we create will be outside the polygon. How can we do that? We'll create a latitude for our new point that is less than the SW latitude.

If the point we're testing is called mypt and our BoundingBox is called box, here's the code to create our testing point:

```
var lat_change = (❶(box.ne.lat - box.sw.lat) / 100);
var pt2 = new mxn.LatLonPoint(box.sw.lat - lat_change, mypt.lon);
```

We don't need to move very far outside the bounding box. To determine how much to change the latitude, I took the number of degrees between the SW and NE ❶ and divided by 100. In the case of Utah, our new point would be 0.05 degrees below the southern border. The smaller the difference between north and south latitudes, the closer the new point will be to the bounding box—but the point will always be outside of the box.

For the longitude of the new point, I set it to be the same as the longitude of the point we're checking. That decision was arbitrary, as any longitude would create a point outside the bounding box, because the latitude is less than the box's smallest latitude.

Check for Line Intersections

Now we have a bounding box and a point outside the box that can be connected with the point we want to test. The final step is to determine how many times the line connecting those two points crosses the polygon. To do this, we need to know how to check whether two lines intersect.

The code becomes a little confusing because there are many variables, despite only working with two line segments. We have four separate points or eight different values. From two to four to eight. Like I said, things become confusing quickly.

Add in a little vector math (based on a solution written in Visual Basic and available at *http://www.vb-helper.com/howto_segments_intersect.html*), and the code starts to look complicated. Here is the JavaScript code to test whether a line segment from point A to B intersects with another from point C to D:

```
    function check_intersection(A, B, C, D) {
❶      var latdiff1 = B.lat - A.lat;
        var latdiff2 = D.lat - C.lat;
        var londiff1 = B.lon - A.lon;
        var londiff2 = D.lon - C.lon;

        // Make sure lines aren't parallel
❷      if (londiff2 * latdiff1 - latdiff2 * londiff1 != 0) {
            var segtest1 = (londiff1 * (C.lat - A.lat) + latdiff1 * (A.lon - C.lon))
                        / ❸(londiff2 * latdiff1 - latdiff2 * londiff1);
```

```
      var segtest2 = (londiff2 * (A.lat - C.lat) + latdiff2 * (C.lon - A.lon))
                       / (latdiff2 * londiff1 - londiff2 * latdiff1);
❹    if (segtest1 >= 0 && segtest1 <= 1 && segtest2 >= 0 && segtest2 <= 1) {
        return true;
      }
    }
    return false;
  }
```

The first thing the code does is calculate how far away the ends of each line are, such as the distance between the latitudes of point A and B ❶. These values become the foundation of the vector computations that will determine whether the lines intersect.

With just the latitude and longitude distances, we can make sure the lines aren't parallel ❷. Determining this saves us further computation because parallel lines will never intersect. More importantly, we won't divide by zero with our first segment test ❸.

The segtest1 and segtest2 variables compare line AB to CD, then vice versa. The value determines where the two lines intersect. Because they aren't parallel, they *will* intersect somewhere. If both of the segment tests are between 0 and 1 ❹, then we know the intersection happens within our line segments.

Perform the Hit Test

At this point, we've found the bounding box of the polygon, drawn a line from the point outside the polygon to our point in question, and learned how to determine whether two line segments intersect. Do you feel like we've lost track of the original plan to find out whether our point is within the polygon? Okay then, let's put it all together and perform the hit test.

Remember our point is within the polygon if the line that we created intersects an odd number of lines that make up the polygon. We'll need to test each and every segment against our line that we know at least *starts* outside the polygon.

Here is the function, using the pieces we've put together earlier in this project, to determine whether a point is within a polygon:

```
function check_polygon(mypt, polypts) {
❶    var box = points_to_bounds(polypts);
❷    if (box.contains(mypt)) {
      var lat_change = ((box.ne.lat - box.sw.lat) / 100);
❸      var pt2 = new mxn.LatLonPoint(box.sw.lat - lat_change, mypt.lon);
      var intersections = 0;
❹      for (var i = 1; i < polypts.length; i++) {
        var seg1 = polypts[i-1];
        var seg2 = polypts[i];
```

```
❺        if (check_intersection(seg1, seg2, mypt, pt2)) {
           intersections++;
         }
       }
❻    if (intersections % 2 == 1) {
         return true;
       }
     }
   return false;
}
```

The hit test function is passed the point to check and the array of points that make up the polygon. From the latter, we're able to determine the bounding box of the polygon ❶. Then, of course, we don't have to do anything unless our point is within this box ❷. The point cannot be within the polygon if it isn't within the polygon's bounds.

Now we're ready to check whether the point is inside the polygon. To do this, we create a temporary line between our point and a point outside the bounding box ❸. Then we need to check where this line intersects with the polygon. To do this, we'll loop through the polygon's points ❹, checking for intersections with this temporary line.

Each time through the loop, we make two line segments from four points. The first segment is made from two consecutive points from the polygon. The other segment is created with our point and the point we found outside the bounding box.

We pass these points to the function we created to check for intersections ❺. If the two segments cross, we increase the intersection count. Either way, we then move on to the next trip through the loop.

When the loop finishes, we'll know whether our point is within the polygon. If the intersection count is odd, the point is inside. If the count is even, our point is outside. A number is odd if, when dividing it by two, you have a remainder of one. The modulus operator, %, gives us the remainder ❻. A remainder means we have an odd number of intersections, and we return true because the point is within the polygon. In all other cases, we return false because the point is not within the polygon.

You Clicked in Utah!

Now that we're able to check whether a point is within a polygon, let's incorporate it into a map. At the beginning of this chapter, we created a series of points shaped like the state of Utah. We'll use that, along with all the other code shown so far, to report whether the user has clicked inside the polygon described by the utah variable.

Create a basic map and add in the polygon points. We'll need the functions we've created so far, too. Make sure to include the check_polygon, check_intersection, and points_to_bounds functions. Then add the following code, replacing the create_map function that already exists:

```
function create_map() {
  mapstraction = new mxn.Mapstraction('mymap', 'google');
  mapstraction.setCenterAndZoom(new mxn.LatLonPoint(39.5, -111.7), 6);
  mapstraction.addSmallControls();
❶ mapstraction.click.addHandler(function(event_type, event_source, event_args) {
    var clickpoint = event_args.location;
    var intersects = check_polygon(clickpoint, utah);
❷  if (intersects) {
      msg = "You clicked in Utah!";
    }
    else {
      msg = "That's not Utah!";
    }
❸  var m = new mxn.Marker(clickpoint);
    m.setInfoBubble(msg);
    mapstraction.addMarker(m);
    m.openBubble();
  });
}
```

The first few lines create the new map, center it on Utah, and add zoom controls. Then we need to wait for the user to click somewhere on the map ❶. When is the user clicks, we initiate an inline, anonymous function, with the click point passed as an argument, as shown in "#27: The User Clicks the Map" on page 103.

The difficult work of checking for whether a point is within a polygon is passed off to the check_polygon function. This function, which we wrote in a previous section, returns either true or false. If the function returns true ❷, we create a text variable to tell the user "You clicked in Utah!" Otherwise, the user gets a message saying "That's not Utah!"

Now we need to report the click and the outcome. We do this by creating a marker at the click point ❸ and putting the text inside a message box. Then we add the marker to the page and open the message box.

Try it out for yourself or see Figure 6-13. See if you can trick the test by clicking in the NE corner of the state, where Wyoming appears to intrude into Utah's bounding box. Sure enough, if you click outside of Utah, you'll see the correct message. Ditto when clicking inside of Utah. The hit test gets the right answer every time.

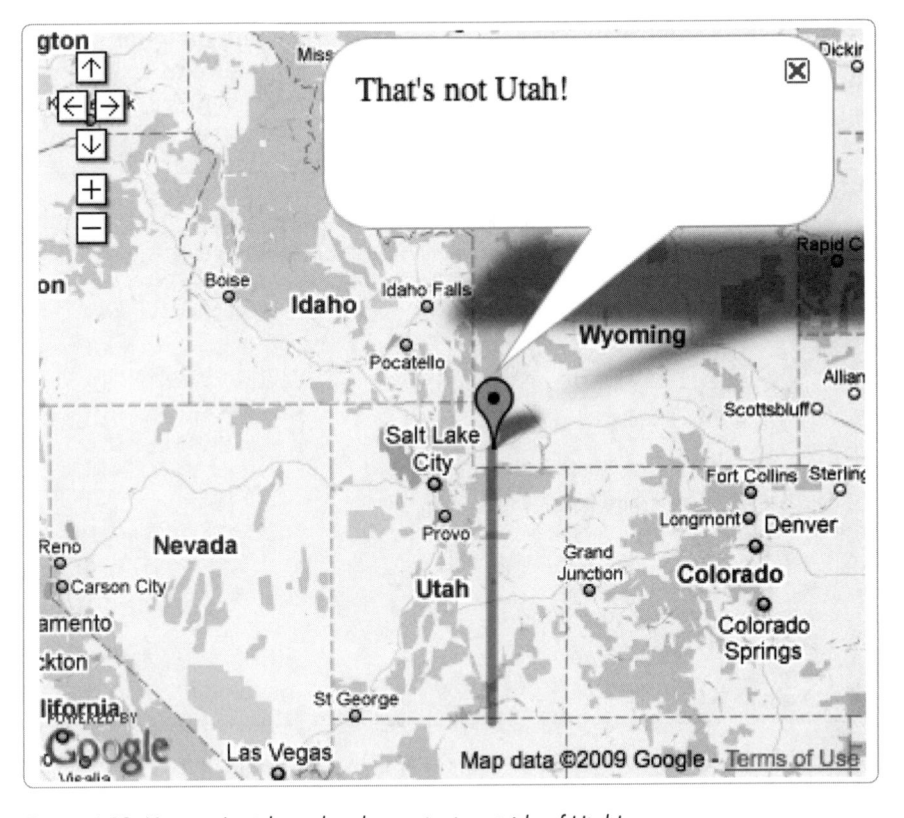

Figure 6-13: You can't trick math—that point is outside of Utah!

#46: Get Nearest Locations from Your Own Database

Earlier in this chapter, I showed how to calculate the distance between two points and how to determine the closest marker to a point. Arguably more useful is what we'll be doing in this project: getting the nearest location to a point from a list of many possibilities stored in a database.

To look up locations in a database, we need to have something in the database in the first place. For this example, we'll use the database table from "#63: Store Locations to a Database" on page 219. Although we're using MySQL as an engine, most databases will work with the SQL statements here. *Structured query language (SQL)* is a syntax to communicate with a database server.

Because we're looking for the nearest locations to a single point, we need to determine what that point is. I've chosen a point near me in Portland, Oregon, with a latitude of 45.517 and a longitude of –122.649. Now we'll plug this into the Haversine formula—that's the same bit of trigonometry we used in JavaScript, but this time we'll use SQL.

From either the MySQL command interpreter or phpMyAdmin, type the following query:

```
SET @earthRadius = 6371;
SET @lat = 45.517;
SET @lon = -122.649;
SET @radLat = RADIANS(@lat);
SET @radLon = RADIANS(@lon);
SET @cosLat = COS(@radLat);
SET @sinLat = SIN(@radLat);
SELECT *,
  ( @earthRadius❶ * ACOS( @cosLat * cosRadLat *
  COS( radLon - @radLon ) + @sinLat *
  sinRadLat ) ) AS dist
FROM places
ORDER BY dist;
```

We select all the fields from the places table, plus an additional field, as described by the entire section in bold. That's a lot of code! It calculates the distance between our point and the points in the database using the latitude and longitude values stored with each place.

The distance, which becomes a column named dist, is expressed in kilometers. As with the previous implementation of the Haversine formula, we multiply by the radius of the earth, which is 6371 km. For miles, replace the number ❶ with its mile equivalent: 3958.

When you run this SQL query, your results will be the same as those shown in Table 6-2. Because we ordered by the distance, the places nearest to our point come first in the table. Therefore, the nearest place to the point we selected is Old Faithful.

Table 6-2: Results of Nearest Place SQL

ID	Name	Latitude	Longitude	Distance
1	Old Faithful Geyser	44.4605	– 110.828	936.12
2	St. Louis Arch	38.6247	– 90.1851	2765.97

7

USER LOCATION

Creating a location-based website requires a starting point. Sometimes this point comes as data from your database or from your site's focus on a small geographic area. Even in these cases, you can benefit from knowing a user's location.

You can retrieve this information in a number of ways, which I'll cover in this chapter. The methods vary in complexity and accuracy. In some cases, you'll need to make a simple call in JavaScript. In others, you'll install a database so your server can determine the location.

Finding a user's location also depends on how much permission you need from him or her. An IP address, for example, is something every Internet user has. You can find a city-level location for most users without them even knowing you looked. For methods where the browser accesses another data source, you'll need the user's permission. In all cases, of course, you should do your part to ensure user privacy.

We'll start with perhaps the simplest method of determining a user's location, something that has been around as long as the Web itself.

#47: Ask Users Where They Are

Does this seem obvious? Asking users where they are may not be a flashy method of determining their location, but this method is bound to produce results the user expects. Plus, it has the built-in benefit of being only as specific as the user wants. In other words, the user can provide a full address, postal code, or simply a city name. If you're counting on knowing your users' whereabouts, at least include this project as a fallback when you cannot otherwise determine their location.

Of course, what you want is latitude and longitude coordinates. Our maps expect those coordinates, and that's how so much geographic data is stored. We can't ask for latitude and longitude directly (go ahead and try that on your friends and see how many know their current geocodes); instead, we ask for the text representation of those coordinates. Once users give you this information, you'll probably need to feed it to a geocoder. This section won't cover that part, but you can learn all about it in Chapter 3. In this project, I'll show how to get the input into variables in both JavaScript and PHP.

Get Input Using JavaScript

When we rely upon JavaScript to accept input, you can use the data without having to reload the entire page. Also because mapping providers work with JavaScript, you only need one programming language, which simplifies things a bit.

To accept user input, we'll incorporate an HTML form into the site. The form will have a simple text input box and a Submit button, as shown in Figure 7-1.

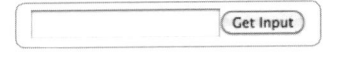

Figure 7-1: Request location or other input with JavaScript.

Add the following code to a new HTML page:

```
<!DOCTYPE html "-//W3C//DTD XHTML 1.0 Strict//EN" "http://www.w3.org/TR/
xhtml1/DTD/xhtml1-strict.dtd">
<html xmlns="http://www.w3.org/1999/xhtml">
  <head>
    <title>Get Input from a Form with JavaScript</title>
    <script type="text/javascript">
      var f;
❶     function prepare() {
        f = document.getElementById("myform");
❷       f.onsubmit = function() {
          var userinput = ❸f.wheretext.value;
```

```
            // Do something with userinput
❹          return false; // avoids form submission
        };
    }
  </script>
</head>
<body onload="prepare()">
  <form id="myform">
    <input type="text" name="wheretext" />
    <input type="submit" name="butnew" value="Get Input" />
  </form>
</body>
</html>
```

When the page is loaded, the prepare function is called ❶. This method is similar to the create_map function in other mapping projects. The name of this function can be whatever you want, as long as it matches the name you use to call it.

First, you need to attach a submission event to the form ❷. You want to stop the form from submitting to the server, however, and instead use the data within JavaScript. In this example, I've used an inline, anonymous function instead of a named function for submitting the form. Otherwise, the prepare function would be a single line.

Also, I'm referencing the form by its index, which, in this case, is zero. It is the first and only form on this page. If other forms were on the page, it might be the second and its index would be one (because JavaScript array indexers start at zero). You could also give the form a name or ID and access it that way.

To obtain the user input, I refer to the text input field by name from the form object ❸. Including the .value portion is important, as that retrieves the text the user typed, as opposed to the input field object. Once you have the text, what you do with it is your decision; for instance, you might display it on the site or determine its coordinates using "#12: Geocode with JavaScript" on page 46.

The final line ❹ of the submission function is also important. This line stops the browser from sending the form's input to the server, which is what we *want* to happen in the next section.

Get Input Using PHP

Let's be clear: Users type their input inside a browser. The difference between using JavaScript to get input and using PHP (or any server-side language) is that we allow the data to be submitted to the server. The original intention of an HTML form is to send data to a server-side script that then replies with additional HTML.

Because most of the notable stuff happens within a PHP script, the HTML for getting input is fairly simple. Add the following lines to a new HTML file:

```
<!DOCTYPE html "-//W3C//DTD XHTML 1.0 Strict//EN" "http://www.w3.org/TR/xhtml1/DTD/xhtml1-
strict.dtd">
<html xmlns="http://www.w3.org/1999/xhtml">
  <head>
    <title>Get Input from a Form with PHP</title>
  </head>
  <body>
    <form ❶method="POST" ❷action="input.php">
      <input type="text" name="wheretext" />
      <input type="submit" name="butnew" value="Get Input" />
    </form>
  </body>
</html>
```

This code is essentially the same HTML as in the JavaScript example, but the JavaScript has been removed. The major difference is that the `<form>` tag receives a few more attributes.

I've declared a method ❶, which tells the browser how to send the input to the server. The two major options here are GET, which sends input inside the URL as a query string. I chose POST, which passes the data in the body of the HTTP message, so the user doesn't see it.

Another important attribute is the form's action ❷. This action is the destination URL for the form data. If the action is omitted, the current page will be assumed. If you're sending from a regular HTML file, this result is definitely not what you want because the server-side language will be unable to parse the data. I've used a PHP file in this case, as that's how I'll be reading in the input.

Now we need to make that PHP code, so add the following code to a new file named *input.php* (or to match your action attribute):

```
<?
  $userinput = $_POST["wheretext"];
  // Do something with userinput
?>
```

Pretty simple, right? All you need to do is pass the name of the input box to the $_POST variable, which is an associative array. PHP does the hard work of deciphering the header text and deciphering the encoded text.

If you're going to use the value within a database, make sure you verify the data is good. If you expecting a postal code, make sure the data is in the correct format. If you have an address, watch out for strange characters that don't belong in addresses—semicolons come to mind. You don't want to be the victim of a SQL injection attack, where user input is co-opted to create a hazardous query.

If you're going to use the input elsewhere, such as in "#13: Geocode with an HTTP Web Service" on page 49, you might be able to rely on its security. But most of the time, do as much as you can on your side to ensure data integrity.

#48: Get Location Using JavaScript

Many web browsers can now report your user's location with a lot more precision than you get with an IP address. Using the coordinates, you can save users the hassle of having to tell you their location, and you could, for example, automatically search nearby.

The Worldwide Web Consortium, often called the W3C, is an organization working for standards on the Web. In these examples, I will use the W3C's recommended syntax. Whether using a desktop, laptop, or mobile phone, the code that you will use is the same.

So, let's get to it. From anywhere in your JavaScript code, add the following line:

```
navigator.geolocation.getCurrentPosition(foundLoc, noLoc);
```

This function begins the geolocation process. The browser will request the user's permission to share his or her location with you. When the user approves, the browser will call a callback function, which is the first argument passed to getCurrentPosition. A second callback function is available when the location cannot be determined or the user rejects your request.

I made up the names of those functions, and you can use whatever name you want. Whatever you call them, however, you'll then need to write the functions, so the browser has something to reference. If you prefer anonymous, inline functions, you can use those in place of the named functions.

In the same file that you used to make the location request, let's add those two functions:

```
function foundLoc(❶pos) {
  var lat = ❷pos.coords.latitude;
  var lon = pos.coords.longitude;
❸ alert('Found location: ' + lat + ', ' + lon);
}
function noLoc() {
❹ alert('Could not find location');
}
```

The first function, which is called when the browser is able to find a location and the user approves sharing it, is passed a position object ❶. We can use this to get at the latitude ❷, longitude, and some other data (more on that later). Once we have snagged both coordinates, we create a

JavaScript alert, showing the location ❸. This alert is not especially useful, but we're just proving it works right now.

If no location can be found (or if the user doesn't want to share his or her location), we create a JavaScript alert that says so ❹. In a full application, you might choose to do nothing in this case. Or depending on how your site is designed, you could create an option to enter the location manually when it can't be determined.

Before we do something a little more interesting, let's talk about how an ordinary browser can even access your location.

Where Does the Data Come From?

The source and accuracy of the location data varies by source. A cutting-edge smart phone is certainly fitted with global positioning satellite (GPS), so the browser has a pretty good idea where you are if that's the source. What about on a laptop or desktop though?

Most computers do not have GPS. Instead, they rely on Wi-Fi to find your location. A handful of companies have driven around the world's largest cities (and some small ones, too!) and "sniffed" for wireless Internet. Whenever they find a signal, they add its unique ID to their database, along with the latitude and longitude.

Then, when a browser requests a location, it sniffs the available Wi-Fi. Armed with an ID, it asks a server to reply back with coordinates. Are you skeptical? In urban areas, this method is extremely accurate in finding a location because so many Wi-Fi access points are available. Also, wireless is only supposed to go a few hundred feet, so for most uses it's still fairly accurate. And in many cases, Wi-Fi is more reliable than GPS, which has a difficult time accessing signals indoors. You can see the accuracy of different methods in Table 7-1.

Table 7-1: Accuracy of Geolocation Methods

Method	Accuracy
GPS	Within feet
WiFi	Within a block
Cell towers	Within a few miles
IP address	ZIP- or city-level

When neither of these options is available, you need a fallback plan. A mobile device can sometimes use cell tower triangulation. A standard web browser, on the other hand, will always have an IP address. Whether the fallback is used depends on the implementation.

Another thing that varies with the device being used and the way the browser implements the location code is what additional data is available.

What Other Data Can We Get?

The W3C created a standard that could work in all situations. As you've seen, a number of data sources and devices can be used to determine a location. Mobile phones, especially, can provide some interesting data.

Previously, I described how to grab a location's coordinates using JavaScript. Here are some other values you may be able to access:

- Time the location was acquired
- Accuracy of the location, in meters
- Altitude of the location
- Accuracy of the altitude, if it exists, in meters
- Speed, in meters per second
- Heading, the direction in degrees relative to true north

Not every device will be able to provide all this information. For example, if the user is on a laptop, latitude and longitude may be all that is available. If the data comes from GPS, however, you may be able to access all these fields.

Use the Location on the Map

Now that you can get the user's location, you probably want to *do something* with it. The easiest example is to use it as the center of your new map. You could also add a marker at that spot. Heck, why don't we do both?

This example will be slightly different than the others in that the map won't be created until we know that we have a location. Because of this, let's start with a fresh HTML file, instead of the basic map. Add these lines to your new file:

```
<html>
  <head>
    <title>W3C Geolocation Map</title>

    <script type="text/javascript"
            src="http://maps.google.com/maps/api/js?sensor=false"></script>
    <script type="text/javascript" src="mxn.js?(googlev3)"></script>
    <style>
      div#mymap {
        width: 400px;
        height: 350px;
      }
    </style>
    <script type="text/javascript">
      navigator.geolocation.getCurrentPosition(❶create_map, ❷function() {});

      function create_map(❸pos) {
        var pt = new mxn.LatLonPoint(pos.coords.latitude, pos.coords.longitude);
        mapstraction = new mxn.Mapstraction('mymap', 'googlev3');
```
❹

```
        mapstraction.setCenterAndZoom(pt, 15);
        var marker = new mxn.Marker(pt);
        marker.setInfoBubble('You Are Here');
        mapstraction.addMarker(marker);
❺      marker.openBubble();
      }
    </script>
  </head>
  <body>
    <div id="mymap"></div>
  </body>
</html>
```

Because we only want to call the create_map function when we have
a location, nothing is called when the page loads. Instead the call to
getCurrentPosition happens within bare JavaScript, and then the map initialization function is used as a callback ❶. If no location is found, we don't
want to do anything, so we create an empty inline function ❷. In the future,
you might want to do something, so this leaves a template to remind you
that something can go here.

When the create_map function does get called, the position ❸ the
browser found is passed to it. The first thing we'll do with that position,
which is an object in the W3C format, is convert it to Mapstraction's object
for describing a point ❹. Then centering the map and creating the marker
is as easy as the examples shown in the first two chapters.

For a little extra fun, we give the marker a message box that says "You
Are Here." After adding the marker to the map, we automatically display
the message ❺. When I ran this in my hometown of Portland, I got the
result shown in Figure 7-2.

From here, you could plot local results on a map or get driving questions using the found location as a starting point.

Receive Continual Updates

If your application will be used on a mobile device, then a user's location
may change as he or she moves around. Depending on what you're doing
with the data, receiving an initial location may not be enough—you may
want updates.

The W3C has accounted for this need with a second function to access
the user's location. Rather than getCurrentPosition, you can use this line:

```
var geoid = navigator.geolocation.watchPosition(foundLoc, noLoc);
```

The two function references passed as arguments are used just as
they are with a single location request. The difference here is the browser
will periodically call your functions without the code performing another
request. Frequency is determined by the browser and may be every minute
or so. Mobile browsers will likely send updates more often.

Figure 7-2: Location coordinates plotted on a map

You could implement this yourself by calling the single request every so often. The browser might prompt the user with every request, however; the watchPosition function's permission lasts until the user reloads the page.

If you want the application to stop tracking the user's location, you can clear it with this function:

```
navigator.geolocation.clearWatch(geoid);
```

Note the function accepts one argument. This variable is an identifier output by the watchPosition function. In order to stop watching, store this identifier in a variable.

Additional Geolocation Options

The two functions mentioned in the previous sections accept a third argument that I haven't covered yet. You can set additional options, such as how old a location can be and whether you want the highest accuracy possible.

Here is an example geolocation call that includes options:

```
var locOptions = {
  enableHighAccuracy: true,
  timeout: 5000,
  maximumAge: 60000
}
navigator.geolocation.getCurrentPosition(foundLocation, noLocation,
locOptions);
```

I created a variable to hold the location options, which are stored as a JavaScript object. The options can be entered in any order, and you don't have to include them all. In this case, I've used all three potential options.

First, `enableHighAccuracy` is a boolean that expects either `true` or `false` as a value. When set to `true`, the browser will provide the most accurate location it can, even if more time is required to do so (for example, a lock on additional GPS satellites). In previous examples where we did not use the options parameter, high accuracy was *not* enabled for efficiency reasons.

We can also give the browser a time limit for the location lookup using the `timeout` option. This option is set in milliseconds. Because there are 1000 milliseconds in 1 second, the example shows a 5-second timeout.

The final option, `maximumAge`, provides the browser with instructions for sending cached locations. Depending on your needs, you may want a very recent location, or you may not care as much. Like the timeout, this value is passed in milliseconds. In this example, I've shown a `maximumAge` of 60,000 milliseconds, or 1 minute.

The options object can be passed as the third argument to either `getCurrentPosition` or `watchPosition`. If you use the latter requesting continual updates, the options will be followed *every* time the browser returns a location.

#49: Use Fire Eagle to Get Location

You can retrieve your user's location in several ways, some of them with very precise output. Many services that ask and store a user's current whereabouts are also available. Fire Eagle, a product from Yahoo!, is a broker for those services. When you write a Fire Eagle application, you can set or receive the user's current location, which then makes it available to all other Fire Eagle applications, as long as the user gives permission.

In this project, I'll show how you can gain access to your user's location using Fire Eagle. And once a user has approved your application for access, you'll be able to get the user's latest location at any time, even when he or she isn't online.

Of course, some application has to set the location for it to be accurate. Remember all those sites I mentioned that help users share their location? We'll let them worry about setting the location in Fire Eagle, so let's dive into using Fire Eagle to retrieve a location. The application we write will use PHP, which I cover in more depth in Chapter 9.

NOTE *There are many other services for sharing location. By the time you read this, there are probably more. See a list and links to tutorials at* http://mapscripting.com/location-apis.

Get the Fire Eagle Essentials

Yahoo! has some tools that make writing Fire Eagle applications much easier. Before you can use them, you'll want to register your application with Fire Eagle, so you get the codes that will make your program work. One is an API key, much like other services use; the other is a "secret code." If it helps, you can think of it as joining a secret club. Really, you're just filling out a form.

You'll need a Yahoo! account. Once you have that, head over to this page to register your app: *https://fireeagle.yahoo.net/developer/create.*

Don't worry about being perfect. You can edit this application later. Plus, Fire Eagle lets you register multiple applications, so let this one be a dress rehearsal for the one you'll write later.

Fire Eagle has two important settings to pay attention to as you create your application. First, you're going to use **Auth for Web-based Services** for authentication. Next, you'll need to set a callback URL. The URL can be named anything you want, but for this simple example, let's use **callback.php**. Fire Eagle wants to know a full URL, so you'll insert something like **http://yoursite.com/fireeagle/callback.php**. For testing purposes, you can even use your local machine instead of your server.

Once you register your application, Fire Eagle will show you some special keys, the API, and the secret code I mentioned earlier. You can get back to them any time by visiting this page: *http://fireeagle.yahoo.net/developer/manage.*

One last thing before you can leave the site for a little while: You need the API kit. Fire Eagle has prepackaged code for various web programming languages that makes coding applications much easier. Download the PHP kit from this page: *http://fireeagle.yahoo.net/developer/code/php.*

You absolutely need two files from this package: *fireeagle.php* and *OAuth.php.* Store these inside a directory called *lib* (which stands for library) because we'll be accessing them soon.

Authenticate the User

As the name of one of these files suggests, Fire Eagle uses OAuth to authenticate users. If you haven't used OAuth before, it might seem a little strange, but I've come to appreciate its simplicity and security.

The process to authenticate a user begins by requesting a *token* from Fire Eagle. This token actually comes in two pieces: *public* and *private.* We redirect the user to Fire Eagle, along with the public token. Then, when the user approves us for access, we can use the public and private tokens together to prove to Fire Eagle that we're the approved application.

Let's see how it looks in code. Create a new file called *authorize.php* and add the following lines:

```php
<?
require_once "lib/fireeagle.php";

$key = "YOURKEY";
$secret = "YOURSECRETCODE";

❶ $fe = new FireEagle($key, $secret);
❷ $response = $fe->getRequestToken();

session_start();
$oauth_token = $response["oauth_token"];
$_SESSION['oauth_token'] = $oauth_token;
$_SESSION['oauth_secret'] = $response["oauth_token_secret"];
❸ $_SESSION["signed_in"] = 0;

❹ header("Location: " . $fe->getAuthorizeURL($oauth_token));
?>
```

To start, we use the key and secret code to create a new Fire Eagle object ❶. The key and secret code are different from the tokens I described. The key and secret code identify your application itself and will never change. The tokens are different for each user.

Using the Fire Eagle object we created, now we request the public and private tokens ❷. We store these as session variables, which is how PHP maintains data for a user from one page to the next. Then we create another session variable that tells us the user has not signed in yet ❸.

Finally, using the public token, we redirect the user to a Fire Eagle URL ❹. This page is where the user will approve our application.

Answer the Call

Once the user agrees to give us access, Fire Eagle will redirect back to our callback URL. Remember that from the settings? When the user comes to this page, chances are pretty good he or she has authorized our application.

The callback page is where the user will officially log in. How you set this up will vary depending on what type of application you are creating. For example, if users have accounts stored in a database, you might maintain their Fire Eagle tokens there. Here we will simply update the session variables.

Add the following code to your *callback.php* file:

```php
<?
require_once "lib/fireeagle.php";

$key = "YOURKEY";
$secret = "YOURSECRETCODE";

session_start();
```

```
❶ $fe = new FireEagle($key, $secret,
                    $_SESSION["oauth_token"], $_SESSION["oauth_secret"]);
❷ $response = $fe->getAccessToken();

  $oauth_token = $response["oauth_token"];
  $_SESSION["oauth_token"] = $oauth_token;
  $_SESSION["oauth_secret"] = $response["oauth_token_secret"];
❸ $_SESSION["signed_in"] = 1;

❹ header("Location: getloc.php");
  ?>
```

We create a Fire Eagle object ❶ again using the PHP kit that Yahoo! provided. This time we include the user's public and private tokens, in addition to our application's key and secret. Remember, this information proves we're the same application the user just approved.

If all these keys and tokens are confusing, get ready. One more pair is coming. Once a user approves an application, the public and private tokens aren't needed. Instead, they're replaced by *access tokens* ❷. We overwrite our previous session variables with new ones. And because the user has now successfully signed in, we can set that session variable appropriately ❸.

This process may seem like a long one to follow to access a user's location, but keep in mind it only needs to happen once. And the steps are all required in the name of security, which users appreciate. Plus, this callback page will appear instantly to the user.

The final line redirects the user to the page we'll use to retrieve his or her location ❹. That's what this whole thing is really about, after all. So let's get down to it.

Get the User's Location

The user has given us access to his or her location. We can even check the session variable that we set to make sure. Now we're going to retrieve the user's location.

Add the following code to the *getloc.php* file:

```
<?
require_once "lib/fireeagle.php";

$key = "YOURKEY";
$secret = "YOURSECRETCODE";

session_start();
❶ if ($_SESSION["signed_in"] == 1) {
    $fe = new FireEagle($key, $secret,
                    $_SESSION["oauth_token"], $_SESSION["oauth_secret"]);

❷  $loc = $fe->user();
❸  $toploc = $loc->user->best_guess;
❹  $lat = $toploc->latitude;
    $lon = $toploc->longitude;
```

```
    $datetime = date("M j, g:i A", strtotime(❺$toploc->located_at));
  }
  ?>
  <p>
❻ Your current location: <strong><?=$lat?>, <?=$lon?></strong>
  (as of <?=$datetime?>)
  </p>
```

The code starts much like other pages have, by including the PHP API kit and declaring our application's key and secret code. Then we check our session variable to make sure the user really has given us permission ❶. If the signed-in variable is still 0, we could redirect to the authentication page, or show an error.

As in the previous section, we create a Fire Eagle object using the application keys and the access tokens. Because we're pretty sure we can access the user's location at this point, we then ask Fire Eagle for the location object ❷. From there, we can retrieve its best guess for the user's location ❸, the most granular level of data the user is willing to share.

Now we have access to several pieces of data, including the latitude ❹ and longitude. We can also get an idea of how long ago the user shared that location ❺. To improve legibility, I used the PHP date function to format the time stamp.

Finally, in the HTML, we output the data ❻ we retrieved from Fire Eagle. Of course, this is just an example, not a great Fire Eagle application. The great one is the one you'll write. Right?

#50: Get Location by IP

All users on the Internet can be identified with a number that stays the same for at least a single online session and can be static—never changing. This number, called an *IP address*, is owned by the Internet provider, who usually has an entire block (or more) of similar numbers. With a database of these numbers tied to locations, you can usually determine at least the city your user is located in, if not the postal code.

I'll demonstrate other projects in this chapter that get at more granular data, determining a user's precise location. But knowing a geographic area is generally enough to do some interesting things. Plus, you can geolocate most of your users by using IPs, and you don't have to ask their permission.

What is an IP address? An IP address is a series of four numbers, each from one to three digits. For example, it might be *208.54.34.3*. Each computer connected to the Internet has its own IP address, though sometimes an address is shared across a local area network.

For this project, we'll look at two services that provide geographic coordinates based on the user's IP address. One must be used on the server, whereas the other runs in the browser using JavaScript. Which you choose depends on how you want to use the data. For example, if you store the result to a database, you will likely want the server-side version. But if you just want to center your map on the user's location, the JavaScript version will do just fine.

Use the HostIP Web Service

For this example, I'll use the hostip.info API. A number of web services provide IP-based geolocation, including a commercial service called MaxMind. I picked HostIP, however, because it is easy to use, and the database is maintained by a community of developers and users.

We'll be using PHP to call the API, including some concepts described in Chapters 8 and 9. I'll do my best to make understanding them easy, but you may want to flip ahead if something looks strange.

Before we can start our PHP code, we need to get a feel for how we are going to get the data back from HostIP. Luckily, the site makes trying out the API within your browser easy. Try loading this URL into your address bar: *http://api.hostip.info/?ip=12.215.42.19.*

Your results should look something like this:

```
<?xml version="1.0" encoding="ISO-8859-1"?>
<HostipLookupResultSet ... >
  <gml:description>This is the Hostip Lookup Service</gml:description>
  ...
  <gml:featureMember>
    <Hostip>
      <gml:name>Sugar Grove, IL</gml:name>
      <countryName>UNITED STATES</countryName>
      <countryAbbrev>US</countryAbbrev>
      <ipLocation>
        <gml:PointProperty>
          <gml:Point srsName="http://www.opengis.net/gml/srs/epsg.xml#4326">
            <gml:coordinates>-88.4588,41.7696</gml:coordinates>
          </gml:Point>
        </gml:PointProperty>
      </ipLocation>
    </Hostip>
  </gml:featureMember>
</HostipLookupResultSet>
```

Right in the middle of it all, shown in bold, are the latitude and longitude coordinates we want (note that here longitude comes first). Getting at those numbers means parsing the result and extracting the numbers. This process is shown in detail in "#52: Use XML" on page 174. Let's put the latitude and longitude into two variables using PHP. Create a new file and add the following lines of code:

```
<?
❶ $ipaddr = $_SERVER["REMOTE_ADDR"];
❷ $xmltxt = get_url("http://api.hostip.info/?ip=$ipaddr");
```

```
❸ $xmlobj = simplexml_load_string($xmltxt);
❹ $coords = $xmlobj->xpath("//coordinates");
❺ list($lon, $lat) = preg_split("/\,/", $coords[0]);

   // cUrl functions
❻ function get_url($url) {
    ...
   }
   ?>
```

Before we can make a call to HostIP, we need to determine the user's IP. Luckily, the IP is made available to PHP via a server variable, which we place into a local variable ❶.

The rest of the code is relatively spartan, despite all that it does, mainly because it counts on other functions to do the heavy lifting. For example, we load the XML text in a one-line call ❷, passing the HostIP URL, which includes the user's IP address. To turn the text into an object we can use, we call the SimpleXML parsing function ❸ that converts the XML. Now that we have an easy-to-access object, we use the xpath function to return all <coordinates> tags ❹. We only have one, so we then pass it off to a string-splitting function to insert it into our two variables ❺.

Most of these functions rely on internal PHP, but one of them ❻ I wrote myself. You can see this entire function in "#61: Retrieve a Web Page" on page 215.

Use Google's ClientLocation JavaScript Object

If you don't need the user's location on the server, you can easily get it if you use Google's Ajax Loader. This is an alternate way to load Google's JavaScript APIs, including Maps and Search. The ClientLocation object is available even without loading a specific API, which makes for minimal overhead considering the data it provides.

As with the standard Google Maps API, you need to include the call to Google's JavaScript within the header of your HTML file:

```
<script type="text/javascript" src="http://www.google.com/jsapi?key=yourkey"></script>
```

Then, anywhere within your JavaScript code, you can access google.loader.ClientLocation.latitude and google.loader.ClientLocation.longitude (in addition to a few other data items, such as the city name).

NOTE   *At press time the Ajax Loader only supports Google Maps version 2. To use this example, you will need a Google Maps API key. You can find that, as well as updated information about the Ajax Loader at* http://code.google.com/apis/ajax/documentation/.

Seeing it on a map is always easier, so let's create a new Mapstraction map using Google as the mapping provider. Instead of the standard Google Maps, we'll use the Ajax loader. Add the following code to a new HTML file:

```
<html>
  <head>
    <title>ClientLocation Map</title>
    <script type="text/javascript"
            src="http://www.google.com/jsapi?key=yourkeyhere"></script>
    <script type="text/javascript" src="mxn.js?(google)">
    <style>
      div#mymap {
        width: 400px;
        height: 350px;
      }
    </style>
    <script type="text/javascript">
❶      google.load("maps", "2");
       function create_map() {
❷        var pos = google.loader.ClientLocation;
❸        var pt = new mxn.LatLonPoint(pos.latitude, pos.longitude);
         mapstraction = new mxn.Mapstraction('mymap', 'google');
         mapstraction.setCenterAndZoom(pt, 10);
         var marker = new mxn.Marker(pt);
         marker.setInfoBubble('You Are Here');
         mapstraction.addMarker(marker);
         marker.openBubble();
       }
    </script>
  </head>
  <body onLoad="create_map()">
    <div id="mymap"></div>
  </body>
</html>
```

The JavaScript's very first line tells the Google Ajax Loader to load in the Maps API ❶. Then, once it—and the rest of the page—has loaded, the create_map function gets called.

To access the location, we copy the ClientLocation object into a local variable ❷, making accessing it easier. Then we create a point ❸ using the latitude and longitude from the new object. From there, the code is much like previous JavaScript examples, where we use this point as the center of the map and create a marker.

#51: Roll Your Own IP Database

Are you the type who would refuse help if you took a spill in a public place? Then you're probably also the type who wants to host your *own* IP database, rather than depend on someone else's service. Of course, you might simply be someone who cares about performance or doesn't want to worry about network latency. Whatever the case, this project will help you geolocate users by IP using your own server.

Where does the data come from? We'll use a free service called IPInfoDB, which updates a streamlined MySQL database dump every month. Download the latest database at *http://ipinfodb.com/ip_database.php*.

You have a number of choices for database types. For this example, we'll use the small, city-level database with a single table. The table should contain about 1.4 million records, which will result in a database file a little over 100MB. (The file will be much smaller when you download the compressed version.)

Import IP Data

Now that you have downloaded the SQL file, you need to import it. The file will be far too big to use phpMyAdmin, so you will need to use the command interpreter, which you can usually get to via the `mysql` command on a server.

You may be able to ask your system administrator to help you get to your MySQL database's command interpreter. Or, if you are using MAMP, you can run `Library/bin/mysql -u root -p` within the MAMP directory (the password is also root). On WAMP, the location may vary, but it can commonly be found at `C:\wamp\bin\mysql\mysqlversion\bin\mysql`. In either case, you will need to access the interpreter via the command line: Terminal (on Mac) or CMD (on Windows).

Open the command interpreter and select your database, or create a new one (see "#63: Store Locations to a Database" on page 219). To begin the process of importing your data, type the following command:

```
\. /path/to/ipdata.sql
```

Make sure you include the full path to the SQL file you downloaded. As it imports, you'll see messages like this:

```
Query OK, 0 rows affected (0.00 sec)
Query OK, 0 rows affected (0.00 sec)
Query OK, 11068 rows affected (0.35 sec)
Records: 11068  Duplicates: 0  Warnings: 0
```

When the messages end, you can leave the command interpreter and return to phpMyAdmin, if you wish. Now that we've added the data, let's access it.

Find an IP's Location

What information is available with the IP database, and how is it stored? From phpMyAdmin, click through to your database and then to the ip_group_city table that you've just imported. Click the Browse tab and you'll see the first 30 records in the database.

Among the interesting fields available are city, latitude, and longitude. You'll also see the IP address itself, stored as a very large number, which is different than the period-separated version you're used to seeing. The difference is because you need to do a little preprocessing, which makes the lookup process much more efficient.

Where the IP is A.B.C.D, the number can be expressed as ((A*256+B)*256+C)*256. So *71.59.208.255* would become *1195102208*. As would anything in the *71.59.208.X* block. Notice the formula does not have a D; that's because IPs come in blocks, so everything in the range will likely have the same location.

This process of converting an IP to a number is fairly standardized. In fact, MySQL has a helper function, INET_ATON, which makes it super easy. Click the SQL tab in phpMyAdmin, or use the command interpreter, and add the following query:

```
SELECT * FROM ip_group_city
WHERE ip_start <= INET_ATON('71.59.208.255')
ORDER BY ip_start DESC LIMIT 1
```

Remember to replace the IP address I used with one of your own. Here, I've requested all the fields for the closest IP address in the database. In order to keep from getting all 1.4 million records back in order, I limit the results to one row—the one I want.

Now we'll connect it to a PHP script, something covered in "#65: Use MySQL from PHP" on page 225.

8

DATA FORMATS

Working with maps usually means interacting with a lot of geographic data. Along
with descriptive information, you need to
know where a place is so you can plot it on
your map. Chances are good that most of the time
you'll need to get data from someone else. You might
also need to share your data with someone.

Several standard formats have been adopted to make passing around
geographic data even easier. In this chapter, I'll go over a few ways to share
the basic pieces of geography you'd put on a map: points, lines, and shapes.

We'll also go over a couple formats that are popular on the web for
exchanging information. More and more, your sources will be websites that
make their data available with an API. In most cases, the format you'll need
is covered in this chapter.

Let's get started and learn some data formats.

#52: Use XML

The *Extensible Markup Language (XML)* is the building block of much of the Web's data and of several other formats discussed in this chapter. It looks a lot like HTML, because some HTML actually *is* XML. This section will stay away from specific flavors of XML, however, as I'll be covering some in their own sections. Here, I'll focus on how to recognize and use generic XML.

First, what does it look like? XML is made up of tags, which are words inside pointed greater-than and less-than brackets, ‹ and ›. Understanding what the words inside the brackets stand for is usually easy, but sometimes they are abbreviations or acronyms. Tags can contain other tags, as well as *key=value* pairs, which are called *attributes*. Tags containing other tags or text end with a matching closing tag that includes a / before the tag name.

Consider this short example XML file:

```
❶ ?xml version="1.0" encoding="UTF-8"?>
❷ root>
    <child ❸name="first">
      ❹<grandchild>text could go here</grandchild>
    </child>
    <child name="second" ❺/>
  </root>
```

XML files usually start off in a similar way, with a processing instruction declaring it as XML ❶ and providing version and encoding information. This special tag does not have a corresponding end tag. With this header out of the way, we get straight to the data.

The root element ❷ can be named anything, but you can only have one. For example, HTML only has one ‹html› tag. Within the starting and ending root tags comes the real XML content. In this case, the XML has two child elements. Again, the tags can be named anything, but I've used names that help describe XML terms in this example.

XML is hierarchical, and accessing the data requires understanding its structure. The first child element has a single attribute ❸ and a child element ❹ of its own. The second child element also has an attribute, but it contains no children. When this is the case, we can abbreviate the closing tag ❺.

Now we want to get at this data inside the XML. Reading in the tags and converting them to a structure the computer can understand is called *parsing*. Most languages have some built-in way to parse XML. Next I'll show two JavaScript examples and one using PHP, a server-side programming language.

Parse XML with JavaScript

Every modern browser comes with a way to read in XML content, which makes sense seeing as so much of the Web is built upon the technology. Unfortunately, the various browsers have their differences. Also, getting at deeply nested elements can be a pain.

Before showing an easier way, we'll give it a go in this section using the XML example just described. Rather than loading in an XML file (which I'll get to in the next section), we'll use XML that is stored as a string of text.

Because we are using JavaScript, the file needs to live inside a web page. Everything we'll be doing will be in the JavaScript portion, so the web page will otherwise be blank. Add these lines into a new file:

```
<html>
<head>
<script>
❶   var xmltxt  = "<?xml version=\"1.0\" encoding=\"UTF-8\"?>\n";
      xmltxt += "<root>\n";
      xmltxt += "  <child name=\"first\" />\n";
      xmltxt += "  <child name=\"second\">\n";
      xmltxt += "    <grandchild>text goes here</grandchild>\n";
      xmltxt += "  </child>\n";
      xmltxt += "</root>\n";
   var x = null;
   var output = "";

❷   if (window.ActiveXObject) { // Internet Explorer
     x = new ActiveXObject("Microsoft.XMLDOM");
     x.async = false;
     x.loadXML(xmltxt);
   }
❸   else if (window.DOMParser) { // Other browsers
     var p = new DOMParser();
     x = p.parseFromString(xmltxt, "text/xml");
   }
   else {
       // Can't load XML

   }

   if (x) {
❹     var children = x.getElementsByTagName("child");
❺     for (i=0; i<children.length; i++) {
❻       output += children[i].getAttribute("name") + "\n";
     }
   }
   alert(output);
</script>
</head>
<body></body>
</html>
```

The bold lines are the ones that get at the data. Everything else is pure setup. To be fair, getting the XML text ready ❶ does take seven lines. We could reduce this to a single line, but I've expanded it for clarity.

Parsing the XML requires a multistep approach. First, we need to try the Internet Explorer way ❷. This method will fail if we are using another browser. Then, we get to the use the more widely adopted method ❸. Hopefully this one works, because if it doesn't, we can't parse the XML.

The x variable should contain an XML object after those two tries. This variable is used by the bold section to extract the names of the children. First, we look through the XML for all the child tags ❹. Then, we loop through all of those tags ❺. We can tell which step we're on by the i variable, which starts at zero and counts up each step. Each time through the loop, we add the name of the current child to the text we will output ❻.

If you load this file into a web browser, you should see a JavaScript alert with the names "first" and "second." You've successfully parsed XML with plain ol' JavaScript. Now let's check out how you parse it with the JavaScript library jQuery.

Parse XML with jQuery JavaScript Library

The single principle behind jQuery is to write less code. The hard work is left to the library, which itself is very small (currently less than 20K). When it comes to fetching and parsing XML, jQuery keeps things predictably simple.

Like the plain JavaScript example, we'll be parsing the XML in an otherwise empty HTML file. However, in this case, we'll load our XML straight from a file, which is a common situation. Make sure you have a file named *example.xml* containing the XML from earlier, and then add these lines to a new file in the same directory:

```
   <html>
   <head>
❶   <script src="http://ajax.googleapis.com/ajax/libs/jquery/1.3/jquery.min.js"></script>
   <script>
     var output = "";
❷   $.get("example.xml", {}, ❸function(xml) {
❹     $("child", xml).❺each(function(i) {
         output += ❻this.getAttribute("name") + "\n";
       });
       alert(output);
     });
   </script>
   </head>
   <body></body>
   </html>
```

The first thing you'll notice is that we need to load the jQuery JavaScript file ❶. You can download it to your own server from *http://jquery.com/* or reference a version hosted by Google, as I did in this example. In either case, we get access to the library's many features, which include using Ajax to load files with JavaScript and parsing XML.

The jQuery library makes use of many techniques to decrease the amount of JavaScript you need to write. Among them is the *dollar sign object*, which allows you to access much of jQuery's functionality with very simple syntax. For example, loading an XML file is accomplished by calling the $.get function ❷.

To implement an Ajax call without jQuery requires trying different methods depending on the browser, much like our XML parsing example in the previous section. Instead, jQuery does the work to ensure we can get at the data.

Loading the XML also shows an example of another technique for decreasing code: inline, *anonymous functions*. These functions are part of the standard JavaScript language but become especially useful with the way jQuery simplifies code. When performing an Ajax call, such as the one we use to load our XML file, JavaScript needs a callback function. Rather than creating a named function just to receive the XML results, we can write one inline ❸.

Inside the anonymous function (so named because it doesn't have a name), we use another jQuery shorthand to parse the XML. The parsing happens so fast, you might not even realize it's happening. The dollar sign function is passed the tag name we want, along with the XML variable that holds the content we got back from the Ajax call ❹. Then we chain the jQuery each function to the result, and we can loop through all the child elements ❺. We don't have to use an explicit for loop, nor do we need to determine the number of children. That happens within jQuery.

What we do each time through the jQuery loop is determined by another anonymous function. Again, we just keep everything inline because having a named function for one line of code doesn't make sense. Of course, the code is only one line because we're using jQuery. The this variable holds the current child element, and then we use the same getAttribute function we used in the non-jQuery example to grab the name attribute ❻.

In about half the lines as the previous example, we achieved the same result. If you load the file in your web browser, a JavaScript alert will print the names of the child tags, "first" and "second." jQuery makes it easy to do the stuff you'll do often as you work with APIs and parse data formats, many of which use XML.

Parse XML with PHP

In many cases, you'll want to retrieve XML on your server. To do this, you won't use JavaScript, because you usually write JavaScript inside a web browser; you'll use PHP. PHP is a popular programming language for coding server-side applications. For more about PHP and making sure you have it available on your server, be sure to read Chapter 9.

Let's parse the example XML from the previous sections using PHP. Make sure you have a file named *example.xml* on your server. Create a new PHP file in the same directory and add these lines:

```
<?
❶ $xmltxt = join("\n", file("example.xml"));
❷ $xmlobj = simplexml_load_string($xmltxt);
```

```
foreach (❸$xmlobj->child as $childobj) {
  print($childobj->❹attributes()->name . "\n");
}
?>
```

The first thing we do is load our example XML file into the $xmltxt variable ❶. In many cases, we'll actually be loading the XML from an API. Either way, the XML content ends up in a variable, ready to be parsed.

We pass the work of going through the XML to PHP's SimpleXML class, which is included automatically in PHP 5. The simplexml_load_string function converts the textual XML into a useful object ❷ for accessing the data inside the XML. A simplexml_load_file function is also available, but again, most of the time you'll be converting a string that you retrieved from an API.

Once the XML is in object form, we can look for the name attribute within the child elements. We need to loop through all the child elements ❸, placing the current child inside its own object. Then, we get the attributes ❹ and find the one called name.

The code to query the XML will make more sense if you see what the object that PHP creates looks like. Use print_r($xmlobj) to see a textual representation of the hierarchical object:

```
     SimpleXMLElement Object (
❶     [child] => Array (
        [0] => SimpleXMLElement Object (
❷         [@attributes] => Array (
            [name] => first
          )
        )
        [1] => SimpleXMLElement Object
          [@attributes] => Array (
            [name] => second
          )
❸         [grandchild] => text goes here
        )
      )
     )
```

First of all, everything is inside a single SimpleXMLElement object, just as all the XML is within the root tag. Additional SimpleXMLElement objects are included as well, which is similar to having tags within tags. The SimpleXML class essentially converts XML into a series of arrays.

To begin, a numerical array of all the child elements ❶ is created. In this case, only two child elements are included, numbered 0 and 1, because, as with JavaScript, array indexes in PHP start at zero. Each child has an attributes array ❷, which is associative, meaning it ctontains key and value pairs. The key is the attribute name, in this case name.

Finally, if tags within the tag exist, they're listed. In this case, the second child tag contains a grandchild tag ❸. This tag contains only text, so it's represented as a key and value pair, too. If it contained tags or attributes underneath it, we'd have yet another `SimpleXMLElement`. Again, the `SimpleXML` class is all about finding a way to represent XML inside a PHP object.

Even Simpler XML with XPath

Traversing the `SimpleXML` object works fine in basic cases where the XML file is short and does not include a deep nesting of tags within tags. If you are swamped with XML content, you might find querying with XPath simpler.

Like XML, XPath is a web standard. You can use XPath to traverse down through the XML to the data you want. All you need to do is call the `xpath` function on the `SimpleXML` object and tell it the "path" you want to access.

All three of the following examples find the same element, the grandchild tag, which is nested within two levels of hierarchy.

You can use the full path to the element:

```
$xmlobj->xpath("/root/child/grandchild")
```

Or prepend a double slash to get every grandchild tag, regardless of what tags surround it:

```
$xmlobj->xpath("//grandchild")
```

Or mix and match. Here, we grab any grandchild tag that exists below a child tag:

```
$xmlobj->xpath("//child/grandchild")
```

XPath can help you quickly access XML in even more ways, such as querying for specific values, but I won't cover them here. You can find out more about XPath and `SimpleXML`, in general, at *http://php.net/simplexml*.

I've shown you several methods for accessing XML: JavaScript, the jQuery library, and PHP. What you use depends on where you're getting your XML, how complicated the XML is, and what languages you're already using.

Alternatively, you may grow weary of parsing XML and porting it to your JavaScript maps. Many programmers prefer working directly with a format called JSON that is closer to true JavaScript. Read on to learn about that format, and see "#57: Convert from XML to JSON" on page 198 to learn about turning XML into the easier-to-use JSON.

#53: Use JSON

With JavaScript's ever-increasing popularity on the Web, JSON is quickly becoming the preferred data format for developers. That's because JSON stands for *JavaScript Object Notation* and almost no parsing is necessary to use it in JavaScript. Plus, JSON takes fewer characters than XML to express the same data because it has no closing tags

You aren't restricted to any one language. You can parse JSON in many server-side programming languages. I'll give an example using PHP later. Most modern languages have a data structure that makes converting JSON easy. This, along with JavaScript's popularity, have made this format widely used for interchanging data.

Enough about JSON's usefulness: Let's see an example of what JSON looks like. The following shows how the XML in the previous project might be expressed in JSON:

```
❶ {"child": [
❷   {"attributes": {"name": "first"}},
❸   {"attributes": {"name": "second"}, "grandchild": "text goes here"}
    ]}
```

This basic example is a bit more complex than it needs to be, but it showcases many of the ways data can be organized in JSON. The building blocks are a series of key and value pairs inside braces, a structure called an object in JavaScript. The fun comes with the definition of a value.

In this example, our main object ❶ has only one key, child. The value is an array, declared by the brackets. An array can itself contain a list of values. In this case, the values are yet more objects.

The first object in the array ❷ contains a single key, attributes, and yet another object within it. Finally, the new object, which is three levels deep now, contains a key name and value of first. The second object in the array ❸ has a similar first key-value pair and then a second key, grandchild, which has a textual value.

So, a value can be an array, another object, or plain text. It could also be a number, a boolean, or a null, though I haven't shown that in this example.

Are you confused by the circular definition of what makes a value? That complication is intentional, but it actually ends up being an easy way to express many types of data. Because an object can contain arrays, objects, or even arrays of other objects, many types of hierarchical data can be expressed with JSON in a very small amount of space.

Now that you have an idea of how JSON looks, let's start using it.

Parse JSON with JavaScript and jQuery

Remember what JSON stands for? JavaScript Object Notation. This data format was not only made *for* JavaScript but also made *from* it.

If you are hard-coding JSON into JavaScript, you don't need to do anything to use the data inside it. It is ready to go as written. Here, we access the first child in the example JSON using JavaScript:

```
var obj = {"child": [
  {"attributes": {"name": "first"}},
  {"attributes": {"name": "second"}, "grandchild": "text goes here"}
]};
alert(obj.child[0].attributes.name);
```

I added the portion of the code in bold. Otherwise, this code is the exact JSON from earlier. All I did was assign it to a variable (obj), end the declaration with a semicolon (;), and then alert a specific value from the object.

Of course, JSON is not likely to be written directly into JavaScript. Instead, you'll probably receive it as output from an API. In other words, you might have JSON in text form.

If you trust the data, you can use the JavaScript eval function to convert JSON from text to object. Ensuring you have good data is a smart idea, however, because eval will execute any JavaScript text, not just text in the JSON format.

To avoid potentially large security issues, the parseJSON function has been added in some browsers. But this function is only really useful if it works in every browser. You can use a JavaScript file available at *http://json .org/* to fill the gaps while waiting for every browser to support the latest JavaScript version.

Another option is use the jQuery JavaScript library, which has an easy way to fetch data with Ajax. In fact, you can retrieve and parse JSON within a single line of jQuery.

Add these lines to a new HTML file:

```
<html>
<head>
❶ <script src="http://ajax.googleapis.com/ajax/libs/jquery/1.3/jquery.min.js"></script>
<script>
$.getJSON(❷"example.json", ❸function(jobj) {
    alert(❹jobj.child[0].attributes.name);
  });
</script>
</head>
<body>
</body>
</html>
```

To access the many useful jQuery functions, we need to include the jQuery JavaScript file ❶. Although you can download this file to your server from *http://jquery.com/*, you can also reference a Google-hosted version, as I've done here.

jQuery does much of the difficult work for you and makes writing very short JavaScript that performs advanced functions possible. One of its more apparent ways of reducing code is to introduce the dollar sign object. Much of what happens in jQuery goes through $.

For example, we use the $.getJSON jQuery function to create an Ajax call to download and parse a JSON file. The most important information we need to provide is the JSON URL ❷. This URL can be a local file or a call to an external API.

Next, jQuery requires a function reference. In this case, we use an inline, anonymous function ❸ to describe what we want to do with the JSON result. Again, jQuery is about reducing code, but understanding what is happening here is still important. Ajax fetches our JSON, which is then parsed into an object. That object is returned to the anonymous function, where we can do whatever we want with it. In this case, I create an alert ❹ with the first child's name, just as I did when the data was hard-coded.

NOTE   *If you are calling an external API that returns JSON, for security reasons, that API will need to accept a callback function name. To see an example of this in action, check out how I retrieve JSON from Yahoo! Pipes in "#69: Create a Weather Map" on page 237.*

Building on top of jQuery can save you time and allow you to focus on higher-level issues with your mapping projects. You also get an added layer of complexity because you have one more piece of JavaScript to include in your HTML. Hopefully its benefits make up for this minor cost in loading time.

Parse JSON with PHP

Sometimes you just need the data on the server. If the data is in JSON format, you won't be able to use JavaScript because it's almost always written inside a web browser. Most languages can easily read JSON though, so you'll find it's a reasonable format to use on a server, as well as on a client.

I'll use PHP again as an example server-side programming language because of its availability on most web hosts. If you're new to PHP, I provide an introduction to using PHP for geo projects in Chapter 9.

At the beginning of this project, I said that most languages have a JSON-like data structure. The JavaScript object, with its key-value pairs, is represented as an associative array in PHP. Similarly, PHP also has standard arrays, in addition to strings of text and numbers. In other words, all the pieces are here to represent JSON fully.

Here is some sample PHP that declares the exact same data I used in the sample JSON file:

```php
<?
$obj = array("child" => array(
  array("attributes" => array("name" => "first")),
  array(
    "attributes" => array("name" => "second"),
    "grandchild" => "text goes here")
));
?>
```

Now that we know representing JSON in PHP is possible, how do we go about parsing from text to associative array? Beginning with PHP 5, you can parse JSON with a single call.

Here's an example accessing the name of the first child, with the JSON text hard-coded. Yours will likely come from an API, or possibly a file, instead:

```php
<?
$jtxt = "{\"child\":[" .
        "{\"attributes\":{\"name\":\"first\"}}," .
        "{\"attributes\":{\"name\":\"second\"}," .
        "\"grandchild\":\"text goes here\"}]}";
$jobj = ❶json_decode($jtxt);
print ($jobj->❷child[0]->attributes->name);
?>
```

Yes, all the work is passed off for the internal PHP function ❶ to perform. Instead of using associative arrays, as we did previously, json_decode uses a PHP object. This object is slightly different but has a similar way of expressing data.

The keys, such as child ❷, are instance variables of the object and are referenced with the -> arrow. All other types of data, including regular arrays, go through as-is. Just as with all other examples, the name of the first child can be found three levels down.

The curious reader might be wondering if another function exists to create JSON text from PHP data structures. Of course! The opposite of json_decode is json_encode. You could pass the $obj variable from the first example or the $jobj variable from the second example, and the result would be identical to the JSON text stored in the $jtxt variable.

You will likely need to decode JSON more often than encode it. That said, you'll be glad that function exists when you need it. For an example of encoding JSON, check out "#71: Search Music Events by Location" on page 260.

Though my most recent examples have used PHP, JSON is a rising star of data formats because it incorporates so easily with JavaScript—JSON essentially *is* JavaScript. Now that you know how to read in JSON data securely, you may find yourself on the lookout for APIs that use the format. JSON makes moving on from data parsing easy, so you can do what you really want to do: create awesome, data-filled web maps.

#54: Use GeoRSS

Location is only one tiny piece of information being pushed around the Web. A list of points is much more useful if you include context for what they mean. GeoRSS is a way to add location and other geographic information to content feeds, creating geo-tagged content.

The content itself is commonly blog posts or photos, though it can be anything. Blogs are prime candidates for geo-tagging because most are already syndicated with an RSS feed, a way to get the latest posts without visiting the website.

Although named after RSS, GeoRSS can be used inside formats other than RSS. For example, the United States Geological Survey publishes an Atom feed of recent earthquakes, including the location and depth of each quake. GeoRSS can be added to any XML feed to attach geographic data to other content.

Let's see an example of GeoRSS inside an RSS feed:

```
<?xml version="1.0" encoding="UTF-8"?>
<rss version="2.0" xmlns:georss="http://www.georss.org/georss">
  <channel>
    <link>http://mapscripting.com</link>
    <title>Feed Title</title>
    <description>Feed Description</description>
    <item>
      <pubDate>Thu, 01 Jan 2010 00:01:23 +0000</pubDate>
      <title>Item Title</title>
      <description>Item Description</description>
      <author>Item Author</author>
      <georss:point>45.256 -71.92</georss:point>
    </item>
    ...
  </channel>
</rss>
```

Most of the text is standard RSS. The bold sections are the GeoRSS hooks that add location data to the feed. At the top, you need to include the GeoRSS namespace, which allows you to use the georss: prefix for tags.

In this example, we've declared a point, which is a geographic coordinate. Inside the tag, we put the latitude first, followed by a space, and then the longitude. Sometimes you may see a comma between the numbers. Both are permissible.

GeoRSS has several ways to declare shapes, as well. These shapes are made up of multiple points and often represent a route, border, or other boundary. GeoRSS refers to them as lines, polygons, and boxes.

Lines and polygons are both declared as a sequence of latitude and longitude points:

```
<georss:line>45.256 -110.45 46.46 -109.48 43.84 -109.86</georss:line>
<georss:polygon>
  45.256 -110.45 46.46 -109.48 43.84 -109.86 45.256 -110.45
</georss:polygon>
```

As in this example, a line is at least two coordinates, but it can be many more. In this way, a line could describe a route.

A polygon is declared similarly, but the final point must be the same as the first point. In other words, a polygon is a circular route. It could, for example, be used to describe the outside walls of a house or the border of a country.

A box, on the other hand, will always create a rectangular shape and is declared with only two coordinates:

```
<georss:box>42.943 -71.032 43.039 -69.856</georss:box>
```

If you're confused, that's okay. A rectangle has four corners, so shouldn't a box have four coordinates? It's just like Mapstraction's BoundingBox, covered in "#19: Draw a Rectangle to Declare an Area" on page 71. GeoRSS uses only two corners to determine the box's location. The minimum data you need is the southwest and northeast corners. From those two points, you can extrapolate the northwest and southeast points.

Now that you are a little familiar with GeoRSS, let's use it in a different type of feed. Here is an example of GeoRSS inside the Atom format:

```
<?xml version="1.0" encoding="utf-8"?>
<feed xmlns="http://www.w3.org/2005/Atom"
      xmlns:georss="http://www.georss.org/georss">
  <title>Feed Title</title>
  <updated>2010-01-01T00:01:23Z</updated>
  <author>
    <name>Feed Author</name>
    <email>feedemail@example.com</email>
  </author>
  <id>tag:mapscripting.com,2009-01-01:feedid</id>
  <entry>
    <title>Entry title</title>
    <link href="http://example.org/entry_link"/>
    <updated>2010-01-01T00:01:23Z</updated>
    <summary>Entry summary</summary>
    <georss:point>45.256 -71.92</georss:point>
  </entry>
  ...
</feed>
```

Atom is an alternative to RSS and is a widely supported format. As you can see, for our purposes, it is very similar to RSS. Again, the GeoRSS portions are bold.

You will see GeoRSS most often in RSS and Atom formats. The examples I've shown, however, are the simple version of GeoRSS. The format sometimes looks a bit different, yet it is still GeoRSS. Read on for some examples of alternate GeoRSS encodings.

Use Alternate GeoRSS Encodings

The GeoRSS demonstrated in the previous section is sufficient for most needs and is likely the most common encoding you'll run across. Understanding its shortcomings and recognizing other ways of representing location data is important, however.

GML is the *Geography Markup Language* and is a superset of GeoRSS. GML was created to express any form of geographic information, including topology and coordinate systems other than the latitude/longitude system we've been using (called WGS84).

To make your GeoRSS compatible with GML, you need additional tags. For example, the single tag required to declare a point becomes three tags:

```
<georss:where>
  <gml:Point>
    <gml:pos>45.256 -71.92</gml:pos>
  </gml:Point>
</georss:where>
```

The data communicated with these tags is the same as the simple GeoRSS example. The additional tags are not extraneous, but included because GML allows for more specific uses. For example, the `<gml:Point>` tag is where you would declare another coordinate system.

GML equivalents of the geometric objects used in the simple GeoRSS are available. The method for polygons, lines, and boxes is similar to points. The GML code is wrapped in `<georss:where>` tags. You can find out more about all the options at *http://www.georss.org/gml*.

Whenever you write XML that includes tags with a colon in the name, you'll need to make sure the word before the colon (the namespace) is declared at the top of your XML. Because this example uses both GeoRSS and GML, we need to include both namespaces:

```
xmlns:georss="http://www.georss.org/georss"
xmlns:gml="http://www.opengis.net/gml"
```

Add this code inside the root tag of your XML. For RSS, the root is `<rss>`, and for Atom, it is `<feed>`. Both are necessary because the GML version of GeoRSS uses georss: and gml: tags.

The two forms of GeoRSS shown so far are the most likely encoding methods you'll run into with new data feeds. An old version is still in somewhat wide use, however.

The Basic Geo Vocabulary is an encoding developed by the Worldwide Web Consortium (W3C), an organization that watches over the development of HTML and CSS, among other standards. The development of GeoRSS made the W3C's geo-tags obsolete, but you'll run into them often enough to need to recognize them.

```
<geo:lat>55.701</geo:lat>
<geo:long>12.552</geo:long>
```

The biggest difference between the W3C geo-tags and the ones shown earlier is that the latitude and longitude is declared separately. Because this encoding is popular, this method is yet another allowed to write GeoRSS. You'll need a different namespace to be able to use the geo: tags, however:

```
xmlns:geo="http://www.w3.org/2003/01/geo/wgs84_pos#"
```

Now that you know about the many encodings of GeoRSS, let's see how to use GeoRSS directly with your map.

Display GeoRSS on a Map

Mapstraction makes adding GeoRSS to your map easy. Through a single function, you can layer the GeoRSS without having to parse the XML yourself.

To display GeoRSS, all you need is a publicly accessible feed and a map on which to display it. Toss these lines into a new HTML file to see GeoRSS in action:

```
<html xmlns="http://www.w3.org/1999/xhtml">
  <head>
    <title>Example GeoRSS Map</title>
    <script src="http://maps.google.com/maps/api/js?sensor=false" type="text/javascript">
</script>
    <script src="mxn.js?(googlev3)"></script>
    <style>
    div#mymap {
      width: 550px;
      height: 450px;
    }
    </style>
    <script type="text/javascript">
    var mapstraction;
    function create_map() {
      mapstraction = new Mapstraction('mymap', 'google');
      mapstraction.addOverlay(
❶      "http://mapscripting.com/example-georss.xml", ❷true);
```

```
    }
  </script>
</head>
<body onload="create_map()">
  <div id="mymap"></div>
</body>
</html>
```

Most of this is standard map code; the important lines are in bold. You can see we use Mapstraction's addOverlay function. The first argument is the GeoRSS URL ❶. This address must be available on the public Web, not on your local computer or a password-protected development server. The reason the feed has to be accessible is the underlying mapping provider will make an Ajax call to load the feed. The mapping provider can't make the call if it can't access the URL. If you don't have your own feed, you can use my example from the companion website.

The second argument ❷ is optional. This argument is a boolean, meaning the value is either true or false. It controls whether the map is auto-centered and zoomed in to show only the GeoRSS content.

Load the previous HTML into your browser, and you should see the GeoRSS content on your map. If you're using my example, you'll see routes across several Portland bridges, plus markers that identify landmarks.

Now you're a little more familiar with the GeoRSS format and its trio of encodings. In this section, I've shown how they can be used in RSS and Atom, the two most popular web feed formats. Also, you've learned how, in one line of Mapstraction code, to layer your GeoRSS feed on your map. To see an example of digging into GeoRSS, read "#70: Display Recent Earthquakes Worldwide" on page 247.

#55: Use KML

Google Earth, a three-dimensional geographic browser, popularized KML as a language to share geo-data. The acronym *KML* stands for *Keyhole Markup Language,* named after the company (acquired by Google) who invented it. Nevertheless, KML is an open standard based on XML. KML stores single locations, lists of points, and polygon shapes, among other features. The biggest factor that separates KML from other geographic data formats is that KML can also include styling information, so you can stipulate the color of lines or use custom marker icons.

KML has a special schema, meaning elements are declared in a specific way.

Here's a very basic KML file, containing one location, called a *Placemark*:

```
❶ <?xml version="1.0" encoding="UTF-8"?>
❷ <kml xmlns="http://www.google.com/earth/kml/2">
  <Document>
❸   <Placemark>
❹     <name>Eiffel Tower</name>
❺     <description>The most recognizable place in Paris</description>
```

```
      <Point>
❻       <coordinates>2.29293460923931,48.85819570061303,0</coordinates>
      </Point>
    </Placemark>
  </Document>
</kml>
```

As you put your KML files together, you can view them in Google Earth or on the Google Maps website, as long as the KML is accessible on the web. Try viewing this example at *http://maps.google.com/?q=http%3A//mapscripting.com/example.kml.*

Now let's examine what's inside that example KML file. As with every XML file, a KML file starts with the XML declaration ❶. Then the file points to the KML namespace ❷ to clearly specify we're speaking a particular XML language. With those technical bits out of the way, we can dive into the actual KML content.

The geographic data in a KML file all falls within the `<Document>` tag. Inside that, I add a `Placemark` ❸, which will contain location and other data for a single place. Each Placemark has a name ❹, which is essentially the equivalent of a title in GeoRSS. Similarly, each Placemark also has a description ❺, which can be plain text (as shown) or HTML (with < and > brackets written as < and >).

Arguably the most important piece of data for a Placemark is the actual geographic point. To declare this, we use a `<Point>` tag and then include the coordinates ❻ within it. Note we include three numbers, as opposed to the usual two. The last number represents altitude and is actually optional. We could increase the number, for example, if we wanted our Placemark to declare the top of the Eiffel Tower.

One final, important note about the first two coordinates: Unlike most other geographic data formats, *KML lists longitude before latitude.* This setup is easy to recognize in examples like this and in North America, where longitudes are always negative. But you definitely want to make sure you get these numbers in the right order.

A document generally contains multiple Placemarks, but in this simple example, I only use one. Adding another is easy—just include an additional pair of `<Placemark>` tags.

Now that you've seen a simple location, let's look at some other ways KML marks up geographic data.

Lines in KML

The single point is the basic feature of geographic data—and that holds for KML, as well. Sometimes a point isn't the best way to describe a place. What single point represents a country or a city? A single point can't; you need many points. This is where lines and polygons become useful.

Rather than use a different tag, KML declares both lines and polygons as Placemarks. Unlike the ones shown previously, these Placemarks do not contain a `<Point>` tag because we're actually declaring multiple points at once to represent a single place.

Consider this example, which shows the path of the Golden Gate Bridge in San Francisco:

```
<Placemark>
  <name>Golden Gate Bridge</name>
  <description>A San Francisco landmark, for sure.</description>
❶  <LineString>
❷    <coordinates>
❸      -122.479485,37.827675,0
       -122.477562,37.811028,0
    </coordinates>
  </LineString>
</Placemark>
```

I've omitted the tags that declare this a KML document and instead focused on the Placemark. I include a name and description, just as in the single point example. To describe the bridge, we first add some KML to say this Placemark is a line ❶, and then we insert a series of coordinates ❷ to describe the line.

Of course, a bridge has two ends, so the line is a very simple one using two points. If this were a more advanced line, such as describing a trail or the route of a race, we would just continue adding coordinates in an order such that they could later be connected by line segments.

As in the single point example, we declare three coordinates ❸, listed in longitude, latitude, and altitude order. The altitude is optional, but this coordinate may provide interesting data in some cases, showing the gradient of a trail, for example. This data is hard to show on a two-dimensional web map, but remember KML data is used in other ways, such as in Google Earth.

Polygons in KML

You may recall that in GeoRSS, as well as Mapstraction, a polygon is simply a line that ends at the same point where it begins. The same is true in KML, though the definition can also get a little more advanced with its description of a shape.

Let's stick with something simple here and continue with the world landmark theme. Consider this bit of KML that describes the outer edges of the Parthenon in Greece:

```
<Placemark>
  <name>Parthenon</name>
  <description>A symbol of ancient Greece.</description>
❶  <Polygon>
❷    <outerBoundaryIs>
❸      <LinearRing>
        <coordinates>
          23.726295,37.971539,0
          23.726376,37.971287,0
          23.727116,37.971420,0
```

```
        23.727024,37.971672,0
        23.726295,37.971539,0
      </coordinates>
    </LinearRing>
   </outerBoundaryIs>
  </Polygon>
</Placemark>
```

Notice that inside the polygon declaration ❶ I've include several levels of tags before getting to the familiar coordinates list. The reason for those additional levels is that KML's polygons are much more powerful than this example can communicate.

For example, here I've declared an outer boundary ❷ for the Parthenon, meaning I'm describing the outside walls. If I also use an inner boundary, I can create a rectangular donut to show just the columns of the Parthenon.

Inside a boundary, I use a linear ring ❸ to tell KML that I am creating a line that ends at its starting point. Here KML's polygon begins to look similar to GeoRSS, but with different syntax.

As with the simple line example, the coordinates are a list of longitude, latitude, and altitude (optional) values. We have four corners of the Parthenon to connect, which requires five points. Why not four? The first and the last must be identical—to complete the ring.

Now that you understand basic Placemarks, including lines and polygons, let's see where KML diverges from other geographic data formats: let's get stylish.

Style KML

Describing points, lines, and shapes is a basic building block of communicating geography. You can put these three types of data together and get plenty of information about a place. KML also lets you describe how you want the data to look, which separates it from other formats. Read on to learn how to style your KML.

If you know how HTML and CSS interact, KML styles will seem familiar. As with HTML, you can create styles inline or reference them globally with declarations at the top of your KML file.

A style tag is available for each of the three types of geographic data we've seen so far: <IconStyle>, <LineStyle>, and <PolyStyle>. Within the tag, you can declare an icon graphic, color, line width, and opacity. Here's an example of styles added inside the Eiffel Tower Placemark:

```
<Style>
  <IconStyle>
    <Icon>
      <href>http://mapscripting.com/icons/modernmonument.png</href>
    </Icon>
  </IconStyle>
</Style>
```

This code is the KML equivalent of "#5: Create a Custom Icon Marker" on page 29. However, if you have a document with many points, you could end up with a lot of redundancy if most points share the same marker graphic, which makes declaring styles at the top of the code useful.

You can move the entire <Style> block up, as an immediate child of the <Document> tag. Then, if you give the tag an id attribute, you can reference it below. For example, here is the Parthenon example filled in with white:

```
<?xml version="1.0" encoding="UTF-8"?>
<kml xmlns="http://www.google.com/earth/kml/2">
<Document>
  <Style id="stoneBuilding">
    <LineStyle>
❶    <color>cccccc</color>
    </LineStyle>
    <PolyStyle>
      <color>ffffff</color>
      <fill>1</fill>
❷    <outline>1</outline>
    </PolyStyle>
  </Style>
  <Placemark>
    <name>Parthenon</name>
    <description>A symbol of ancient Greece.</description>
❸    <styleUrl>#stoneBuilding</styleUrl>
    <Polygon>
      <outerBoundaryIs>
        <LinearRing>
          <coordinates>
            23.726295,37.971539,0
            23.726376,37.971287,0
            23.727116,37.971420,0
            23.727024,37.971672,0
            23.726295,37.971539,0
          </coordinates>
        </LinearRing>
      </outerBoundaryIs>
    </Polygon>
  </Placemark>
</Document>
</kml>
```

The portion of the KML that produces the style is in bold. As you can see, most of the styling is already declared by the time we get to the Placemark. Along with the white-shaded polygon, I add a LineStyle to give it a light gray outline ❶. Then, I also make sure the PolyStyle has outlines turned on ❷ via the boolean (1 is on; 0 is off).

Finally, we reference the styles ❸ from the Placemark itself. This reference is created much like a reference to an id within CSS, by prepending a # in front of the style id.

Display KML on a Map

With your KML file on the Web, you can display it on a map in many ways. Earlier, I showed how you can use the Google Maps website to show KML. You can also open it in Google Earth. In this section, we'll see instead how to layer a KML file into your embedded map using Mapstraction.

Start with a brand-new HTML file and add the following code:

```
<html xmlns="http://www.w3.org/1999/xhtml">
  <head>
    <title>Example KML Map</title>
    <script src="http://maps.google.com/maps/api/js?sensor=false" type="text/javascript">
</script>
    <script src="mxn.js?(googlev3)"></script>
    <style>
    div#mymap {
      width: 550px;
      height: 450px;
    }
    </style>
    <script type="text/javascript">
    var mapstraction;
    function create_map() {
      mapstraction = new Mapstraction('mymap', 'google');
      mapstraction.addOverlay(
❶       "http://mapscripting.com/example.kml", ❷true);
    }
    </script>
  </head>
  <body onload="create_map()">
    <div id="mymap"></div>
  </body>
</html>
```

Most of this is a pretty basic map. The part that loads the KML file is in bold. Just like for the GeoRSS, we use Mapstraction's addOverlay function. The first argument is the KML URL ❶. As I've mentioned, this address needs to be available on the public Web, not on your local computer or a password-protected development server. The reason the feed has to be accessible is the underlying mapping provider will make an Ajax call to load the feed. This call won't work if the provider can't access the URL. If you don't have your own feed, you can use my example from the companion website.

The second argument ❷, which is optional, is a boolean, meaning the value is either true or false. This controls whether the map is auto-centered and zoomed in to show only the KML content.

Load this HTML into your browser and you should see the KML content on your map. If you're using my example, you'll see a polyline surrounding the Parthenon.

#56: Use GPX

Are you a hiker, a runner, or a mountain biker? You could use the GPS exchange format, GPX, to track your favorite trails and routes. Most modern GPS devices, which use satellites to triangulate their location, can store this data and output it in GPX format. Even if the data did not originate on a GPS device, this format is useful for sharing any sequence of latitude and longitude points.

GPX really is just another way to store *polylines*, a series of coordinates to connect on a map. Where the format is different is that it also contains useful metadata to make more sense of the dozens of points.

GPX is separated into three types of data:

Tracks A record of a particular trip, including the time at each step

Routes A suggested trip meant to be shared with others, which does not include time information

Waypoints A single point, often used for landmarks or other points of interest

From a technical standpoint, GPX is just XML. Its schema is special, however, and elements are declared in a specific way. Here is an example GPX file:

```
❶ <?xml version="1.0" encoding="UTF-8"?>
❷ <gpx version="1.0" xmlns:xsi="http://www.w3.org/2001/XMLSchema-instance" xmlns="http://
   www.topografix.com/GPX/1/0" xsi:schemaLocation="http://www.topografix.com/GPX/1/0 http://www
   .topografix.com/GPX/1/0/gpx.xsd">

   <trk>
     <name>Dog Walk</name>
❸    <trkseg>
❹      <trkpt lat="45.521270" lon="-122.626111">
❺        <ele>7.125</ele>
❻        <time>2010-09-06T00:14:34Z</time>
       </trkpt>
       <trkpt lat="45.521292" lon="-122.625950">
         <ele>6.831</ele>
         <time>2010-09-06T00:14:37Z</time>
       </trkpt>
       ...
     </trkseg>
   </trk>

</gpx>
```

Most XML files begin in a similar way ❶ to show they contain XML. Then the code points to the GPX schema ❷. With the formalities out of the way, let's dive into the actual data.

This example is showing a track, so we begin by wrapping everything in a <trk> tag. A track has at least one segment ❸, which contains the individual track points ❹. The latitude and longitude are stored as attributes of the <trkpt> tag, with the elevation ❺ and timestamp ❻ as subelements.

A program going through the track points uses differences in the latitude and longitude to determine the distance between points. Similarly, the number of seconds or minutes between timestamps can be used to determine the approximate speed. The elevation numbers can determine the trail's grade. We can learn a lot from the metadata.

Examples of GPX

In addition to trail enthusiasts plotting and sharing their escapades, GPX has other even more useful applications. GPX is bringing geographic data that wasn't included before to rich content like photos and video. A world of volunteer cartographers also use it to map streets and cities.

Walking around snapping shots is something most photographers do with regularity, whether hiking through nature or walking urban streets. By synchronizing the internal times on a GPS and camera, you can get latitude and longitude coordinates for your photos.

Digital cameras usually timestamp each photo. If you have a record of a path, like the one stored in a GPX file, cross-referencing the two is straightforward. Just find the track point with a timestamp closest to the photo's. Update the photo metadata to include the coordinates, and you have now geo-tagged the photo. You can install many programs on your computer that will do this for you.

OpenStreetMap uses GPX to map the world. It sends volunteers to walk the streets with GPS units. Then, the track points, along with other information like street names, are used to create maps that are available for anyone—without licensing fees.

In many countries, such as the United States, much of this street data is already available. OpenStreetMap volunteers, in these cases, are checking accuracy and filling in what's missing. In some places, OpenStreetMap is all there is, so the GPX tracks become incredibly important to the project.

Display GPX Tracks on a Map

Once you have a GPX file, you'll want to do something with it, like show it on a map. Getting at the track points requires parsing the XML and then "connecting the dots" with polylines in Mapstraction.

XML parsing can be painful. I discussed it in detail in the earlier in this chapter. We'll use the jQuery method here, which is as easy as it gets, but it does require a small JavaScript library.

To start, let's lay the groundwork for the GPX map by preparing the basic HTML, CSS, and JavaScript to display a simple map. Put this code into a new HTML file:

```
<html xmlns="http://www.w3.org/1999/xhtml">
<head>
  <title>GPX on a Map</title>
  <script src="http://maps.google.com/maps/api/js?sensor=false" type="text/javascript">
</script>
❶  <script src="http://ajax.googleapis.com/ajax/libs/jquery/1.3/jquery.min.js"></script>
  <script src="mxn.js?(googlev3)"></script>
  <style>
    div#mymap {
      width: 600px;
      height: 450px;
    }
  </style>
  <script type="text/javascript">
  var mapstraction;
  function create_map() {
    mapstraction = new Mapstraction('mymap', 'google');
❷    mapstraction.setCenterAndZoom(new LatLonPoint(0,0), 2);
    mapstraction.addControls({"zoom": "large"});
❸    parse_gpx("gpxfile.gpx");
  }
  </script>
</head>
<body onload="create_map()">
  <div id="mymap"></div>
</body>
</html>
```

We haven't quite parsed the GPX yet. This code just prepares a basic map. Make sure you include your Google Maps API key. Otherwise, everything is ready to go. Before moving on, however, I'd like to point out a few bits.

First, I've included the jQuery JavaScript framework ❶. We'll use it for the Ajax call that will download the GPX file. Also, jQuery makes XML parsing easier, so we'll use it to get at the GPX data.

The eventual location for the map will be determined by the latitude and longitude values inside the GPX file. Because we don't know what those are yet, I centered the map in the middle of the globe ❷. Assuming we're able to load data, that location will only stay for a short time. If you know what city the data will be in, a good practice is to use the coordinates of the city center.

Finally, I make a call to the parse_gpx function ❸, passing a filename. Make sure *gpxfile.gpx* exists in the same directory and has some GPX data. You can find example files at *http://mapscripting.com/gpx-files*.

But wait . . . where is the parse_gpx function? We haven't added it yet, so let's write it! Add these lines below the create_map function:

```
function parse_gpx(filename) {
❶   jQuery.get(filename, {}, function(xmltxt) {
      var pdata = {"color": "blue"};
      var pts = [];
❷     jQuery("trkpt", xmltxt).each(function(i) {
        var lat = ❸parseFloat($(this).attr("lat"));
        var lon = parseFloat($(this).attr("lon"));
❹       var thispt = new LatLonPoint(lat, lon);
❺       pts.push(thispt);
      });
❻     mapstraction.addPolylineWithData(new Polyline(pts, pdata));
❼     mapstraction.autoCenterAndZoom();
    });
}
```

The parse_gpx function is really just a wrapper for the jQuery Ajax call ❶. It grabs the passed filename and returns the XML results to an anonymous, inline function. This is where the real stuff happens. You can see how one of my GPX files looks when added to the map in Figure 8-1.

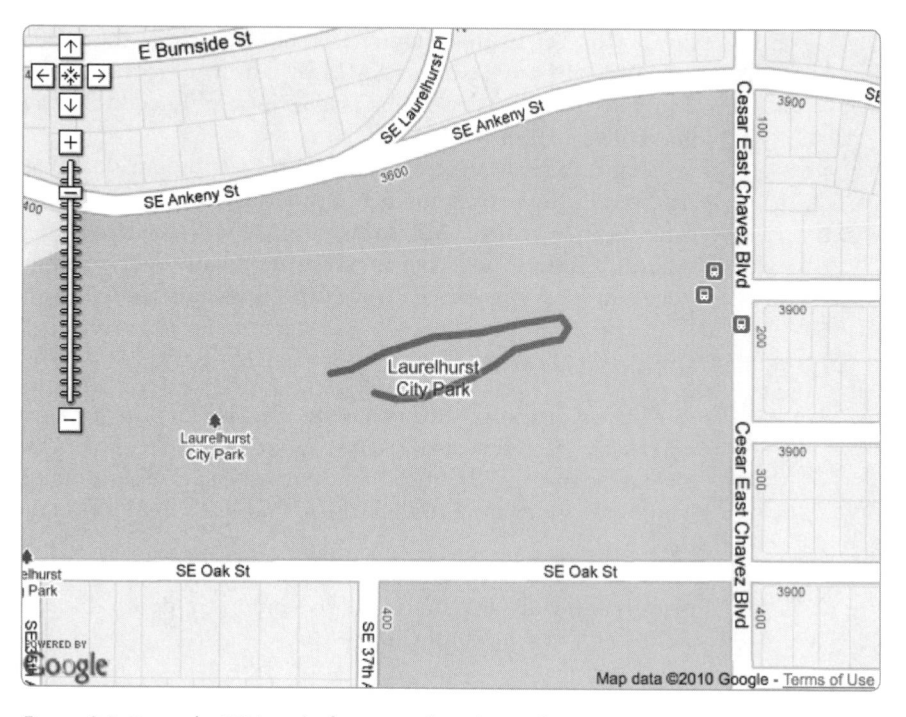

Figure 8-1: Example GPX tracks from a walk in the park

After creating a few variables, the function uses jQuery to look for every `<trkpt>` in the GPX file ❷. For each track point, it calls yet another anonymous function, which is sort of equivalent to a `for` loop. Each time through the loop, the function parses the latitude and longitude of the current track point.

The `parseFloat` JavaScript function ❸ takes the text from the GPX file and turns it into the decimal number (also called a *floating point number*) needed. Again, the function uses jQuery to parse the GPX, but it uses the shorthand dollar sign method.

Before we draw the track on the map, we need to have all the data points to pass to Mapstraction at the same time, as shown in "#16: Draw Lines on a Map" on page 62. We'll use an array to collect the points. Once we have the latitude and longitude of the current track point, we create a `LatLonPoint` with the two values ❹. Then we add the point to the `pts` array ❺.

Once we're outside the loop, we pass our data to draw the Polyline ❻ and then zoom the map automatically to show our entire Polyline ❼. Now we have, in the case of most tracks, a tight view of the GPX data.

#57: Convert from XML to JSON

As I've mentioned, XML is not always the easiest format to use with JavaScript. Yet, as this chapter has shown, most of the formats you'll be working with are flavors of XML. By now you probably prefer JSON, right? To make things easier on the JavaScript, we'll need to do a little extra work and convert from XML to JSON.

A number of ways are available for getting our data from XML to JSON. And really, the conversion is not that difficult an operation. For example, once we load either XML or JSON into PHP, the data is very similar. In this section, I'll show how you can convert on your own server and also introduce you to a nifty service from Yahoo! called Pipes.

Convert Using PHP

Most Unix or Linux servers have a copy of PHP already running, which makes it a great server-side language to learn. We'll use PHP to read in and parse some XML and then turn around and encode it into JSON. The whole process takes just a few lines, thanks to helper functions included in PHP 5.

Even if you don't have a server, or PHP is not accessible, you can likely install it on your own machine. For a more in-depth discussion of PHP, you'll want to check out Chapter 9.

To start converting, create a new PHP file and add these lines:

```php
<?
$xmltxt = ❶get_url("http://mapscripting.com/example.xml");
❷ $xmlobj = simplexml_load_string($xmltxt);
$jtxt = ❸json_encode($xmlobj);
print $jtxt;
?>
```

Like I said, this code isn't very complicated, is it? To get the XML text, I use a helper function ❶ I wrote, which is explained in "#61: Retrieve a Web Page" on page 215. You could also read in the file directly, as we did when parsing XML with PHP.

Once we have the XML text, we convert it first to a PHP object ❷. This parses the hierarchy of the XML file into a format PHP can understand directly. Because JSON is so close to data structures found within PHP, a simple call ❸ is all that's needed to encode the JSON. Then we print it and voilà—we have converted data formats.

Convert Using Yahoo! Pipes

Don't have server-side chops, or just don't want to deal with additional code? Many folks are turning to a service from Yahoo! called Pipes. Pipes reads in various data formats, lets you massage the data if you want, and then outputs it as either XML or JSON.

Why use Yahoo! Pipes instead of your own server? For one, the conversion process is even easier than using PHP. Plus, no code is required because Pipes has a graphical, drag-and-drop interface. You also get the benefit of Yahoo!'s infrastructure. Yahoo! decides how often to check for new content and deals with caching the most recent copy—something we didn't do at all in the PHP example.

The downside to relying on Pipes? It introduces another point of failure. Even if your server is humming along, your map might not work if Pipes crashes. Although you can likely count on Yahoo! for uptime, what if the company decides the Pipes product isn't worth keeping around? You'd be hung out to dry.

To me, the ease of using Pipes outweighs the detractions. Let's see just how easy converting from XML to JSON with Pipes is.

You'll need a Yahoo! account to store your Pipes. Log in at *http://pipes.yahoo.com/pipes* and click **Create a Pipe** to go to a blank canvas, with options on the left. First, Pipes requires a data source, so drag a Fetch Feed source on to the canvas. Paste your feed URL into the box, or use *http://mapscripting.com/example.xml*.

Now a second box called Pipe Output should also appear at the bottom of the workspace. Drag the circle at the bottom of the Fetch Feed box to the circle at the top of the Pipe Output. This connects the elements to create a complete Pipe, as shown in Figure 8-2. Go ahead and try it and you should see sample output in the debugger at the bottom of the workspace.

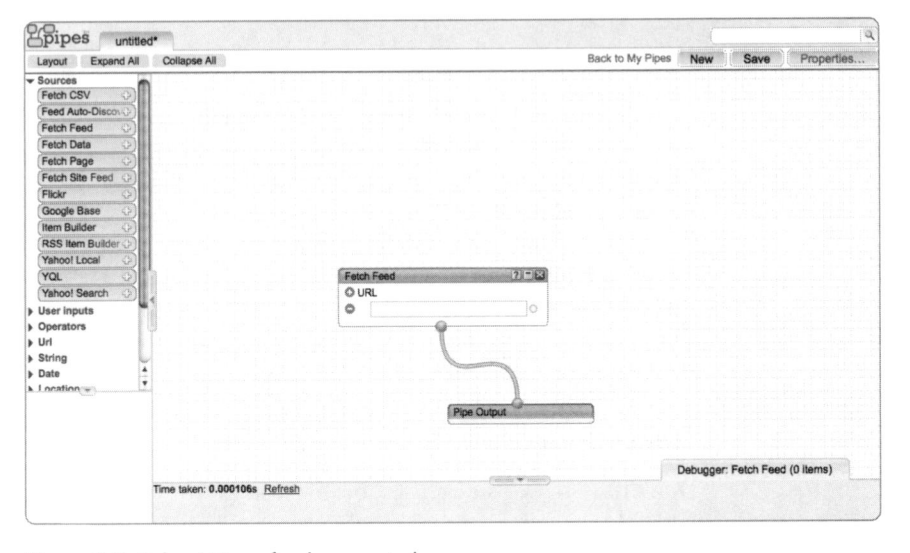

Figure 8-2: Yahoo! Pipes feed connected

Here's where things get really interesting: *You're done.* Save the Pipe, and then click **Run Pipe**. You should see your content within the Pipes interface. At the top of your content, you'll see a Get as JSON link. That's the URL to your converted data run through Yahoo!'s servers. Now you can order new business cards because you're a certified data plumber!

#58: Filter, Merge, and Sort Data with Yahoo Pipes!

APIs and RSS feeds are becoming commonplace. So much of the Web's content is now available in a format that programmers are quickly able to use, which is great. The downside is that another problem has been created: Getting at just the right information can be tough.

Sometimes a feed is a fire hose when a garden variety hose would do. Other times you have to combine multiple sources before you get the information you really need. Yahoo! Pipes has an easy interface for solving both issues—by filtering and merging data.

Much of this data-munging is stuff programmers have been doing manually using server-side scripts. Sometimes that will still be necessary, but Yahoo! Pipes is able to solve the common scenarios. Plus, for reasons described in the previous project, offloading some of this work onto Yahoo!'s servers provides some major benefits.

Before you create a Pipe, you'll need at least one data source. This source is often an RSS feed and, for map-related projects, may be GeoRSS. A Pipe is a way to transform data sources. The data comes in the Pipe, some stuff happens, and then the data flows out of the Pipe. If you have a data source, then let's start working on that "stuff" part. You can begin by editing the Pipe we created in the previous section.

Filter Your Feed's Content

Rather than simply running our feed through Pipes, let's try filtering out certain content. To do this, we'll need to drag a Filter box from the Operators menu. You can place the box anywhere in the workspace, but placing it between the Fetch box and the Output box may make the most sense.

Next, you'll need to connect the feed to the filter. Drag the circle at the bottom of the Fetch box to the top of the Filter box. Then connect the Filter box to the Pipe Output by dragging the filter's bottom circle to the output's top circle.

Of course, the filter isn't useful unless it's actually filtering some content. You can do this two ways with Pipes: You can filter *in* or filter *out*. At the top of the Filter box, you can select **Block** to filter out and **Allow** to filter in.

Pipes can filter based on any fields in the feed. A common choice is the title, which, for RSS, is *item.title*. Click the arrow next to the first text area in the filter box (see Figure 8-3) and you'll see a list of available fields. Then you can type the words you want to filter in the second text field. The drop-down box lets you perform some basic types of filtering on the field, including greater-than/less-than for numbers.

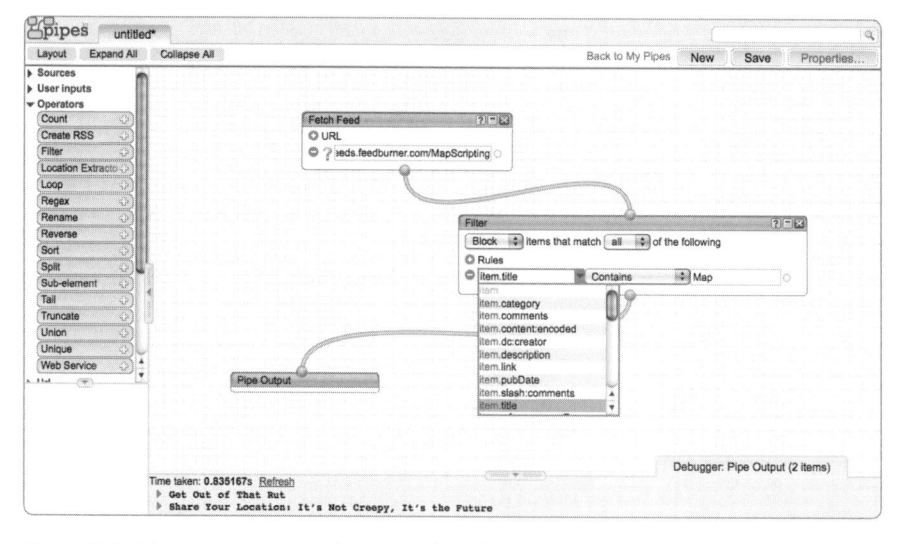

Figure 8-3: Filtering out items with map *in the title*

If you want additional filters, just click the plus sign next to Rules. Otherwise, your Pipe is complete. Save it, and then click **Run Pipe**. Your filtered feed will be shown within the Pipes interface. To get this new feed, choose **Get as RSS** or **Get as JSON**. If you are reading the feed in to use with JavaScript, JSON is probably your best choice.

Merge Two or More Feeds

What if you have two similar feeds that you want to combine? Pipes is very good at this! Create a new Pipe and drag two Fetch Feed boxes to the canvas (see Figure 8-4). Choose two feeds (if you're short of examples, you should be able to find an RSS feed from your favorite blogs or websites) and insert their URLs into the Fetch Feed boxes.

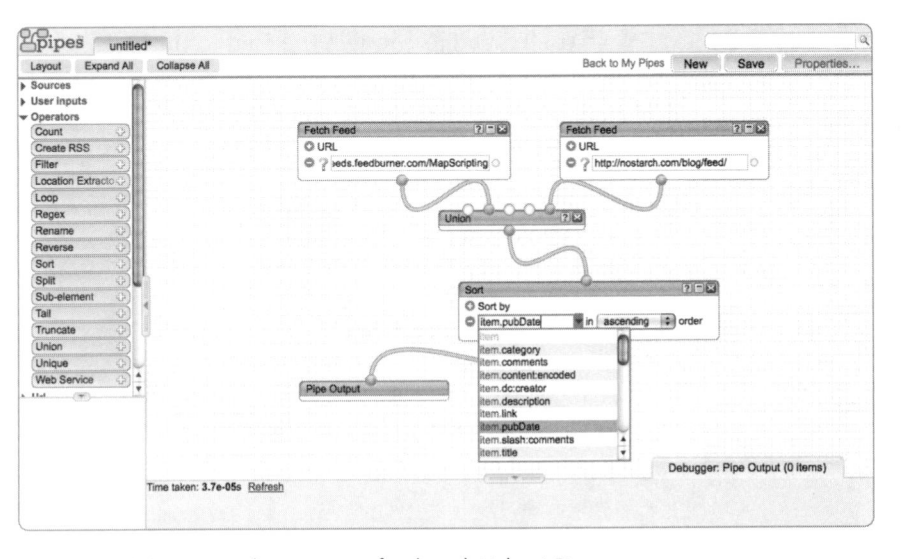

Figure 8-4: Merging and sorting two feeds with Yahoo! Pipes

If the feeds are of the same variety and you don't plan to filter anything, you can actually use a single Fetch Feed box. Just click the plus sign next to URL. In many cases, you'll want to have the option to perform more advanced operations, so I recommend using a Fetch Feed for each individual feed.

To combine the two feeds, we'll need a Union box from the Operators menu. Drag the Union box to the canvas below the two Fetch Feed boxes. Drag the circle below each feed to one of the five circles at the top of the Union box. Finally, drag the circle at the bottom of the Union box to the Pipe Output.

Your feeds are combined in the order they were added to the Union box (left to right). In other words, the second feed's content is only seen after the entire contents of the first feed. This arrangement is not ideal. Most likely, you usually want to see the content in the order it was published. Pipes can do the sorting for you.

Drag a Sort operator to the canvas. Connect the bottom circle of the Union box to the top of the Sort box. Then connect the bottom of the Sort box to the Pipe Output. You'll need to choose a field to sort by clicking the arrow next to the text field within the Sort box. To use the date, select **item.pubDate**. Now save the Pipe and you're done.

You've now filtered, merged, and sorted with Yahoo! Pipes. You can transform data into whatever you want it to be. In fact, if you dig through the documentation a bit (*http://pipes.yahoo.com/pipes/*), you'll realize Pipes is even more powerful than the few examples I've shown. You can load feeds dynamically, use web services, and even extract location from text. Best of all, when you're done, the data is in a format that is easy to read in and plot on a map.

9

GO SERVER-SIDE

Mapping APIs are popular because they bring a lot of power to the web browser that used to be much more difficult for the average developer to achieve. Plenty of situations still exist, however, where your application will benefit from scripts that run *outside* of the browser. This is when you'll need to go server-side.

In this chapter, we'll look at two popular technologies that run on a server: PHP, a programming language used mostly to output web pages; and MySQL, a database for storing text, numbers, and a whole lot more. As opposed to the numerous other available technologies, I've chosen these two for their ubiquity—almost all web hosts support them. They are also solid platforms used by many including, most notably, Yahoo!.

Entire books have been devoted to PHP and MySQL, together and separately. I'll only provide a very quick primer to get you started. Then we'll dive into how each can help you make better maps, including storing locations and finding the nearest locations from your database.

#59: Install PHP

PHP is an extremely popular programming language for easily creating dynamic web pages and applications. You can install it on your computer for testing or on a server for sharing with the world. In fact, if you have web hosting on a server, PHP may already be installed.

You need to use PHP in conjunction with a web server, the most common of which is Apache. Requests come from a web browser to your web server, which then looks to see if the page being requested uses PHP. If it does, then the page is sent to PHP for processing.

Next I show several ways to install PHP—or to determine if it is already installed. In only one situation will you have to also worry about installing Apache. Read on and we'll get you up to speed with PHP.

Check Your Web Host for PHP

If you already have web hosting, you almost certainly have PHP installed already. The easiest way to check is to create a simple PHP file and then try accessing it with a web browser.

You'll want to put this new file where you already know HTML files can be accessed. Your site administrator (who could also confirm whether you are able to access PHP) can point you to your public directory where web pages are stored.

Create a new PHP file in your web directory and add these few lines:

```php
<?php
  print phpinfo();
?>
```

Easy enough. Give the file a name ending in *.php* (I creatively chose *test.php*), and then from your web browser, go to its public web address. For example, I might go to *mapscripting.com/test.php*.

If you see your own code when you load that file, then you probably don't have PHP. You'll need to ask your administrator to install it or find another way to use PHP. You'll know PHP is installed, however, if you see an information page like the one shown in Figure 9-1. Remember to delete the file from your server when you're done.

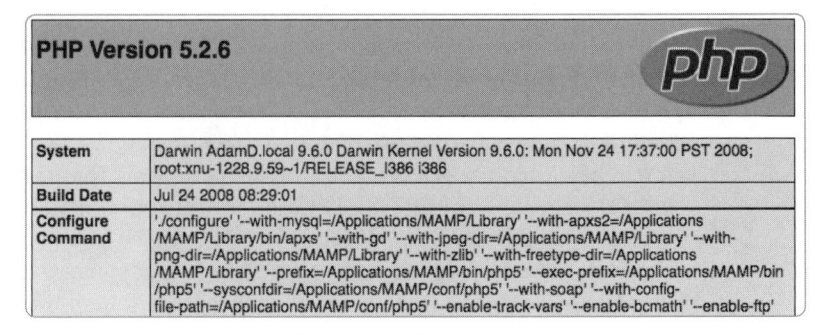

PHP Version 5.2.6	
System	Darwin AdamD.local 9.6.0 Darwin Kernel Version 9.6.0: Mon Nov 24 17:37:00 PST 2008; root:xnu-1228.9.59~1/RELEASE_I386 i386
Build Date	Jul 24 2008 08:29:01
Configure Command	'./configure' '--with-mysql=/Applications/MAMP/Library' '--with-apxs2=/Applications /MAMP/Library/bin/apxs' '--with-gd' '--with-jpeg-dir=/Applications/MAMP/Library' '--with-png-dir=/Applications/MAMP/Library' '--with-zlib' '--with-freetype-dir=/Applications /MAMP/Library' '--prefix=/Applications/MAMP/bin/php5' '--exec-prefix=/Applications/MAMP/bin /php5' '--sysconfdir=/Applications/MAMP/conf/php5' '--with-soap' '--with-config-file-path=/Applications/MAMP/conf/php5' '--enable-track-vars' '--enable-bcmath' '--enable-ftp'

Figure 9-1: The PHP info dumped by my local machine

If you're new to PHP, you might want to skip ahead to "#60: A Quick PHP Introduction" on page 208. Otherwise, you need to check whether you have MySQL installed, too (see "#62: Install MySQL" on page 217), or connect PHP to MySQL (see "#65: Use MySQL from PHP" on page 225).

Use a Packaged Installation of PHP

The easiest way to install PHP on your own computer is to download a package for your operating system. The upside to this method is that you'll also get Apache and MySQL at the same time, which is useful.

The names of the packages are patterned after the popular server architecture, *LAMP*, which stands for *Linux*, *Apache*, *MySQL*, and *PHP*:

- Windows (WAMP): *http://www.wampserver.com/*
- Macintosh (MAMP): *http://www.mamp.info/*

Either of these packages should install on your computer without needing much information from you (though you may have to enter an administrator password).

Open WAMP/MAMP once the install process has completed. The program should open two windows. First, it will open a small status dashboard, as shown in Figure 9-2. Second, the application will also create a new web browser window pointed at *localhost*, the name of the server on your own computer. By default, you'll see a welcome screen.

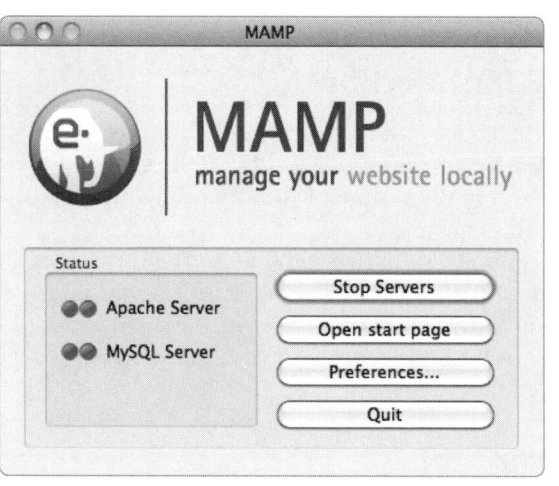

Figure 9-2: The MAMP console

You'll want to change the directory that WAMP/MAMP uses to look for your files. To do this, click the **Preferences** button, which will open a new pane with more options. Click the Apache (web server) tab, and then select a new document root, as shown in Figure 9-3.

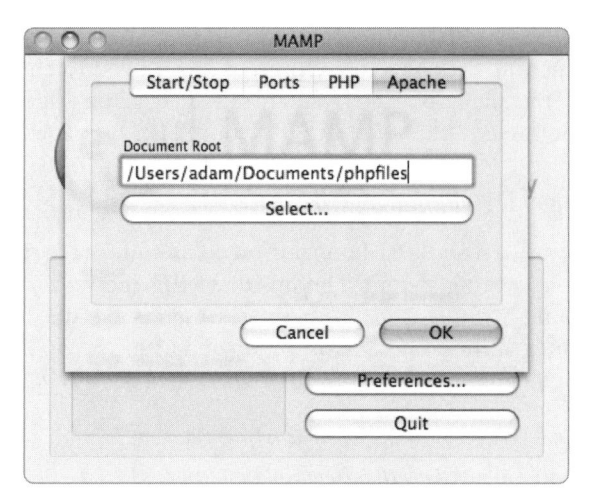

Figure 9-3: Change the MAMP document root.

Install PHP Yourself

If you're using an operating system for which a package is not available, you'll need to install PHP yourself. Too many variations exist to describe in this chapter, but many tutorials are available on the Internet to help you.

The PHP website is the first place to start: *http://php.org/*.

#60: A Quick PHP Introduction

Some very thick books—much thicker than this one—are dedicated to teaching you how to program with PHP. This project will provide the boost necessary to use PHP in some of your mapping projects. It will not, however, make you a master.

In the sections that follow you'll learn the very basics about structuring PHP code. I'll also show you how to use conditionals, often called *if statements*. Next, you'll learn how to work with arrays and then use loops. Finally, I'll show how to create your own functions to reduce the amount of PHP you need to write.

The Nitty Gritty

PHP code is usually added to a file that ends with a *.php* extension. When the program is finished running, the output is most often HTML (though it can also be XML, JSON, or any text that can be transferred using HTTP). As such, PHP can be interspersed with plain HTML.

The PHP portions of the code are surrounded by a special *twi-character blocks*, <?php and ?>. For example, try this small bit of code, which combines PHP and HTML:

```
<html>
<body>
<?php
  print "This text comes from PHP!";
?>
</body>
</html>
```

This code is abbreviated HTML, of course. But from it, you should get an idea of how PHP works. And the code will load into a browser and simply display the text within the quotes, which is output by PHP's print function. Note the semicolon—most lines of PHP end with a semicolon. Exceptions exist, however; if you write a command on a single line, chances are it needs a ; at the end.

Variables store values that can be changed or accessed later. They can hold numbers, text, and more and usually have a descriptive name, always starting with a dollar sign. For example, $mynum could be a variable for holding a single number.

Here is some code similar to the previous code, but containing a few variables:

```
   <html>
   <body>
   <?php
❶   $msg = "This is text";
❷   $mynum = 5 + 1;
❸   $msg = $msg . " and a number: " . $mynum;
     print $msg;
   ?>
   </body>
   </html>
```

When you run this example, it produces the following output:

```
This is text and a number: 6
```

The code starts with a text variable ❶, often called a *string*. This variable starts the line that will eventually be the code's output. Next, you create a number variable ❷. I could have simply set this variable to 6, but I wanted to show how to add two numbers together.

In the final line ❸ before outputting our message, I set the string equal to itself and then concatenate it with more text, before finally tacking the number onto the end. Note that to combine strings, you use a period, but to combine numbers, use a plus sign.

If we replaced the plus in line ❷ with a period, the number output at the end of the message would be 51 (five followed by a one, instead of the number five added to the number one). If we replaced the first period in line ❸ with a plus sign, the entire message would be 06, because the number representation of text is zero.

Using the correct operator to combine numbers and text is important because the operator you use can change your output a great deal.

Taking Input

You can accept input from the user in two ways: from the URL itself or through a form. Regardless of which possibility you choose, the method for accessing this data within PHP is very similar.

If input is being passed in the URL, you'll see something like this:

```
yourfile.php?msg=Hello+there&num=42
```

To get at this info, you'll need to use a special PHP variable called $_GET. $_GET is an associative array, which is a collection of key-value pairs accessed using bracket syntax. Generally, you'll want to take the value from this array and put it into a new variable.

For example, here is some PHP to access the two pieces of input:

```
<html>
<body>
<?php
  if ($_GET["msg"] != "" && $_GET["num"] != "") {
❶    $msg = $_GET["msg"];
❷    $mynum = $_GET["num"];
❸    print "Your message is " . $msg . " and your number is " . $mynum;
  }
?>
</body>
</html>
```

Here's the output of this PHP program:

```
Your message is Hello there and your number is 42
```

To grab the message ❶, I put the key used in the URL (i.e., msg=Hello+there) inside brackets after the $_GET variable.

NOTE *The name of the variables do not need to match the names used in the URL, though they can.*

Now I want to get at the number, which is the `num=42` section of the URL. I use the same method as in the previous code ❷, even though this is a number. Finally, I print out both of my new variables, along with some descriptive text ❸. Notice the periods used to concatenate the portions of the output.

Retrieving data from a form is very similar. Instead of `$_GET`, you use the variable `$_POST`. The only tricky part is that the form must have been sent to this page using the `action` attribute in HTML.

If This Is True, Then Do That

Your PHP programs need to make decisions. Because they aren't able to do this on their own, you need to tell them how to decide what to do. You do this using a *conditional*—or *if* statement.

We'll build upon the previous example, where we received input in the URL, but we'll just use the number portion. We want to look at the number and provide different output if the number is a double digit number (10 or greater).

Our URL will look something like this: *yourfile.php?num=42*.

And here is the code, including our two conditions:

```
    <html>
    <body>
    <?php
❶    $mynum = $_GET["num"];
     if (is_numeric($mynum)) {
❷    if ($mynum < 10) {
       print "Your number is less than 10!";
     }
❸    else {
       print "You have double digits!";
     }
     }
    ?>
    </body>
    </html>
```

First, we grab the number that was passed in the URL ❶. This number is stored in a variable that can now be used in the rest of the program. We use this variable to create an `if` statement ❷, which checks if the number is less than 10. If it is, a message to that effect is output.

Notice the curly braces, { and }, after the `if` statement. These hold all the code that is run when the `if` statement holds true. Otherwise, everything in the curly braces after the `else` ❸ is run instead. You can have an `if` without an `else`, but in this case, we want to do something in either of the cases, not just one.

Table 9-1: Comparison Operators

Operator	Description	When used
==	Equal	Numbers or text
!=	Not equal	Numbers or text
>	Greater than	Mostly numbers
<	Less than	Mostly numbers
>=	Greater than or equal	Mostly numbers
<=	Less than or equal	Mostly numbers

There are six operators, shown in Table 9-1, to use when comparing variables. The operators are most useful to compare numbers, but can also be used to compare text.

Quite the Array

So far I've shown two types of variables: text and numbers. Two other common types are available, which I'll introduce in this section.

The first is an *array*. An array is a single variable that holds many other variables so you don't have to name them individually. A simple array tracks the values it holds by index, which starts counting at zero. You can declare an array like so:

```
$beatles = array("John", "Paul", "George", "Ringo");
```

In this example, I used text. An array can also hold numbers, or a combination of numbers and text. It can also hold other arrays and objects, but let's keep it simple for now. Notice that the array function takes any number of values, separated by commas.

Here is the line of code to print George (the third option):

```
print $beatles[2];
```

Notice the index is 2, instead of 3. That's because the index starts at 0. And the index goes inside square brackets [and] when accessing the values.

The other kind of array I want to show you is called an *associative array*. Instead of using an index to track the values inside the array, it uses a textual key.

For example, you could access George using an associative array in this way:

```
print $beatles["guitarist"];
```

We still use the bracket notation, but instead of our index, we use our text key. And here is how that associative array may have been declared:

```
$beatles = array("singer" => "John", "bassist" => "Paul",
                 "guitarist" => "George", "drummer" => "Ringo");
```

As with a standard array, the items are separated by commas inside the array function. In this case, however, key => value pairs are used to declare how each item in the array will be accessed.

In the next section, I'll show how you could loop through array values.

Feelin' Loopy

If you want to do the same thing many times, you can achieve this by using a loop structure. This section will include the for and foreach loops in PHP. We'll visit each value in an array and output its contents.

Consider this simple array:

```
$bandmates = array("Simon", "Garfunkel");
```

Now let's loop through it and print out each name:

```
$upperBound = count($bandmates) - 1;
for ($idx = 0; $idx <= ❶$upperBound; ❷$idx++) {
❸   print $bandmates[$idx];
❹   if ($idx < $upperBound) {
      print " and ";
    }
}
```

When you run this code, it will print out the name of the band:

```
Simon and Garfunkel
```

We do this by creating an index variable, starting at zero. The program goes through the loop until that index variable is no longer less than the total number of items in the array ❶. The increment operator ++ is used to increase the index by one each time ❷.

To print the name simply means accessing the current index in the array variable ❸. Then, it also prints some text between the names, but only when the index is less than the total number minus one ❹. Because the total number is two, this will only happen during the first time through the loop, when zero is less than one.

If you add your last name as a third item in the $bandmates variable and run the code again, you'll see another and thrown in (and you'll have put yourself in the band).

Let's use another loop to go through an associative array. We'll stick with the same band, but focus our attention on their hair instead. Is it straight or curly? Consider this associative array:

```
$bandhair = array("straight" => "Simon", "curly" => "Garfunkel");
```

Now let's loop through this array to share what we know about their hair:

```
foreach ($bandhair as $description => $name) {
  print $name . " has " . $description . " hair. ";
}
```

Finally, here's the output:

```
Simon has straight hair. Garfunkel has curly hair.
```

In this case, we're accessing both the key and the value in each element of the associative array. Then, at each step, we're printing them both out.

Get Functional

Creating your own functions in PHP can save you time typing. You'll also find it's good practice. The way you create PHP functions is quite similar to JavaScript, so you may be closer than you realize to being able to use your own functions.

For this example, we'll create a function that takes a number as input and returns that same number quadrupled. This function may not be especially useful, but it is just simple enough to teach how functions work in PHP.

Within your PHP brackets, <?php and ?>, include this code:

```
     function quadruple(❶$somenum) {
❷      $newnum = $somenum * 4;
❸      return $newnum;
     }
```

Like I said, a simple function: It contains a name and is passed a single variable ❶. This variable is local to just this function, meaning it doesn't have to exist elsewhere. You can name the variable whatever you want.

Then I created another variable ❷ to hold the quadrupled value. This variable is also local, so we're just using it inside the function. Note that the multiplication operator is an asterisk. Armed with our new value, we need to pass it back out ❸ to whichever line of code called our new quadruple function.

Now let's call our function. And to show how useful this function is, we'll call it on several numbers in a row using an array and a loop. Create a new PHP file with this code:

```
<html>
<body>
<?php
  $allnums = array(4, 18, 21);
  foreach ($allnums as ❶$thisnum) {
❷  $quadnum = quadruple($thisnum);
  print $thisnum . " quadrupled is " . $quadnum . "! ";
}

function quadruple($somenum) {
  $newnum = $somenum * 4;
  return $newnum;
}
?>
</body>
</html>
```

Here I've used a foreach loop on a regular, nonassociative array. To do this, I simply use one value ❶ instead of a key-value pair. Then, for every item in the array, I use the new function to quadruple the number ❷.

When all is said and done, here is the output:

```
4 quadrupled is 16! 18 quadrupled is 72! 21 quadrupled is 84!
```

And with that, you know the basics of PHP. You've interspersed it with HTML. You learned several types of variables: numbers, text, arrays, and associative arrays. You can help your code think with conditionals, and you can use loops and functions to keep your code small and reusable.

To learn how to grab web pages or connect PHP to a web service, continue to the next section. And to connect PHP to a database, you'll want "#65: Use MySQL from PHP" on page 225.

#61: Retrieve a Web Page

One of the most common reasons to use a server-side language like PHP is to be able to make calls to web services. Some services provide a result that can be read directly into the browser with JavaScript. Taking these calls server-side gives you more freedom to use or store the results, however.

Calling a web service is exactly like loading a web page. You pass a URL to a server, and it responds with code (HTML for a web page, usually XML for a web service). In PHP, the code is put into a string variable, which holds a bunch of text. From there, you can do whatever you want with the web page—print it out, cut it apart, parse it into data, store it away. But first, let's just work on *getting* the web page.

PHP 5 comes with a standard library called *cUrl*. The library is all about making network connections. In earlier versions of PHP, you might have used the file function to do this, which was kind of duct-taped on. Switch to cUrl—it's made for doing URL grabbing.

Of course, the file function is so easy. Just one line and you had the content from a web page. As you'll see, cUrl is a little bit more involved. Let's make our own function, however, so we can reuse it in many places (as I have done several times in this book). Then we'll have all the convenience of file with the power of cUrl.

In an empty PHP file, add the following code:

```php
<?php
// Additional code may go here

// cUrl function
function get_url(❶$url) {
❷    $c = curl_init();
❸    curl_setopt($c, CURLOPT_URL, $url);
❹    curl_setopt($c, CURLOPT_RETURNTRANSFER, 1);
     $content = trim(❺curl_exec($c));
❻    curl_close($c);
❼    return $content;
}
?>
```

Our function, which I've named get_url, has one parameter, the URL ❶. This input is what it needs to do its job, which is to fetch a web page. Once inside the function, we need to initialize a cUrl object ❷, so we can begin using it.

Now let's tell cUrl what we need by setting options. First, we tell it the URL we want to fetch ❸. Then we explain that we want to get back the content the URL will send ❹. Some people use cUrl to send information only, in which case they don't care about the reply. We do.

Notice that each time we set options, we passed the $c variable that we created when we initialized cUrl. That variable is important because it keeps track of the options we set and the status of our cUrl session.

With the options set, we make the call to the URL ❺ with the content stored in a normal variable. First, we run it through the trim function to remove any spaces or carriage returns from the beginning and end of the file. Otherwise, we get the exact data that a web browser would get.

Now we'll clean up our mess, so we tell cUrl that we're done ❻. Then the most important part: We return the content ❼ from this function. This is how we get the results of the web page out of the function and into whatever variable we declare.

Let's test our new function. Below the `Additional code may go here` line, let's add this line, which will grab the home page of the book's website:

```
$htmlcode = get_url("http://mapscripting.com");
print $htmlcode;
```

If you load your PHP file into a browser, you should get a web page. The web page is coming from your new function! Open *http://mapscripting.com/* in another browser window, and you'll see almost the same thing, though styles and images might be missing from your copy—that's because you're only loading the HTML.

What's the big deal with using PHP to show the stripped-down version of this book's website? It isn't a big deal; this is just a proof of concept. The really great stuff comes when you download XML from a web service. I show more of how that works in "#52: Use XML" on page 174.

Include Your Function in Other Scripts

One way to make your get_url function accessible in other PHP scripts you write is to copy and paste it in every time. Of course, cutting and pasting each time is the hard way and difficult to keep up-to-date if you change the function; you would have to change it everywhere that you pasted it.

Instead, create an include file that you can call from other scripts. Take the previous code, not including the two lines we used to test the function, and put them in a new file. I named the file *net_func.inc.php*, thinking I might add more network-related functions down the road. I gave a non-*.php* extension to the file because I didn't want it to be mistaken for something that can be shown directly to a web browser.

Now start a new PHP file, so you can test including your new function file:

```
<?php
include("net_func.inc.php");
$htmlcode = get_url("http://mapscripting.com");
print $htmlcode;
?>
```

The results from this test should be the same as the previous test. Only now the code for the get_url function is separate from the code that calls it, which will allow us to use it easily in many places.

#62: Install MySQL

MySQL is a popular database platform that is available across most operating systems. You can install it on your own computer, and you can also run it on a web server, which means using it as a data source for applications is easy.

For the uninitiated, a *database* contains one or more tables that are used to store data. At a very crude level, you can think of a database as a spreadsheet, like a Microsoft Excel file, that can be accessed in part or whole and filtered for only the stuff you care about. Instead of worksheets, you have tables. Every row of a worksheet is a new *database record*. The columns across the top of most worksheets are the *database fields*—they describe the data that goes in that column. In fact, when people talk about databases, they often speak about rows and columns.

The SQL part of MySQL stands for *structured query language*, the syntax to communicate with a database server. MySQL and many other database servers use a standard set of statements (called SQL-92), though each also has its own dialect.

You will find MySQL most useful when combined with some other technologies. The examples in this chapter use PHP for a programming language and Apache for a web server. Read on, however, to get the details about using MySQL by itself.

Check Your Web Host for MySQL

If you have web hosting, you may have MySQL installed already. You'll want to look in your control panel or double-check with your administrator that MySQL is available and set up for your account. Ask about one or both of these two common methods for using MySQL:

phpMyAdmin   A web dashboard for accessing MySQL. As the name implies, PHP must also be installed. By using this method, you can create database tables and look at data in a visual, point-and-click manner that beginners often prefer.

Command Interpreter   A command-line utility that lets you access MySQL from a text interface. Creating database tables and all other operations occur via typed commands.

All examples in this chapter will be shown using both methods. In some cases, the differences are minimal because you will need to type commands into phpMyAdmin as well.

If MySQL is installed, you're ready to move on to "#63: Store Locations to a Database" on page 219.

Use a Packaged Installation of MySQL

To install MySQL on your own computer, the easiest method is to download a package for your operating system that is ready to go. When you follow this route, you'll also get PHP and Apache at the same time, which is useful.

The names of the packages are patterned after the popular server architecture, LAMP, which stands for *Linux*, *Apache*, *MySQL*, and *PHP*:

- Windows (WAMP): *http://www.wampserver.com/*
- Macintosh (MAMP): *http://www.mamp.info/*

Either of these packages should install on your computer without much information from you (though you may have to enter an administrator password).

Open WAMP/MAMP once the install process has completed. The program should create a new web browser window pointed at *localhost*, the name of the server on your own computer. By default, a welcome screen will appear, as shown in Figure 9-4.

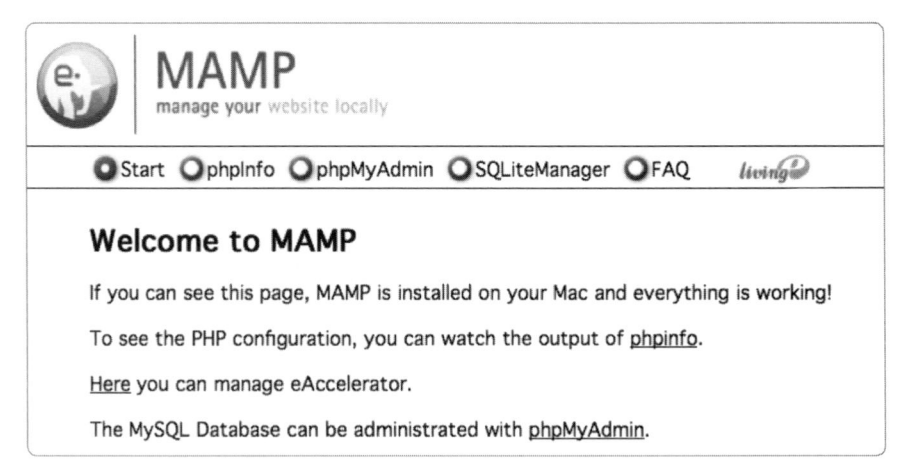

Figure 9-4: The MAMP welcome screen

To administer your MySQL installation, click the **phpMyAdmin** link. Now you're ready for the next project.

Install MySQL Yourself

If you're using an operating system that does not have a package available, you will need to install MySQL yourself. Too many variations exist to describe in this chapter, but many tutorials are available on the Internet to help you out.

The MySQL website is the first place to start: *http://mysql.org/*.

When you are up and running, keep on reading for geographic-specific instructions.

#63: Store Locations to a Database

To build extremely powerful mapping applications, you'll want to use a database. By maintaining your own data, your site will be quicker and you can do more interesting things. First, however, you'll need to create the database and add some locations to it. This section will describe how to get started with a MySQL location database.

At this point, we need to get our jargon straight. That data, which lives in a database, actually resides in a database *table*. Before you can create a table, you need to have a database. MySQL is a database management system that can contain many individual databases, which themselves have many tables.

Create a New Database

If you're using MySQL through a hosting provider, you likely already have a database assigned to you. Even your database contains other tables already (say, for blogging software), you can still use it for this project. We will simply be creating an additional database table.

If you don't have a database, creating one is easy in phpMyAdmin. From the main screen, simply type the name of your database into the form (I chose *mapscripting*) and click the **Create** button (see Figure 9-5). Or, using the MySQL Command Interpreter, type `create database("mapscripting");`.

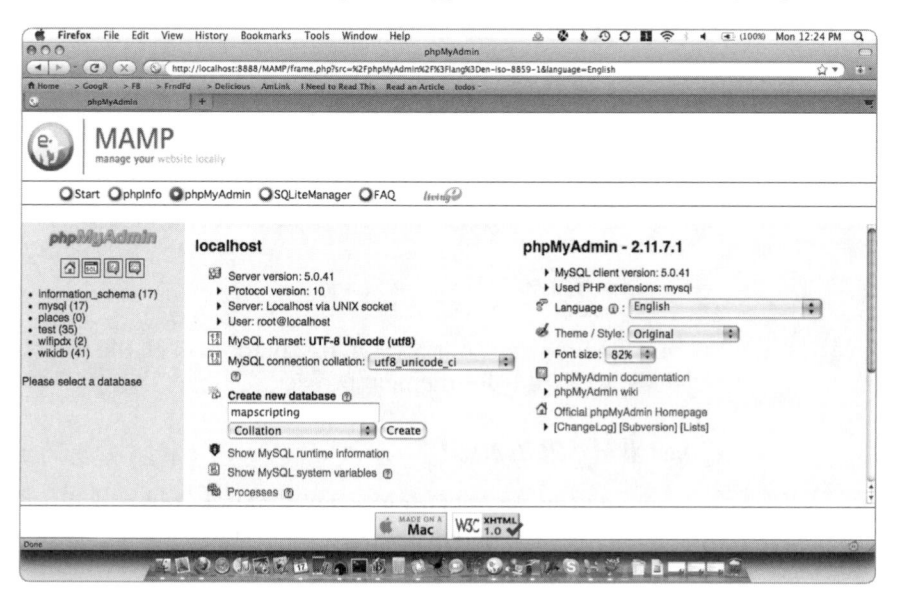

Figure 9-5: Create a new database.

Once completed, you need to select the database name, by clicking it or typing `\u mapscripting` in the interpreter. Now you're ready to create the database table.

Create a Database Table

Now that you have a database, you can begin adding tables. I'm keeping this example simple, so we're only going to have one table.

To create a new table in phpMyAdmin, you fill out the form on the database's main page. You need to give the table a name and choose a number of fields. I'm calling my table *places*, and it will have four fields, which are types of values that every place will contain. Click the **Go** button to further define the table.

As you can see in Figure 9-6, we need to name each field and give it a type. The four fields I'm adding to our basic place table are *id* (unique identifier), *label* (a name for the place), *latitude*, and *longitude*.

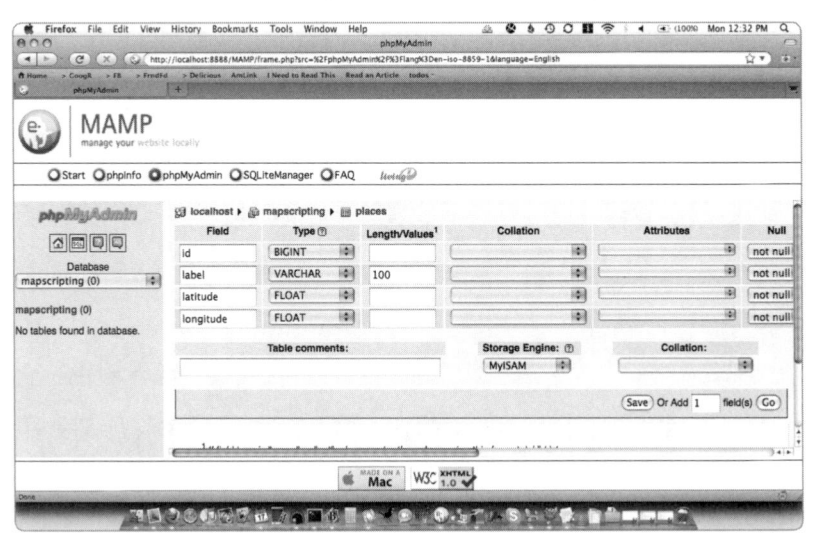

Figure 9-6: Create a table with four fields.

The identifier is a good idea for any database table because it makes distinguishing one piece of data from another easy. I've made the identifier a *bigint*, meaning it is an integer that can get very large (up to 9 quintillion—that's 18 zeros). We don't want to worry about counting the number ourselves, however, so we need to make sure MySQL does it for us.

Look on the far right in phpMyAdmin (you may need to scroll horizontally), and you'll find the Extra column. Select the drop-down for the id row and choose **auto_increment**. Then, also click the option directly to the right, the one with the icon that looks like a key. See Figure 9-7 for an example. Selecting this will make the identifier the primary key. Both of these steps are necessary for MySQL to do the counting for you.

The remaining fields are fairly simple. The label is a short (100 character) description of the place and then the location is stored as two floating point (decimal) numbers: latitude and longitude, no doubt quite familiar to you by now.

Click the **Save** button and you've created a table. To do the same in the Command Interpreter (or using phpMyAdmin's SQL window), type the following:

```
CREATE TABLE places (id BIGINT NOT NULL AUTO_INCREMENT PRIMARY KEY,
                label VARCHAR(100), latitude FLOAT, longitude FLOAT);
```

Now that you have a table, let's start adding data to it.

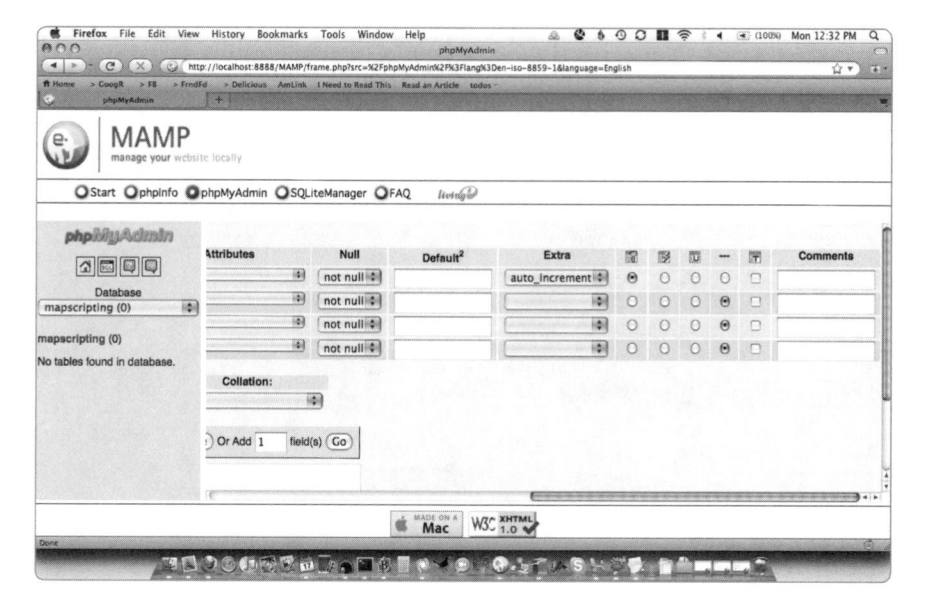

Figure 9-7: Make the identifier field auto-increment.

Add Data to Your Places Table

Your places table, with its four fields, is sitting happily inside your database, but you have a problem. The table is empty. It doesn't have any data. Let's add some.

Within phpMyAdmin, click the table name and then the Insert tab. You should see another form (as shown in Figure 9-8) with four fields. This time, instead of names, which are already listed, you'll enter values.

Leaving the id value empty is important. MySQL will create that value because it's counting (auto-incrementing) for us. In the other boxes, type a descriptive name, followed by latitude and longitude. Then click **Go**.

You don't have to add data via phpMyAdmin. You can also use plain SQL (such as in the Command Interpreter). To add Old Faithful to the places table, type the following:

```
insert into places (label, latitude, longitude)
          values ('Old Faithful geyser', 44.46054, -110.82834);
```

Notice that I don't include the id here at all. I want MySQL to deal with it. The other three fields are first listed by name and then by the values I want to add to them.

After performing these tasks, you've added a single place to your places database table. Add a few more, varying the labels, latitude, and longitude. You have yourself an up-and-coming location database now. Within php-MyAdmin, click the Browse tab to see your places, or type this SQL in the Command Interpreter: `select * from places;`.

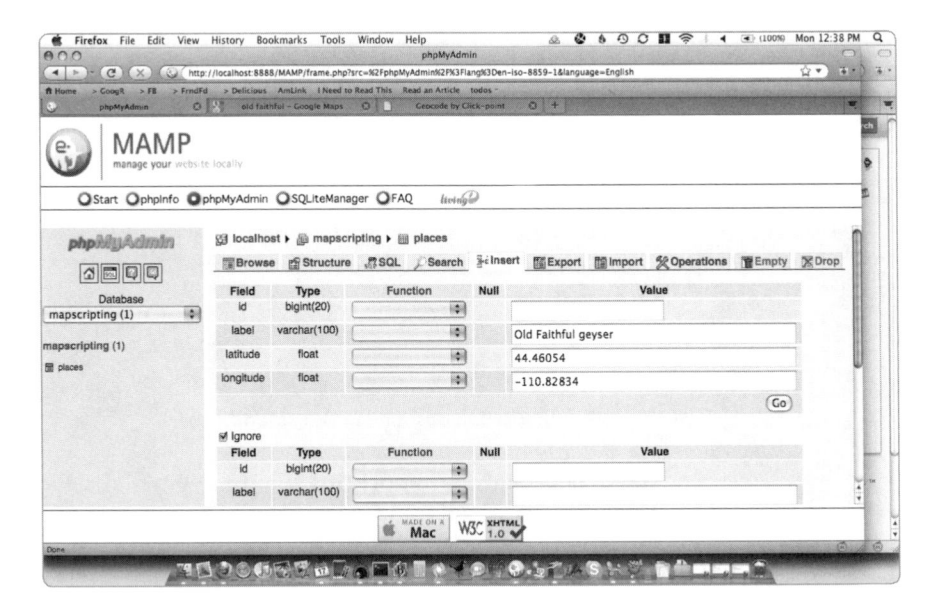

Figure 9-8: Enter values in your places table.

Now you can do something interesting with the location database, such as plot locations from a database or get the nearest locations from a database.

#64: Import Data from a Spreadsheet

If you're sold on getting your location data into a database (and I hope you are), you'll want a way to make it easy. Filling out form after form or writing out SQL inserts by hand is tedious. In this section, I'll show how to use a spreadsheet, convert it to CSV, and then import it directly into MySQL.

Earlier I compared a database table to a spreadsheet. Both have columns, which in a database are also referred to as field names. Both have rows, which we call database records. The easiest way to prepare a lot of data for a database is to use a spreadsheet, such as Excel or OpenOffice Calc. Work on your spreadsheet as you normally would. Figure 9-9 shows an example of how the places database I created in the previous project might look as a spreadsheet.

Make sure you have a few rows filled out, and then save a copy of your spreadsheet. Instead of saving as the normal spreadsheet format, scroll through your list of file types, and choose **Comma-Separated, .csv**. This format is a simple, universal one for storing data.

I chose the name *places.csv* for my file, which looks like this when I open it in a plain-text editor:

```
"label","latitude","longitude"
"Old Faithful geyser",44.46054,-110.82834
"St. Louis Arch",38.62470,-90.18510
```

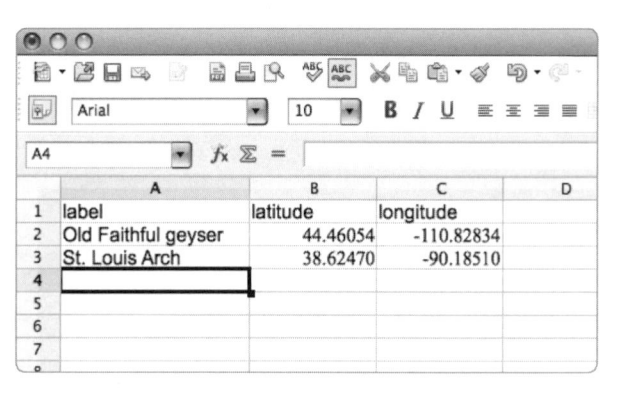

Figure 9-9: A database table is similar to a spreadsheet.

Now you're ready to import this comma-separated values (CSV) version of the database table. Within phpMyAdmin, navigate to the places table and click the Import tab. First, you'll select the file to import, so click the **Browse** button and choose your CSV file. If your file has a header row, as mine does, be sure to fill out the form to skip one record because you don't want to import the field names as values.

Scroll down to the File Import section. It is probably set to SQL because that's the main way MySQL expects to read in files. Choose **CSV** instead. Then fill out the options as shown in Figure 9-10. Fields are terminated by a comma; fields are enclosed by a double quote character; and fields are escaped by backslash. You can let line terminators be determined automatically.

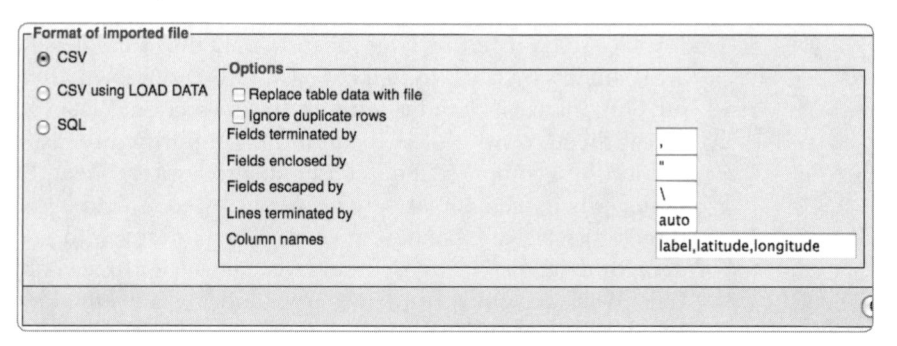

Figure 9-10: Import a comma-separated file into MySQL.

The final option is a list of fields to import. If you are importing every field in the table, you may not need to enter these. We have an automatically generated identifier, however, so we need to specify the columns we are importing, which is everything except the id column.

Click the **Go** button and your data should be imported. To check, click the Browse tab, which will show you the current contents of the places table.

You can also import using the Command Interpreter:

```
LOAD DATA LOCAL INFILE 'places.csv' INTO TABLE places
FIELDS TERMINATED BY ',' ENCLOSED BY '"' LINES TERMINATED BY '\n'
IGNORE 1 LINES (label, latitude, longitude);
```

The CSV file will need to be accessible to the machine running MySQL. If you're using the interpreter on a server, you'll need to upload the file to the server.

Using a spreadsheet to create your data is the easiest method when you have more than just a few records. Also, you may find plenty of other data available in this format, so knowing how to import from CSV can help you use other people's data, as well.

#65: Use MySQL from PHP

Many programming languages have ways to connect to MySQL. PHP includes many functions in its default installation, making PHP and MySQL a popular pair. In this section, I'll introduce you to the most common functions for accessing your MySQL database from PHP.

The following example assumes you have a location database table like the one we created in "#63: Store Locations to a Database" on page 219 with at least one place added to the database. Once you have your table ready to go, let's write some PHP to grab all the place descriptions.

Create a new PHP file with the following content:

```
    <?php
❶  $db = mysql_connect('localhost', 'username', 'password');
❷  mysql_select_db('mapscripting', $db);
    $sql = "select label from places";
❸  $res = mysql_query($sql, $db);
    while (❹$row = mysql_fetch_assoc($res)) {
      print ❺$row["label"];
    }
❻  mysql_close($db);
    ?>
```

Everything that begins with mysql_ (shown in bold) is a function associated with accessing MySQL from PHP. Many more functions are listed at *http://php.net/mysql.*

In this example, you first connect to MySQL using a server, username, and password ❶, which are likely provided by your site administrator. If you're using MAMP, you can find the login info on your installation's start page. These values establish the connection to MySQL and ensure not just anybody can access your data.

Because MySQL can have many different databases, we need to tell it which one to use ❷. Here I've chosen the mapscripting database I created previously. Also, I pass along the database connection variable from the previous line.

Now we're ready to get some data from the database. We use SQL to do this, similar to what happens behind the scenes on the Browse tab in php-MyAdmin. When using MySQL with PHP, you need to write the SQL yourself, which I've put into the variable $sql, which gets passed to a query ❸ along with the database connection variable.

You can fetch data from a query in many ways, all using the object that is returned from the previous line. In this example, we use a while loop to look at each result one at a time. Whenever the $row variable no longer has a value, the while loop will end.

The value for each result is an associative array ❹, so the results are stored as key-value pairs. The table's field name is the key, so we put that inside square brackets to get at the value ❺. To finish, we close the connection to the database ❻, which frees up resources.

When you run this PHP code, you should see the description of every place you added print out, one after another, in no particular format. The output may not be pretty, but you have now made a very simple connection to your MySQL database from PHP. Better yet, any data you want can now be connected to the Web. Are you feeling powerful yet? You should be.

Continue reading to do something a bit more useful with the data in your location database.

#66: Plot Locations from a Database

This project is the one you've been waiting for. You patiently put in your time learning the basics of MySQL and PHP. All you really wanted to do was put some points on a map without having to hand code it. Once you master the skills in this project, your mapping projects will be much more powerful because they'll be driven by data.

Believe it or not, you already have the knowledge necessary to plot locations from a database. The concepts we'll be using combine "#65: Use MySQL from PHP" on page 225 and the parsing portion of a data formats project, "#53: Use JSON" on page 180, which put the JavaScript framework jQuery to work for us.

This project has two parts: creating the JSON on the server using our database and interpreting the JSON in the browser. Let's go at 'em in that order.

Output All Places as JSON

We'll be using PHP that is only slightly more advanced than what you've written in other projects. Rather than printing out each result as we come across it, we'll store it. Once we have all the data, we'll print it out as JSON with help from a built-in PHP function.

Whenever you are getting data from your database, consider what you need. Here, we're going to be plotting our locations on a map, so we'll need, at the very least, the latitude and longitude of each place. Having a description of each, too, would be nice so we'll also grab our label. Depending on what you're doing, you might also like the unique id.

How many rows do you want? For our example, let's get them all. Bear in mind that if your table is very large, you could be setting your users up for quite a long download. In that case, you might choose to only get the nearest locations from a database, but that's another project. Onward!

Create a new PHP file and add the following code:

```php
<?php
$db = mysql_connect('localhost', 'username', 'password');
mysql_select_db('mapscripting', $db);
❶ $sql = "select label, latitude, longitude from places";
$res = mysql_query($sql, $db);
❷ $allrows = array();
while ($row = mysql_fetch_assoc($res)) {
❸   array_push($allrows, $row);
}
mysql_close($db);
❹ print json_encode($allrows);
?>
```

We begin with connection details and then go straight to the SQL ❶. I have listed the three field names we want to get from the database. Before looping through the results, I've created an empty array ❷. We'll use this to hold all the results.

As we loop through every row that the database returns, we use a PHP function to "push" the result to the end of our array ❸. You may remember that each result from the database is itself an associative array, with values stored with field names as keys. So the array containing all the rows is really an array *of arrays*. A bit confusing, perhaps, but perfectly suited for JSON.

After all of the results are stored in our massive array, we'll convert the variable to JSON text and print it out. We can do all of that in one single line ❹, assuming we have the JSON extensions (included in all recent PHP installations).

Here is the JSON output from my database, which has two rows:

```
[
  {"label":"Old Faithful geyser","latitude":"44.4605","longitude":"-110.828"},
  {"label":"St. Louis Arch","latitude":"38.6247","longitude":"-90.1851"}
]
```

Very likely your results will be all squished together on one line, but I've split up the pieces to make more sense of them. When we parse this into JavaScript, we'll have an array (defined by square brackets) of objects (defined by curly brackets).

Once the data is put into JavaScript, we'll be able to plot it on a map. Let's get going.

Plot Places from JSON

Using PHP we have output all the places in our location database as JSON. Now we need to create a map that reads in the data and creates a new marker for every place. On the surface, this map is just like any other map we've created before. In this case, however, we won't even initialize the map until we hear back from the database.

Before we get to parsing the JSON results, we need to include the jQuery JavaScript framework. Add the following to the header code of a basic Mapstraction map:

```
<script src="http://ajax.googleapis.com/ajax/libs/jquery/1.3/jquery.min.js"></script>
```

Now replace any JavaScript code with the following function to initialize the map:

```
    var mapstraction;
    function create_map() {
❶     $.getJSON("allplaces.php", function(jobj) {
❷       mapstraction = new Mapstraction('mymap', 'google');
❸       for (var i=0; i < jobj.length; i++) {
❹         var place = jobj[i];
          var mk = new Marker(new LatLonPoint(place.latitude, place.longitude));
          mk.setInfoBubble(place.label);
          mapstraction.addMarker(mk);
        }
        mapstraction.autoCenterAndZoom();
      });
    }
```

Unlike other times we've used a create_map function, we don't start by making a new Mapstraction map. We save this for later, once we've received data. Instead, the first thing we do is use jQuery to create an Ajax call to our PHP file (which I've called *allplaces.php*) ❶.

Once we have a result, *then* we create the map ❷, so we can start adding the data to it. Here, we've used a for loop to go through each place ❸. We can then save that object ❹, which has three attributes: label, latitude, and longitude. Those values are used to create a marker and give the marker a message box.

Finally, outside of the for loop (so it only happens once), we automatically center the map based on our markers. Figure 9-11 shows what my map, which has two landmarks as places, looks like.

If I add a third place to the database and reload the page, I'll have a third marker. That's the beauty of a database-driven map!

Figure 9-11: Database-driven places map

#67: Get Nearest Locations from a Database

In Chapter 6, we looked at several projects concerning what's nearby. I showed how to calculate the distance between two points and how to determine the closest marker to a point. Arguably more useful is what we'll be doing in this project: getting the nearest location to a point from a list of many possibilities stored in a database.

To be able to look at locations in a database, we need to have something in the database in the first place. For this example, we'll be using the places database table from "#63: Store Locations to a Database" on page 219. Although we've been using MySQL as an engine, most databases will work with the SQL statements that follow.

Because we're looking for the nearest locations to a single point, we need to determine what that point is. I've chosen a point near me in Portland with a latitude of 45.517 and a longitude of −122.649. Now we'll plug this into the Haversine formula—that's the same bit of trigonometry that we used in Chapter 6 to determine distance. There, we used JavaScript, and in this example, we'll use SQL.

From either the MySQL Command Interpreter, or in phpMyAdmin, type the following query:

```
SELECT *,
  ( 6371❶ * ACOS( COS( RADIANS( 45.517 ) ) * COS( RADIANS( latitude ) ) *
  COS( RADIANS( longitude ) - RADIANS( - 122.649 ) ) + SIN( RADIANS( 45.517 ) ) *
  SIN( RADIANS( latitude ) ) ) ) AS dist
FROM places
ORDER BY dist;
```

Here we're selecting all the fields from the places table, plus an additional field, described by the entire section in bold. That's a lot of code! This code calculates the distance between our point and the points in the database using the latitude and longitude values stored with each place.

The distance, which becomes a column named dist, is in kilometers. As with the previous implementation of the Haversine formula, we multiply by the earth's radius, which is 6,371 km. For miles, replace the number ❶ with its mile equivalent (3,958).

When you run the SQL query, your results will be those shown in Table 9-2. Because we ordered by distance, the places nearest to our point come first in the table. Therefore, the nearest place to the point we selected is Old Faithful geyser. Of course, more useful examples will be from a places database with many locations all within the same city. Then, based on a point within that city, you can find the closest places, which will likely be within a few miles.

Table 9-2: Results of Nearest Place in SQL

ID	Label	Latitude	Longitude	Distance
1	Old Faithful geyser	44.46	−110.83	936.12
2	St. Louis Gateway Arch	38.62	− 90.19	2765.97

Improve Your Query's Performance

Database experts will have some big problems with the SQL we used in the previous section. You know all that math we used: COS this and RADIANS that? Those are being calculated for each row in the database, even if the value isn't changing. The result is a query that will not make your server very happy once you've stored many places. In computer science terminology, the query has *poor performance*.

Let's improve performance by storing some values that won't change in SQL variables. The process is similar to PHP variables, but the syntax is a bit different. Alter the query from the previous section to look like this:

```
SET @earthRadius = 6371;
SET @lat = 45.517;
SET @lon = -122.649;
```

```
❶ SET @radLat = RADIANS(@lat);
  SET @radLon = RADIANS(@lon);
  SET @cosLat = COS(@radLat);
  SET @sinLat = SIN(@radLat);
  SELECT *,
    ( @earthRadius * ACOS( @cosLat * COS(RADIANS(latitude)) *
    COS( RADIANS(longitude) - @radLon ) + @sinLat *
    SIN(RADIANS(latitude)) ) ) AS dist
  FROM places
  ORDER BY dist;
```

The SET command is used to store a value into a variable. The variables themselves start with the @ sign. The first three variables are used to hold numbers that were previously written directly into the query, making the distance portion of the query (again, in bold) easier to read.

The other four variables, beginning with ❶, also improve readability and make the query considerably shorter. Even better, performance improves as well. The values stored in the variables are only calculated once—when the variable is created.

A number of calculations are still happening as the query runs, which will bog down your server. Code like COS(RADIANS(latitude)) can be avoided, but only if we change our database table. In the next section, I'll show you how you can further improve your query's performance.

Precalculate Values in New Columns

The changes you're making to your SQL won't be noticeable until you have many locations stored in your database. The flip-side is that with many locations stored applying this query becomes more interesting, which could attract more users to your site. And that's definitely not the time you want your server to be slow.

Some things *have* to be calculated on-the-fly, otherwise the result would be the same for every location. You'll be returning different results for every pair of latitude and longitude coordinates. We'll focus on precalculating these three values from the previous section:

* COS(RADIANS(latitude))
* RADIANS(longitude)
* SIN(RADIANS(latitude))

For every place stored in the database, these values will be different. Once the values are set, however, they will remain the same. That's a perfect case for adding three columns to your table. We'll name them cosRadLat, radLon, and sinRadLat and make them all type FLOAT.

Here's the SQL version to add these columns through the Command Interpreter:

```
ALTER TABLE places ADD cosRadLat FLOAT, ADD radLon FLOAT, ADD sinRadLat FLOAT;
```

Once you've added these three columns, you need to fill in the values for all the places currently in your table:

```
UPDATE places set
  cosRadLat = COS(RADIANS(latitude)),
  radLon = RADIANS(longitude),
  sinRadLat = SIN(RADIANS(latitude));
```

Finally, now that you've added values to new columns in your table, you can use this optimized query to get the nearest locations from your database:

```
SET @earthRadius = 6371;
SET @lat = 45.517;
SET @lon = -122.649;
SET @radLat = RADIANS(@lat);
SET @radLon = RADIANS(@lon);
SET @cosLat = COS(@radLat);
SET @sinLat = SIN(@radLat);
SELECT label, latitude, longitude
  ( @earthRadius * ACOS( @cosLat * cosRadLat *
  COS( radLon - @radLon ) + @sinLat *
  sinRadLat ) ) AS dist
FROM places
ORDER BY dist;
```

The result is an even shorter, much faster query. A few calculations still need to happen on the fly, but the rest has been precalculated and stored in either variables or columns in the places table.

The only other change is that we are explicitly naming the fields to select, which is another database best practice. Plus, now that we added the three precalculated columns, we don't want to muddy our results with those additional values. Those numbers are just to improve speed and aren't particularly useful outside of that.

#68: Get Nearest Locations to a Postal Code

Big businesses often have store locators on their website. To use one, you type in your postal code and then you get a list of locations nearest yours. In this project, I'll show you how to perform the SQL database calls to reproduce this feature on your own site.

On one hand, the code to find places near a postal code is the same as the previous project. All you need to do is determine the latitude and longitude point of a particular postal code, which you can get from most geocoder services, and you'll be able to find the closest places.

Of course, having a postal code table in your own database is even more useful. This process is described in "#15: Get Postal Code Coordinates" on page 58, and I have links to database sources at *http://mapscripting.com/postal-code-database*. Installing your own database will save one step in the process, so you can find the ZIP Code's coordinates and its closest places in one call to the database.

Create a new database table, which I'll be calling *postals*. It will have three columns: *code*, *latitude*, and *longitude*. As you can see in Figure 9-12, the postal code itself is a five-character string (*varchar*) because that's what is used in the United States, where ZIP Codes are five digits.

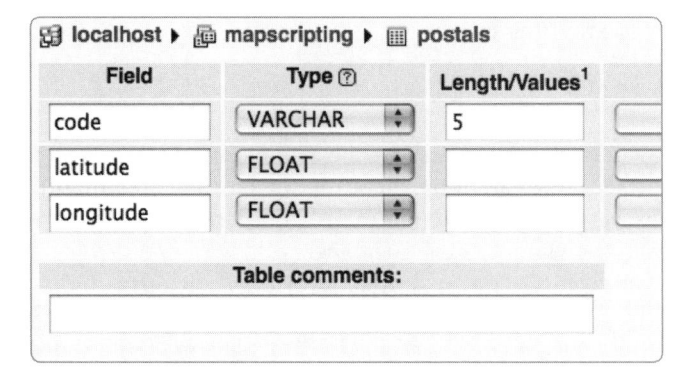

Figure 9-12: Create a ZIP Code table.

The postal code is represented as text to account for the situation when the code starts with a zero. If you store the code as a number, which is more efficient, you will need to account for the starting zero with every lookup. Latitude and longitude are floating point numbers, just as they are in the places database.

Here is the SQL version to create this table in the command interpreter:

```
CREATE TABLE postals(code VARCHAR(5), latitude FLOAT, longitude FLOAT);
```

Now you're ready to add some postal codes to your database. You can do a few by hand just for this test, using a geocoder to determine the correct latitude and longitude points. A better long-term solution would be to download a full postal code database and use "#64: Import Data from a Spreadsheet" on page 223.

At this point, your database should have two tables: *places* and *postals*. We'll use both together in one SQL call to determine the nearest places.

From either the MySQL Command Interpreter or phpMyAdmin, type the following query:

```
SELECT @lat:=latitude, @lon:=longitude FROM postals WHERE code='90210';
SET @earthRadius = 6371;
SET @radLat = RADIANS(@lat);
SET @radLon = RADIANS(@lon);
SET @cosLat = COS(@radLat);
SET @sinLat = SIN(@radLat);
SELECT label, latitude, longitude
  ( @earthRadius * ACOS( @cosLat * cosRadLat *
  COS( radLon - @radLon ) + @sinLat *
  sinRadLat ) ) AS dist
FROM places
ORDER BY dist;
```

Most of the query is the same as the optimized version from the previous project. Instead of hard-coding the latitude and longitude, the first line selects it from our *postals* database. The portion in bold stores the coordinates in the @lat and @lon variables.

The results of our example query are shown in Table 9-3. Again, because I've chosen a location on the west coast of the United States, Old Faithful geyser is closest. As for finding places near a point, the really interesting stuff comes when you have many places all within one city.

Table 9-3: Results of Nearest Place SQL

Label	Latitude	Longitude	Distance
Old Faithful geyser	44.46	−110.83	1322.32
St. Louis Gateway Arch	38.62	− 90.19	2566.23

10

MASHUP PROJECTS

Throughout this book, I've demonstrated how to perform some common tasks with web maps and geographic data. Now I'll put many of these lessons together in example projects. The mashups in this chapter show how to retrieve, convert, and utilize external data sources.

We'll also create interfaces that go beyond just showing a few locations on a map. Using events to capture clicks and mouse movements, we'll add some interactivity to the maps.

What Is a Mashup?

The Web is much more than a collection of interconnected documents. Millions of applications are creating, collecting, and consuming data all the time. When these applications talk to each other, sharing this data with application programming interfaces (APIs), the resulting feature is called a *mashup*.

The name comes from music. Musically, a mashup is created when a DJ layers two or more songs together to make something new. This analogy describes what programmers and designers are creating with web mashups. They combine APIs to create something new, often an enlightening way of envisioning the underlying data.

We've been using a different type of API throughout this book. Maps, in addition to graphing and charting APIs, are used for visualizing data, either from your own or other APIs. Most APIs, however, are used to make data available to developers. Those that I'll use in this chapter provide publicly available location data.

The Projects

The five projects in this chapter will get you started creating mashups. They were chosen for their conceptual diversity, so you can learn a number of techniques in this single chapter. Here's a brief overview of the projects:

Weather

Just like your daily newspaper, this map shows weather conditions across the United States—only this weather map is interactive and updated each time the page loads. See *http://mapscripting.com/weather*.

Earthquakes

You'll get geological and create a map showing last week's earthquakes plotted across the globe. Using the Richter scale measure of a quake's intensity, you can see where the big ones were and zoom in on the world's seismic hotspots. See *http://mapscripting.com/earthquakes*.

Concerts

Turn this mashup to 11! We'll create a tool to search a city or surrounding area for concerts. We'll even let users be frugal and declare their budget before searching. We'll filter only the results that match their criteria. See *http://mapscripting.com/concerts*.

Twitter

Help users find tweets near their location, or anywhere they search. Optionally, users can add a keyword to the search to zero in on both the *what* and *where* stored in Twitter status messages. See *http://mapscripting.com/twitter*.

Midpoint search

Meet in the middle! Just searching for coffee isn't enough. The final mashup shows you how to first find the midpoint of a route and then search for coffee near that midpoint. That way, you don't have to be the one to drive across town when you find a place to meet in the middle. See *http://mapscripting.com/middle*.

These five projects use many of the concepts you've learned earlier in this book. Complete them and you will definitely be on your way to map mashup mastery. Let the mashing begin!

#69: Create a Weather Map

A big map with current conditions isn't just for your local meteorologist. Using the Yahoo! Weather API, you can make a visual forecast of a region, a country, or the whole world. In this example, I'll show how I created a US weather map with icons of current conditions marked for major regional cities.

As you'll see, most of the effort to create the weather map involves manipulating data. Once the data is in a format that JavaScript can easily access, all we need is a basic map with some custom markers. Things get a little tricky when we zoom in on a city and show its forecast in an overlay, but even that should be a cinch for a map master like you. By the end of this project, your map will look like Figure 10-1.

Figure 10-1: Complete US weather map

Prepare a Basic US Map

What are the essential elements of a web map? A center point and a zoom level. Okay, so you also need the HTML with a div for your map and some basic styles. Plus, you'll need to load some JavaScript files. Once that foundation is in place, however, you just need to setCenterAndZoom.

I decided early on that I only wanted to show the continental United States. Sorry Alaska and Hawaii—I'll make it up in the earthquake example later in this chapter. I arrived at the center and the zoom level with a little guess and check. Drag the map to where you want it and set the zoom to the perfect level. Then, call getCenter and getZoom (or do this automatically whenever the map is dragged).

The center I arrived at has a latitude of 38 and a longitude of −98. Although not the exact center of the United States, it looked best. I chose a zoom level of four, which is enough to see major cities and highways. Here is the code to create the basic map that we'll build on in upcoming sections:

```
<html xmlns="http://www.w3.org/1999/xhtml">
  <head>
    <title>Weather Map Mashup</title>
    <style>
      div#mymap {
        width: 800px;
        height: 450px;
      }

    </style>
❶   <script src="http://ajax.googleapis.com/ajax/libs/jquery/1.3/jquery.min.js"></script>
    <script type="text/javascript" src="http://maps.google.com/maps/api/js?sensor=false">
</script>
    <script src="mxn.js?(googlev3)"></script>
    <script type="text/javascript">
      var mapstraction;
❷     var center = new mxn.LatLonPoint(38,-98);
❸     var zoom = 4;

      function create_map() {
        mapstraction = new mxn.Mapstraction('mymap', 'googlev3');
        mapstraction.setCenterAndZoom(center, zoom);
        mapstraction.addControls({"zoom":"large"});

      }
    </script>
  </head>
  <body onload="create_map()">
    <div id="mymap"></div>

  </body>
</html>t
```

Most of this code likely looks familiar from other simple maps. We'll add to it soon but you can already spot signs that this code is looking ahead: I included *jQuery* ❶, a JavaScript framework that makes applying effects and using Ajax to retrieve data easy. I also set center ❷ and zoom ❸ variables globally, so we'll be able to return users to the original view after zooming in.

The basic map, as seen in Figure 10-2, is now ready for markers. Before we can plot the weather conditions on the map, however, we'll need some data in an accessible format.

Figure 10-2: Basic US weather map

Convert Weather Results to JSON

To make our map a mashup, we need some data, specifically current weather condition data. Yahoo! has an easy-to-use weather API that accepts a postal code or a proprietary location identifier. The result comes as GeoRSS, which is a plaintext XML file.

Let's look at an example call to the Yahoo! Weather API. To get the current conditions and forecast for Minneapolis, Minnesota, we fetch this URL: *http://weather.yahooapis.com/forecastrss?p=**USMN0503***.

The bold portion of the URL is the location ID. The API will also accept a postal code, but in this example, we'll use the ID. When we plot the conditions on the map, I'll explain where to get the location IDs.

If you visit this URL, the result will look similar to this abbreviated version of the XML that is returned:

```
<rss version="2.0" xmlns:yweather="http://xml.weather.yahoo.com/ns/rss/1.0"
xmlns:geo="http://www.w3.org/2003/01/geo/wgs84_pos#">
<channel>
...
<item>
<title></title>
<geo:lat></geo:lat>
<geo:long></geo:long>

</item></channel></rss>
```

Not to be too picky about the format of free data, but parsing XML with JavaScript can be troublesome, as I discussed in "#52: Use XML" on page 174. Many APIs now offer JavaScript Object Notation (JSON), a format that can be immediately plugged into JavaScript. Yahoo! Weather only provides XML, but another Yahoo! product can convert the data for us.

Yahoo! Pipes can perform many complex operations to merge, filter, and sort data. In this example, we won't be pushing the boundaries. All we want to do is read in XML from the API and output JSON. This is easy using Pipes. You could also use Yahoo! Query Language or run the XML through a process on your server. I'll show the second method in a project later in this chapter.

Create a New Pipe

Because all we have to do is convert from XML to JSON, we'll be creating about as simple a pipe as we can make. You can see a more in-depth version of this example in "#57: Convert from XML to JSON" on page 198, where you'll also find more advanced uses for Pipes.

From the Pipes home page at *http://pipes.yahoo.com/*, click **Create a Pipe** to get a brand new, empty pipe. On the left, you'll see pieces of "plumbing" that you can use. Drag a **Fetch Feed Source** to the workspace. This point is where the data will flow in.

What is the feed's URL? We'll be making several calls to the Weather API, one for each city we want to look up. The calls will be routed through Pipes, which means the feed URL cannot be static. To accept input to the pipe, drag a **Text Input** to the workspace. Name the input **location**, and set the prompt to something like, **Enter a location**. For default and debug values, use your postal code or city name. You could also use a location ID, such as the one for Minneapolis, **USMN0503**. This helps you confirm the pipe is working.

Now that you've set up the text input to provide a location value, you're ready to create the URL. To merge the static and dynamic portions of the URL, we'll use one final piece of piping. Drag a **String Builder** to the workspace. For a first value, add the beginning of the Weather API URL: *http://weather.yahooapis.com/forecastrss?p=*.

Drag the output of the **Text Input** to the second value of the **String Builder**. This action will append the location ID to the end of the call to the Weather API. Now you have a complete feed URL. Drag the output of the **String Builder** to the **Fetch Feed URL** line. Finally, drag the **Fetch Feed** output to the **Pipe Output** at the bottom of the workspace.

You've just created a Yahoo! Pipe! The final product should look something like Figure 10-3. At the bottom of the screen in the Debug Output section, you should see some sample results based on the location you entered as the debug value for the Text Input.

To use your pipe, you need to save it. Once you've saved it, you can run it to retrieve more example results by entering different locations. From the sample results screen, click **Get as JSON**. You may need to right-click (CTRL-click on Mac) and copy the link. The Pipes URL will look something like this: *http://pipes.yahoo.com/pipes/pipe.run?_id=sGDQu...&_render=json&location=USMN0503*.

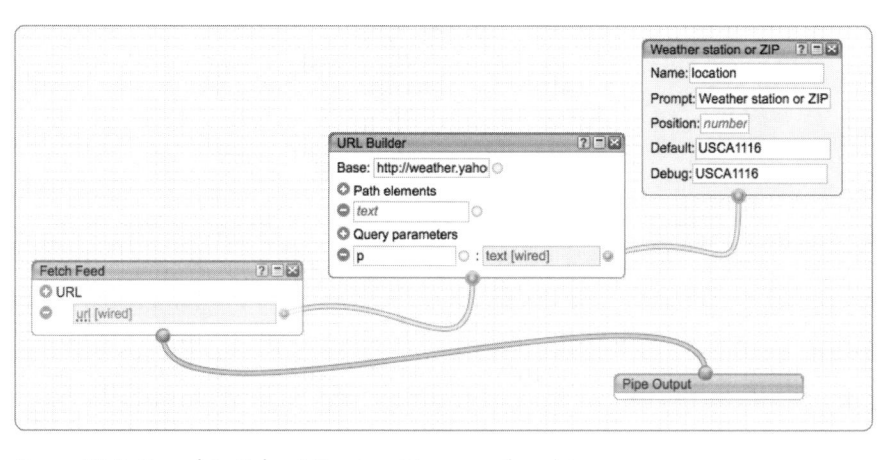

Figure 10-3: Complete Yahoo! Pipe to retrieve weather data

This URL will retrieve the weather conditions for Minneapolis in JSON format. Here is an abbreviated version of what it returns:

```
{"count":1,"value":{"items":[{"geo:long":"-93.26","geo:lat":"44.98",
"description":"<img src=\"http:\/\/l.yimg.com\/a\/i\/us\/we\/52\/26.gif\"\/>
<br \/>\n<b>Current Conditions:<\/b><br \/>\nCloudy...","yweather:condition":
{"temp":"50","text":"Cloudy",...,"code":"26"}}]}}
```

That URL is what we'll use to get weather conditions for several cities, replacing the Minneapolis-specific location ID. In fact, that's what we're ready to do now that we've converted the XML results to JSON.

Plot Conditions on the Map

With our JSON feed ready to go, let's dive into the JavaScript to retrieve the weather conditions and plot them on our US map. First, you need to decide which cities to plot. I chose 11 prominent places, focusing on geographic diversity.

To gather the location IDs for my cities, I went to *http://weather.yahoo .com/* and typed each city name into the search box. The result forwards to a URL like this: *http://weather.yahoo.com/forecast/**USMN0503**.html.*

The part of the filename without the extension, the bold portion, is the location ID. Once I had the IDs for all of my cities, I created a variable at the top of my JavaScript to hold the values:

```
var weatherids = [
  "USIL0225", // Chicago
  "USTX0327", // Dallas
  "USCO0105", // Denver
  "USFL0316", // Miami
  "USMN0503", // Minneapolis
```

```
     "USTN0357", // Nashville
     "USNY0996", // New York City
     "USAZ0166", // Phoenix
     "USM00787", // Saint Louis
     "USCA0987", // San Francisco
     "USWA0395"  // Seattle
];
```

The weatherids variable is an array, which holds a list of values. I spread the variable declaration over several lines to improve readability and make adding or removing cities easy. The city names are comments, so you can easily tell which location ID corresponds to which city.

When the map loads, we want to cycle through each city and look it up in our piped version of the Yahoo! Weather API. Add this loop code to the create_map function:

```
var pipeid = "Sbcb8u8J3hGNdOcopgt1Yg";for (var i=0; i < weatherids.length; i++) {
   var pipeurl = "http://pipes.yahoo.com/pipes/pipe.run?_id=" + pipeid;
   pipeurl += "&_render=json&location=" + weatherids[i] + "&_callback=?";
   jQuery.getJSON(pipeurl, add_weather);}
```

The variable i holds the index of the array, which begins at zero and counts up to 10 (Nashville, the 11th item in the array). Each time through the loop, we create a URL to call our pipe using the location ID value of the current weather station.

To fetch the JSON from our pipe, we use jQuery, a small JavaScript framework. When we set up the basic map previously, we included a reference to the jQuery file, so we're all set; most of the work of creating the Ajax call is done for us by jQuery's getJSON function with the URL we just created.

In addition to the location parameter, we add a new argument to the URL, _callback=?. This security feature lets us get JSON from a site other than our own. Yahoo! Pipes will wrap the results so only our callback function has access to the data. The question mark is a holding place for the function, which we pass along as the second parameter for getJSON.

When jQuery gets results from the Weather API, those results are passed to our add_weather function, which we now need to write:

```
function add_weather(data) {
   jQuery.each(data.value.items, function(i, item) {
      var lat = item["geo:lat"];
      var lon = item["geo:long"];
      var code = item["yweather:condition"].code;
      var imgsrc = "http://l.yimg.com/a/i/us/we/52/" + code + ".gif;

      add_marker({"lat":lat, "lon":lon, "code":code, "imgsrc":imgsrc});
}
```

The JSON data is automatically passed as a parameter to our callback function. In this case, I've used a variable called data to hold the response from the pipe. The weather conditions we want to get at are inside the first result of an array called items, which is itself inside an object named value. Sure, we've got some unnecessary overhead, but these are XML remnants.

The main data we need is latitude, longitude, and description. Wherever possible, I use JavaScript dot notation like item.description. Several field names in this feed contain a colon, which would be interpreted incorrectly with dot notation. In this case, I use the bracket notation to retrieve the properties from item instead.

Every weather condition has a numbered code that matches a particular description. The number allows machines to interpret a forecast easily without needing to parse text. The code is also used by Yahoo! Weather to call up the image designated for each condition. For example, a code of 30 means the sky is partly cloudy. The corresponding graphic is stored at *http://l.yimg.com/a/i/us/we/52/30.gif.* I piece together this image URL into the imgsrc variable.

Once we have the data we need, we wrap it inside an object with curly braces and pass it off to the add_marker function to do the work of plotting this marker on the map:

```
function add_marker(options) {
  var marker = new mxn.Marker(new mxn.LatLonPoint(options["lat"], options["lon"]));
  marker.setIcon(options["imgsrc"], [52,52]);
  marker.setShadowIcon('❶blankshadow.png', [0,0]);
  mapstraction.addMarker(marker);
}
```

Why did I pass the data as a JavaScript object (the options variable) instead of individual parameters? You could use parameters, but four parameters would be a lot to pass along to a function. Every time we called it, we would need to double-check the order. Is description third or fourth? Also, JavaScript objects are commonly used to share data between JavaScript functions, so using them is good practice.

The rest of the add_marker function creates a straight-forward custom marker. The only line that might look strange is the shadow icon ❶, which I want to be empty. Because a shadowless marker is not an option, I used one transparent pixel for the shadow icon.

Now we have all the pieces to plot the conditions for our list of cities. Put them together and you have a complete weather map, with a little graphical representation of the current weather hovering above each city. Here's a brief recap of everything that happens as the mashup loads:

1. The HTML page is loaded, the create_map function is called, which sets up the basic map and calls the get_weather function for each location ID in the weatherids array.

2. The JSON is retrieved from the Yahoo! Pipe, the data gets passed to the add_weather function.

3. The important bits get extracted from the JSON into a JavaScript object, which is itself passed to the add_marker function.

4. Custom markers are created and placed on the map.

Now let's make this mashup a little more interactive. When the user clicks a marker, the map will zoom in on the forecast details for that location.

Add a Forecast Details Pane

A visual representation of current conditions is great, but we cannot show much content from the Weather API. In this section, we'll add a Forecast Details pane. For added interactivity, we'll make the pane appear when the user clicks a marker, as shown in Figure 10-4.

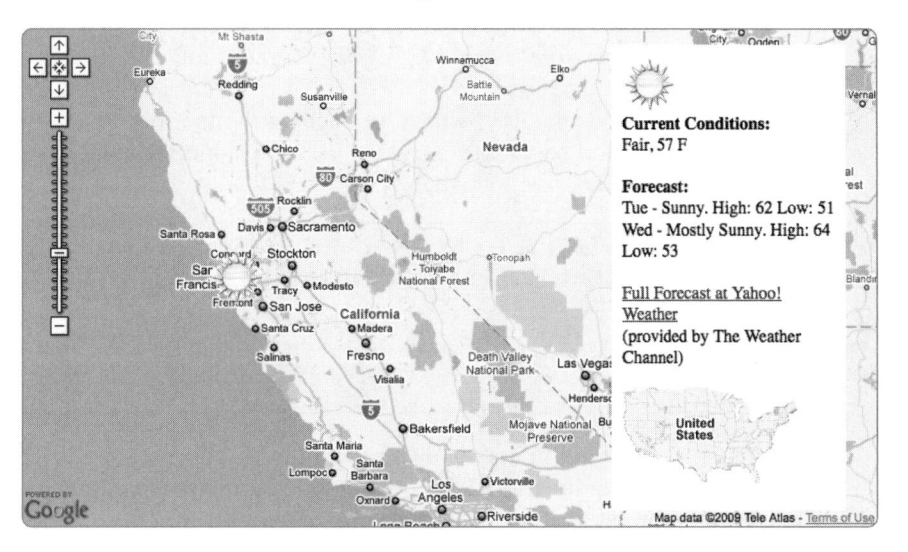

Figure 10-4: Forecast pane for our weather map

To start, we need to add the HTML shell for the new content. Right below the map div, add this line:

```
<div id="forecast"></div>
```

Like the map, the shell is empty. We'll use JavaScript to load it with content. Because we want to overlay the forecast details on the map itself, we'll use CSS to position the new div. In the <style> section of the header, add these lines:

```
div#forecast {
  position: relative;
  width: 200px;
  height: 400px;
  background-color: #fff;
```

```
    top: -435px;
    left: 550px;
    padding: 10px;
}
```

This CSS creates a thin, tall, white box to the right side of the map. In fact, save your file, load it in a browser, and from Michigan east will be obscured with the box. That's certainly not what we want. We want the forecast pane only to show up when a city is selected. By default, we'll need to hide it.

We can do that by adding this one line of jQuery to the create_map function:

```
$('#forecast').hide();
```

Here we call the jQuery hide function on the forecast div. When the map is first loaded, the pane will be hidden, waiting for a user to click.

Now we can use Mapstraction to fill the Forecast Details pane with content. Rather than creating infoBubbles when a marker is clicked, we'll instead call setInfoDiv with the forecast data from the API.

First, we actually need to get at that data. An entire description of the current conditions plus a forecast is passed from the Weather API in the description field. We need a fifth variable in the add_weather function. After the imgsrc line, add this:

```
    var desc = item.description;
```

Now you'll alter the call to add_marker by adding another option to the passed object:

```
add_marker({"lat":lat, "lon":lon, "code":code, "desc":desc, "imgsrc":imgsrc});
```

Then you'll use the new value inside the add_marker function. Add this line before the call to addMarker:

```
marker.setInfoDiv(❶options["desc"] + "<p><a href=\"javascript:return_center()\">"
    + ❷"<img src=\"usmap.png\" border=\"0\" alt=\"Return to full map\" />"
    + "</a></p>", ❸"forecast");
```

Here we set the Forecast Details pane to contain the description ❶ from the API, plus a clickable US map image ❷ that calls a new JavaScript function to return the map to the center and clear the Forecast Details pane. How does Mapstraction know which div to use? We pass its id as the second variable ❸.

To see the Forecast Details pane in action, we need to write code to show the hidden div when a marker is clicked. Add this line after the call to addMarker, as we'll be working with the marker object we've just created:

```
marker.click.addHandler(marker_clicked);
```

Now we are listening for a click event on a marker and then responding with a function reference. Let's write the marker_clicked function, which will be called whenever any of our markers is clicked:

```
function marker_clicked(event_name, event_source, event_args) {
❹   mapstraction.setCenterAndZoom(event_source.location, 6);
    var bounds = mapstraction.getBounds();
    var diff = ((bounds.ne.lon - bounds.sw.lon)/4);
❺   mapstraction.setCenter(
      new mxn.LatLonPoint(mapstraction.getCenter().lat, bounds.ne.lon - diff));
❻   $('#forecast').show();
});
```

When any marker is clicked, we set it to the center of the map and zoom in ❹. We use the clicked marker's location as the center, which comes to the function via the event_source argument. Then, to account for the Forecast Details pane on the right side of the map, we shift the map center to the west ❺, so the marker will appear centered in the visible portion of the map. Finally, we make sure the Forecast Details pane is visible ❻.

Save your file and load it in a browser. Now you should be able to click a marker and zoom in to see the forecast. The only piece that isn't connected is the ability to zoom back out and see the whole contiguous United States again. To do this, we'll need to write the return_center function called whenever you click the US map.

Add this function to the JavaScript section:

```
function return_center() {
  mapstraction.setCenterAndZoom(center, zoom);
  $('#forecast').hide();
}
```

This housekeeping function returns the map to its original center and zoom level and then hides the Forecast Details pane. Now we can see the whole US map again.

With the house cleaned, the mashup is complete. You pulled in data from Yahoo! Weather using Yahoo! Pipes to convert to JSON. Then you displayed the conditions for several cities, along with a descriptive graphic, on a map. Finally, upon clicking the marker, you zoomed the map into the city and displayed the forecast in its own overlaid info pane.

The best part, of course, is that you no longer need to read the weather page in the newspaper. You have an online, always-updating replacement.

#70: Display Recent Earthquakes Worldwide

Are you an aspiring geologist? Or maybe you're just looking for a quick way to see what's shaking in the world? In this mashup, I'll show you how to use a public data source to make sense of the world around you. We'll plot a week's worth of earthquakes, as tallied by the United States Geological Survey (USGS).

Lucky for us, the USGS logs earthquake data not just for the United States, but for the whole world. Even luckier for us, they're hip to the latest data formats. The organization publishes an XML feed that is geographically encoded as GeoRSS. It covers earthquakes that register 2.5 or greater on the Richter scale. That should still give us plenty of earthquakes to reveal some interesting trends on our map, as shown in Figure 10-5.

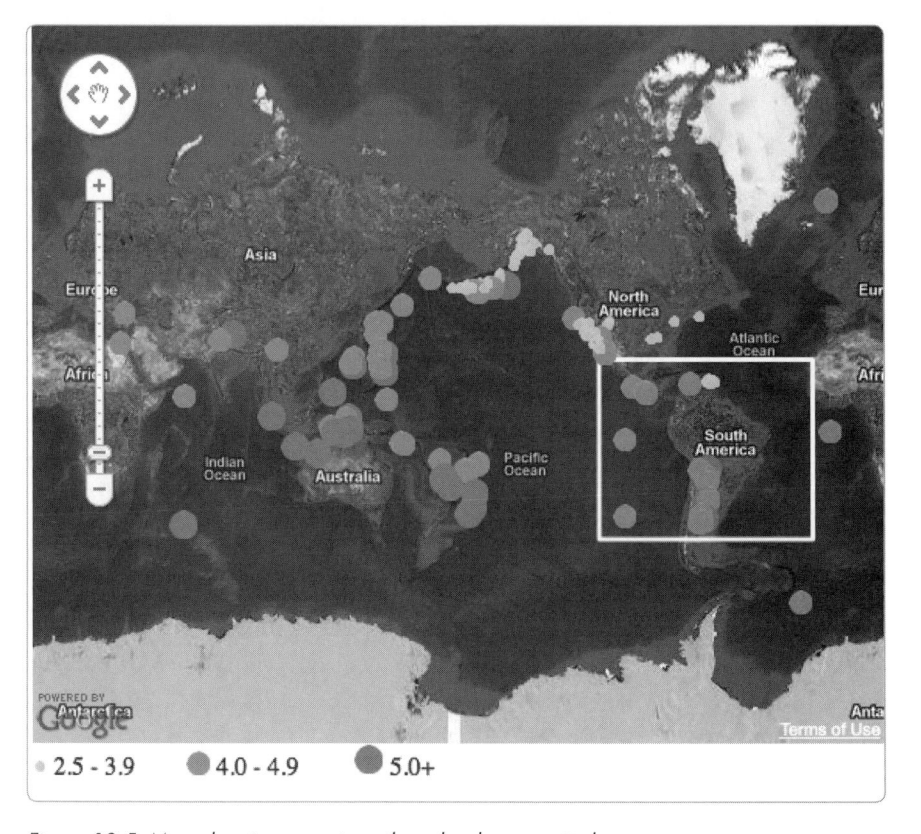

Figure 10-5: Map showing recent earthquakes by magnitude

You can load the feed into a web browser to view the content directly: *http://earthquake.usgs.gov/eqcenter/catalogs/7day-M2.5.xml.*

Many browsers will display a "pretty" version by default. View its source to get a glimpse at all the data it sends along with it. Here is an abbreviated version of the XML file from the USGS:

```
<feed xml:base="http://earthquake.usgs.gov/" xmlns="http://www.w3.org/2005/Atom"
      xmlns:georss="http://www.georss.org/georss">
<title>USGS M2.5+ Earthquakes</title>
<subtitle>Real-time, worldwide earthquake list for the past 7 days</subtitle>
<entry>
  <id>...</id>
  <title>M 2.6, Washington</title>
  <updated>YYYY-MM-DDTHH:MM:SSZ</updated>
  <link rel="alternate" type="text/html" href="/eqcenter/recenteqsww/Quakes/..."/>
  <summary type="html">...</summary>
  <georss:point>46.4078 -119.2521</georss:point>
</entry>
<entry>
...
</entry>
...
</feed>
```

That's some good stuff. Let's start using that data on our maps. First, we'll automatically parse GeoRSS, a feature that Mapstraction makes look easy. Then, if that basic visualization isn't enough, we'll create a completely custom solution.

Show Earthquakes with GeoRSS

Okay, you've chosen the quick version. You simply want to see these earthquakes get tossed up on a map. And you want to see this done using the fewest lines of code possible.

Add these very few lines to a new HTML file:

```
<html xmlns="http://www.w3.org/1999/xhtml">
  <head>
    <title>Earthquake GeoRSS Map</title>
    <script src="http://maps.google.com/maps?file=api&amp;v=2&amp;key=YOURKEY"
type="text/javascript"></script>
    <script type="text/javascript" src="mxn.js?(google)"></script>
    <style type="text/css">
    div#mymap {
      width: 550px;
      height: 450px;
    }
    </style>
    <script type="text/javascript">
    var mapstraction;
    function create_map() {
      mapstraction = new mxn.Mapstraction('mymap', 'google');
      mapstraction.setCenterAndZoom(❶ new mxn.LatLonPoint(0, 0), 0);
      mapstraction.addControls({zoom: 'large'});
```

```
      mapstraction.addOverlay(
        "http://earthquake.usgs.gov/eqcenter/catalogs/7day-M2.5.xml");
      mapstraction.autoCenterAndZoom();
    }
    </script>
  </head>
  <body onload="create_map()">
    <div id="mymap"></div>
  </body>
</html>
```

As always, remember to use your own API key. Otherwise, the code
is ready to go. Save and load it in a browser to see something similar to
Figure 10-6. The actual location of the markers will differ based on the past
week's geological activity.

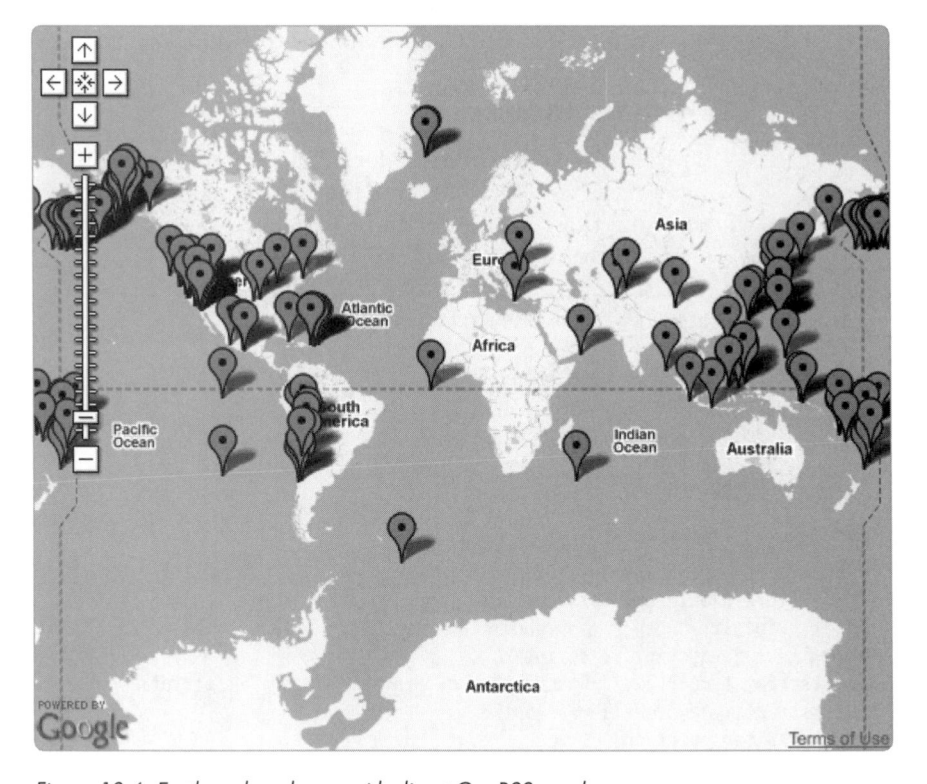

Figure 10-6: Earthquakes shown with direct GeoRSS overlay

Did you catch all those zeroes on the line where we set the center and
zoom ❶? Those aren't typos. A latitude of zero is the equator. A longitude
of zero is roughly the international dateline, running through London.
Finally, a zoom level of zero shows the whole world.

The money line, which loads the earthquake data, is shown in bold.
Mapstraction's addOverlay function does most of the work. It creates dozens
of markers and even adds infoBubble content to them. Unfortunately, the

fun stops here. Once we outsource all that work to a single function, we've handcuffed our ability to make exactly what we want.

To give this earthquake map our personal touches, we need to get deeper into the code. We need to go custom.

Create a Custom Earthquake Map

If all you want to do is visualize where earthquakes are, using Mapstraction's built-in GeoRSS support gets the job done easily. On the other hand, if you want to prefilter content or show different icons based on quake intensity, you'll need a more custom solution.

In this section, I'll show you how to convert the GeoRSS to JSON using Yahoo! Query Language. Then you'll choose a marker icon based on the earthquake's Richter value. Finally, you'll get extra clever and zoom in on zones that usually have considerable earthquake activity.

To start, you need a basic view of the world on the map.

Prepare Basic World Map

The basic map of the world doesn't need to be much different from the map in the GeoRSS version of the earthquake mapper. We need to load the map and then set a center and zoom level.

Add the following code to a new HTML file:

```
<html xmlns="http://www.w3.org/1999/xhtml">
  <head>
    <title>Earthquake Map Mashup</title>
    <style type="text/css">
      div#mymap {
        width: 550px;
        height: 450px;
      }
    </style>
❶  <script type="text/javascript"
src="http://ajax.googleapis.com/ajax/libs/jquery/1.3/jquery.min.js"></script>
    <script src="http://maps.google.com/maps?file=api&amp;v=2&amp;key=YOURKEY"
type="text/javascript"></script>
    <script type="text/javascript" src="mxn.js?(google)"></script>
    <script type="text/javascript">
    var mapstraction;
❷  var defaultloc = {"point": new mxn.LatLonPoint(14.604847155053898, -177.1875),
                      "zoom": 1};

    function create_map() {
      mapstraction = new mxn.Mapstraction('mymap', 'google');
      mapstraction.setMapType(mxn.Mapstraction.HYBRID);
      mapstraction.addControls({"zoom":"large"});
      view_world();

    }
    function view_world() {
```

```
❸        mapstraction.setCenterAndZoom(defaultloc["point"], defaultloc["zoom"]);
    }
  </script>
</head>
<body onload="create_map()">
  <div id="mymap"></div>
</body>
</html>
```

Save the file, load it into a browser, and you'll see a markerless map of the world, like Figure 10-7. I've made a few changes to the code to look ahead as we customize the map. For one, I included jQuery ❶, the JavaScript framework that makes applying effects and using Ajax to retrieve data easy.

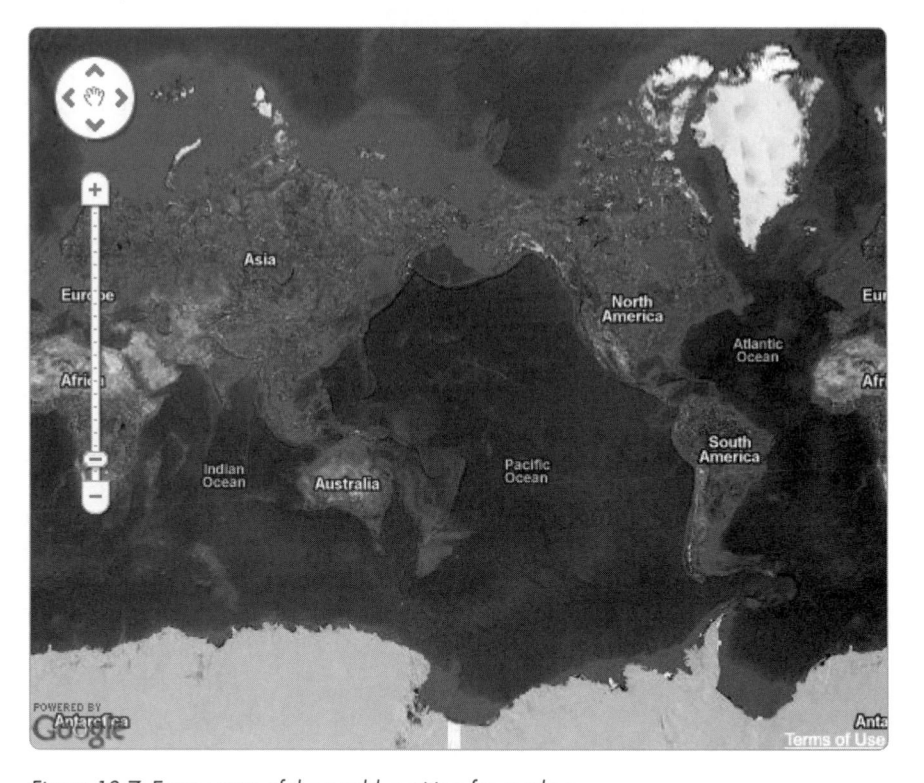

Figure 10-7: Empty map of the world, waiting for markers

I created an object variable to hold the default location and zoom level ❷, rather than individual variables. The values I chose were based on guessing and then checking to find a good location where the entire world would be visible and the location of the earthquakes would make the most sense. Because a world map is a two-dimensional view of a three-dimensional object, problems can crop up with where markers and polylines wrap. I chose the center of our basic map so our hotspot regions are completely within view globally.

Finally, I created an entire function ❸ to use the default center and zoom values. Later with this mashup, we'll zoom into those hotspot regions, but afterward we need a way to zoom back to the original center. We might as well reuse code where we can.

Convert Earthquake Data to JSON

Now that the basic map is set up, we need to start thinking about data. The USGS provides an XML feed. JavaScript can parse XML, but we would need to download the XML to a server first for security reasons. If we can get the data as JSON, our job is so much easier.

We have a number of options for converting the earthquake data from XML to JSON. In the weather mashup, we used Yahoo! Pipes. In this case, we'll use another Yahoo! product, Yahoo! Query Language (YQL). Among many other uses of the technology YQL makes converting any GeoRSS feed to JSON easy.

YQL's syntax is similar to SQL, the language used to query a database. You can try out commands in the YQL console at *http://developer.yahoo.com/yql/console/*. Instead of querying a database table, we'll work against the USGS GeoRSS URL we used in the previous section. Here's the query to grab all the data from that feed:

```
select * from atom where
  url='http://earthquake.usgs.gov/eqcenter/catalogs/7day-M2.5.xml'
```

Type that command in the YQL console, select the JSON output, and click the **Test** button. As shown in Figure 10-8, you'll see the results in the pane below. If you prefer to see a more structured view, click the **Tree View** tab to peruse the data. From there, you can see the items we'll have available to us when we load the data into our map.

Figure 10-8: YQL Console showing results from earthquake feed

Copy the long URL at the bottom of the console under The REST Query and store it somewhere. We'll use that URL in the next section.

Plot Earthquakes on Map

As you've seen, simply plotting earthquakes on a map requires a single line call to a GeoRSS feed. That's too basic for us, however. The purpose of this mashup is to create something more customized. We want to provide a visual way to see the intensity of earthquakes at a glance by using bigger icons in places the Richter value is higher.

The following two JavaScript functions will load the data from the YQL JSON URL we found in the previous section, determine which icon to use, and plot the marker on the world map. Add this code to your basic map following the create_map function:

```
// Data and marker functions
function get_quakes() {
❶    var jsonurl = "http://query.yahooapis.com/v1/public/yql"
     + "?q=select+*+from+atom+where+url%3D'http%3A%2F%2Fearthquake.usgs.gov"
     + "%2Feqcenter%2Fcatalogs%2F7day-M2.5.xml'"
     + "&format=json&diagnostics=true&callback=?";
     jQuery.getJSON(jsonurl, function(data) {
❷      jQuery.each(data.query.results.entry, function(i, item) {
         // Get Lat/Lon point
         var lltxt = item.point;
❸        var llarr = lltxt.split(" ");
         // Get Richter value
         var richter = item.title;
❹        richter = richter.substr(2, 3);
         var majorrichter = richter.substring(0, 1);
         var iconvals = get_icon(majorrichter);
         // Find link
         var link;
         if (item.link[0]) {
           link = item.link[0].href;
         }
         else {
           link = item.link.href;
         }
         // Create marker
         var marker = new mxn.Marker(new mxn.LatLonPoint(llarr[0], llarr[1]));
         marker.setIcon(iconvals.name, iconvals.size);
❺        marker.setShadowIcon('blankshadow.png', [0,0]);
         var eqdate = item.updated.substr(0, 10);
❻        marker.setInfoBubble('<strong>' + item.title + '</strong><p>On ' + eqdate +
         ' (<a href="' + link + '">more info</a>)</p>');
         mapstraction.addMarker(marker);
       });
     });
}
```

```
function get_icon(majorrichter) {
  var identifier;
  var size;
  if (majorrichter < 4) {
    identifier = "low";
    size = [10, 10];
  }
  else if (majorrichter == 4) {
    identifier = "med";
    size = [15, 15];
  }
  else {
    identifier = "high";
    size = [20, 20];
  }
  return {"name": "richter-" + identifier + ".png", "size": size};
}
```

The get_quakes function is actually a single line, but it's a really long line. It calls the getJSON function in jQuery. The JavaScript framework requires two variables to retrieve our JSON from YQL. The first is the URL to call. The second is a reference to a callback function. I used an anonymous, inline function. This callback function is what takes up most of the space in the get_quakes function.

The YQL URL ❶ is spread out over a few lines as a single, long string that is almost exactly the same as you copied from the YQL console. The only change is that the callback argument (the last part of the URL) is a question mark. By including a question mark, jQuery replaces it with the callback function for us.

Once we have a result, it is passed to the anonymous function as the data variable, which will be a JavaScript object. Within the object, data.query.results.entry refers to the array of all earthquake results. Using jQuery's each function ❷, we iterate through every result. Each earthquake is passed to yet another anonymous function.

For each earthquake, we first retrieve the geographic coordinates from the point value. As you may recall from the USGS XML, both the latitude and longitude are stored as a single value, with a space between. Our code splits them into two values ❸ and stores the result in an array. The first item in the array (with an index of zero) is the latitude; the second is the longitude.

Next, we need to find the Richter value. The *Richter value* is the measurement of an earthquake's intensity and is usually given a decimal value less than 10. Unfortunately, the USGS does not directly pass this value, even though it's sitting right there in the title. For example, M 2.6, Washington. By sucking out a substring from the title, we can find the Richter value. In this case, we want 2.6 and nothing more.

The Richter value begins at the third character in the string, which is referred to as *slot two* because textual strings, like arrays, start counting at zero. Then the Richter value continues for three characters. So our call to substr ❹ begins at slot two and continues three characters. The value of the richter variable is now 2.6 in this example, just like we wanted.

With the Richter value in hand, we can determine which icon to use by passing it to the get_icon function. I selected three levels and created a graphic for each of them. If an earthquake is relatively small, less than four, I assign it the smallest icon. If the earthquake is between four and five, it gets a medium-sized icon. Anything five and greater gets the largest icon. The icons are also colored differently among the levels, so the earthquake markers get bigger and redder with greater magnitude.

Using the latitude/longitude array that we split from the data, we create a marker for this earthquake. We give it a custom icon based on the Richter value, and then give it no shadow ❺. I used one transparent pixel for the shadow icon and set the width and height to be zero. As you'll see, our map will have so many earthquakes, we won't have room for shadows.

To finish, I added a very simple message inside the infoBubble ❻. The message shows the full title, the date, and a link to the page on the USGS site where the user can get more information about this earthquake.

Create a Legend

In just a few lines, this map is easier to read than the one generated by the GeoRSS. The many earthquakes take up less space because of the smaller markers. We have shown that some earthquakes are more noteworthy than others by changing the size and color of the icons. Will the map make sense to someone who doesn't know the method to our Richter-based madness?

Let's create a legend, like the one shown in the finished map (Figure 10-5), below the map to show what each icon means. Following the map div, add this ordered list, which describes the different icons:

```
<ol id="legend">
  <li><img src="richter-low.png" /> 2.5 - 3.9</li>
  <li><img src="richter-med.png" /> 4.0 - 4.9</li>
  <li><img src="richter-high.png" /> 5.0+</li>
</ol>
```

We don't want the legend to look like an ordered list because that takes up too much space. Most of the time, something like this will be shown along one line. Enter a little CSS to make it look the way you want. Add this to your stylesheet:

```
ol#legend {
  list-style: none;
  margin: 0;
  padding: 0;
}
ol#legend li {
  display: inline;
  padding-right: 30px;
}
```

Now the ordered list exists on a single line. Each list item is padded to the right, so which icon goes with which description is still obvious. Now that we've made it clear what the icons mean, let's add a little interactivity to this map.

Zoom to Hotspot Regions

As you can tell from this mashup, some areas of the world are more seismically active than others. These spots are fairly predictable regions. Some, like California, may be more obvious than others. Due to the clustering of many markers in these areas, having a way to zoom in for a better view would be useful.

I identified four of these regions and created a system that makes adding others easy. In the variable section of your code, add these lines to create an object containing the regions' boundaries:

```
var regions = {
  "California": new mxn.BoundingBox(30, -136, 45, -101),
  "Alaska": new mxn.BoundingBox(48, 164, 68, -125),
  "Latin America": new mxn.BoundingBox(-47, -112, 24, -15),
  "Southeast Asia": new mxn.BoundingBox(-33, 52, 39, -167)
};
```

At its most basic level, the regions variable holds text keys that correspond to Mapstraction BoundingBox objects. For our purposes, the key is a unique identifier for the region. The four numbers used to create the bounds are the minimum necessary to describe the region. The first pair describes the southwest corner of the box. The second describes the northeast corner. The other two corners of the box can be extrapolated from these values.

As the user mouses around the map, we want to determine when the cursor is hovering over one of these regions. If it is, we'll highlight the region by drawing a box around it. Then, if the user clicks, we'll zoom in to that region, like in Figure 10-9.

To achieve this, we need to listen for two events: mouse moving and clicking. Add these lines to your create_map function:

```
❶ google.maps.event.addListener(mapstraction.getMap(), 'mousemove', check_hover);
❷ mapstraction.click.addHandler(function() {
    if (highlighted) {
❸     set_region(highlighted);
    }
  });
```

The first ❶ listens for mouse movement and highlights a region if the mouse is within its bounding box. We have to use Google's native addListener function, because the mousemove event is not supported by Mapstraction. An event object is passed along to the check_hover function.

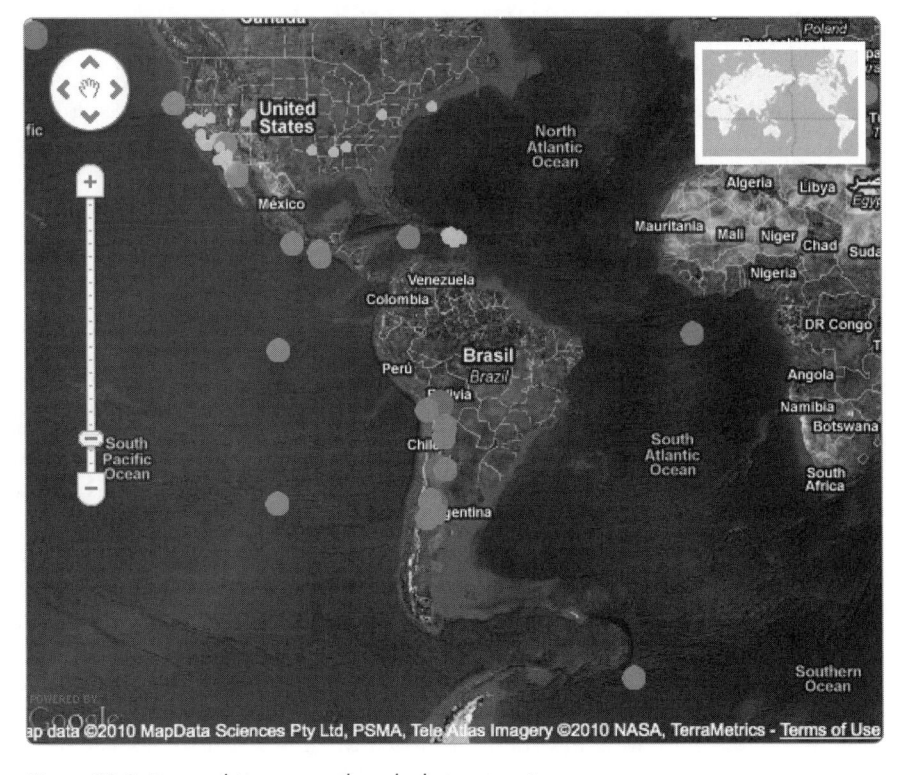

Figure 10-9: Zoomed into an earthquake hotspot region

Though we used a little Google-specific code, we are still able to use Mapstraction for everything else. The second ❷ event listens for a click somewhere on the map. If a region is already highlighted, it zooms in ❸ to give a closer look at the quakes.

Now let's write the two functions (in bold) that are called from our event code. First, we'll write the code to determine whether the mouse is hovering over any of our identified regions. Add this to your JavaScript:

```
// Region highlight functions
var highlighted = "";
function find_region(cpt) {
  for (var k in regions) {
    if (k != "World") {
❶      if (regions[k].contains(cpt)) {
        return k;
      }
    }
  }
  return "";
}
function check_hover(google_event) {
  // Google-specific code to convert event to Mapstraction LatLonPoint
  pt = new mxn.LatLonPoint(google_event.latLng.lat(), google_event.latLng.lng());
```

```
      // Mapstraction code to highlight appropriate region
      var regionin = find_region(pt);
      if (regionin) {
❷       if (highlighted != regionin) {
          highlighted = regionin;
          highlight_region(regionin);
        }
      }
❸     else if (highlighted) {
        highlighted = "";
❹       mapstraction.removeAllPolylines();
      }
    }
```

In addition to the check_hover function, we also have a helper function.
Together, this duo determines whether the user is hovering over a region
and, if so, which region. The find_region function does most of this work.
It loops through the region's array and compares the mouse's latitude/lon-
gitude to the four edges of the bounding box ❶ using the handy contains
function.

If the user is hovering over a region, the name of the region is returned
to check_hover. Assuming we aren't already highlighting that region❷, we
pass the name along to the highlight_region function, which draws the box.
If the mouse is not over a region, but one was previously highlighted ❸,
then we know the user moved the mouse outside of the region. Therefore,
we can remove the box from the screen ❹.

We haven't created the function to add the box, so we'll do that now:

```
function highlight_region(name) {
  var bounds = regions[name];
  if (bounds) {
    mapstraction.removeAllPolylines();
❺   var pdata = {"color": "white"};
    var poly = BoundingBox_to_Polyline(bounds);
    mapstraction.addPolylineWithData(poly, pdata);
  }
}
function BoundingBox_to_Polyline(box) {
  var points = [box.sw, new mxn.LatLonPoint(box.ne.lat, box.sw. Lon),
                box.ne, new mxn.LatLonPoint(box.sw.lat, box.ne.lon),
                new mxn.LatLonPoint(box.sw.lat, box.sw.lon-.0001)];
  var poly = new mxn.Polyline(points);
  return poly;
}
```

The process of highlighting is fairly simple, though I have separated it into
two functions. I have reprinted the second function, BoundingBox_to_Polyline,
from "#19: Draw a Rectangle to Declare an Area" on page 71.

The box created in the highlight_region function uses a white polyline ❺. You may wish to change the polyline to another color. The rest is
simply drawing the box on the map.

At this point, as a user moves the mouse around the map, regions will be highlighted. Now we need to make something happen when a user clicks while a region is highlighted. In other words, we need to set the current region and zoom in, fulfilling the second function called by the event listeners.

Add this to your JavaScript:

```
function set_region(name) {
  var bounds = regions[name];
  if (bounds) {
    mapstraction.setBounds(bounds);
  }
}
```

Quite simply, if the region exists in our array, we set the map's boundaries to include only the selected region. The map zooms in and is centered to show the earthquakes in the region.

Now we need a way to get back to the world map. Very early on in this mashup, we created a `view_world` function. How do we call it? We'll use a graphic of the world and call the function whenever the image is clicked.

Adding this functionality is something that touches several sections of the mashup. So we need to include a few lines in a number of places. First, add the graphic to your HTML between the map and the legend:

```
<a href="#" id="reset"><img src="worldmap.png" /></a>
```

You can find this image, along with the marker icons I've used in this example at *http://mapscripting.com/earthquake-mashup*.

Next, we need to add some CSS so the graphic appears in the upper-right corner of our map:

```
#reset img {
  border: 5px solid white;
  position: relative;
  top: -435px;
  left: 430px;
}
```

Let's use jQuery to respond to a user clicking the image. Add this code to the `create_map` function:

```
$("#reset").click(view_world);
```

This retrieves the link element, which surrounds the image using CSS selector syntax and tells the browser to call the `view_world` function whenever that object is clicked.

If we weren't picky, we'd stop here. In a perfect world, the clickable graphic would only be visible when the map is zoomed in. Let's see if we can't make this world a little more perfect, again using some jQuery functions.

Because we want the graphic to disappear whenever we're viewing the whole world, we'll need to add this line inside the view_world function:

```
$("#reset").hide();
```

The image will now be invisible all the time. Of course, we want it to appear when we've zoomed in. Inside the set_region function, directly under the setBounds line, we add this line:

```
$("#reset").show();
```

With that, we've incorporated a better interface into our interactive earthquake map. Zooming in by region is cool, as long as you can return to the map. We may not have made a perfect world, but this world map mashup is close to perfect.

We converted USGS data from XML to JSON. Then we read in every earthquake in the past week, determined its intensity, and gave it an appropriate icon. Finally, we implemented zooming into hotspot regions. The only thing left to do is monitor tectonic movements; at least now you have a tool to do that.

#71: Search Music Events by Location

Want to check out a concert tonight? Where shall we go and who's playing? This information is out there. Let's get our hands on it and plot it on a map.

For this mashup, we'll be using Yahoo!'s Upcoming API. Upcoming is an events calendar showing conferences, concerts, user group meetings, and more. We want to search only for music, an option made possible by using the API's tag-based search.

Unless we can count on users all being from the same city, we'll need to provide a way to search by location. Lucky us—that's also an option with Upcoming. Because some people are willing to drive farther than others, we also want users to be able to specify distance. Yep, that option is also supported.

Some people are more frugal than others. You may be willing to drop $75 to see an aging rocker, but I prefer to pay a small cover to see a local band at a bar. We'll need to plan for different price ranges. Alas, Upcoming does not directly support this option. We can query free concerts, but I'm not a total cheapskate; I'll pay five or ten bucks. Seeing as Upcoming does pass along ticket cost, however, we can handle price filtering ourselves.

This mashups requires a lot of features. You can see in Figure 10-10 that they all come together nicely.

Now we have a game plan so let's jam! Before we get into the data itself, we'll get a feel for the interface we'll create for users.

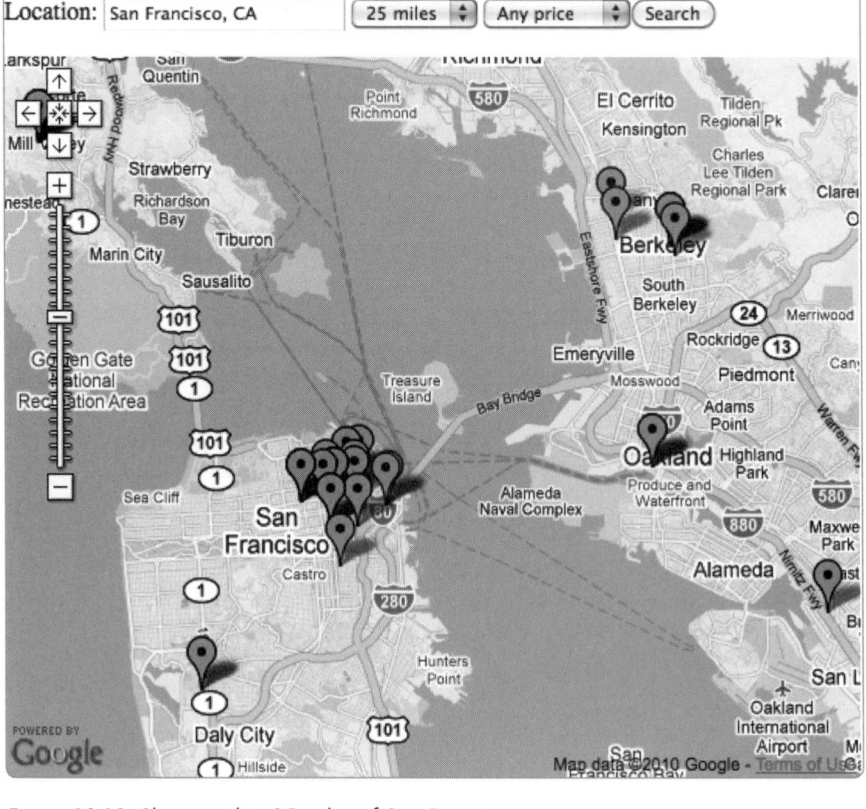

Figure 10-10: Shows within 25 miles of San Francisco

Prepare HTML for Search Interface

This being a map mashup, the map will be the center of our experience. The user will need to let us in on his or her whims regarding location and price. We'll need to put the search functions close to the map, so it's obvious that one controls the other.

Open up a new file and add this code to create a basic map and form fields:

```
<html xmlns="http://www.w3.org/1999/xhtml">
<head>
  <title>Upcoming Music Map Mashup</title>
  <script type="text/javascript"
  src="http://ajax.googleapis.com/ajax/libs/jquery/1.3/jquery.min.js"></script>
  <script src="http://maps.google.com/maps?file=api&amp;v=2&amp;key=YOURKEY"
  type="text/javascript"></script>
  <script type="text/javascript" src="mxn.js?(google)"></script>
  <style type="text/css">
  div#mymap {
    width: 550px;
    height: 450px;
  }
```

❶

```
    </style>
    <script type="text/javascript">
      var mapstraction;
      function create_map() {
        mapstraction = new mxn.Mapstraction('mymap', 'google');
        mapstraction.addControls({"zoom":"large"});
        mapstraction.setCenterAndZoom(new mxn.LatLonPoint(45.5, -122.5)❷, 10);
      }
    </script>
</head>
<body onload="create_map();">
<p>
<form onsubmit="search_upcoming(); return false;">
Location: <input type="text" name="location" value="Portland, OR"❸ size="20" />
<select name="radius" onchange="search_upcoming();">
  <option value="1">1 mile</option>
  <option value="5"❹>5 miles</option>
  <option value="10">10 miles</option>
  <option value="25" selected="selected">25 miles</option>
  <option value="50">50 miles</option>
</select>
<select name="cost" onchange="filter_select(this);">
  <option value="9999"❺>Any price</option>
  <option value="25">$25 or less</option>
  <option value="10">$10 or less</option>
</select>
<input type="submit" value="Search" />
</form>
</p>
<div id="mymap"></div>
</body>
</html>
```

Much of this HTML will look familiar. As with most maps, I've loaded the Google Maps and Mapstraction JavaScript libraries. I also included jQuery ❶, which makes applying effects and using Ajax easy.

The search location text defaults to Portland, Oregon, in this example. When the map first loads, it is centered on Portland. You can change the center to your city, but you'll need to edit multiple places. First, I used geographic coordinates ❷ to set the center. You've memorized these for your city now, right? Second, you need to change the value of the text field ❸. Of course, your user may edit the location, but starting with a logical default makes sense. For me, I used my hometown.

The radius and cost fields are drop-down boxes. The values hold the maximums. For example, if you choose a radius of five miles ❹, nothing even a foot farther than five miles will show in the results. The same goes for price values. For the option of showing results regardless of cost ❺, we're hoping no concert is charging more than $9,999.

Creating the basic interface for a mashup, as we have here, can help you figure out everything you need to do. Look back at the code listing and note the function names in bold. You need to write those—one to search and another to filter—at the very least to be able to convert this interface into a working mashup.

Before we start building the functions we need, let's look at the data we'll be using. To do that, we need to become familiar with the Upcoming API.

Perform an Upcoming API Search

Upcoming uses a REST API, which means we can play around with it in the browser before coding anything. As a first step, you need a Yahoo! account to sign into Upcoming. Then, you need to get an Upcoming API key. This key is different than ones you've used for any other Yahoo! service.

While logged into Upcoming, request a key here: *http://upcoming.yahoo .com/api/url.*

Now that you have an API key, try out this Upcoming search by copying this URL into your browser: *http://upcoming.yahooapis.com/services/rest/?api_ key=YOURKEY&method=event.search&location=Portland,+OR.*

Here is a sample of the results from this simple search:

```
<rsp stat="ok" version="1.0" resultcount="12">
<event id="1234567" name="Some Band Name" description="..."
start_date="2011-04-15" latitude="45.5409" longitude="-122.6637"
geocoding_precision="address" geocoding_ambiguous="0"
venue_name="Wonder Ballroom" venue_address="128 NE Russell St"
venue_city="Portland" venue_state_name="Oregon" venue_state_code="OR"
venue_zip="97212" ticket_url="..." ticket_price="$25-$40" ticket_free="0" />
<event .... />
...
</rsp>
```

The search term has merely restricted to a location. We need to add more options to the search before it will find the data we seek. See Table 10-1 for a description of the arguments we'll use. Many more are listed in Upcoming's documentation.

Table 10-1: Upcoming API Event Search Option

Argument	Description
api_key	Your API key (required)
location	City and state to search for events
radius	How far away from center of location to search
min_date	What date to start searching for events
max_date	What date to stop searching for events
tags	The metadata keywords to filter results

Retrieve Event Data Server-Side

Now that we know what to expect from the Upcoming API, we're ready to connect to it. Rather than use JavaScript to get directly at the data, we'll run the data through a server-side PHP script. If you're unsure about whether you have PHP or how to use it, go check out Chapter 9.

We're using PHP to pass the results to JavaScript for two reasons: First, we have to take into account security issues with accessing outside APIs directly with JavaScript. In many cases, browsers won't allow it. Second, we can do some preprocessing to the data. We need to find the concert cost and put the price in a format that will make filtering results easier. Also, even though the API provides XML, we'll output as JSON with the server-side script. JSON can be read directly into a JavaScript object, which again will make our lives easier.

The PHP code we'll use to access the Upcoming API is about 60 lines long. Rather than display it all at once, I'll go through one section at a time. That way I can describe what's happening, and you'll understand each piece before moving on to the next.

To start, let's create a new PHP file on your server and retrieve arguments from the query string:

```php
<?php
$apikey = "YOURKEY";
$dateformat = "Y-m-d";
// Get arguments from querystring
$location = $_GET["location"];
$radius = $_GET["radius"];
$timeframe = $_GET["timeframe"];
$tags = $_GET["tags"];
// Determine the timeframe as a timestamp, set max/min date variables
❶ $mindate = date($dateformat);
$maxdate = "";
switch($timeframe) {
  case "1d":
    $timestamp = ❷time();
    break;
  case "1m":
    $timestamp = strtotime("+1 month -1 day");
    break;
  case "1w":
  default:
    $timestamp = ❸strtotime("+1 week -1 day");
    break;
}
❹ $maxdate = date($dateformat, $timestamp);
```

Even though we're using someone else's API, writing a middleman PHP script like this is sort of like creating our own API. Most of our query string arguments (in bold) will be passed unchanged to Upcoming. The timeframe argument, however, is my own creation.

This argument specifies how far in the future to search. This simple version allows three options: one day (1d), one week (1w), and one month (1m). Because Upcoming does not have this option, we need to convert the timeframe to a maximum date by finding the timestamp that represents a day in the future.

We already set the minimum date to be today ❶. PHP's date function, if a second argument isn't included, assumes the current date. We can achieve the same result by passing time() as the second argument. In fact, with a timeframe of one day, we simply set the timestamp equal to time() ❷. That leaves the minimum date as today and the maximum date as today, just like we want.

In the case of a week or month, we need to do a little date math. PHP has a strtotime function that takes many different types of input. In this example ❸, the function starts at today and adds a week. Then it subtracts a day. Why? Because otherwise we'd have eight days, which is more than a week. The same is true of the month option.

Finally we convert our timeframe to a timestamp format the computer understands. Now all we need is to set the $maxdate variable by passing the timeframe to the date function ❹.

Now that we've figured out all the variables that we're sending to the Upcoming API, we're ready for the next bit of code. In this section, we actually retrieve data and preprocess it:

```
     // Get XML results from Upcoming
❺  $url = "http://upcoming.yahooapis.com/services/rest/?api_key=$apikey";
     $url .= "&method=event.search&location=$location&radius=$radius";
     $url .= "&tags=$tags";
     $url .= "&max_date=$maxdate&min_date=$mindate";
❻  $xmlobj = get_xml($url);
     $outobj = array();
     // Loop through results
     foreach (❼$xmlobj->event as $event) {
❽    $attribs = $event->attributes();
       $id = (int) $attribs->id;
       $lat = (float) $attribs->latitude;
       $lon = (float) $attribs->longitude;
       $title = (string) $attribs->name;
       $date = (string) $attribs->start_date;
       $cost = "";
       // Convert ticket price range into number value we can use in JavaScript
❾    preg_match_all("(\\\$\d+)", (string) $attribs->ticket_price, $dollars);
       if (count($dollars) > 0 && count($dollars[0]) > 0) {
         $cost = $dollars[0][count($dollars[0])-1];
       }
       $cost = str_replace("$", "", $cost);
       // Put all results into an array of associative arrays
       $eventobj = array(
         "id" => $id,
         "latitude" => $lat,
         "longitude" => $lon,
         "title" => $title,
```

```
      "date" => $date,
      "cost" => $cost
   );
❿   array_push($outobj, $eventobj);
}
```

Using the variables we created in the previous section, we piece
together the URL to call Upcoming's API ❺. The content from the URL
will come through as XML, which we convert into a SimpleXML object. In
"#61: Retrieve a Web Page" on page 215, we wrote the get_xml function to
perform this task. We might as well save ourselves some time and reuse that
function here ❻.

With the XML now easily accessible, let's loop through all the events
that the Upcoming API returned. We'll grab each <event> tag ❼ one at a
time. The data about the event is stored as the event tag's attributes. We can
grab all the attributes at once ❽ and then pick and choose only the ones we
want: the unique id assigned by Upcoming, latitude, longitude, the event's
title, its date, and its cost. Most of these are straightforward, but we'll need
to do a little voodoo to get the price of the event in the format we want.

Upcoming includes a dollar sign in front of the ticket price, and many
events have a price range instead of a single amount. To filter by the cost in
our JavaScript code, we need our PHP code to return a simple number.

Here, I used a regular expression to look for all instances of a dollar
sign followed by one or more digits ❾. This way, we can take the last dollar amount, which should be at the highest end of the range if one exists.
If tickets are just one price, the expression will find that, too. Finally, we
remove the dollar sign, so we return only a number.

Now that we have the data from the event we need, we put it into an
associative array, $eventobj. That new array then gets "pushed" onto the
end of the results object ❿, which is a normal array. I've named the results
object $outobj because we'll print it. In fact, with all the preprocessing com-
plete, we can do that now:

```
// Output values as JSON
print header("Content-type: application/json");
print json_encode($outobj);
?>
```

We first print the header to declare that we're sending plain text. PHP
defaults to HTML. Next, we print out the results object, but we make sure
it is JSON-encoded. That way, we're giving our JavaScript code something
easy to digest.

Remember when we used the get_xml function to retrieve the Upcoming
URL and convert the XML content to a SimpleXML object? We never actually
included the function in our code. Let's do that now:

```
<?
//cUrl functions
function get_url($url) {
```

```
  $c = curl_init();
  curl_setopt($c, CURLOPT_URL, $url);
  curl_setopt($c, CURLOPT_RETURNTRANSFER, 1);
  $content = trim(curl_exec($c));
  curl_close($c);
  return $content;
}
function get_xml($url) {
  $xml = get_url($url);
  return simplexml_load_string($xml);
}
?>
```

Hey! That's two functions!

You caught me. Because one calls the other, we need to include them both. If you find yourself using these functions often, adding them to their own file is probably worthwhile. Then you can make them part of your project as needed with the PHP include function.

And that's that. We've written some PHP to call the Upcoming API. From the XML returned by Upcoming, we take only the stuff we want and output it as JSON. I saved the PHP file as *upcoming.php* in the same directory as the HTML search interface we created earlier. Now let's return to that HTML file, so we can use JavaScript to connect to our newly created PHP file.

Plot Event Search Results on a Map

Now that you know how to get data from Upcoming, let's put that data on our map. We'll connect to the PHP file we just created, sending it the information it needs.

You may recall from setting up the HTML that we need to create two functions. First, we write the search_upcoming function to perform the Ajax call to our PHP. Add these lines in the JavaScript below the create_map function:

```
function search_upcoming() {
❶   var tags = "music,concert";
    var timeframe = "1w";
❷   var data = {
      "location": f.location.value.replace(", ", ",").replace(" ", "_"),
      "radius": f.radius.value,
      "tags": tags,
      "timeframe": timeframe
    };
❸   $.get("upcoming.php", data, ❹plot_upcoming);
}
```

Before we can search Upcoming, we need to retrieve the user's values from the form. To do this, I used the document.getElementById function, doing a little data cleanup for the location.

I hard-coded some values that are options in our PHP file that we don't currently use as input from the user. For example, the tags ❶ that we look for can be changed to something else if you aren't looking for concerts. The timeframe defaults to one week, which seems the most useful for planning impromptu entertainment.

The values that I hard-coded, plus a couple from the form, are put into a JavaScript object ❷. The jQuery getJSON function ❸ that calls our PHP file using the data variable to include values requires this format. The last parameter is a function reference to plot_upcoming ❹. That's one we need to write.

In this new function, we want to loop through all the results in the JavaScript object. As we find each event, we plot it on the map. Add this code to your JavaScript:

```
function plot_upcoming(jobj) {
  if (jobj.length > 0) {
    mapstraction.removeAllMarkers();
❺    for (var i=0; i < jobj.length; i++) {
      var ev = jobj[i];
❻      var url = "http://upcoming.yahoo.com/event/" + ev.id;
      var marker = new mxn.Marker(new mxn.LatLonPoint(ev.latitude, ev.longitude));
      var cost = ev.cost;
      if (cost != "") {
❼        marker.setAttribute('cost', parseInt(cost));
        cost = " ($" + cost + ")"; // Format cost for infoBubble
      }
      else {
        marker.setAttribute('cost', 9999); // Set a way too high value
      }
      var bubbletext = ev.date + " <a href=\"" + url + "\">" + ev.title
                      + "</a>" + cost;
      marker.setInfoBubble(bubbletext);
      mapstraction.addMarker(marker);
    }
❽    filter_select(document.forms[0].cost);
  }
  else {
    alert('no results for this search');
  }
}
```

This function unpacks the variables that are output by the PHP and uses them to add a marker for every Upcoming event the API returned. Remember, we used an array holding many associative arrays. The JavaScript object is also an array. We iterate through it with the for command ❺, putting each event result into the ev variable.

Using the id returned from Upcoming, we can piece together the URL ❻ where the user can find out more information about the event. Other data, like the latitude and longitude, we put directly into variables that we use to create the marker.

If the PHP was able to determine the cost of the event, we add an attribute to the marker with that information ❼. This information will be useful when we filter by ticket price. In fact, at the end of this function, once all the markers have been added to the map, we call that filter function ❽, which means we better go write it.

Filter Results by Ticket Price

When the results are returned, they contain all the music events in an area, not just the ones that match the user's budget. The Upcoming API has no way to query for events under a specific ticket price, though it does provide the price in the results, if available. The PHP we wrote takes the ticket price and produces a numeric cost that we can use as a filter.

In the previous section, we added a cost attribute for every marker containing the ticket price. Just having the attribute is not enough to remove overpriced concerts. We also need to apply the filter, which comes from a drop-down box in the HTML form.

The filter_select function is called when all the markers are added to the page, or whenever the value in the drop-down box changes. Add these functions to your JavaScript code:

```
  function filter_select(selobj) {
❶   var cost = parseInt(selobj.options[selobj.selectedIndex].value);
    filter_cost(cost);
  }
  function filter_cost(amt) {
❷   mapstraction.removeAllFilters();
    mapstraction.addFilter('cost', ❸'le', amt);
    mapstraction.doFilter();
❹   mapstraction.visibleCenterAndZoom();
  }
```

As with other examples, two functions perform this one task. The first retrieves the value from the drop-down box ❶ and then passes the cost to the second. The filter_cost function does the actual filtering work.

Before creating a new filter, we need to remove any previous filters ❷. Why? Mapstraction's filtering is additive, meaning a second filter does not replace the first, but instead is applied in addition to the first. In this case, we only want to use a single filtering method, we remove all filters before adding new ones.

To apply a filter requires three pieces of information: the attribute to be filtered by, the operator to use (in this case le for less than or equal to ❸), and finally the value to compare. Markers don't actually get filtered until Mapstraction's doFilter function is called.

Now with only the markers matching our filter being displayed, we can make sure they're all visible on the map. Mapstraction has a function specifically for situations like this ❹. We don't want to set the center and zoom based on all the markers; we simply want to use the visible markers.

These filtering functions are called from our mashup whenever the user searches for concerts. We also save a little bandwidth whenever the user changes the value in the ticket price drop-down box. Because we've stored concerts for all price ranges, we call these filtering functions to show only the ones that match, as shown in Figure 10-11.

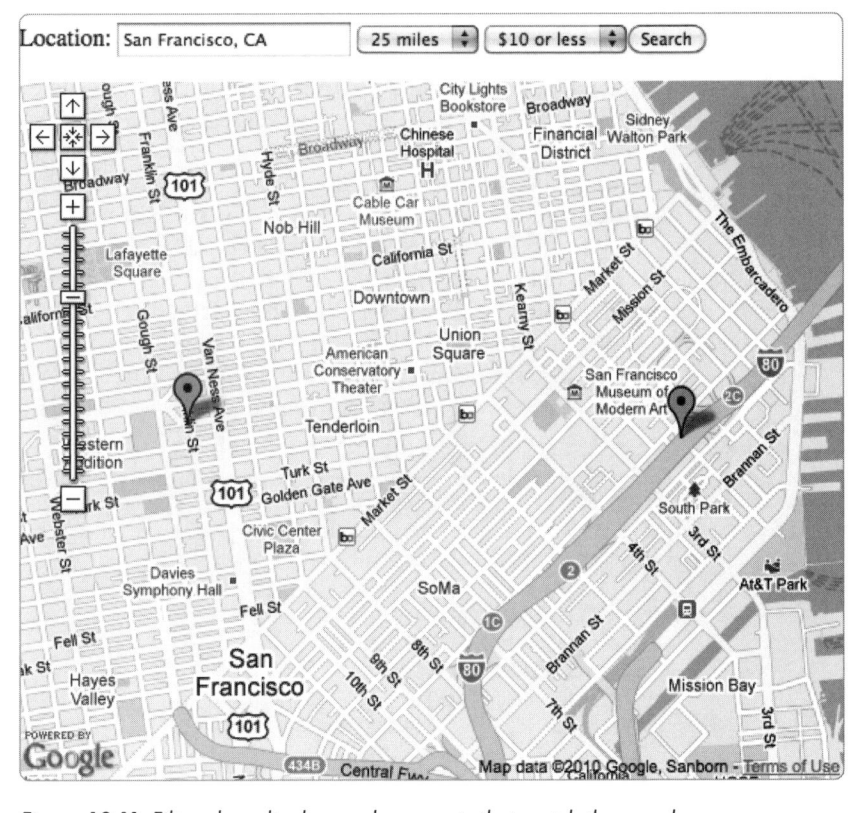

Figure 10-11: Filtered results show only concerts that match the search

If you look back to Figure 10-10, you can see all the results for concerts within 25 miles of San Francisco. Then, in Figure 10-11, you see only the two concerts that are $10 or less. The map automatically zooms to show only the concerts that match our filter criteria. Pretty slick. Now which band are we going to hear?

#72: Plot Twitter Geo-Tweets

Twitter is a popular service for sharing short messages with friends. In 140 characters or less, people send rants, links, photos, or whatever else they feel like. Optionally, those messages (called *tweets*) can be geo-tagged. When content is tied to a location, you can do some interesting things with that data.

In this mashup, we'll create a tool for users to search for geo-tagged tweets by city name, ZIP Code, or address. We'll also create an optional way to search by keyword. Do you want all the geo-tagged tweets nearby that mention *lunch*? You can do that! Just take a look at Figure 10-12.

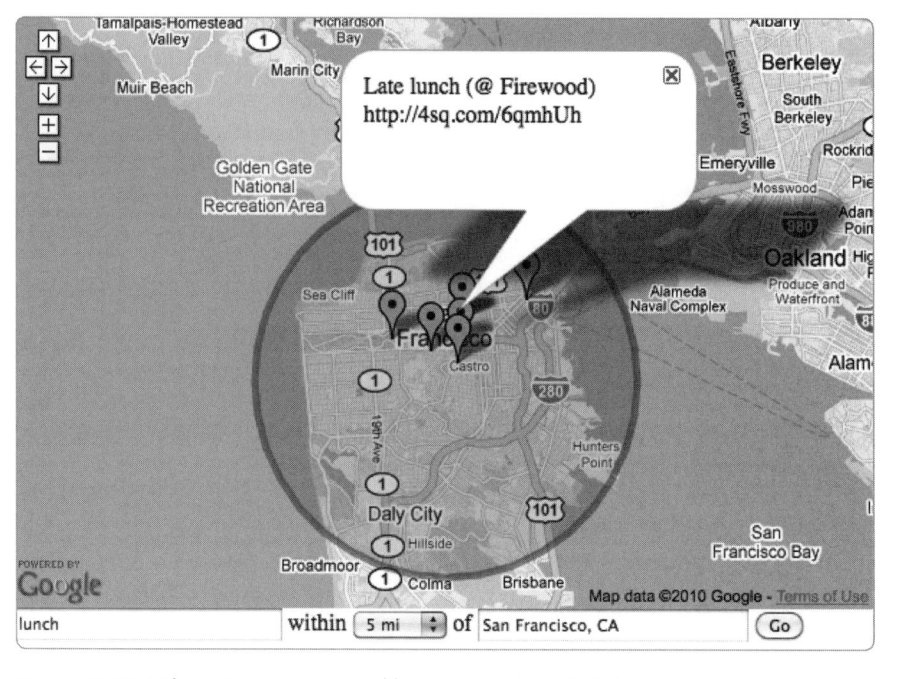

Figure 10-12: Where San Franciscans like to tweet about their lunch

Along with searching tweets, we'll integrate a few other projects from earlier in the book. Because we need the user to enter a location, we'll need a geocoder to translate the name of a place to latitude and longitude coordinates. For that, we'll use "#12: Geocode with JavaScript" on page 46. And because we need to start somewhere, I've used "#50: Get Location by IP" on page 166 to guess where the user is.

But first we need to create the HTML for the page where our map will reside. Let's get started.

Prepare the Map with User Location

Most maps we've created start with a default location. That's the biggest difference between this map and the others. Here, we'll use Google's ClientLocation to guess the user's city. If that's not available, we'll instead show a map of the entire United States. In either case, the form below the map will be accessible to set a new location or other search term.

In an empty file, add the following code:

```
<html xmlns="http://www.w3.org/1999/xhtml">
  <head>
    <title>Show Geocoded Tweets</title>
    <style>
      div#mymap {
        width: 600px;
        height: 400px;
      }
```

```
      </style>
❶    <script type="text/javascript"
       src="http://ajax.googleapis.com/ajax/libs/jquery/1.3/jquery.min.js"></script>
❷    <script type="text/javascript" src="http://www.google.com/jsapi?key=YOURKEY"></script>
     <script type="text/javascript" src="mxn.js?(google)"></script>
❸    <script type="text/javascript" src="mxn.google.geocoder.js"></script>
     <script type="text/javascript">
❹      google.load("maps", "2");

        var mapstraction;
        var radius_field, location_field, kw_field;
        function create_map() {
          mapstraction = new mxn.Mapstraction('mymap', 'google');
          mapstraction.addControls({"zoom":"large"});

          // Store form field objects
          radius_field = document.getElementById('radius');
          location_field = document.getElementById('loc');
          kw_field = document.getElementById('keyword');

          // Get position from ClientLocation
          var pos = google.loader.ClientLocation;
          if (pos) {
            var posloc = new mxn.LatLonPoint(pos.latitude, pos.longitude);
            var cityname = pos.address.city + ", " + pos.address.region;
            get_twitter_geo(posloc, 5);
            mapstraction.setCenterAndZoom(posloc, 11);

❺          location_field.value = cityname;
          }
          else {
❻          mapstraction.setCenterAndZoom(new mxn.LatLonPoint(40, -92), 3);
          }
        }
     </script>
   </head>
   <body onload="create_map()">
     <div id="mymap"></div>
     <form onsubmit="geocode_form();return false;">
       <input type="text" id="keyword" name="keyword" size="25" /> within
       <select name="radius" id="radius">
         <option value="1">1 mi</option>
         <option value="5" selected>5 mi</option>
         <option value="10">10 mi</option>
         <option value="25">25 mi</option>
       </select>
       of <input type="text" id="loc" name="loc" size="25" />
       <input type="submit" value="Go" />
     </form>
   </body>
 </html>
```

First, we include the jQuery library ❶, which we'll use to make the Ajax call to Twitter. Then we load the generic Google JavaScript API script ❷.

This distinction from the normal way of loading the Google Maps API is important; we use this alternate method so we can retrieve the user's location. Because we will also be using the JavaScript geocoder, we need to include that, too ❸.

At this point, we've loaded all our scripts the standard way. All we've included from Google, however, is a script that loads other scripts. The first thing we need to do in the JavaScript section is load Google Maps ❹.

When we create the map, we need to check whether we can determine the user's location. If we can, then we can set the center of the map based on the coordinates retrieved from ClientLocation. We'll also prepopulate the search form with the name of this location ❺ and call to the get_twitter_geo function, which retrieves search results from Twitter.

If we can't determine the user's location, we'll just zoom out so the entire United States is shown on the map ❻. And calling for search results from this view is futile, so we'll wait for the user to search manually. How does that happen? Read on.

Geocode User Input

Accepting user input is an important part of this mashup. Users want to interact with the map and the data, which requires the ability to look for any location. The form we created in the previous section has inputs for a keyword, radius, and place. Twitter can use all of these to find tweets, but first we need to convert the place into the latitude and longitude coordinates that Twitter expects.

When the user submits the form, the browser will call the geocode_form function, which is used to initiate a call to the JavaScript geocoder. Let's create this function by adding the following lines to your JavaScript section, outside any other functions:

```
function geocode_form() {
  var loctxt = location_field.value;
❶  if (loctxt == "") {
    call_twitter_geo({point: mapstraction.getCenter()});
  }
  else {
    geocoder = new MapstractionGeocoder(❷call_twitter_geo, 'google');
    var address = { address: loctxt };
❸    geocoder.geocode(address);
  }
}
```

If the user has left the location field empty ❶, we assume they want to search using the center of the current map. Otherwise, we create a geocoder and set the callback function ❷. Then, we perform geocoding ❸ using the location the user entered.

In either case, the next function that will be called is call_twitter_geo (either directly or as a callback from the geocoder), which passes the point and other criteria to our get_twitter_geo function, which does the heavy lifting. Let's create the first and simpler of those two functions now. Add the following code within the JavaScript section, but not within another function:

```
function call_twitter_geo(❹loc) {
  mapstraction.setCenterAndZoom(loc.point, 11);
  var kw = kw_field.value;
  var rad = radius_field.options[radius_field.selectedIndex].value;
❺ get_twitter_geo(loc.point, rad, kw, 1, 100);
}
```

The argument expected is a location object ❹, which is a `point` attribute containing a Mapstraction `LatLonPoint`. Even though we sometimes call this function directly, it is designed to accept the results of the JavaScript geocoder.

We gather the rest of the form fields (keyword, radius) and pass them off to be used to retrieve geo-tweets ❺.

With that, we're through with the overhead. Now we're ready to search tweets.

Retrieve Geo-Tweets from Twitter

So far we have only determined (in various ways) a point around which to search, but we haven't performed the actual search. That's what we'll do here: Send our requirements to Twitter, and receive tweets in return.

Twitter's search API does not require a key, so you can get started right away. The base URL is *search.twitter.com/search.json*, and you can use a number of parameters to call it. The ones we'll use are listed in Table 10-2.

Table 10-2: Some Twitter Search Parameters

Argument	Description
q	Search query/keyword
geocode	Coordinates in lat,lon,radius format
page	Page of results to retrieve
rpp	Results per page

You can search in your browser by adjusting the URL. Here are some abbreviated example results:

```
{"results":[
  {"from_user":"mapscripting", "created_at":"Thu 15 Jul 2010 12:30:12",
   "text":"This is an example tweet, shown in the API",
   "geo":{"coordinates":[45.5228,-122.6485],"type":"Point"},
   ...},
  {"from_user":"adamd", ...
   "geo":null, ... },
  ...
], ... }
```

You can see that the results contain the username, tweet text, and date. Also, the geo attribute contains information about geocoded tweets. Not every tweet will contain this data, however, even when we send the `geocode` argument in the search query. We'll need to watch for that as we create the function to plot geocoded tweets. In fact, because so many non-geocoded tweets are out there, we may need to go through many pages of results before we get enough tweets to plot on our map.

Much more data than I have shown is sent along with the tweet, such as the client used to create the tweet and the profile image of the user who wrote it. You can find full documentation of the search API on Twitter's site at *http://dev.twitter.com/doc/get/search*.

Now that you better understand the data you'll get from Twitter's API, let's write the get_twitter_geo function that we call from our mashup. Add the following code to your JavaScript, outside any other functions:

```
function get_twitter_geo(loc, rad, kw, pg, rpp) {
  // Set default values
  if (rpp == null) {
    rpp = 100;
  }
  if (rad == null) {
    rad = 5; // radius in miles
  }
  // Clear the map on first page
  if (pg == null || pg == 1) {
    pg = 1;
    mapstraction.removeAllMarkers();
    mapstraction.removeAllPolylines();
❶  polygon_circle(loc, rad);
  }
  mapstraction.autoCenterAndZoom();
  // Construct URL
  var url = "http://search.twitter.com/search.json?page=" + pg;
  if (kw != null && kw != "") {
    url += "&q=" + kw;
  }
  url += "&geocode=" + loc.lat + "," + loc.lon + "," + rad + "mi" + "&rpp=" + rpp;
❷  url += "&callback=?";

  $.getJSON(url, function(jobj) {
    var resarray = jobj.results;
    for (var i=0; i<resarray.length; i++) {
      var res = resarray[i];
❸    if (res.geo) {
        var coords = res.geo.coordinates;
        var mk = new mxn.Marker(new mxn.LatLonPoint(coords[0], coords[1]));
        mk.setInfoBubble(res.text);
        mapstraction.addMarker(mk);
      }
    }
  }
```

```
❹    if ((pg * rpp) < 1500 && resarray.length == rpp) {
       get_twitter_geo(loc, rad, kw, ❺pg+1, rpp);
     }
   });
 }
```

The function contains five parameters, but only one (the location) is required. The others—radius, keyword, page, and results per page—are set to defaults if need be.

Whenever the search is for the first page of results, we know that this is a new search, so we have to remove previous results from the map. Then, based on the center point, we draw a circle around the search area. I've used a polygon to approximate a circle, as described in "#18: Add Circles to Show Search Radius" on page 67. For convenience, the polygon_circle ❶ function is reprinted at the end of this section.

Using the function arguments (or the defaults), we then create the URL for a Twitter search. At the end, we include the callback parameter ❷ with a question mark that will be filled in by jQuery with a generated function name.

Once we get query results, we loop through until we find a tweet that is geocoded ❸. Then we grab its coordinates (an array, with latitude before longitude) and create a marker with them. I've given the marker a message box containing the text of the tweet. You could also include more data about the tweet if you want.

When we've looped through all the results, we aren't necessarily done. Because not every tweet is geocoded, we need to view many pages. Twitter will only return 1,500 tweets. The number of pages will depend on the results per page. As long as we're below the limit and still receiving a full set of tweets ❹, we want to keep searching. In some areas, especially without searching by keyword, your tweet map will get pretty full, like in Figure 10-13.

This get_twitter_geo function is what computer scientists call *recursive*, meaning it calls itself. This can be dangerous, because if you aren't careful about the conditions when you make another call, you've got the potential for an infinite loop. Perhaps the most important part of the function is that we increase the page number ❺ with each call. Doing so will ensure that eventually we'll stop calling the function.

That's it! Before your code will work, you'll need to include the code, which I am reprinting from Chapter 4:

```
function polygon_circle(center, radius) {
  var rad = new mxn.Radius(center, 10);
  var poly = rad.getPolyline(mxn.util.milesToKM(radius), '990066');
  mapstraction.addPolyline(poly);
}
```

Now you've written a mashup that geocodes a location and searches Twitter for tweets near that place. You've tapped into the geographic hive-mind. Now start using it to uncover some interesting data. Where in your city are people tweeting about lunch?

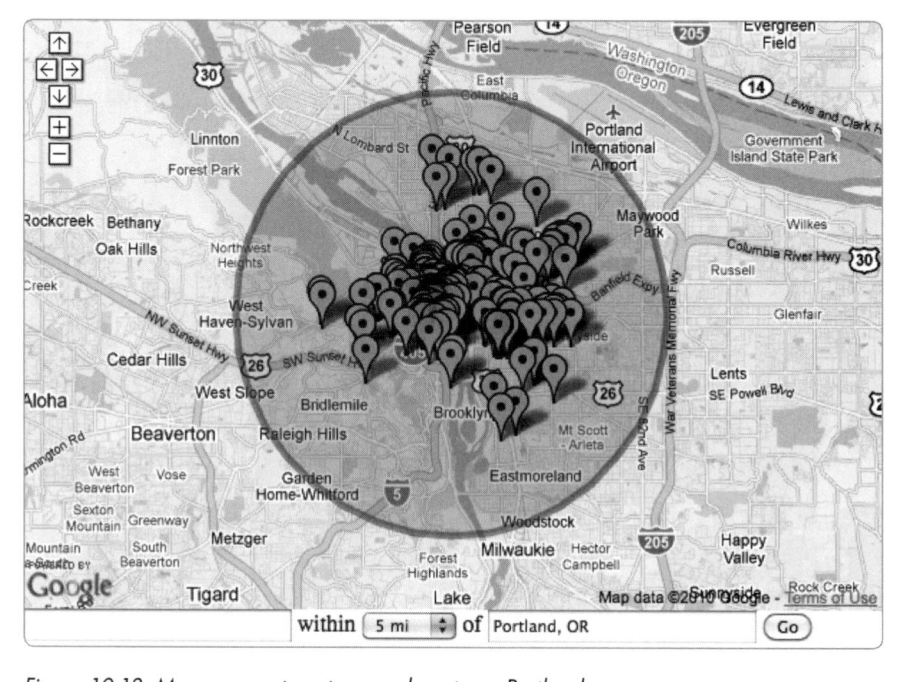

Figure 10-13: Many, many tweets near downtown Portland

#73: Find a Coffee Shop to Meet in the Middle

Meeting in the middle is the secret to a happy marriage and the key to passing kindergarten. And when it comes to physically finding a place to meet, meeting in the middle makes for a great map mashup. Whether you and a friend are just across town or many miles apart, we'll make a map that will find coffee shops as close to the midpoint between your two locations as possible, as shown in Figure 10-14.

The map we create will use several examples covered earlier in this book. First, we'll take input from the user and determine the route, as I showed in "#37: Find True Distance with Routing" on page 120. Then we'll go through each step of the driving directions to determine when we're about halfway. To find the exact midpoint, we'll use another method described in "#40: Find a Point Along a Line" on page 128. Finally, we'll use the midpoint to perform a local search using the review service Yelp's API.

Armed with this game plan, read on to get started.

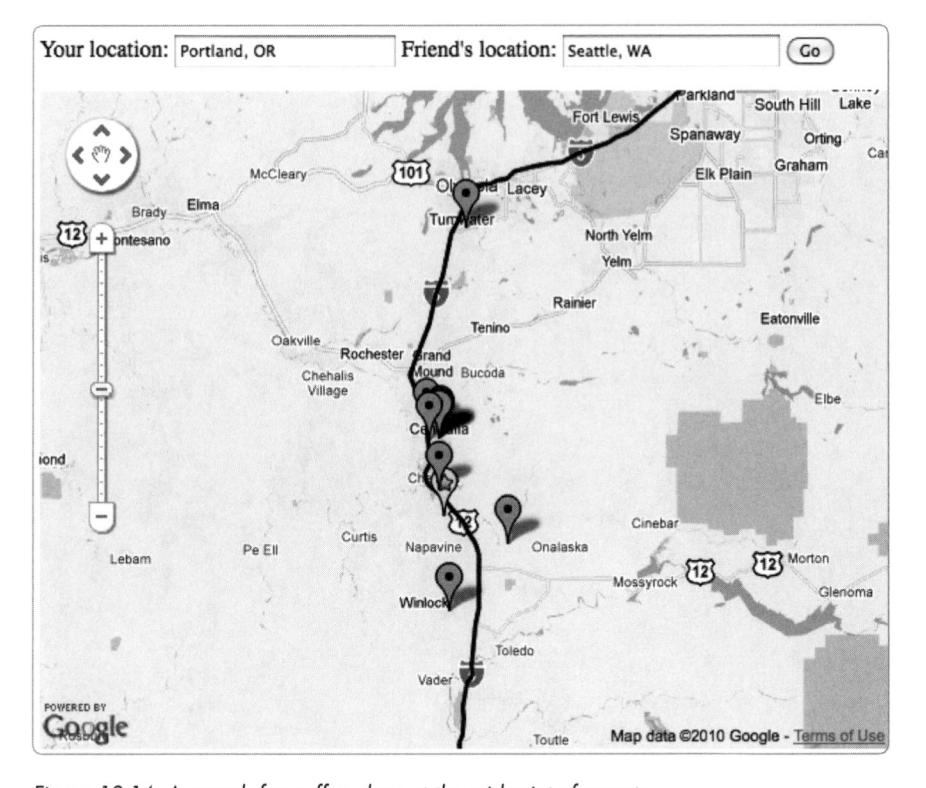

Figure 10-14: A search for coffee shop at the midpoint of a route

Prepare the Map and Form

Before we can incorporate the other examples from Chapter 6, we need to think about the pieces to include on our web page. Obviously, we need to include a map. We also need a way to get two locations from the user.

Open a new file, and add the following HTML to create a map with a view of the entire United States and the input fields we need to get user input:

```
<html xmlns="http://www.w3.org/1999/xhtml">
  <head>
    <title>Coffee in the Middle</title>
    <style>
      div#mymap {
        width: 600px;
        height: 450px;
      }
    </style>
    <script type="text/javascript"
      src="http://ajax.googleapis.com/ajax/libs/jquery/1.3/jquery.min.js"></script>
    <script src="http://maps.google.com/maps?file=api&amp;v=2&amp;key=YOURKEY" type="text/
javascript"></script>
    <script type="text/javascript" src="mxn.js?(google)"></script>
    <script type="text/javascript">
```

❶

```
        var mapstraction;
❷       var gdir;

        function create_map() {
          mapstraction = new mxn.Mapstraction('mymap', 'google');
          mapstraction.addControls({"zoom":"large"});
          mapstraction.setCenterAndZoom(new mxn.LatLonPoint(40, -92), 3);

        }
      </script>
    </head>
    <body onload="create_map()">
      <form id="myform" onSubmit="❸goDir();return false;">
        Your location: <input type="text" id="start" />
        Friend's location: <input type="text" id="end" />
        <input type="submit" value="Go" />
      </form>
      <div id="mymap"></div>
    </body>
    </html>
```

I have included the jQuery JavaScript library ❶, which we'll use later to connect to Yelp. Looking ahead, I added the gdir variable ❷ to hold driving directions from Google. Save and load the file, and it will look like Figure 10-15.

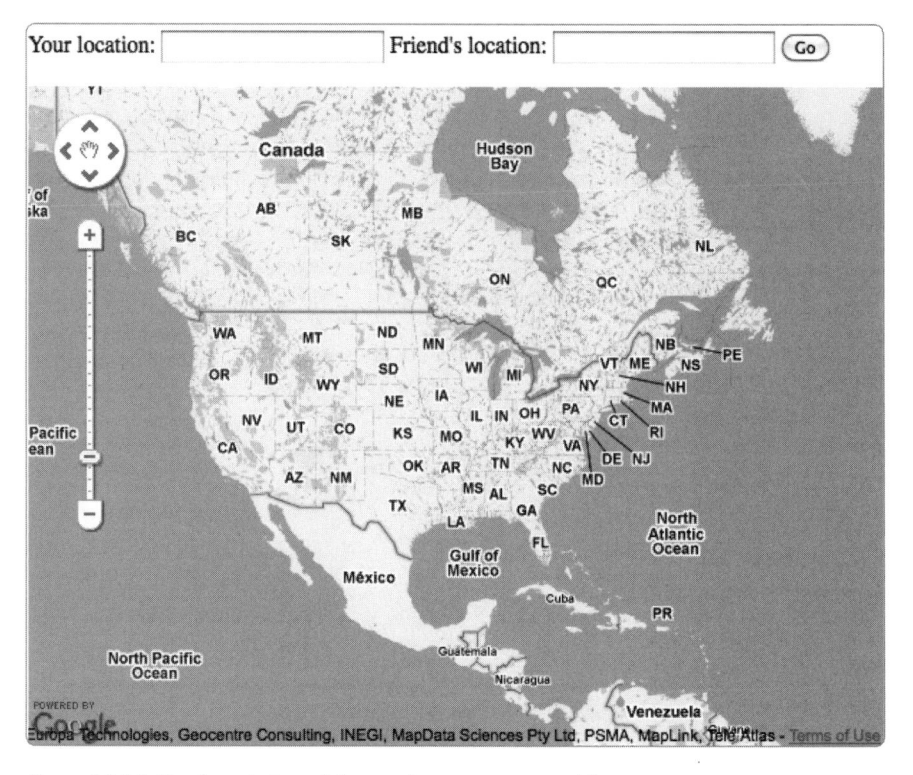

Figure 10-15: The foundation of the mashup: our map and form

Note that the form doesn't do anything right now. If you click the Submit button or press ENTER within a text field, it will attempt to call the goDir() function, as instructed in the HTML ❸. The function does not exist yet, however, so the next step is to create it. We'll do that and retrieve driving directions from the user's input in the next section.

Retrieve Driving Directions

This mashup *could* have found the midpoint between two start and end points, but that would have only been the middle if you and your friends are crows. Or pilots. You are much more likely to drive than to fly, so we'll use Google's driving directions API.

As you may recall from Chapter 6, to retrieve driving directions we first need to tell Google to load the appropriate code. In the create_map function, add the following lines to prepare for driving directions:

```
❶ // Google-specific code for driving directions
❷ gdir = new google.maps.DirectionsService();
```

First, we've created a comment ❶ to note that we're writing provider-specific code; in this case, the code only works with Google. If you ever need to convert this mashup to use a different mapping provider, including this will be helpful.

In order to use driving directions, we must create a DirectionsService object ❷. Later, we can call functions on that object or pass it to other functions.

Now that we are ready to look up driving directions, let's write the goDir function. This function gets called when the user fills out the form. Add this code to the JavaScript section but outside the create_map function:

```
function goDir() {
  var start = document.getElementById('start').value;
  var end = document.getElementById('end').value;

  // Remove Markers and Polylines
  mapstraction.removeAllMarkers();
  mapstraction.removeAllPolylines();

  // Google-specific: load directions
❸  var diropt = {
      origin: start,
      destination: end,
      travelMode: google.maps.DirectionsTravelMode.DRIVING
    }
❹  gdirroute(diropt, addDir);
}
```

The purpose of the goDir function is to hand off the two locations to the driving directions service. We first store the text the user entered into variables. In case this is a subsequent search and the map already contains results, we need to clear the map of markers and polylines before calling for directions.

Now we are ready to pass the locations to Google's directions. We include them in a special options object ❸. Then we can call the directions service using the options and also give Google a callback function ❹.

Before we find the midpoint, let's add the directions to the map. Here is the code for the callback function:

```
function addDir(response, status) {
  if (status == google.maps.DirectionsStatus.OK) {
❺   var gpts = response.routes[0].overview_path;
    var polypts = [];
    for (var i=0; i<gpts.length; i++) {
❻     polypts.push(new mxn.LatLonPoint(gpts[i].lat(), gpts[i].lng()));
    }
    // Add polyline to map
    var poly = new mxn.Polyline(polypts);
    mapstraction.addPolyline(poly);
    mapstraction.autoCenterAndZoom();
    // Find distance
❼   var dist = response.routes[0].legs[0].distance.value / 1000;
    // Find midpoint
❽   findMidpoint(polypts, dist);
  }
}
```

This function is passed the results from the Google driving directions service. From the results, we can get the points ❺ that make up the route. Then, loop through those points, adding each to a new array of points ❻ after converting each into a Mapstraction LatLonPoint.

When we have all the points in the route, we can use them to create a new polyline. The line will serve as a visual of the entire route between the two locations, as shown in Figure 10-16. We're almost ready to find the midpoint, but we need one more thing from the Google directions: the total route distance (in km) ❼. Then, we pass the new array of points and the distance to the findMidpoint function ❽.

In the next section, we'll create that function, which does most of the real work involved in this mashup.

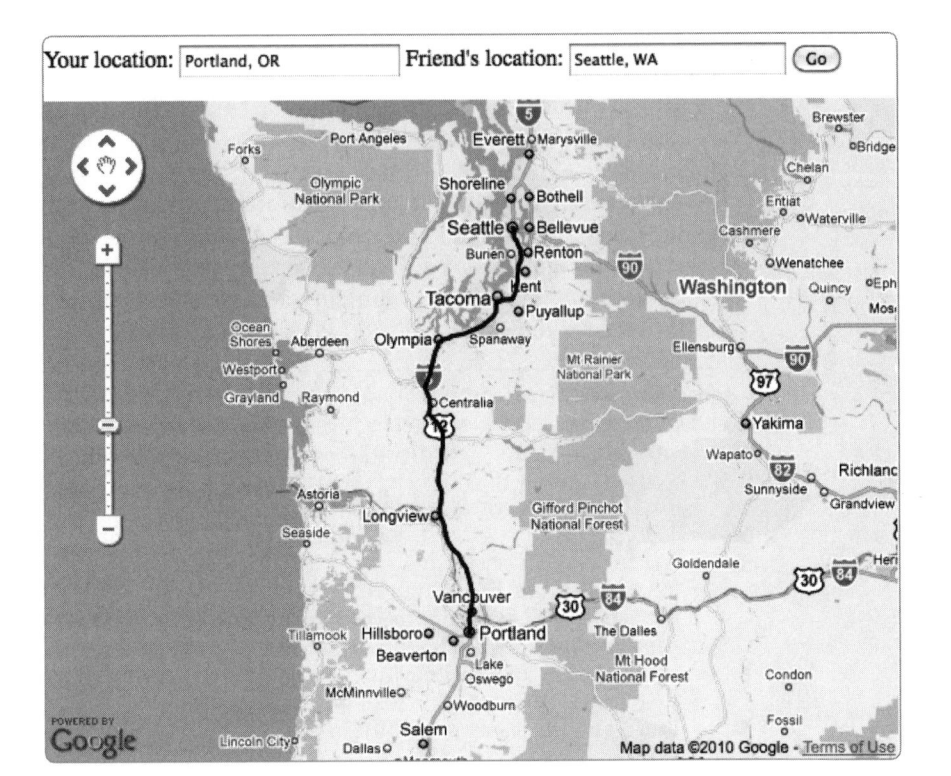

Figure 10-16: The full directions shown while we find coffee shops

Find the Route's Midpoint

Now that we've set up the web page and retrieved the route from Google's directions service, we need to write the code to traverse the route data returned. As we go through each point in the directions, we'll add the total distance traveled so far, stopping when we've gone half the total distance.

The findMidpoint function receives two arguments, the route points and the total distance. Add the function to your JavaScript code but outside other functions:

```
function findMidpoint(allpts, totaldist) {
    var midicon = 'http://chart.apis.google.com/chart?chst=d_map_pin_icon&chld=star|00FF00';

    // Determine distance needed
    var halfdist = totaldist / 2;
    var distsofar = 0;

    // Loop through points, adding up distance so far
    for (var i=1; i < allpts.length; i++) {
```

```
        var pt1 = allpts[i-1];
        var pt2 = allpts[i];
        var thisdist = pt1.distance(pt2);
❶      if ((distsofar + thisdist) < halfdist) {
          distsofar += thisdist;
        }
        else {
❷        var distneeded = halfdist - distsofar;

          // Determine point that is "distneeded" along the line between pt1 and pt2
          var bearing = get_bearing(pt1, pt2);
          var midpt = get_destination(pt1, distneeded, bearing);
❸        var midmk = new mxn.Marker(midpt);
          midmk.setIcon(midicon);
          mapstraction.addMarker(midmk);

          // Determine search radius
          var radius = 1+ totaldist / 10;
          if (radius > 25) {
            radius = 25;
          }
❹        loadYelp("coffee", midpt, radius);
          break; // stop the loop, we're halfway!
        }
      }
    }
  }
```

Each time through the loop, we look at two points—the previous point and the current one. Because we need two points, our loop begins at 1 (the second point) instead of 0. We calculate the distance between these two points. As long as the distance between all points so far is less than half the total distance ❶, we just add the distance between the two points to a running total and move on to the next point in the loop.

Once we have found a halfway point, the real work begins. Most likely the point we found is actually *farther* than halfway. Because we are looking at each point in order, however, we know the two points that our midpoint is between. And we can calculate how far between the two points ❷ we need to go for the midpoint.

Now that we have two points and a distance from the first to the second, we have all the information needed to use the example from "#40: Find a Point Along a Line" on page 128. The two functions from that project, get_bearing and get_destination, are reprinted at the end of this section.

When we have the midpoint, we can use it to create a marker ❸, which we add to the map. Then we will also use that point to search Yelp. But first we need to determine what radius to send to search. Yelp will accept anything that is 25 miles or less. If our user is only searching a route across town, 25 miles is probably a longer search than the entire route. Yet, if we choose too small a radius, we run the risk of there not being any coffee nearby when the midpoint is in a more rural area.

I've chosen to make the search radius at least one mile, but then I add ten percent of the total distance. That way, small distances have proportionally small search radii. And, if my users are driving across the country, a radius of 25 miles is reasonable.

Finally, we send all this information to Yelp ❹. Before we get to that, here are the reprinted functions from Chapter 6:

```
function get_bearing(pt1, pt2) {
  var lat1 = degrees_to_radians(pt1.lat);
  var lat2 = degrees_to_radians(pt2.lat);
  var lon_diff = degrees_to_radians(pt2.lon - pt1.lon);
  var y = Math.sin(lon_diff) * Math.cos(lat2);
  var x = Math.cos(lat1) * Math.sin(lat2)
        - Math.sin(lat1) * Math.cos(lat2) * Math.cos(lon_diff);
  var bearing = Math.atan2(y, x);
  return (radians_to_degrees(bearing)+360) % 360;
}
function get_destination(pt, dist, bearing) {
  var R = 6371; // radius of earth (km)
  var lat1 = degrees_to_radians(pt.lat);
  var lon1 = degrees_to_radians(pt.lon);
  bearing = degrees_to_radians(bearing);
  var cosLat1 = Math.cos(lat1);
  var sinLat1 = Math.sin(lat1);
  var distOverR = dist / R;
  var cosDistOverR = Math.cos(distOverR);
  var sinDistOverR = Math.sin(distOverR);
  var lat2 = Math.asin( sinLat1 * cosDistOverR
          + cosLat1 * sinDistOverR * Math.cos(bearing) );
  var lon2 = lon1 + Math.atan2( Math.sin(bearing) * sinDistOverR * cosLat1,
          cosDistOverR - sinLat1 * Math.sin(lat2) );
  lon2 = (lon2 + Math.PI) % (2 * Math.PI) - Math.PI;
  lat2 = radians_to_degrees(lat2);
  lon2 = radians_to_degrees(lon2);
  return new mxn.LatLonPoint(lat2, lon2);
}
function degrees_to_radians(deg) {
  return deg * Math.PI / 180;
}
function radians_to_degrees(rad) {
  return rad * 180 / Math.PI;
}
```

Now the only thing missing from this mashup is the call to Yelp. We'll write that in the next section.

Search for Coffee on Yelp

This mashup isn't just about finding a midpoint; it's about finding a place to meet near that midpoint. As the title of the mashup suggests, we're searching for coffee shops, though you could have your mashup search for any keyword you want. To perform the search, we'll use Yelp, a site that catalogues local businesses.

Yelp has an API that makes searching based on a latitude and longitude point easy. Better yet, the response from Yelp is in JSON, a format that makes incorporating it into our mashup quick. Before you can use the API, you'll need to get an access key, just as you did for maps. Sign up as a Yelp developer at *http://yelp.com/developers*. Now you're ready to make your first call to the Yelp API. The base URL is *api.yelp.com/business_review_search*, but we'll also include the parameters shown in Table 10-3.

You can try out a few searches in your browser and see the text for the JSON results. For example, here's a snippet response:

```
{"message": {"text": "OK", "code": 0, "version": "1.1.1"},
 "businesses": [
   {"name": "Somewhere Coffee", "latitude": 12.3456, "longitude": 123.4567, ... },
   {"name": "Someplace Jo", "latitude": 12.3456, "longitude": 123.4567, ... },
   ...
 ]
}
```

Table 10-3: Yelp API Search Options

Argument	Description
ywsid	Your API key (required)
num_biz_requested	Number of search results
term	Keyword(s) to search
lat	Latitude of search point
long	Longitude of search point
radius	Radius to search (in miles—25 or less)

Let's dive in and create the `loadYelp` function that we've already called in earlier code. Add the following function to your JavaScript section, being careful to place it outside all other functions:

```
function loadYelp(kw, loc, rad) {
  var url = "http://api.yelp.com/business_review_search";
  url += "?ywsid=YOURKEY&num_biz_requested=10&term=" + kw";
  url += "&lat=" + loc.lat + "&long=" + loc.lon + "&radius=" + rad;
❶ url += "&callback=?";
```

```
    $.getJSON(url, ❷function(x) {
      if (x.message.text == "OK") {
        if (x.businesses.length != 0) {
          var res = x.businesses;
          var allpts = [];
          for (var i = 0; i < res.length; i++) {
❸           var place = res[i];
❹           var thisloc = new mxn.LatLonPoint(place.latitude, place.longitude);
            allpts.push(thisloc);
            var html = "<strong>" + place.name + "</strong><br />" + place.address1;
            html += "<br />" + place.city + ", " + place.state;
            // Create and add marker to the map
            var mk = new mxn.Marker(thisloc);
            mk.setInfoBubble(html);
            mapstraction.addMarker(mk);
          }
❺         mapstraction.centerAndZoomOnPoints(allpts);
        }
      }
    });
  }
```

The loadYelp function requires three arguments: the keyword to search, the location to search (as a Mapstraction LatLonPoint), and the radius (in miles). The first thing the function does is use the arguments to create the URL for Yelp's API. We include the callback parameter ❶ with a question mark that will be filled in by jQuery with a generated function name.

To interpret the results from Yelp, we'll use an anonymous, inline function ❷ that accepts a single parameter, x, to hold the JSON object results. Once we've confirmed that we have usable data, we loop through all the results and grab each business listing ❸. From there, we can also find the business' location ❹ and other information.

In this example, I created a message box with some simple business information and basic styling. You could go wild here and include any HTML you want inside the message box. Yelp also provides some fun data in its response that I haven't included here. You can get the distance from the search point, average reviews, and even pictures of some locations.

When we're done looping through the results, we'll have a marker for each business. Then we center and zoom on just those markers ❺, passing an array of points we collected during the loop. This function is different than one shown in "#8: Determine the Correct Zoom Level to Use Based on Markers" on page 34. The autoCenterAndZoom function takes polylines into consideration, too, which shows the entire route.

You can see an example search in Figure 10-17, where the mashup finds a few Kansas coffee shops between Boulder and Little Rock.

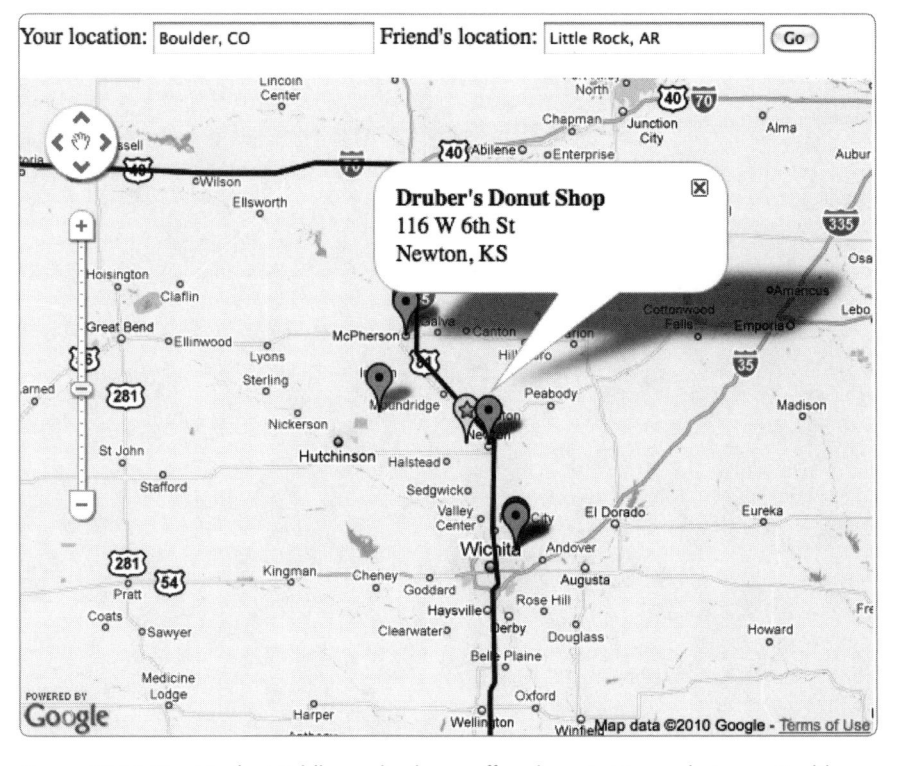

Figure 10-17: Meet in the Middle results show coffee shops in Kansas between Boulder, Colorado, and Little Rock, Arkansas.

The next time you want to meet a friend, either across town or across the country, neither of you has to drive the whole way. You can meet halfway, thanks to driving directions, a little math, Yelp, and this little mashup you've just created.

A

JAVASCRIPT QUICK START

 All the mapping APIs covered in this book are based on JavaScript. To use them, you need to program JavaScript from your web page to interact with the maps. However, as you'll see in this appendix, it's a programming language that is easy to learn.

I'll cover a very basic approach to JavaScript—enough not to be confused by the examples elsewhere in the book. If you're looking to learn the complete ins and outs, pick up *The Book of JavaScript* (thau!, No Starch Press, 2000).

Where JavaScript Goes

JavaScript is added to HTML pages via the <script> tag. Sometimes code is placed between this tag and its closing tag. Other times, the tag calls to an external file from the attributes. I'll show both versions in this section.

Technically, you can put your ‹script› tag anywhere within an HTML document. For analytics services the bottom of a page may be optimal. JavaScript for widgets may need to be placed at the exact location where you want the widgets to appear. With the JavaScript you write, however, including it in the ‹head› of your document whenever possible makes sense from a standards compliance and best practice point of view.

Here's an example of some very basic JavaScript on an even more basic web page:

```
<html>
<head>
  <title>My Simple JavaScript Example</title>
  <script type="text/javascript">
    alert('Testing JavaScript');
  </script>
</head>
<body>
  <h1>Hello World</h1>
  <p>Did you see the JavaScript alert?</p>
</body>
</html>
```

JavaScript code goes between the ‹script› tags. Here I've used alert, a JavaScript function that will create a message window in your web browser using the text inside the parentheses. Using an alert is a handy way to show simple examples and to debug, but moving beyond it is best for more complex scripts and for public-facing web pages.

TIP *Want to send a special message to browsers without JavaScript? Include ‹noscript› tags and the browser will display any content within.*

A ‹script› tag can include as many lines of JavaScript as you want, though too much can start to weigh down your HTML file, so most scripts that are more than a few lines are stored in external files. Consider the following, slightly altered example:

```
<html>
<head>
  <title>My External JavaScript Example</title>
  <script type="text/javascript" src="js/test.js"></script>
</head>
<body>
  <h1>Hello World</h1>
  <p>My JavaScript is stored in a file.</p>
</body>
</html>
```

Here, I've loaded the JavaScript via the src attribute of the ‹script› tag, which is similar to the way images are referenced in HTML. By convention, the file has a *.js* extension. Also, to keep things organized, most developers keep JavaScript files in a directory off the web root. In this example, I have used a directory named js.

The contents of the file are the same as when you include the JavaScript directly on the page. But you do not need the <script> tags. Continuing the previous example, *test.js* would contain only a single line:

```
alert('Testing JavaScript');
```

Using this method has the distinct advantage that the script file is cached separately by the user's browser. If you use the same script on many pages, as the user navigates around your site, the script will only have been downloaded once.

As in the first example, this code runs as soon as it is loaded. To run code at different times, you'll need to use functions, described later in this appendix. But first, let's get a feel for other pieces of JavaScript syntax, such as variables, conditionals, and loops.

Variables

Variables store values that can be changed or accessed later. You can hold numbers, text, and more inside variables. In this section, I'll show some simple values, as well as more complex structures like arrays and objects.

First, you need to be able to identify variables. They look like ordinary words. Sometimes variables are more than one word, though they can't include spaces. Often the first time a variable is used it will be set to a value, for example:

```
var age = 21;
```

Here I have created a new variable using JavaScript's var keyword. This variable is called age, but you can use just about any name you want, as long as it isn't one of the words reserved by the language. Like most lines of JavaScript code, this one ends with a semicolon.

The equals sign declares that the variable on the left side will now be set to the value on the right side. In this case, I've used a literal number. You could also use text, another variable, or even a combination of other variables and literal values.

Here is an example using multiple variables, one dependent on the others:

```
var cost_per_person = 3;
var num_people = 7;
var total_cost = cost_per_person * num_people;
```

The var keyword should only be used the first time you reference a variable. In fact, you do not even need to use it at all, though if you don't, the variable is then assumed to be *global*. "Variable Scope" on page 298 will explain what this means and why it's a good idea to declare your variables explicitly. You can even do so without creating a value:

```
var tbd;
```

When setting variables that hold text, you need to use quotes on each end of the value, for example:

```
var name = 'Adam';
```

You can use either single (') or double (") quotes to define your text literals, but you can't mix them. If you want to include the quote within your string, you need to escape it with a backslash.

```
var name = 'Adam\'s apple';
```

Another idiosyncrasy about text variables is covered in the next section.

Arithmetic

In the previous section, I showed an example that calculated the total_cost by multiplying one variable times another, using an asterisk (*) character.

The +, -, *, /, and = signs are your tools when it comes to changing variable values. We've already seen that = sets a variable as *equal* to a value. Addition uses the plus sign, +. Subtraction uses the minus, -. Multiplication and division are accomplished by the asterisk, *, and slash, /, respectively.

Here's a more complex example:

```
var num = 10 * 2 / 4 + 8; // num is 13
```

The *mathematical order of operations* is followed, which means multiplication and division is performed first and everything is calculated left to right. You can force ordering by enclosing some operations within parentheses:

```
var num = 10 * (2 / 4 + 8); // num is 85
```

To save you some typing, a few shorthand arithmetic conventions are shown in Table A-1. Use these when you need to alter a variable's value by some amount relative to its current value.

Table A-1: Arithmetic Shorthand

Shorthand	Long Version
num += 3;	num = num + 3;
num++;	num = num + 1;
num -= anothernum;	num = num - anothernum;
num--;	num = num - 1;
num *= 2;	num = num * 2;
num /= 4;	num = num / 4;

The plus sign, +, can also be used to *concatenate*—add together—text strings, for example:

```
var her = 'Eve';
var him = 'Adam';
var together = him + ' and ' + her;
```

Three separate strings are all combined here. The first and last are the him and her variables. The middle one is a literal string, which begins and ends with a space. If you were to alert the together variable, it would read *Adam and Eve.*

NOTE *You can also use the += shorthand to concatenate strings. For example: name += ' Smith' will add the string to the end of the text in the name variable.*

Arrays

So far I've covered two types of variables—numbers and text. Here I'll introduce a special kind of variable that holds multiple values. Or, put another way, it can contain an *array* of values.

The values can be numbers, text, or a combination. You can also include other arrays or even objects (covered in the next section) within an array. Here is an example of an array declaration:

```
var herbs = ['Parsley', 'Sage', 'Rosemary', 'Thyme'];
```

The values are separated by commas. The list is surrounded by square brackets, [and]. The same brackets are used to access the individual values according to where they appear in the list. For example, to pull Rosemary from the herbs variable, you use the following:

```
herbs[2]
```

In JavaScript, as in most programming languages, array indexes begin at zero. Therefore, even though Rosemary is the third item in the list, you access it with number 2.

To determine how many items are in a list, you use the length attribute:

```
herbs.length
```

In "Loops" on page 296, I'll show how to access each item in the array.

Objects

Like arrays, objects hold multiple values. The difference is that you can express more structured data than a simple list. To do this, objects contain key and value pairs. Keys are word-like labels, but values can be numbers, text, arrays, or other objects.

Here's a simple example representing a car:

```
var car = {
  make: 'Ford', model: 'Mustang', year: 1965, color: 'red'
}
```

To access the values within the object, you use dot notation:

```
car.model
```

Now that you have seen the different ways of expressing data in JavaScript, let's do something with it.

Conditionals

Conditionals help you compare variables to other values (including other variables). This comparison happens in a *conditional statement*. Using conditionals is the basis of much programming, because they contain the logic that helps a computer "make decisions."

The most common conditional is an if statement. You use it to provide code that is only used in a situation where the condition is true, for example:

```
if (num == 5) {
  // code to run if true
}
```

The code inside the { and } braces will only run if the num variable is exactly 5. The == operator is used to provide the *equals* comparison—in contrast to the single equals, which is used to *assign* a value.

You can use other comparison operators, as shown in Table A-2, for cases where you don't want the values to be exactly equal.

Table A-2: Conditional Operators

Operator	Description
==	Equal
!=	Not equal
>	Greater than
<	Less than
>=	Greater than or equal
<=	Less than or equal

If you want to do something else if the condition is false, you can include an else statement immediately after an if:

```
if (num > 0) {
  // code to run if true
}
else {
  // code to run if condition is false
}
```

The code within the { and } after the else statement only runs if the condition in the if statement is not true. In this example, the else code runs when num is zero or less. The if code runs in the other case (where num is greater than zero). You won't encounter an occasion where both if and else code runs.

NOTE *An else statement cannot exist without an accompanying if statement. You can, however, have if statements without else statements.*

You can also have an if statement without any operator. In those cases, the variable within the statement is called a *boolean*, which is either true or false. Here's an example:

```
var is_cool = true;
if (is_cool) {
  // code to run if true
}
```

The if (is_cool) code is shorthand for the much longer if (is_cool == true). You can also compare a variable to false in shorthand, using an exclamation point to mean "not," as in this example:

```
if (!is_cool) {
  // code to run if is_cool is false
}
```

Sometimes a non-boolean variable can be a conditional, too. In that case, *empty* values are considered false. Empty values are 0 for numbers, "" (empty string) for text, and null for objects. Also, any undefined variable is false.

Loops

Loops are like special conditionals that run the code over and over until the condition is no longer true. I will cover two types of loops in this section: for loops and while loops.

In most cases, a loop has a number to count how many times you have used the loop. Here's an example that runs 10 times:

```
for (❶var i=0; ❷i < 10; ❸i++) {
  // Code to run each time
}
```

Three pieces are included inside the parentheses of the for statement. The initial value ❶, the condition under which the loop continues ❷, and the increment portion ❸. The first time through the loop, i is 0. Then 1 and so on, as long as i is *less than* 10. When i equals 10, the loop stops. But since we started at 0, the loop will have run 10 times.

The same can be achieved with a while loop using the following code:

```
var i=0;
while (i < 10) {
  // Code to run each time
  i++;
}
```

In fact, if you look at the segments of the code in bold, you'll notice they match with the three pieces of a for statement. This while loop is logically equivalent.

NOTE   *When you know how many times a loop will run, using for is probably easiest. When you don't know in advance the number of iterations needed (such as when you're searching for a value), use while.*

Remember the herbs variable from the array section? To refresh your memory, we declared it like so:

```
var herbs = ['Parsley', 'Sage', 'Rosemary', 'Thyme'];
```

Now let's use a loop to do something with each value in the array. Because we know the total number of *iterations* (the length of the array), we'll use a for loop. Here's the code:

```
var allherbs = '';
for (var i=0; i < herbs.length; i++) {
  allherbs += herbs[i] + ' ';
}
```

Each time through the loop, we tack the current herb (the one in the index determined by the number i) to the end of the allherbs string. At the end of the loop, this is what is stored in that variable:

```
Parsley Sage Rosemary Thyme
```

We've used a loop to concatenate the four values held in our array. This concept is used throughout the book, only not usually for adding strings together; instead, we use it to create hundreds of map markers in just a few lines or output all the results of a search.

Loops are an important tool in limiting the code you need to write. But functions are perhaps the best tool to achieve simple, reusable code. Read on to see what I mean.

Functions

If you're ready to upgrade your JavaScript programming abilities, writing functions is a good place to start. A function is a packaged-up piece of code for performing a particular operation. They can accept one or more variables and return a value if necessary. With functions, you can make your code more reusable and break your application into smaller pieces.

For a basic example, we'll create a function that outputs the greater of two numbers. This function already exists as Math.max (which can accept many values to compare), but it's still a good example. Here's the entire code for the function:

```
function biggest(num, another) {
  if (num > another) {
    return num;
  }
  else {
    return another;
  }
}
```

Every function begins with the function declaration, followed by the name of the function. Then, within parentheses, you declare the parameters—variables—that your function will accept. In this case, we have two that I've named num and another.

The rest of the function, which resides inside { and } braces, should look familiar; it's just ordinary JavaScript code. When the function is called, you pass two variables, and the code runs based on that input. When you're ready to send a value back, you use the return statement to immediately exit the function and make its output equal to the variable (or literal value) you put after return.

I can probably explain it best with an example. Here's how you might call the new biggest function:

```
var somenum = 7;
var bigone = biggest(somenum, 11); // After the biggest function, bigone is 11
```

I've passed a variable (somenum) and a literal number to the function. I can use any combination of literal or variable values. And the names of my variables don't need to match those used within the function. They have different *scope*, as I'll explain in the next section.

For normal boolean, number, and text variables, JavaScript makes a copy of the value and sends it to the function. That means if you make any changes to the values within the function, the original variables outside are unaffected. The same is not true of objects and arrays; in these cases you will be modifying the value of the original variable—even if the variable is not in the return.

At the very beginning of this section, I mentioned that a function does not need to take parameters. In these instances, the function needs empty parentheses. Here's a mapping-related example:

```
function recenter_map() {
  mapstraction.setCenter(stored_center);
}
```

This function would be used to set the map to a stored center point, as long as you have the variable in memory. I used a similar approach in "#34: Return to the Center When the Message Box Is Closed" on page 109. The only way for it to work as shown is if stored_center is a global variable, visible from any JavaScript on the page.

Variable Scope

In the previous sections, I demonstrated how to create variables. I also explained that the var keyword, although optional, is recommended. The reason behind this advice has to do with a variable's visibility—or its scope.

If you use a variable without including the var statement, the variable will automatically be considered *global*, as opposed to *local*. Global variables can be seen from any JavaScript on the page, including other functions. You can also explicitly make a variable global by declaring it outside a function, usually at the beginning of your JavaScript section.

Consider this example:

```html
<html>
<head>
  <title>JavaScript Variable Scope Example</title>
  <script type="text/javascript">
❶   var firstvar = 1; // explicit global variable
    function call_first() {
❷     secondvar = 2; // implicit global variable
❸     var thirdvar = 3; // local variable
      then_me();
      alert('First: ' + firstvar + '\nSecond: ' + secondvar
          + '\nThird: ' + thirdvar);
    }
    function then_me() {
❹     firstvar = 10;
❺     var secondvar = 20;
❻     thirdvar = 30; // implicit global variable
    }
  </script>
</head>
<body onLoad="call_first()">
  ...
</body>
</html>
```

What will the values of the three variables be when the JavaScript alert shows them? Let's walk through the code. When the page loads, we create a global variable ❶ and then we call the call_first function.

Within the first function, we set a variable's value without using the var keyword ❷, making the variable, implicitly, a global variable. The third variable ❸ we create is a local variable because the var keyword is used within a function.

With these three variables created in different ways, we then call our second function from within the first function. In this new function, we reset a global variable ❹, create a new local variable ❺, and create a new global variable ❻.

When we return to our spot in the first function, the only variable that has changed for this scope is firstvar. The secondvar variable within the then_me function is local, so it does not alter the global secondvar. And even though then_me's thirdvar is global, that does not alter a local variable with the same name inside the call_first function.

TIP *To make things easier on yourself, be clear and always use the var keyword to declare variables explicitly.*

It's okay if it seems confusing. The good news is the process is logical, if you can follow it.

Anonymous Functions

A special kind of function gets used often in modern JavaScript, especially when reading in data (as you often do with maps). This function is called an anonymous function because it has no name. These functions are often passed as parameters to other functions.

Here's a very basic example:

```
function start_here() {
  call_another(function() {
    alert('Anonymous function message!');
  });
}
function call_another(❶fn) {
❷  fn();
}
```

The portion in bold is the anonymous function. It looks exactly like any other function, except a name is missing. Another strange thing is that here the function is slapped inside the parentheses of a call to another function, call_another. In that second function, we have one variable ❶, which holds the *reference* to our anonymous function. Then we can call it with the name of the reference variable ❷.

Sure enough, if you load that up and call the start_here function, you'll see an alert message from your anonymous function—via the second function.

Here's an example of a more common use for an anonymous function, reading JSON in from a web service using jQuery:

```
jQuery.getJSON(url, function(obj) {
  // Code to access the obj variable
});
```

We're passing two values to jQuery's getJSON function. The first is the URL of the JSON we want to retrieve. The second is our anonymous function—this time with a variable being passed to it. When evaluating the JSON data (see "#53: Use JSON" on page 180), jQuery puts it into a JavaScript object, which is then passed to our anonymous function.

Using anonymous functions is, in a way, shorthand. Here's a longer version of this jQuery example:

```
jQuery.getJSON(url, get_results);
function get_results(obj) {
  // Code to access the obj variables
}
```

Sure, you don't save *that much* time typing, but your code is often more readable. Littering your JavaScript with single-purpose functions isn't very clean. But perhaps the best reason to understand anonymous functions is that you'll probably see many of them in other people's code—including in this book.

Anonymous functions should only be used in the situations where they're most useful, however. If you find yourself writing a lot of code in an anonymous function, you might make it a named function. Also, watch out for creating anonymous functions inside a long loop. You're essentially creating new functions every time through the loop, which is inefficient. And doing this is also counter to the purpose of functions: to write code once and run it many times.

Using jQuery

In several places in this book, I make use of the JavaScript framework, jQuery. jQuery simplifies common tasks and provides a single interface to actions that are implemented inconsistently in different browsers. Perhaps the most common use of jQuery, especially in this book, is reading in files or other data from web services. This section is meant to give a quick introduction to using jQuery.

Before you can use jQuery, you need to include it in your web page. You can do so by downloading the latest version at *http://jquery.com/* or by grabbing a Google-hosted version by adding the following to the <head> section of your HTML file:

```
<script src="http://ajax.googleapis.com/ajax/libs/jquery/1.3/jquery.min.js"></script>
```

One advantage to using the Google-hosted version is that many other sites do as well. That means when people come to your site, they may already have jQuery stored in their browser's cache. Even if they don't, they can download it quickly—currently the file is under 20KB.

Once you have included jQuery in your document, you can use its functions via two global variables: jQuery and its shorthand, $.

Query Document Objects

Among its many uses, jQuery is very good at quickly and easily extracting elements from your HTML page into JavaScript code. You can query by id, tag name, CSS class, or combinations of these factors. jQuery makes this task easier, so you can focus on what you want to do with those elements.

To grab a single piece of the page, such as the map <div>, you call it by its id. Much of jQuery's syntax is borrowed from CSS, which may look familiar. Here is how you would call an object with an id of mymap:

```
var mapdiv = $('#mymap');
```

Notice I'm using the dollar-sign shorthand. Then I add parentheses because $ is a variable and a function (jQuery stretches the bounds of JavaScript in ways that you and I probably won't). Inside the function, we pass a string with the CSS we'd use to style the map div, #mymap.

You've now used your first jQuery function to query for a specific element. You can achieve the same result with JavaScript's standard document.getElementById function, but jQuery's method is faster to type. Plus, the result using $ allows you to chain other jQuery functions, such as visual effects.

jQuery can also do more than just query individual elements; it can gather multiple elements in a single call. Here are a few examples:

```
var imgs = $('img');            // all the images on a page
var allmaps = $('.map');        // every element with class="map"
var mapimgs = $('#mymap img');  // all images that are within #mymap element
var firstp = $('p:first');      // first paragraph on a page
```

Each of these examples shows a different type of querying—and many more are possible. You can learn about what jQuery calls *selectors* at *http://api.jquery.com/category/selectors/*.

Insert and Hide Content

Once you have one or more elements from the page using jQuery, you'll want to do something to them. In this section, I'll show you a way to add or replace the content inside a page element. And I'll also demonstrate an effect that will hide the content, so later, you can make it reappear.

Let's say you want an element on your page where you can show the results of some calculation. You can add the element with HTML using something like this:

```
<div id="results">Results:</div>
```

When you're ready to add the results, you can use jQuery to find the element and then display the results. If you want to display the content of a variable called total, you could use this single line of jQuery:

```
$('#results').html(total);
```

This line will find the element on the page with the id of results and then replace its inner HTML with the value in the total variable. If you just want to add additional content to the element, use this line instead:

```
$('#results').append(total);
```

Now the results section will look something like this (if the total variable is 42):

```
Results: 42
```

You've seen how to insert content, but what about making that same content disappear? For example, before adding the results, a page with just Results: without anything after it looks a bit funny. So when the page loads (you'll learn how in the next section), run the following code to hide the results element:

```
$('#results').hide();
```

And when you're ready to display the results to the user, include this code:

```
$('#results').show();
```

These two functions are simple (and very useful) examples of jQuery effects. Many more effects are listed on the jQuery website at *http://api .jquery.com/category/effects/*.

Use Browser Events

Earlier in this book, I spent an entire chapter on events that happen on maps, such as clicking or dragging. You can also react to events anywhere in the browser, and jQuery makes reacting a simple process.

To respond to an event, you first need to be listening for it. When your page first loads, you register your intention to react to an event. You can do this by adding a JavaScript function to the onload attribute of your <body> tag. Or you can do this with a special jQuery event.

Although creating an event to register other events may seem counterintuitive, it works. Here's an example that waits until the page is ready:

```
$(document).ready(register_events);
```

Notice that the element we're querying for is a little different than in the past. Instead of a string inside the parentheses, we've inserted a standard JavaScript object, document. When enough of the page has loaded that the browser knows all the objects it contains, we call the register_events function. That function doesn't exist, however, so we need to write it. Or, instead, we could react to the same event with an anonymous function:

```
$(document).ready(function() {
  // Code to register events
});
```

As with most anonymous functions, you usually want to keep it to just a few lines. If you have many events to register, you are probably best served with a named function.

NOTE   *A big difference exists between using your browser's onload attribute and jQuery's ready event. With onload, you wait until the entire page is loaded, including images and other external files. With $(document).ready, you can run code, such as registering events and hiding objects, the moment the browser is ready. Using jQuery here often translates to a better user experience.*

Now that you've waited for the browser to be ready to register other events, let's register them. Here's the basic pattern for jQuery events:

```
$(element).event(function);
```

The *element* portion is usually a selector, such as an element's id (though it can also be any browser object, as shown in the ready example). The *event* piece is the name of the function, as declared by jQuery. Finally, *function* is the function reference, either an anonymous function or the name of the function to call.

Here's how you'd listen for a particular element to be clicked:

```
$('#myid').click(function() {
  alert('Clicked on myid');
});
```

If you're familiar with JavaScript events included in HTML, you might be wondering where the on, as in onClick, went. In jQuery, events are referenced with only the action.

You can also get additional information about the event. The information available may be a little different depending on the event. Here's how you find out where the user has double-clicked on a page:

```
$(document).dblclick(function(❶e) {
  alert('Double-clicked at ' + ❷e.pageX + ', ' + ❸e.pageY);
});
```

Instead of a click event, I used a dblclick event. Because we want more information about the event, I included an optional parameter ❶ to the anonymous function. Within the function, I can use that variable to get information, such as where the user clicked. This data comes in two pieces: the number of pixels from the left side of the page ❷ and the number from the top of the page ❸.

You can see a sampling of available events in Table A-3, along with the additional information that is passed in the optional parameter to each event.

Table A-3: Some Useful jQuery Events

Event Name	Objects Available	Additional Information
click	Any	Page location: pageX, pageY
dblclick	Any	Page location: pageX, pageY
mousemove	Any	Page location: pageX, pageY
keydown	document, window	Key code: which
focus	Form elements	

Events will make your web pages much more interactive, whether or not they contain maps. For a full list of events (and additional event information available), see jQuery's documentation at *http://api.jquery.com/category/events/*.

Load Files and Data

If you want to interact with data outside of your current HTML file, jQuery has some excellent tools for doing these sorts of Ajax calls. Though Ajax is short for *Asynchronous JavaScript And XML*, you can access any type of data with Ajax.

To load a file with jQuery, you use the get function. get needs at least two parameters: the URL you want to load and the function to which you want jQuery to send the results. Here's a simple example for loading a text file:

```
$.get(❶"test.txt", function(txt) {
  alert(txt);
});
```

The URL ❶ I provided is just the name of a file. In this case, the file is text, but it could be a bit of HTML code or another type of content. In "#52: Use XML" on page 174, I show how to parse XML results with the get function.

You aren't restricted to only loading simple files. You could include directory names or even a full URL. Whatever you load needs to be on the same domain that you are making the call on. For security reasons, browsers will not let you retrieve data from someone else's site, even if that data is meant to be public. You can get around this by loading the file server-side (as shown in "#61: Retrieve a Web Page" on page 215) and then accessing the local copy.

A special case exists that allows you to load data from another site. If the site provides JSON data and it allows you to specify a callback function in the URL, then you can load the data remotely using jQuery's getJSON function. Here's the basic structure:

```
jQuery.getJSON(❷url, function(obj) {
  // Code to access the obj variable
});
```

The URL you send to the getJSON function ❷ needs to contain a question mark in place of the name of a function. Then jQuery will create a function and call your anonymous function (or named function, if you choose) from its new function.

Another way getJSON is different from get is in the type of data passed in the parameters to your callback function. Rather than the plain text returned to the URL, jQuery passes you parsed JSON in the form of a JavaScript object.

You'll find a more complete example of getJSON in "#53: Use JSON" on page 180. Also, you can see examples of the function used in a real project in several of the mashups in Chapter 10.

B

MAPSTRACTION REFERENCE

The Mapstraction library makes it easy to create maps that work with any provider. This appendix provides details of Mapstraction's many classes and functions. Use it as a reference as you develop your own maps.

This appendix is organized by Mapstraction class—the way the library itself is separated. Within each class, I've covered its constructor, other functions, and any class variables. The classes include:

- mxn.Mapstraction, the main class used to create and control the map
- mxn.BoundingBox, used to describe rectangular areas (bounds)
- mxn.LatLonPoint, a class for storing and referencing a single coordinate
- mxn.Marker, which maintains data for a single point of interest
- mxn.Polyline, a class for collections of connected points (shapes or lines)
- mxn.util, a utility class for useful functions

The contents of this section are based on the official documentation generated from the Mapstraction source files. Though I have expanded most sections with examples and more detailed descriptions, a big thanks goes out to the Mapstraction developer community for maintaining the docs.

As with all things Mapstraction, you can find the latest documentation at *http://mapstraction.com*.

Class mxn.Mapstraction

This is the main class; it's always your first stop with Mapstraction. You use `mxn.Mapstraction` to create a map object which then provides the main interface through which the map is altered.

In this section, you'll find the constructor, which makes a new map object. The other functions are used to perform map-level actions, such as setting the center and adding layers to the map. Much of this class is covered in Chapter 1.

Function mxn.Mapstraction

This is the constructor for the `Mapstraction` class. The function initiates a map with some API choice into the HTML element given. Every Mapstraction map will begin with this line:

```
mxn.Mapstraction(element, api, debug)
```

Parameters

element (**string**)   An HTML DOM element or the `id` of an HTML DOM element which will contain the map.

api (**string**)   Mapstraction's name for the API to use. Options include: 'cloudmade', 'geocommons', 'google', 'googlev3', 'map24', 'mapquest', 'microsoft', 'multimap', 'openlayers', 'openstreetmap', and 'yahoo'.

debug (**boolean**)   An optional parameter to turn on debugging support. If this parameter is true, Mapstraction will use alert panels for unsupported actions. This may be useful during development, but is not useful for production. Defaults to false.

Returns

The Mapstraction object, which can be used to make calls to `mxn.Mapstraction` fields and methods. Referred to in this section as `mxnobj`.

Example

```
var mxnobj = new mxn.Mapstraction('mymap', 'googlev3');
```

Function addControls

This function adds multiple controls, such as zoom and map type, to the map, using only one call. You can specify which controls to add in the object that is the only argument.

```
mxnobj.addControls(args)
```

Parameter

> *args* (**object**)   Which map controls to display. Options include: pan, zoom ('large' or 'small'), overview, scale, and map_type. Except for zoom, all options are booleans (true or false).

Example

```
mxnobj.addControls({map_type: true, zoom: 'small'});
```

Function addFilter

This function adds a marker filter to automatically show or hide markers based on attributes you have created. The addFilter function prepares a filter and requires doFilter to perform the filtering. To learn more about Mapstraction's filtering options, see "#9: Filter Out Certain Markers" on page 36.

```
mxnobj.addFilter(name, operator, value)
```

Parameters

> *name* (**string**)   The name of the attribute to place a filter on. Added via *markerobject*.addAttribute.
>
> *operator* (**string**)   The operator used to compare the attribute to a value. Options include: 'ge' (greater than or equal), 'le' (less than or equal), or 'eq' (equal).
>
> *value* (**number, string**)   The value to compare against.

Example

```
mxnobj.addFilter('age', 'ge', 21);
mxnobj.doFilter();
```

Function addImageOverlay

This function adds a geo-referenced image on top of the map at the given location. The graphic is displayed on top of the map imagery, but below markers and polylines, so it can be used as replacement or augmented imagery.

To ensure your image covers the correct area, you will need to *rectify* it, as shown in "#25: Overlay an Image on a Map" on page 83.

```
mxnobj.addImageOverlay(unique, url, opacity, west, south, east, north);
```

Parameters

unique (**string**)   A unique identifier for this overlay, used as the DOM id for the new object added to the map.

url (**string**)   The file location of the image to overlay. This URL can be local or remote, and the file can be any format supported by your browser. Transparent graphics (such as PNG files) work best for augmenting (rather than replacing) map imagery.

opacity (**number**)   A value between 0 (transparent) and 100 (completely opaque) to determine how much of the original map imagery shows behind your graphic.

west (**number**)   The longitude of the most western point of the graphic's bounding box.

south (**number**)   The latitude of the most southern point of the graphic's bounding box.

east (**number**)   The longitude of the most eastern point of the graphic's bounding box.

north (**number**)   The latitude of the most northern point of the graphic's bounding box.

Example

```
mxnobj.addImageOverlay('centralpark', 'centralpark.png', 100,
                       -73.9867415, 40.7622753, -73.9460798, 40.8032834);
```

Function addLargeControls

This function adds a provider's large zoom controls to the map. In some cases it may also include other controls, such as panning controls and a scale.

```
mxnobj.addLargeControls()
```

Function addMapTypeControls

This function allows users to select from the map types available using the provider's controls.

```
mxnobj.addMapTypeControls()
```

Function addMarker

This function adds a marker object (previously created using mxn.Marker) to the map based on the criteria in the marker object. Common options for markers are covered in Chapter 2.

```
mxnobj.addMarker(marker);
```

Parameter

marker (mxn.Marker)   The marker to be added to the map.

Example

```
var mk = new mxn.Marker(new mxn.LatLonPoint(45, -122));
mxnobj.addMarker(mk);
```

Function addMarkerWithData

This function adds a marker object (previously created using mxn.Marker) to the map with a collection of options.

```
mxnobj.addMarkerWithData(marker, options);
```

Parameters

marker (mxn.Marker)   The marker to be added to the map.

options (object)   A hash object of options for the marker, including draggable, groupName, hover, hoverIcon, infoBubble, icon, iconShadow, infoDiv, label, and openBubble.

Example

```
var mk = new mxn.Marker(new mxn.LatLonPoint(45, -122));
var opt = {infoBubble: 'Message box content', draggable: false};
mxnobj.addMarkerWithData(mk, opt);
```

Function addOverlay

This function adds a GeoRSS or KML overlay to the map. Both data formats are covered in detail in Chapter 8.

```
mxnobj.addOverlay(url, autoCenterAndZoom);
```

Parameters

url (**string**)   The full, public URL to a GeoRSS or KML file.

autoCenterAndZoom (**boolean**)   Whether to automatically center the map on the overlay content. Defaults to `false`.

Example

```
mxnobj.addOverlay('http://mapscripting.com/example.kml');
```

Function addPolyline

This function adds a polyline object (previously created using `mxn.Polyline`) to the map based on the criteria in the polyline object. Common options for polylines are covered in Chapter 4.

```
mxnobj.addPolyline(polyline);
```

Parameter

polyline (`mxn.Polyline`)   The polyline to be added to the map.

Example

```
var poly = new mxn.Polyline(
            [new mxn.LatLonPoint(45, -122), new mxn.LatLonPoint(46, -121)]);
mxnobj.addPolyline(poly);
```

Function addPolylineWithData

This function adds a polyline object (previously created using `mxn.Polyline`) to the map, along with a collection of options.

```
mxnobj.addPolylineWithData(polyline, options);
```

Parameters

polyline (`mxn.Polyline`)   The polyline to be added to the map.

options (**array**)   A hash object of options for the polyline, including closed, color, fillColor, opacity, and width.

Example

```
var poly = new mxn.Polyline(
        [new mxn.LatLonPoint(45, -122), new mxn.LatLonPoint(46, -121)]);
var opt = {color: '#ffcc99', width: 3};
mxnobj.addPolylineWithData(poly, opt);
```

Function *addSmallControls*

This function adds a provider's small zoom controls to the map. In some cases, it may also include the small versions of other controls, such as panning.

```
mxnobj.addSmallControls()
```

Function *addTileLayer*

This function adds a tile layer to the map using a parameterized URL. Covered in depth in "#26: Use Custom Tiles" on page 90.

```
addTileLayer(tile_url, opacity, copyright, min_zoom, max_zoom, map_type)
```

Parameters

tile_url (**string**)   The URL template for tiles. Requires a parameterized URL for {X} and {Y} coordinates and zoom level {Z}.

opacity (**number**)   A decimal value between 0 (transparent) and 1 (completely opaque) to determine how much of the original map imagery shows behind your tile layer.

copyright (**string**)   Text to include in the copyright of the map.

min_zoom (**number**)   Minimum zoom level where the tile layer is visible.

max_zoom (**number**)   Maximum zoom level where the tile layer is visible.

map_type (**boolean**)   true if the tile layer is a selectable map type in the layers palette. Defaults to false.

Example

```
mxnobj.addTileLayer('http://tile.openstreetmap.org/{Z}/{X}/{Y}.png',
                    1.0, "OSM", 1, 19, true);
```

Function applyOptions

This function applies the current options settings.

```
mxnobj.applyOptions()
```

Function autoCenterAndZoom

This function sets the center and zoom of the map to the smallest bounding box containing all markers and polylines.

```
mxnobj.autoCenterAndZoom()
```

Function centerAndZoomOnPoints

This function sets the center and zoom of the map to the smallest bounding box containing all points passed to the function.

```
mxnobj.centerAndZoomOnPoints(points);
```

Parameter

> *points* (**array**)   The points (as mxn.LatLonPoint objects) to determine the new center and zoom for the map.

Example

```
mxnobj.centerAndZoomOnPoints([new mxn.LatLonPoint(45, -122),
                              new mxn.LatLonPoint(46, -121)]);
```

Function declutterMarkers

You can declutter the markers on the map and group together overlapping markers with this function. It is not widely supported, though there is another method shown in "#11: Handle Clusters of Markers" on page 39.

Function doFilter

The doFilter function hides or shows markers based on attributes and criteria previously created using the addFilter function. To learn more about Mapstraction's filtering options, see "#9: Filter Out Certain Markers" on page 36.

```
mxnobj.doFilter()
```

Example

```
mxnobj.addFilter('age', 'ge', 21);
mxnobj.doFilter();
```

Function getAttributeExtremes

This function finds the minimum and maximum values set in marker attributes.

```
mxnobj.getAttributeExtremes(attribute)
```

Parameter

attribute (**string**)   The name of the marker attribute.

Returns

A two element array containing the minimum and maximum values of the passed attribute.

Example

```
var minmax = mxnobj.getAttributeExtremes('age'); // return [min, max]
```

Function getBounds

This function retrieves the BoundingBox of the currently viewable map.

```
mxnobj.getBounds()
```

Returns

A mxn.BoundingBox object.

Function getCenter

This function retrieves the center of the currently viewable map.

```
mxnobj.getCenter()
```

Returns

A mxn.LatLonPoint object.

Function getMap

This function retrieves the native map object of the current map. Useful if you need to make proprietary mapping calls.

```
mxnobj.getMap()
```

Returns

A native object depending upon the provider you are using.

Function getMapType

This function retrieves the image type, such as satellite or hybrid, for the current map.

```
mxnobj.getMapType()
```

Returns

A number corresponding to the map type. See "Set Map Type" on page 19 for a description of the available types.

Function getZoom

This function retrieves the current zoom level.

```
mxnobj.getZoom()
```

Returns

An integer corresponding to the current zoom level. The topic is covered in detail in "Set Zoom Level" on page 18.

Function getZoomLevelForBoundingBox

This function retrieves the best zoom level for the bounds given.

```
mxnobj.getZoomLevelForBoundingBox(bounds)
```

Parameter

bounds (`mxn.BoundingBox`)   The bounds for which you want to find the best zoom level.

Function polylineCenterAndZoom

This function sets the center and zoom of the map to the smallest bounding box containing all polylines, ignoring markers.

```
mxnobj.polylineCenterAndZoom()
```

Function removeAllFilters

The removeAllFilters function removes all filters previously added, but does not show previously filtered markers (for that you will need to call the doFilter function again). Because filters are additive, this function is useful when switching from one filtering method to another.

```
mxnobj.removeAllFilters()
```

Function removeAllMarkers

This function removes all markers from the map permanently. To do so temporarily, use the hide function within mxn.Marker.

```
mxnobj.removeAllMarkers()
```

Function removeAllPolylines

This function removes all polylines from the map permanently. To do so temporarily, use the hide function within mxn.Polyline.

```
mxnobj.removeAllPolylines()
```

Function removeFilter

This function removes a filter previously added, but does not show markers previously filtered by the removed filter (for that you will need to call the doFilter function again).

```
mxnobj.removeFilter(name, operator, value)
```

Parameters

name (**string**)   The name of the attribute to remove a filter on.

operator (**string**)   The operator previously used to compare the attribute to a value.

value (**number, string**)   The value to compare against. Can be a number or text.

Example

```
mxnobj.removeFilter('age', 'ge', 21);
mxnobj.doFilter();
```

Function removeMarker

This function removes a marker object (previously created using `mxn.Marker`) from the map.

```
mxnobj.removeMarker(marker);
```

Parameter

marker (`mxn.Marker`)   The marker to be removed from the map.

Example

```
mxnobj.removeMarker(mxnobj.markers[0]); // removes first marker
```

Function removePolyline

This function removes a polyline object (previously created using `mxn.Polyline`) from the map.

```
mxnobj.removePolyline(polyline);
```

Parameter

polyline (`mxn.Polyline`)   The polyline to be removed from the map.

Example

```
mxnobj.removePolyline(mxnobj.polylines[0]); // removes first polyline
```

Function resizeTo

This function resizes the map object via CSS to the dimensions provided.

```
mxnobj.resizeTo(width, height)
```

Parameters

> *width* (**number**)   The new width for the map.
> *height* (**number**)   The new height for the map.

Example

```
mxnobj.resizeTo(800, 600); // 800 pixels wide, 600 pixels tall
```

Function setBounds

This function sets the map to the appropriate center and zoom based on a BoundingBox.

```
mxnobj.setBounds(bounds)
```

Parameter

> *bounds* (**mxn.BoundingBox**)   The BoundingBox to use to determine the new center and zoom level of the map.

Function setCenter

This function sets the center of the map based on a point provided.

```
mxnobj.setCenter(point)
```

Parameter

> *point* (**mxn.LatLonPoint**)   The point to use as the new center of the map.

Example

```
mxnobj.setCenter(new mxn.LatLonPoint(45, -122));
```

Function setCenterAndZoom

This function sets the center and zoom level of the map based on a point and zoom level provided.

```
mxnobj.setCenterAndZoom(point, zoom)
```

Parameters

> *point* (`mxn.LatLonPoint`)   The point to use as the new center of the map.
>
> *zoom* (**number**)   The new zoom level to use for the map. Zoom levels are covered in "Set Zoom Level" on page 18.

Example

```
mxnobj.setCenterAndZoom(new mxn.LatLonPoint(45, -122), 10);
```

Function setDebug

This function determines whether to turn on debug support. When debug support is on, Mapstraction will use alert panels for unsupported actions.

```
mxnobj.setDebug(debug)
```

Parameter

> *debug* (**boolean**)   If this parameter is true, debug support is turned on. This may be useful during development, but it is not useful for production.

Function setMapType

This function declares the imagery type, such as satellite or hybrid, for the current map.

```
mxnobj.setMapType(type)
```

Parameter

> *type* (**integer**)   A number corresponding to the map type. See "Set Map Type" on page 19 for a description of the available types.

Example

```
mxnobj.setMapType(mxn.Mapstraction.SATELLITE);
```

Function setOption

This function sets a single option, such as the scroll wheel zoom or draggable map.

```
mxnobj.setOption(name, value)
```

Parameters

name **(string)**   The name of the option to set. Currently supported options: 'enableScrollWheelZoom' and 'enableDragging'.

value **(boolean)**   Whether an option is set (true or false).

Example

```
mxnobj.setOption('enableDragging', false); // map cannot be dragged
```

Function setOptions

This function uses an object to declare many options, such as the scroll wheel zoom or draggable map, at once.

```
mxnobj.setOptions(opt)
```

Parameter

opt **(object)**   A hash object containing the names and values for the options to set. Currently supported options: 'enableScrollWheelZoom' and 'enableDragging'.

Example

```
mxnobj.setOptions({'enableDragging': false, 'enableScrollWheelZoom': true);
```

Function setZoom

This function sets the current zoom level.

```
mxnobj.setZoom(zoom)
```

Parameter

zoom **(number)**   Number corresponding to the zoom level to set. The topic is covered in detail in "Set Zoom Level" on page 18.

Example

```
mxnobj.setZoom(13); // Roughly city-level zoom
```

Function swap

The swap function hides the previous map and changes the active map to a
different API provider on the fly.

```
mxnobj.swap(api, element)
```

Parameters

api (**string**)   Mapstraction's name for the API to use with the new map.
Options include: 'cloudmade', 'geocommons', 'google', 'googlev3', 'map24',
'mapquest', 'microsoft', 'multimap', 'openlayers', 'openstreetmap', and 'yahoo'.

element (**string, DOM element**)   The id of the HTML element, or the
element itself, to contain the new map.

Example

```
mxnobj.swap('yahoo', 'secondmapdiv');
```

Function toggleFilter

If the marker filter exists, this function removes it. Otherwise, it adds a
marker filter to automatically show or hide markers based on attributes you
have created. It still requires the doFilter function to perform the filtering.
To learn more about Mapstraction's filtering options, see "#9: Filter Out
Certain Markers" on page 36.

```
mxnobj.toggleFilter(name, operator, value)
```

Parameters

name (**string**)   The name of the attribute to place a filter on. Added via
markerobject.addAttribute.

operator (**string**)   The operator used to compare the attribute to a
value. Options: 'ge' (greater than or equal), 'le' (less than or equal), or
'eq' (equal).

value (**number, string**)   The value to compare against. Can be a number or text (only 'eq').

Example

```
mxnobj.toggleFilter('age', 'ge', 21);
mxnobj.doFilter();
```

Function toggleTileLayer

The `toggleTileLayer` function controls the visibility of a previously added tile layer. If the tile layer is visible, this function makes it invisible (and vice versa).

```
mxnobj.toggleTileLayer(tile_url)
```

Parameter

tile_url (**string**)   The exact URL used in the `addTileLayer` function.

Example

```
mxnobj.toggleTileLayer('http://tile.openstreetmap.org/{Z}/{X}/{Y}.png');
```

Function visibleCenterAndZoom

This function sets the center and zoom of the map to the smallest bounding box containing all *visible* markers and polylines. Ignores markers or polylines that have been hidden.

```
mxnobj.visibleCenterAndZoom()
```

Variables in mxn.Mapstraction Class

These variables can be accessed directly via the Mapstraction object. For example, you can loop through all markers added to the map using the *mxnobj*.markers variable, as shown in "#7: Loop Through All Markers" on page 34.

The variables available are:

api (**string**)   The name of the active API for this Mapstraction object. This value is the same as the `api` parameter passed in the `mxn.Mapstraction` constructor.

CurrentElement (**object**)   The DOM element containing the map. Mapstraction sets this value to `document.getElementById(`*mxnobj*`.element)`.

element (**string**)   The original element id passed as the element parameter to the `mxn.Mapstraction` constructor.

markers (**array**)   An array containing all the markers currently loaded on the map (including any hidden).

options (**object**)   Map options currently set using the `setOptions` function.

polylines (**array**)   An array containing all the polylines currently loaded on the map (including any hidden).

Class mxn.BoundingBox

This class creates a BoundingBox and provides methods to access information about the box. A BoundingBox object is used to describe an area with two latitude/longitude points, as described in "#19: Draw a Rectangle to Declare an Area" on page 71.

Mapstraction also uses the BoundingBox class internally for automatically centering the map or retrieving the bounds of the current map. Additionally, you can use a BoundingBox object to perform a simple hit test (see "#43: Check Whether a Point Is Within a Bounding Box" on page 137).

Function mxn.BoundingBox

This is the constructor for the BoundingBox class. Use this function to create a new BoundingBox object from the coordinates of the southwest and northeast corners.

```
mxn.BoundingBox(swlat, swlon, nelat, nelon);
```

Parameters

swlat (**number**)   The latitude of the southwest point.

swlon (**number**)   The longitude of the southwest point.

nelat (**number**)   The latitude of the northeast point.

nelon (**number**)   The longitude of the northeast point.

Returns

A new BoundingBox object, which can be used to make calls to mxn.BoundingBox functions. Referred to in this section as bbobj.

Example

```
var bbobj = new mxn.BoundingBox(45, -122, 46, -121);
```

Function contains

This function is used to perform a simple hit test. That is, it finds whether a given point is within a BoundingBox.

```
bbobj.contains(point)
```

Parameter

point (LatLonPoint)   The point with which to test.

Returns

A boolean (true or false) to describe whether the point is within the bounding box.

Example

```
var pt = new mxn.LatLonPoint(45.5, -121.5);
var hittest = bbobj.contains(pt);
```

Function extend

If a point is not within the bounds, the extend function extends the BoundingBox to include the point.

```
bbobj.extend(point)
```

Parameter

   point (LatLonPoint)   The new point to include in the bounds.

Example

```
var pt = new mxn.LatLonPoint(45.5, -121.5);
bbobj.extend(pt);
```

Function getNorthEast

This function retrieves the most northeast point of the bounds.

```
bbobj.getNorthEast()
```

Returns

A mxn.LatLonPoint object.

Function getSouthWest

This function retrieves the most southwest point of the bounds.

```
bbobj.getSouthWest()
```

Returns

A mxn.LatLonPoint object.

Function isEmpty

This function finds whether the bounds has zero area—that is, whether the southwest and northeast points are the same.

```
bbobj.isEmpty()
```

Returns

A boolean (true if empty, false if the bounds has area).

Class mxn.LatLonPoint

Without this class you couldn't put much on the map. An `mxn.LatLonPoint` object describes a single point on the earth and provides a few functions for using the data, such as the one shown in "#36: Calculate Distance Between Two Points" on page 117.

Mostly, `mxn.LatLonPoint` is a utility player. Every other class depends upon it to hold the latitude and longitude coordinates.

Function mxn.LatLonPoint

This is the constructor for the `mxn.LatLonPoint` class. Use it to create new `LatLonPoint` objects that you can pass as the center of the map, location of a marker and more.

```
mxn.LatLonPoint(lat, lon)
```

Parameters

    lat (**number**)   The latitude of the point you are creating.

    lon (**number**)   The longitude of the point you are creating.

Returns

A new `LatLonPoint` object, which can be used to make calls to `mxn.LatLonPoint` functions. Referred to in this section as `llobj`.

Example

```
var llobj = new mxn.LatLonPoint(45, -122);
```

Function distance

This function calculates the distance, in kilometers, between the current LatLonPoint and a second LatLonPoint.

```
llobj.distance(point)
```

Parameter

point (LatLonPoint)   A second LatLonPoint object.

Returns

A decimal number corresponding to the kilometers between the llobj LatLonPoint and the parameter.

Example

```
var llobj = new mxn.LatLonPoint(45, -122);
var newpt = new mxn.LatLonPoint(44, -121);
var kms = llobj.distance(newpt); // 136.578 km
```

Function equals

The equals function tests if this point is the same as a second LatLonPoint— whether the latitudes and longitudes are both equal.

```
llobj.equals(point)
```

Parameter

point (LatLonPoint)   A second LatLonPoint object.

Returns

A boolean (true or false) answering whether the points are identical.

Example

```
var llobj = new mxn.LatLonPoint(45, -122);
var newpt = new mxn.LatLonPoint(44, -121);
var same = llobj.equals(newpt); // false
```

Function latConv

This function provides the latitude conversion—the distance of one degree of latitude—based on the current projection. It is used within Mapstraction for features like search radii (see "#18: Add Circles to Show Search Radius" on page 67).

```
llobj.latConv()
```

Function lonConv

This function is like latConv, only it returns the longitude conversion—the distance of one degree of longitude—based on the current projection.

```
llobj.lonConv()
```

Function toString

This function gives a textual representation of the point.

```
llobj.toString()
```

Returns

A string (like 45, -122) that shows both the latitude and the longitude contained in the LatLonPoint.

Class mxn.Marker

While mxn.LatLonPoint declares points, mxn.Marker is the most common way to *show* points on the map. Use this class to create new marker pins, including custom icon graphics. Markers are covered in depth in Chapter 2.

Function mxn.Marker

This is the constructor for the mxn.Marker class. Use it to create new markers, then set its options. Then add it to the map with the mxn.Mapstraction.addMarker function.

```
mxn.Marker(point)
```

Parameter

point (LatLonPoint)   The point on the map to place the marker.

Returns

A `mxn.Marker` object, referred to throughout this section as `mkobj`.

Example

```
var mkobj = new mxn.Marker(new mxn.LatLonPoint(45, -122));
```

Function addData

Add data, such as custom icon graphics, to the marker in one handy function. The `addData` function is similar to the `mxn.Mapstraction.addMarkerWithData` function.

```
mkobj.addData(options)
```

Parameter

> *options* (**array**)   A hash object of options for the marker, including `draggable`, `groupName`, `hover`, `hoverIcon`, `infoBubble`, `icon`, `iconShadow`, `infoDiv`, `label`, and `openBubble`.

Example

```
var opt = {infoBubble: 'Message box content', draggable: false};
mkobj.addData(opt);
```

Function getAttribute

This function retrieves the value of a particular attribute from the marker. Attributes are most commonly used in filtering, and they contain data about a particular marker.

```
mkobj.getAttribute(name)
```

Parameter

> *name* (**string**)   The name of the attribute whose value you want to retrieve.

Returns

The value of the attribute.

Example

```
var num = mkobj.getAttribute('age');
```

Function setAttribute

The other side of getAttribute, this function sets the value of a particular attribute in the marker.

```
mkobj.setAttribute(name, value)
```

Parameters

name (**string**)   The name of the attribute whose value you want to set.

value (**varies**)   The value of the attribute you want to set.

Example

```
mkobj.setAttribute('age', 21);
mkobj.setAttribute('address', '123 Main St');
```

Function setDraggable

This function declares whether a marker is draggable—able to be moved from one location to another by the user—if the provider supports this feature.

```
mkobj.setDraggable(draggable)
```

Parameter

draggable (**boolean**)   Set to true if the marker should be draggable (otherwise false).

Function setHover

This function determines whether a marker's message box should be displayed when the mouse hovers over the marker.

```
mkobj.setHover(hover)
```

Parameter

hover (**boolean**)   Set to true if you want a hoverable marker. Otherwise, set to false.

Function setHoverIcon

This function adds a special icon to show when the mouse hovers over the marker. The hover icon inherits the marker size from the main icon.

```
mkobj.setHoverIcon(iconurl)
```

Parameter

iconurl (**string**)   A filename or complete URL to the graphic to use as a hover icon.

Example

```
mkobj.setHoverIcon('highlighted.png');
```

Function setIcon

This function adds a custom icon to the marker. It is covered in "#5: Create a Custom Icon Marker" on page 29.

```
mkobj.setIcon(iconurl, iconSize, iconAnchor)
```

Parameters

iconurl (**string**)   A filename or complete URL to the graphic to use as an icon.

iconSize (**array**)   An array containing the width and height (in pixels) of the icon.

iconAnchor (**array**)   An optional parameter to describe where the graphic points to the map. The array contains the number of pixels to the left and down from the upper-left point in the graphic.

Example

```
mkobj.setIcon('pin.png', [24, 36], [12, 36]);
```

Function setIconAnchor

This function sets the icon's anchor, where the icon points to the map, directly.

```
mkobj.setIconAnchor(iconAnchor)
```

Parameter

> *iconAnchor* (**array**)   Contains the number of pixels to the left and down from the upper-left point in the graphic.

Example

```
mkobj.setIconAnchor([12, 36]);
```

Function setIconSize

This function sets the icon's dimensions directly.

```
mkobj.setIconSize(iconSize)
```

Parameter

> *iconSize* (**array**)   An array containing the width and height (in pixels) of the icon.

Example

```
mkobj.setIconSize([24, 36]);
```

Function setInfoBubble

This function declares the text to be shown inside the marker when the marker is clicked (or moused over if the hover option is activated). Most providers allow this text to be HTML.

```
mkobj.setInfoBubble(text)
```

Parameter

> *text* (**string**)   The text or HTML to show inside a message box.

Example

```
mkobj.setInfoBubble('<em>This</em> is my message!');
```

Function setInfoDiv

This function declares the text to show in a div outside of the map when the marker is clicked.

```
mkobj.setInfoDiv(text, div)
```

Parameters

text (**string**) The text or HTML to show inside the div.

div (**string**) The id of the div in which to show your message.

Example

```
mkobj.setInfoDiv('<em>This</em> is my message!', 'msgbox');
```

Function setLabel

This function declares the short text to show as a tooltip above the marker when a user mouses over the marker.

```
mkobj.setLabel(text)
```

Parameter

text (**string**) The text to show as a tooltip on hover.

Example

```
mkobj.setLabel('Name of Location');
```

Function setShadowIcon

This function adds a shadow icon below the marker's icon, if supported by the provider.

```
mkobj.setShadowIcon(iconurl, iconSize)
```

Parameters

iconurl (**string**) A filename or complete URL to the graphic to use as a shadow icon.

iconSize (**array**) An array containing the width and height (in pixels) of the shadow icon.

Example

```
mkobj.setShadowIcon('pin-shadow.png', [36, 42]);
```

Class mxn.Polyline

When a single point does not describe your data, turn to the `mxn.Polyline` class to describe lines and shapes. The most common use is to describe a route, but a number of other examples are given in Chapter 4.

Function mxn.Polyline

This is the constructor for the `mxn.Polyline` class. Use this function to create a new polyline then set its options. Then add it to the map with the `mxn.Mapstraction.addPolyline` function.

```
mxn.Polyline(points)
```

Parameter

points (**array**)   The `mxn.LatLonPoint` objects that describe the polyline.

Returns

A `mxn.Polyline` object, referred to in this section as `pobj`.

Example

```
var pobj = new mxn.Polyline(
          [new mxn.LatLonPoint(45, -122), new mxn.LatLonPoint(44, -121)]);
```

Function addData

Add data, such as line color and opacity, to the polyline in one handy function. The `addData` function is similar to the `mxn.Mapstraction.addPolylineWithData` function.

```
pobj.addData(options)
```

Parameter

options (**object**)   A hash object of options for the polyline, including `closed`, `color`, `fillColor`, `opacity`, and `width`.

Example

```
var opt = {color: '#ffcc99', width: 3};
pobj.addData(opt);
```

Function setClosed

This function declares whether a polyline is meant to be a polygon—a complete shape.

```
pobj.setClosed(closed)
```

Parameter

closed (**boolean**)   If the polyline is meant to be a complete shape, set to true. Otherwise, false.

Function setColor

This function declares the color of the line directly. It does not affect the color inside the polygon (if the Polyline is closed).

```
pobj.setColor(hex)
```

Parameter

hex (**string**)   A hexidecimal representation of the color value, including a preceding #.

Example

```
pobj.setColor('#ff0000'); // red
```

Function setFillColor

This function declares the inner color of a polygon directly. It does not affect an unclosed Polyline.

```
pobj.setFillColor(hex)
```

Parameter

hex (**string**)   A hexidecimal representation of the color value, including a preceding #.

Example

```
pobj.setFillColor('#0000ff'); // blue
```

Function setWidth

This function declares the width of the polyline (or polygon border) directly.

```
pobj.setWidth(pixels)
```

Parameter

pixels (number)   The number of pixels wide.

Example

```
pobj.setWidth(4);
```

Function simplify

The simplify function reduces the number of points in the polyline, removing those that are near others based on the tolerance you provide. Simplifying the points is a good idea if you are showing a large line at a wide zoom level.

```
pobj.simplify(tolerance)
```

Parameter

tolerance (number)   The distance (in km) that a point needs to be from the previous point in order to be included in the simplified polyline.

Example

```
pobj.simplify(1.5);
```

Namespace mxn.util

Mapstraction has a handful of functions that don't fit into any of the previous classes. These utility functions live in the mxn.util namespace. Unlike the classes, mxn.util does not need to be initialized with a constructor before you can use its functions.

Function mxn.util.$m

The $m function is similar to jQuery's $ function, only it's used solely to look up HTML elements by id. It's a more elegant document.getElementById function.

```
mxn.util.$m(id [, id]*)
```

Parameter

> *id* (**string**)   The element's identifier. Unlike jQuery, this parameter does not require the CSS syntax of a preceding #. Multiple id arguments may be passed.

Returns

The HTML object corresponding to the element id. If multiple id arguments are provided, the matching elements are returned in an array.

Example

```
var mapobj = mxn.util.$m('mymap');
```

Function mxn.util.getAvailableProviders

This function retrieves all providers currently loaded. Most of the time, you'll only be using one provider, but if you get into fancy multi-mapping, this result is useful.

```
mxn.util.getAvailableProviders()
```

Returns

An array containing the provider identifiers.

Example

```
var loaded = mxn.util.getAvailableProviders();
```

Function mxn.util.getStyle

This function retrieves CSS style information. Because not all browsers access styles the same way, Mapstraction provides this cross-browser function.

```
mxn.util.getStyle(htmlobj, style)
```

Parameters

> *htmlobj* (**object**)   The object version, such as the value returned by mxn.util.$m, of the HTML element.
>
> *style* (**string**)   The name of the style you want to retrieve.

Returns

A string containing the style information.

Example

```
var this_style = mxn.util.getStyle(mxn.util.$m('mymap'), 'border');
```

Function mxn.util.KMToMiles

Sure, you could do the math yourself, but Mapstraction provides several functions to convert between measuring systems. This function converts kilometers to miles.

```
mxn.util.KMToMiles(km)
```

Parameter

> *km* (**number**)   The number of kilometers.

Returns

The number of miles.

Function mxn.util.loadScript

This function loads a JavaScript file. This is used internally to read in appropriate Mapstraction files for providers, but you can use it, too.

```
mxn.util.loadScript(scripturl)
```

Parameter

scripturl (**string**)   The location of the script file, either a single file or full URL.

Function mxn.util.loadStyle

This function loads a CSS stylesheet.

```
mxn.util.loadStyle(styleurl)
```

Parameter

styleurl (**string**)   The location of the stylesheet, either a single file or full URL.

Function mxn.util.lonToMetres

The curvature of the earth makes the length of a degree of longitude change based on the degree of latitude at the location. This function converts a longitude to meters at sea level. Note the British spelling of the function name.

A latitude to meters conversion can be achieved by passing the latitude distance as the *lon* parameter and 0 as the *lat* parameter.

```
mxn.util.lonToMetres(lon, lat)
```

Parameters

lon (**number**)   Degrees of longitude to convert to meters.

lat (**number**)   The latitude of the location.

Returns

The number of meters in the specified number of degrees of longitude at the specified latitude.

Function mxn.util.metresToLon

This is the reverse of the `mxn.util.lonToMetres` function. It converts meters into degrees of longitude.

Degrees of latitude are the same as degrees of longitude at latitude 0, so a value of 0 for the `lat` parameter can be used to convert meters for latitude.

```
mxn.util.metresToLon(meters, lat)
```

Parameters

> *meters* (**number**)   The number of meters to convert.
>
> *lat* (**number**)   The latitude of the location.

Returns

The degrees of longitude.

Function mxn.util.milesToKM

This is the reverse of `mxn.util.KMToMiles`. This function converts miles to kilometers.

```
mxn.util.milesToKM(miles)
```

Parameter

> *miles* (**number**)   The number of miles to convert.

Returns

The number of kilometers.

Function mxn.util.stringFormat

Concatenating variables intermixed with text in JavaScript can be a pain, so Mapstraction provides this function to make it easier. Pass a parameterized string along with a number of variables and Mapstraction creates a single string of text.

```
mxn.util.stringFormat(text, var1, var2, ...)
```

Parameters

> *text* (**string**)   The full text, with special numbered parameters inside denoted with { and } brackets.
>
> *var1, var2, ...* (**varied**)   Any number of variables or values matching the number of parameterized values in the *text* variable.

Returns

The full text string, with variables/values inserted.

Example

```
var message = mxn.util.stringFormat('There are {0} tiny {1}', num, 'eggs');
```

INDEX

authenticating users, 163–164
authorize.php file, 164
auto-zooming, 35
autoCenterAndZoom function, 35, 314
AWS Management Console, 92

B

Basic Geo Vocabulary, 187
bearing, 130–131
blogs, geo-tagging, 184
bounding box
    checking if point is within, 137–140
    finding for polygon, 143–145
    getting random point in, 140–142
BoundingBox class, 71
BoundingBox object, 141
    global variable for, 112
BoundingBox_to_Polyline function, 139
bounds, moving map outside preset,
    112–115
boundsInBounds function, 114–115
box, GeoRSS to declare, 185

C

callback function, for Ajax call, 177
callback page, 164
callback URL, for Fire Eagle, 163
callback.php file, 164–165
call_twitter_geo function, 273–274
Cascadenik, 97
Cascading Style Sheets (CSS)
    for earthquake project legend, 255
    to position div element, 244–245
cell tower triangulation, 158
center of map, 8
    preserving previous, 110
    resetting, 20
    retrieving current, 20
    returning to, after closing message
      box, 109–110
centerAndZoomOnPoints function, 314
check_bounds function, 138
check_hover function, 257–258
check_intersection function, 146–147
check_polygon function, 147–148, 149
child elements in XML, 174
circles for search radius, 67–70
    overlaying image, 69–70
city-level coordinates, precision, 6

ClientLocation JavaScript object
    (Google), 168–169, 271
closeBubble function, 29
closeInfoBubble event, 109
closest marker, determining, 125–128
closing message box, 107–108
    returning to center after, 109–110
closing tag in XML, 174
CloudMade, 93
cluster icon, changing, 41
ClusterMarker utility, 40
clusters of markers, 39–41
color
    of polylines, 65
    for states/countries, 74–76
color_state function, 76
combining strings, in PHP, 209
comma-separated values (CSV), 51
    importing to MySQL, 223–224
command interpreter for MySQL,
    170, 218
    adding columns to table, 231–232
    importing data using, 225
comments, 20
    slashes for, 25
comparison operators, in PHP, 212
concatenating strings
    in JavaScript, 293
    in PHP, 209
concerts. *See* Music Events project
conditional statements
    in JavaScript, 294–296
    in PHP, 211–212
constants, in Mapstraction, 19
contains function, 324–325
continual updates, to user location,
    160–161
controls
    adding, 16–17
    custom, 76–78
converting
    between decimal representation of
      coordinates and degree format,
      5–6
    earthquake data to JSON, 252–253
    file format for Mapnik tile
      generator, 97
    textual values to floating point
      numbers, 134
    weather results to JSON, 239–241
    XML, 168
    XML to JSON, 198–200

R

radians, 118
radians_to_degrees function, 284
Radius object, 68
records in database, 218
rectangle, for declaring area, 71–72
recursive function, 276
regular expressions, 266
remainder, 148
removeAllFilters function, 37, 317
removeAllMarkers function, 38, 317
removeAllPolylines function, 317
removeFilter function, 317–318
removeMarker function, 26, 318
removePolyline function, 318
removing
    all markers, 38–39
    markers, 26–27, 106
resizeTo function, 14, 318–319
response.Placemark array, 56
return statement (JavaScript), 298
return_center function, 246
reverse geocoding, 54–58
    in click, 56–57
    with Google web service, 57–58
    with JavaScript, 55–56
Richter value, 254
ROAD map type, 19
road maps, 90
root element (XML), 174
routes
    finding distance with, 120–122
    plotting, 129
    polyline segments for displaying,
      63–64
Royal Observatory (Greenwich,
    London), 4
RSS feed, GeoRSS inside, 184
rubbersheeting, 85

S

SATELLITE map type, 19
satellite view, 90
    control for, 17
scope of variables, 26, 298–299
<script> tag (HTML), 289–290
search, for map location, 133
search radius, circles for, 67–70
search_upcoming function, 267
seconds ("), 3

security
    and access to outside APIs, 264
    and data retrieval, 305
    parseJSON function and, 181
semicolon (;), for PHP, 209
server-side processing, 205
SET command (SQL), 231
setAttribute function, 37, 330
setBounds function, 319
setCenter function, 20, 319
setCenterAndZoom function, 18, 319–320
setClosed function, 335
setColor function, 335
setDDist function, 122
setDebug function, 320
setDir function, 125
setDraggable function, 330
setFillColor function, 335
setHover function, 330
setHoverIcon function, 331
setIcon function, 331
setIconAnchor function, 331–332
setIconSize function, 332
setInfoBubble function, 27, 29, 332
setInfoDiv function, 245, 332–333
setLabel function, 333
setMapType function, 19, 320
setOption function, 320–321
setOptions function, 321
set_region function, 259
setShadowIcon function, 333
setWidth function, 336
setZoom function, 18, 321
shadows
    for markers, 30
    for thumbnails, 82
shapes
    checking for point within, 142–149
    drawing on map, 65–67
    GeoRSS to declare, 185
sharing location, 162–163
show function, 26
SimpleXML class (PHP), 178
SimpleXML function, 168
SimpleXML object, 266
SimpleXMLElement object, 178
simplexml_load_string function
    (PHP), 178
simplify function, 336
size of maps, changing, 15
size of tiles, 13
slot two in string, 254

The Electronic Frontier Foundation (EFF) is the leading organization defending civil liberties in the digital world. We defend free speech on the Internet, fight illegal surveillance, promote the rights of innovators to develop new digital technologies, and work to ensure that the rights and freedoms we enjoy are enhanced — rather than eroded — as our use of technology grows.

PRIVACY EFF has sued telecom giant AT&T for giving the NSA unfettered access to the private communications of millions of their customers. eff.org/nsa

FREE SPEECH EFF's Coders' Rights Project is defending the rights of programmers and security researchers to publish their findings without fear of legal challenges. eff.org/freespeech

INNOVATION EFF's Patent Busting Project challenges overbroad patents that threaten technological innovation. eff.org/patent

FAIR USE EFF is fighting prohibitive standards that would take away your right to receive and use over-the-air television broadcasts any way you choose. eff.org/IP/fairuse

TRANSPARENCY EFF has developed the Switzerland Network Testing Tool to give individuals the tools to test for covert traffic filtering. eff.org/transparency

INTERNATIONAL EFF is working to ensure that international treaties do not restrict our free speech, privacy or digital consumer rights. eff.org/global

EFF.ORG

ELECTRONIC FRONTIER FOUNDATION
Protecting Rights and Promoting Freedom on the Electronic Frontier

EFF is a member-supported organization. Join Now! www.eff.org/support

UBUNTU FOR NON-GEEKS, 4TH EDITION

A Pain-Free, Get-Things-Done Guide

by RICKFORD GRANT *with* PHIL BULL

The new edition of this best-selling guide to Ubuntu for beginners covers Ubuntu 10.04, Lucid Lynx. Topics in the book build on each other in a way that keeps readers moving forward and interacting with their systems, rather than just reading about them. *Ubuntu for Non-Geeks* tackles topics likely to be of interest to the average desktop user, such as installing software; connecting to the Internet; working with flash drives, printers, and scanners; burning CDs and DVDs; playing audio and video; using iPods; customization; and even a bit of the command line. From Open-Office.org for word processing, GIMP for photo editing, and Firefox for web browsing, to other tools for enjoying multimedia or hooking up an iPod, Grant and Bull are masters at getting to the heart of what people actually do with their computers.

JULY 2010, 496 PP., W/CD $34.95, ISBN 978-1-59327-257-9

AUTOTOOLS

A Practitioner's Guide to GNU Autoconf, Automake, and Libtool

by JOHN CALCOTE

The GNU Autotools make it easy for developers to create software that is portable across many Unix-like operating systems. In *Autotools*, author John Calcote teaches readers how to master the Autotools build system to maximize their software's portability. Calcote begins with an overview of high-level concepts and a quick hands-on tour of the philosophy and design of the Autotools. He then tackles more advanced details, like using the M4 macro processor with Autoconf, extending the Automake framework, and building Java and C# sources. He concludes the book with detailed solutions to the most frequent problems encountered by first-time Autotools users. *Autotools* also includes two complete projects that readers will work through with the author to gain a real-world sense of how to become an Autotools practitioner.

JULY 2010, 360 PP., $44.95, ISBN 978-1-59327-206-7

THE BOOK OF™ AUDACITY

The Definitive Guide to Recording, Editing, Mixing, and Mastering with the Free Audio Editor

by CARLA SCHRODER

Audacity is a cross-platform, open source program that allows anyone to turn their computer into a powerful recording studio. *The Book of Audacity* shows readers how to complete fun and useful projects with the Audacity software while demystifying geeky digital audio jargon along the way. Readers will learn how to digitize their vinyl record collections, create podcasts, record live performances, create super-high fidelity recordings, mix and master multi-track recordings, and create ringtones, special effects, and more. They'll also learn how to package their work for online distribution, whether that means distributing a podcast on iTunes or selling an album on CD Baby.

NOVEMBER 2010, 308 PP., $34.95, ISBN 978-1-59327-270-8

LAND OF LISP

Learn to Program in Lisp, One Game at a Time!

by CONRAD BARSKI, M.D.

Lisp is a uniquely powerful programming language that, despite its academic reputation, is actually very practical. *Land of Lisp* brings the language into the real world, teaching readers Lisp by showing them how to write several complete Lisp-based games, including a text adventure, an evolution simulation, and a robot battle. While building these games, readers learn the core concepts of Lisp programming, such as recursion, input/output, object-oriented programming, and macros. And thanks to Lisp's powerful syntax, the example code is short and easy to understand. The book is filled with the author's brilliant Lisp cartoons, which are sure to appeal to many Lisp fans and, in the tradition of all No Starch Press titles, make learning more fun.

SEPTEMBER 2010, 504 PP., $49.95, ISBN 978-1-59327-281-4

THE LINUX PROGRAMMING INTERFACE

A Linux and UNIX System Programming Handbook

by MICHAEL KERRISK

The Linux Programming Interface is the definitive guide to the Linux and UNIX programming interface—the interface employed by nearly every application that runs on a Linux or UNIX system. In this authoritative work, Linux programming expert Michael Kerrisk provides detailed descriptions of the system calls and library functions that readers need to master the craft of system programming, and accompanies his explanations with clear, complete example programs. Extensively indexed and heavily cross-referenced, *The Linux Programming Interface* is both an introductory guide for readers new to the topic of system programming and a comprehensive reference for experienced system programmers.

AUGUST 2010, 1,552 PP., $99.95, HARDCOVER, ISBN 978-1-59327-220-3

PHONE:
800.420.7240 OR
415.863.9900
MONDAY THROUGH FRIDAY,
9 AM TO 5 PM (PST)

FAX:
415.863.9950
24 HOURS A DAY,
7 DAYS A WEEK

EMAIL:
SALES@NOSTARCH.COM

WEB:
WWW.NOSTARCH.COM

MAIL:
NO STARCH PRESS
38 RINGOLD STREET
SAN FRANCISCO, CA 94103
USA

UPDATES

Visit *http://www.nostarch.com/mapscripting.htm* for updates, errata, and other information.

Map Scripting 101 is set in New Baskerville, TheSansMono Condensed, Futura, and Dogma.

The book was printed and bound by Transcontinental, Inc. at Transcontinental Gagné in Louiseville, Quebec, Canada. The paper is Domtar Husky 60# Smooth, which is certified by the Forest Stewardship Council (FSC). The book has an Otabind binding, which allows it to lie flat when open.